Connected Places

Religion/Culture/Critique
Series editor: Elizabeth A. Castelli

How Hysterical: Identification and Resistance in the Bible and Film
By Erin Runions (2003)

Representing Religion in World Cinema: Filmmaking, Mythmaking, Culture Making
Edited by Brent S. Plate (2003)

Connected Places

Region, Pilgrimage, and Geographical Imagination in India

Anne Feldhaus

palgrave
macmillan

First published 2003 by
PALGRAVE MACMILLAN™
175 Fifth Avenue, New York, N.Y. 10010 and
Houndmills, Basingstoke, Hampshire, England RG21 6XS
Companies and representatives throughout the world

PALGRAVE MACMILLAN is the global academic imprint of the Palgrave Macmillan division of St. Martin's Press, LLC and of Palgrave Macmillan Ltd. Macmillan® is a registered trademark in the United States, United Kingdom and other countries. Palgrave is a registered trademark in the European Union and other countries.

ISBN 1–4039–6323–1 hardback
ISBN 1–4039–6324–X paperback

Library of Congress Cataloging-in-Publication Data
Feldhaus, Anne.
Connected places : region, pilgrimage, and geographical imagination in India / Anne Feldhaus
p. cm.
Includes bibliographical references and index.
ISBN 1–4039–63233–1—ISBN 1–4039–6324–X (pbk.)
1. Maharashtra (India)—History 2. Hindu pilgrims and pilgrimages—India—Maharashtra. I. Title.

DS485.M348F45 2003
954′.7923—dc21 2003045977

A catalogue record for this book is available from the British Library.

Design by Newgen Imaging Systems (P) Ltd., Chennai, India.

First edition: December, 2003
10 9 8 7 6 5 4 3 2 1

Printed in the United States of America.

for
Patrick and Suman
Viju and Dilip
James and Miko

Contents

List of Maps

List of Figures

Series Editor's Preface

Religion/Culture/Critique is a series devoted to publishing work that addresses religion's centrality to a wide range of settings and debates, both contemporary and historical, and that critically engages the category of "religion" itself. This series is conceived as a place where readers will be invited to explore how "religion"—whether embedded in texts, practices, communities, or ideologies—intersects with social and political interests, institutions, and identities.

Anne Feldhaus's work, *Connected Places: Region, Pilgrimage, and Geographical Imagination in India*, invites its reader into the world of religious pilgrims in Maharashtra, using the theoretically evocative categories of place, travel, and memory to analyze how religious observance transforms the imaginative and geographical landscapes of the region. Rich in ethnographic detail and sweeping in its historical reach, this study draws the reader into the complexly woven networks of religious practice in a multicultural region where issues of difference and modernity are negotiated by means of religious mapping and commemoration. Pilgrimage, here, is a form of ritual re-enactment of religious narratives, especially divine biographies. It constitutes a way for practitioners to make imaginative connections between themselves, narratives, and the places of memory that they visit. Nature and ritual objects become the artifacts out of which memory becomes materialized. The sacred geography of Maharashtra emerges as a non-static, multidimensional, transforming and transformative place that produces and contests ideas about identity, political regionalism, and religious experience.

Elizabeth A. Castelli
Religion/Culture/Critique Series Editor

New York City
April 2003

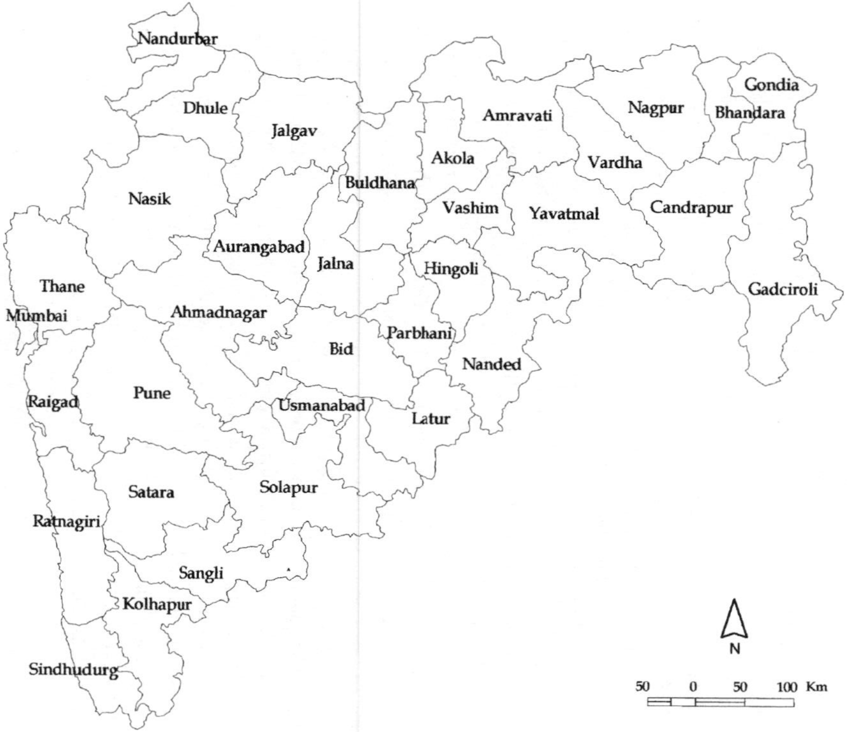

Districts of Maharashtra

Acknowledgments

This book is the product of more than 30 years spent working in and thinking about Maharashtra. Over those years, numerous teachers, friends, and colleagues have prepared me and helped me to gather and analyze the information presented here. Among these people I must mention in particular Sudhir Waghmare, who has accompanied me to virtually all the places and all the festivals described in this book. The anonymous "companions" that I mention from time to time also include Ramdas Atkar and Sakharam Lakade, as well as Jeffrey Brackett, R. C. Dhere, Maruti Gaykwad, Shubha Kothavale, Bhau Mandavkar, V. L. Manjul, Manisha and Dnyaneshwar Mehetre, Asha Mundlay, M. L. K. Murty, Purushottam Nagpure, Candrakant Nimbhorkar, Lee Schlesinger, Thakur Raja Ram Singh, Günther Sontheimer, Sonja Stark-Wild, Ananya Vajpeyi, Pushpa Waghmare, Rajaram Zagade, and Eleanor Zelliot.

Many more people have willingly spent their time patiently explaining things to me, a complete stranger from far away who suddenly appeared in their village, at their temple, or at their festival, trying to understand what was going on. Most of these people remain anonymous in this book, but they include Mahadu Jhagade and his family (chapter 3), the two Bhutojī Telīs (chapter 2), Arjun Kisan Bhagat (chapter 3), and numerous Mahānubhāv monks, nuns, and lay people (chapter 6). I made tape recordings of my conversations with many people who were generous in giving me their time and sharing with me their knowledge and wisdom. For her help in the laborious task of transcribing the tape recordings, I am grateful to my honorary daughter, Manisha Mehetre.

I thank Nikhil Shejwalkar for making most of the maps, Linda Zellmer for teaching me about mapmaking, and Sudhir Waghmare for the map of Ṛddhipūr. Claudia Brown and Kranti Waghmare helped with the illustrations. S. G. Tulpule helped me with reading the Old Marathi texts used in chapters 5 and 6. He and David Carásco, R. C. Dhere, Joel Gereboff, Roland Jansen, V. L. Manjul, K. R. Paradkar, Rajendra Vora, and especially Eleanor Zelliot helped with bibliographical tips and with getting hold of books and articles that I needed. I am very grateful to all of them as well.

Financial and practical assistance came from the American Institute of Indian Studies, the United States Educational Foundation in India (Fulbright), the Bhandarkar Oriental Research Institute (Pune), Arizona State University, the South Asia Institute of the University of Heidelberg, the Alexander von Humboldt Stiftung, the Woodrow Wilson International Center for Scholars (Washington), and the John Simon Guggenheim Foundation. Among the many people at these institutions who have facilitated my work, I especially want to mention Madhav Bhandare, S. D. Laddu, Pradeep Mehendiratta, V. L. Manjul, and Ann Sheffield. My warm thanks also to Claudia Brown in Arizona and Shubha Kothavale in Pune, who have kept watch over my affairs in my two homes, cheerfully enabling my long and repeated absences from each of them.

For reading or listening to all or parts of the manuscript, and for discussing my ideas about Maharashtrian religious geography as they have developed over many years, I am grateful to: Véronique Bouillier; Joel Brereton; Heidrun Brückner; Dilip and Vijaya Chitre; Rose Ann Christian; Eugene Clay; Catherine Clémentin-Ojha; Frank Conlon; David Damrel; James Foard; Joel Gereboff; Irina Glushkova; Jack Hawley; James Laine; Jayant Lele; Meera Kosambi; Philip Lutgendorf; Stephen MacKinnon; Michael Martinez; Christian Novetzke; Patrick Olivelle; Lee Schlesinger; Lorenzo Simpson; Günther Sontheimer; Nick Street; Sani Umar; Ananya Vajpeyi; Rajendra Vora; Mark Woodward; my students in Heidelberg, Paris, Vienna, and Arizona; my colleagues at Arizona State University and at the Woodrow Wilson International Center for Scholars; the participants in the international conference on regions held in Pune in December 2001; and colleagues who have participated with me in various Maharashtra conferences over the past several years.

Some parts of this book have been published elsewhere. In particular, parts of chapter 6 appeared in my articles "Maharashtra as a Holy Land: A Sectarian Tradition" (*Bulletin of the School of Oriental and African Studies, University of London*, 1986) and "The Religious Significance of Ṛddhipur" (in *Religion and Society in Maharashtra*, edited by Milton Israel and N. K. Wagle, 1987). I am grateful to Cambridge University Press and the Centre for Asian Studies at the University of Toronto for permission to reprint materials from these articles. In addition, several articles scheduled to appear in print contain earlier versions of some of the materials in this book. These include articles due to appear in the proceedings of the Third International Conference on Devotional Literature in New Indo-Aryan Languages (Leiden, December 1985), edited by G. Schokker; the proceedings of the Seventh International Conference on Maharashtra: Culture and Society (Sydney, January 1998), edited by Jim Masselos; and the proceedings of the Symposium on Region and Regionalism in India

(Pune, December 2001), edited by Rajendra Vora and Anne Feldhaus. Finally, I am grateful to the Sontheimer Cultural Association (Pune) and the Srimati Nabadurga Banerji Endowment Lecture, Asiatic Society of Mumbai, for permission to use materials from public lectures of mine that they intend to publish.

As I try to show in this book, Maharashtra is made up of many small worlds. I am grateful to those who have admitted me to so many of these worlds, as well as to those who have made the effort to understand what I have learned about them. The book is dedicated to six friends—James and Miko Foard, Viju and Dilip Chitre, and Patrick and Suman Olivelle—who have helped me for decades to connect my own places to one another.

Note on Transliteration and Pronunciation

In order to help the reader pronounce unfamiliar names and terms, I have used diacritical marks on some words. In doing so, I have followed the standard conventions for transliterating the *devanāgarī* script, which is used for both Marathi and Sanskrit. In most cases, I have left out the short "a" when it is not pronounced in Marathi (e.g., I have written "Nāmdev" rather than "Nāmadeva," and "Rāmṭek" rather than "Rāmaṭeka"). Names and terms that are much more familiar in their Sanskrit than in their Marathi forms I have given in the Sanskrit form (e.g., "Śiva" and "Śaiva"), rather than in Marathi ("Śiv," "Śaiv"). I have not used diacritical marks in Indian words that are widely used in English, or in the names of Indian languages, states of modern India, districts of modern Maharashtra, major Indian cities, or most living people (except when I refer to them as the authors of Marathi works).

The following guide should help those unfamiliar with Indian languages to pronounce the names and terms used in this book:

a sounds like "u" in "cup"
ā sounds like "a" in "father"
i sounds like "i" in "hit"
ī sounds like "ee" in "feet"
u sounds like "u" in "put"
ū sounds like "oo" in "root"
ṛ sounds like "ri" in "river"
e sounds like "ay" in "day"
ai sounds like "y" in "fry"
o sounds like "o" in "go"
au sounds like "ow" in "cow"
c sounds like "ch" in "church" or like "ts" in "rats"
g is always hard, as in "go"
j sounds like "g" in "George" or like "z" in "zoo"

ṭ and *ḍ* are retroflex consonants, sounding like "t" and "d" in British pronunciations of "table" and "doctor"

bh, dh, ḍh, gh, kh, th, and *ṭh* are aspirated consonants, pronounced like the corresponding consonant clusters in "club-house," "dog-house," and so on

ś and *ṣ* are both pronounced "*sh*"

In long words, English speakers should put a slight stress on the second-last syllable, if it contains the vowels *ā, ī, ū, e, ai, o,* or *au,* or is followed by two consonants (and not merely by a single aspirated consonant: *dh, bh, ch,* and so on). If the second-last syllable does not have one or both of these characteristics, the stress should be placed on the closest preceding syllable that does. "Mahābhārata," for instance, receives a slight stress on "*bhā,*" and "Himālayas" receives a slight stress on "*mā.*"

Introduction

When I first went to Maharashtra, I didn't even know it existed. Invited to go to India, I thought that a college summer there would be my chance to see the world. I looked up India on a map of the world. India was the country that hung down in a triangle, far west and south of the curving bulge of China and the smaller, sharper bulge of Southeast Asia, southeast of the Arabian peninsula, far to the east of Africa. Then, on a map of India, I searched for Pune (at that time still usually spelled "Poona"), the place where my teacher[1] had said that we would stay. Only later did I learn that I was going to a part of India called Maharashtra, the part where most people's first language is Marathi (map 0.1).

Like most twentieth-century foreigners entering Maharashtra, we arrived first in Bombay (now Mumbai), the booming, polyglot metropolis that India's British rulers had stitched together out of a cluster of small islands halfway down the west coast of the South Asian peninsula. Mumbai is the economic capital of India, the center of the Indian film industry, and also the political capital of Maharashtra—but I knew none of these things when I arrived there one day in early June, 1970. The monsoon had just struck, as it does around that time every year. Rain was teeming down unrelentingly. The gutters, knee-deep with water, overflowed onto the streets and sidewalks. We took refuge in the office of a travel agent who got us train tickets to Pune.

The most famous train from Mumbai to Pune is called the "Deccan Queen." It leaves the posh "Fort" area of Mumbai in the late afternoon, travels for an hour or more through the neighborhoods and suburbs of Mumbai, takes another hour to cross the coastal plain, and then begins to climb almost straight up the mountains called the Sahyādris or Western Ghats. Past cliffs and waterfalls, through clouds and tunnels, the train traverses a dense jungle with dramatic views into wooded valleys below. At the top of the mountains, the air becomes cooler and less humid, as the train reaches a plateau that descends gradually all the way across India to the Bay of Bengal. This is the Deccan Plateau, the place that the train is ultimately named for.[2] Maharashtra extends halfway across this plateau, with spurs of the western mountains alternating with the valleys of rivers that flow from northwest to southeast across the plateau.

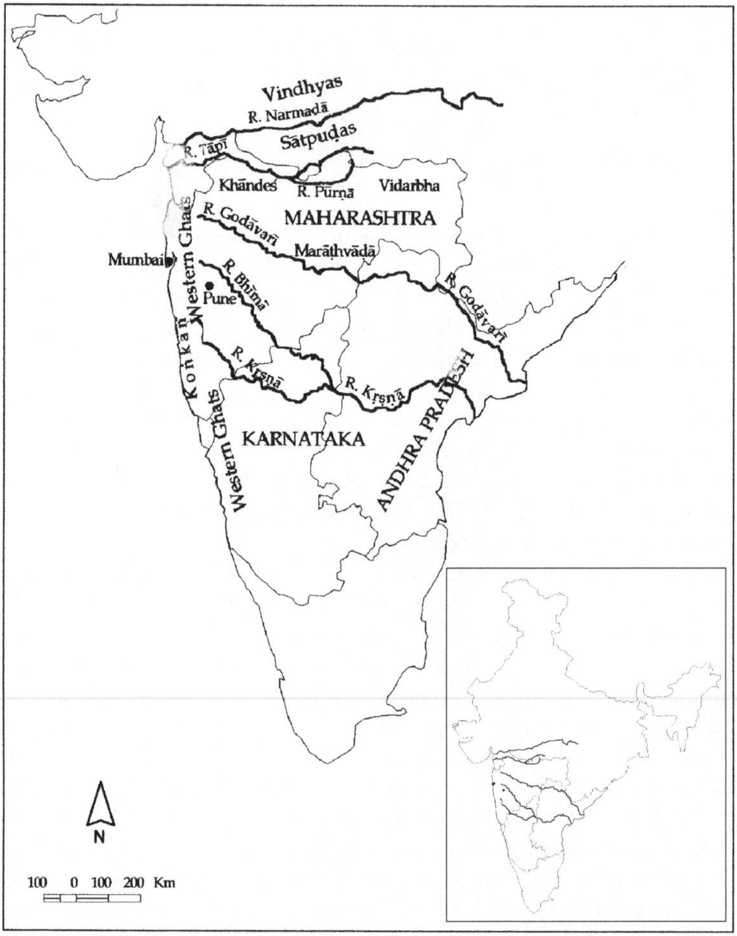

Map 0.1 Maharashtra, Andhra Pradesh, and Karnataka, with major rivers of the Deccan

In the Marathi language, the part of Maharashtra on the Deccan Plateau is called the Deś ("the country," or simply "the land"), and the coastal plain is called the Koṅkaṇ. The contrast between Koṅkaṇ and Deś is the most basic distinction within Maharashtra. It is a physical-geographical distinction and at the same time a cultural one. Semi-nomadic shepherds called Dhangars spend the monsoon season in their homes on the Deś and the eight dry months of each year in fields in the Koṅkaṇ. The two principal kinds of Maharashtrian Brahmans, Deśastha and Koṅkaṇastha, are named for their origins in these two parts of Maharashtra, and people are aware of many other differences—of language and diet, for instance—that distinguish the two areas. Stewart Gordon (1993:21–22) explains the basis for the lively trade between Koṅkaṇ and Deś that existed in the seventeenth century and that still continues to a great extent today:

> The Desh and the Konkan were ecologically complementary regions. Consider the products that grow in the Konkan, but not on the Desh: coconuts . . . , mangoes, jackfruit, betel nuts, dried fish, salt (from seawater), herbs and honey (from the forested regions), rice, sea shells (as ornaments), timber and bamboo. All these products appear in the market documents of the Desh towns of the seventeenth century. Next, consider what the Desh produced which did (and does) not grow in the Konkan: sugarcane (for jaggery, the main sweetener), cotton, onions and garlic, tobacco, turmeric (crucial for fish curing). Perhaps the most important of all were the pulses grown on the Desh. The heavy rains of the Konkan made vegetables available only in limited seasons, and pulses from the Desh were (and are) the basic complement to the rice diet of the Konkan. Except in the heaviest monsoon periods, bullock caravans regularly carried these items of trade (plus items of copper, iron and brass which came from outside Maharashtra) up and down the Ghats to weekly markets in both areas.

On that first day, taking the train from Mumbai to Pune, I experienced for myself this most important geographical contrast in Maharashtra. In subsequent visits during the next three decades, I learned about many more of the geographical traits of Maharashtra, and I experienced, in some measure, the physical boundaries of Maharashtra as a whole. Besides the mountains that run parallel to the west coast of India and separate the Koṅkaṇ from the Deś, there are mountains to the north of Maharashtra as well: the Sātpuḍas and, beyond them, the Vindhyas. These mountains, together with the rivers that flow westward alongside them, form a physical-geographical barrier that separates Maharashtra and the areas to its south from North India. Jungles and tribal areas mark not only this northern edge of Maharashtra but the eastern edge as well. To the south of Maharashtra there is no such pronounced boundary,[3] so that, in physical-geographical terms, Maharashtra blends nearly imperceptibly into the linguistically, culturally, and politically distinct states of Karnataka and Andhra Pradesh.

Pune lies toward the western edge of the Deccan Plateau. It is the headquarters of a contemporary administrative division of Maharashtra called "Western Maharashtra" that was the heartland of the Marāṭhā kingdom in the seventeenth and eighteenth centuries. Today it is the most densely populated part of Maharashtra (except for Greater Mumbai), and the part that, along with Mumbai, dominates the state culturally, economically, and politically as well. In northwestern Maharashtra lies Khāndeś.[4] Historically, the principal residents of Khāndeś have been tribals (primarily Bhils) and pastoralists (especially Ahīrs or Ābhīras). People here speak a distinctive form of Marathi called Ahirāṇī. From 1296, when 'Alā-ud-dīn Khiljī invaded the Deccan, until 1760, Khāndeś was under Muslim rule. The northeastern part of Maharashtra is Vidarbha (formerly also called Varhāḍ[5]). An area mentioned by name in texts as early as the Upaniṣads (*BSK*, Volume 8, p. 687), and famous in Sanskrit literature as the home of Kṛṣṇa's wife, Rukmiṇī, Vidarbha formed part of the territory that Vākāṭaka kings ruled in the first centuries C.E.; its easternmost lands were once ruled by kings belonging to the Gond tribe (Karve 1968:57).

Marāṭhvāḍā is the current name of the central part of Maharashtra. Marāṭhvāḍā is made up of districts that until 1947 were included in the "Dominions" of the Nizam of Hyderabad.[6] This is the area that Cakradhar, the founder of the Mahānubhāv sect, referred to in the thirteenth century as the "Gaṅgā valley" (see chapter 6), that is, the (upper) valley of the Godāvarī, the northernmost of the great rivers that flow from northwest to southeast across the Deccan Plateau. In Cakradhar's time, what is now Marāṭhvāḍā was the core of the Yādava kingdom, with its capital at Devgirī (subsequently called Daulātābād). Paiṭhaṇ, the capital of the much earlier kingdom of the Sātavāhanas (first century B.C.E. to third century C.E.) is also found in Marāṭhvāḍā, on the Godāvarī river, as is Nāndeḍ, the site of the grave of the seventeenth-century Sikh leader Govind Singh. The Mughal emperor Aurāṅgzeb's city, Aurāṅgābād, is now the principal city of Marāṭhvāḍā, which is also home to the Buddhist (and Jain and Hindu) caves at Ajanta and Ellora (called Verūḷ in Marathi) and to the major Sufi shrines at Khuldābād.

As I traveled off and on for over 30 years through these different parts of Maharashtra, slowly sorting out their history and learning about their gods, I became interested in the variety of ways in which residents of Maharashtra conceive of where they live and travel. I was particularly interested in places that Maharashtrians think of as holy. I found and read old texts in Sanskrit and Marathi and newer Marathi pamphlets describing individual holy places or whole sets of them. I went to a number of holy places, sometimes when they were quiet and peaceful and other times when they were filled with huge, often boisterous, festival crowds. At the pilgrimage festivals at these places, I noticed things that the people were doing, and I saw the kinds of objects that groups of people had brought along: large, heavy palanquins with brass images of gods inside; baskets full of gods carried on people's heads; cymbals, drums, and clap-sticks; tall poles and flags; small water pots and large contraptions for carrying water; and in one case a bed for a goddess to lie on. As my command of Marathi improved, I began to talk at these festivals with people I met, learning where they had come from, how they had traveled, what they wanted to do in the festival, and why they thought it was worth coming to. I wrote down the names and addresses of some of the pilgrims and priests, and returned to talk with them at quieter times. In this way, I slowly became familiar with a few of the hundreds of pilgrimage festivals that take place all over Maharashtra every year. The observations I made, the conversations I held, and the readings I did are the sources of the descriptions, interpretations, and analyses in this book.[7]

Region and Place

This book is about ways in which Maharashtrians live in and make sense of their world. It shows that people in Maharashtra inhabit a variety of regions that acquire religious meaning in a number of different ways. A region is a part of the earth that has coherence and meaning in some respect for some people. By calling this book "Connected Places," I am suggesting that a region is a set of places that are connected to one another and that taken together contrast with some other set of places (another region). A region in this sense is not the concern of an "objective" geography that would identify, for instance, the region within which certain flora or fauna are found, the region within which the roofs of houses are made with one, as opposed to another, sort of material, or the region within which a particular script is used for the written form of languages. Rather, the kind of region this book is concerned with is one that is thought of as such by its residents and perhaps also by some others, an area with a distinct identity and significance for people who live in it and for others who think and care about it.[8] In this sense, a region is a kind of place.

Many recent scholars of the humanities and social sciences who are interested in "place"[9] define it in opposition to "space." Whereas space is abstract, homogeneous, unmarked, and neutral, place is concrete, particular, and differentiated. For some theorists of place, the place par excellence is the domestic residence, the home,[10] but the notion of place can also be extended to include a region.[11] In such a usage, a region is simply a large place. It could be a "holler" in West Virginia (Stewart 1996), a neighborhood in Los Angeles (Soja 1989), or a cluster of islands in New Guinea (Munn 1986). The philosopher Edward Casey prefers to think of a region not as a large place, but as an area in which a number of different places are connected with one another. He defines a region as "a concatenation of places that, taken together, constitutes a common and continuous here for the person who lives in or traverses them" (Casey 1993:53).

The kind of geographical awareness involved in a sense of a region as place is not merely knowledge *about* the region. It is not merely, for example, the ability to list and describe all the places in the region. At a more fundamental level, a sense of place is formative of one's cosmology and basic orientation to the world. Such a geographical awareness can be the immediate result of administrative arrangements, of physical geography, or of images and stories.

A prime example of administrative arrangements forming people's orientation is the grid of most of the American landscape. Sack (1980:103) describes the "rectangular land survey" as "the dividing of land into increasingly smaller rectangular counties, townships, sections, half-sections, quarter-sections and so on." He explains: "This ordinance moulded farmstead location and orientation, farm boundaries, transportation networks, and the shapes and locations of settlements and political boundaries." More fundamentally, the grid has also provided the basic, commonsense orientation of the people who have lived within it. John Brinkerhoff Jackson (1994:3–4) describes as follows the grid's effect on people:

> In the early days of commercial aviation many first-time flyers were puzzled by the prevailing rectilinearity and assumed that it was the work of unscrupulous real estate operators laying out some monstrous megacity . . . . The so-called grid system, oriented to the four points of the compass and extending from the Ohio to the Pacific, . . . was an ingenious, if unimaginative, way of creating a landscape, but it was not easy to get used to, and in the beginning settlers from the East or from Europe complained of its monotony and its disregard of the topography; in fact, the grid made no adjustment to rivers or hills or marshlands. Still by now, more than two centuries later, there are millions of Americans so thoroughly at home in the grid that they cannot conceive of any other way of organizing space. I have been in homes in Kansas where they refer to the southwest (or northwest) burner on their stove. They tell you that the bathroom is upstairs, straight ahead south.

On the Deccan Plateau of India, in the Deś area of Maharashtra, people speak not so often of "west" and "east"[12] as of "up" (*var*) and "down" (*khālī*). "Up" and "down" mean "upstream" and "downstream," and refer to the rivers that flow across the Deccan from northwest to southeast, joining the ocean at the far-off Bay of Bengal.[13] Kalyāṇ Kāḷe (1983) describes the ways in which people in his home village indicate directions. This village lies in a part of Maharashtra that (having grown up myself in the "Midwest" of the United States) I would call the "south" bank of the Godāvarī river, and that others (relying on a more immediately body-based sense of orientation) would call the "right" bank of that river. Not only do people in Kāḷe's village and others near it refer to west and east, respectively, as "up" and "down," but they also refer to north as "toward the Gaṅgā" (*gaṅgaṃkaḍaṃ*)—that is, toward the Godāvarī river, widely known in that part of the world to be the southern branch of the Ganges.[14] For "south," people in Kāḷe's village draw on the *Rāmāyaṇa* story. Alluding to the demon Rāvaṇa's kingdom of Laṅkā (now Sri Lanka, the island just off the southern end of the Indian peninsula), they refer to the southern direction as "toward the demon(s)" (*rākisākaḍaṃ*). For "south," then, these people orient themselves not in terms of rivers, but in terms of a traditional story.

Beyond this sort of basic orientation to the world, a sense of place provides an experience of meaning.[15] Meaning involves both the intellect and the emotions. The notion of place, and thus also that of region, generally involves a significant affective element as well as cognitive ones. A person *cares* about places, likes them or dislikes them, longs to go to them, to return to them, to leave them, or not to leave them. In some cases, the sense of region as place includes a sense of the place as one's *own* place, one's home, a place that one belongs to and that belongs to one in some important way. Even further, awareness of *where* one is (or where one comes from) can become an important element in understanding *who* one is: it can become a vital aspect of a person's identity. Ultimately, when shared by a significant portion of a population, such an awareness can become the basis of a separatist movement aiming at regional autonomy or independent nationhood.

Although the meaning people ascribe to a region may be intensely felt and widely shared, there need not be—and often is not—unanimity about what the region means. "Regional consciousness" can also be a matter of contention and opposition.[16] A North American example of ways in which different groups can find opposed meanings for the same area is Canadians' deep disagreement about the far northern reaches of their country. English-Canadian intellectuals generally see the Far North as the "True North Strong and Free" of their national anthem, an "unterritorialised, undifferentiated, 'unconquerable' zone of purity: a white wilderness" to be left alone. French Canadians, by contrast, tend to see northern Québec "as an engineering zone rich in resources and hydro-electric potential" that ought to be developed (Shields 1991:61, cf. 162–206).

Beyond the fact that people can have views of a single region as opposed as those of English and French Canadians with respect to the Far North, there can also be a simpler, less politicized multiplicity of points of view. It is not necessarily, and probably not often, the case that all the people living in or related to a region share the same sense of it as a place, the same traditions about its meaning, or even the same notion of what "it" is—of what area is to count as the region. Most people, in fact, live simultaneously in a number of different regions. As this book will repeatedly show, different regions often overlap in the same area, and different ones of these overlapping regions become salient in different contexts, even sometimes for the same person.

Maharashtra

Maharashtra has been home to at least one movement aiming at some form or degree of regional autonomy. This was a mid-twentieth-century movement called the "United Maharashtra" (Saṃyukta Maharashtra) movement. As a result of this movement, Maharashtra came into being as a single, unified political entity, a state within the modern nation of India. This happened in 1960, 13 years after India became independent from Britain. Thus, in 1970, when I did not know that Maharashtra existed, I was in one sense only ten years out of date.

In another sense, I was many centuries behind the times. The name "Maharashtra" had been in use for a millennium and a half (Tulpule and Feldhaus 1999:xxiv), and there had been Marathi-speaking kingdoms in Western India since the twelfth century C.E. In fact, Maharashtra State is only the most recent of dozens of political entities that have come and gone in the area it covers. Even before the emergence of the Marathi language, a number of different dynasties ruled substantial parts of the area now known as Maharashtra: the Sātavāhanas (first century B.C. to A.D. 250), the Ābhīras (third century A.D.), the Vākāṭakas (A.D. 25–510), the Kalacuris (fifth to sixth centuries A.D.), the Western Cālukyas (A.D. 560–750), the Rāṣṭrakūṭas (A.D. 750–950) and the Śilāhāras (tenth to twelfth centuries A.D.) (Kulkarni 1996:4).

The twelfth- and thirteenth-century Yādavas, with their capital at Devgirī (Daulātābad) and their heartland in the upper valley of the Godāvarī river, were the first dynasty to rule a Marathi-speaking kingdom. It was under them, in part with their patronage, that Marathi literature first arose. After the fall of the Yādavas, who were conquered in 1296 by 'Alā-ud-dīn Khiljī, parts of Maharashtra came under various Muslim sultanates and empires, including the Bāhmanīs (1347–late 1400s), the Sultanate of Bijāpūr (founded in 1489/90), and the Ahmadnagar Sultanate (1489/90–1633).

Maharashtra's most famous ruler was Śivājī, who founded the Marāṭhā kingdom in the mid-seventeenth century. After his death, the kingdom was ruled from Pune by a series of Brahman prime ministers, called Peśvās, with descendants of Śivājī enthroned at Sātārā and Kolhāpūr under the Peśvās' control. The British defeated the Peśvās in 1818 and later took over other princely states. In 1947, when India achieved independence, much of what is now Maharashtra was included in Bombay State, the successor to the British Bombay Presidency. It was Bombay State that was broken up in 1960, its Marathi-speaking portion joining other, contiguous Marathi-language areas to form Maharashtra State.[17]

The grounds of legitimacy of the United Maharashtra movement was the decision of the central government of independent India to delimit states in terms of language. Linguistic definitions of states rest on a kind of geography that is, in one respect, more "objective" than the geographical ideas with which this book is primarily concerned. Objective a criterion though it may be, however, language is hardly one toward which people take a bloodless attitude. Even in the least complicated cases, "the 'mother tongue' . . . becomes the metaphor for the love fellow nationals feel for one another" (Balibar 1991:98). Besides, such uncomplicated cases are rare: a simple congruence between language and nation is seldom found outside of Europe, if even there.[18] In situations like India's, in which a number of different languages are spoken within a single nation-state,[19] the multiplicity can give rise to extremely strong feelings and even to violence. Ramaswamy (1997) illustrates graphically, for example, the kinds of "passions" that modern Tamil-speakers have exhibited for their language in opposition to the "national" language, Hindi.

Moreover, even where a single language is spoken throughout a region or a nation, the language is not simply a basis for unity. Differences in speech that may appear subtle to outsiders can cause or express deep social rifts. In Bengali, for example, as Sudipta Kaviraj (1992b:26) explains:

> The *bhadralok* of Calcutta speak the Bengali standard language, one which has resemblances on one side with the 'high' language in which Tagore wrote his poetry, but also, on the other side of the cultural spectrum, with the language spoken in the bazaar by the fisherman, [by] the maid in the *babu* household, or by criminals in the margins of urban Calcutta.

Marathi speech reflects similar sorts of social differentiation.

In addition, Maharashtra has experienced the kind of tension that arises in borderlands where the language of one region blurs into that of another. For, even to the extent that language *is* an objective criterion for making boundaries, the boundaries it creates are by no means clear-cut. In premodern India, as Kaviraj (1992b:40–41) explains, language difference is "fuzzy," with "dialects slowly and imperceptibly changing, such that, with historical clairvoyance these could be ascribed to what would eventually become . . . distinct vernaculars . . . . Differences would shade off the way distinctly different colours are arranged in a spectrum." Linguistically speaking, says Kaviraj, premodern India is "a world . . . of transitions rather than of boundaries."

The Maharashtra–Karnataka borderland is still, in some respects, such a world. Here the boundaries of language loyalty, fuzzy in any case, become even more indeterminate, as they do not coincide with any particularly marked features of physical geography. Commentaries on the command of the Mahānubhāv sect's thirteenth-century founder, Cakradhar, to stay at "the end of the land" (i.e., in insignificant, out-of-the-way places) interpreted this as referring to the mixing of languages at the edges of the Marathi language region.[20] Seven centuries after Cakradhar, when the boundaries of Maharashtra were created, the primarily Marathi-speaking city of Belgaum became part of Karnataka because Belgaum was surrounded by a countryside in which most people spoke Kannada, the language of Karnataka. Since 1960, the location of the boundary line between Maharashtra and Karnataka has remained a contentious issue that has led to a number of "language riots."

Geographical Stories

Besides physical geography, political history, and language, another way to think about Maharashtra is in terms of what might be called its mythological geography. Stories abound telling of gods, goddesses, heroes, and heroines who have lived or visited here and who have left their mark on the landscape. Telling or hearing such stories provides a way for people to see meaning in Maharashtra as a whole and in various regions within it. This book will present many stories of this sort about a large number of different regions. Here we need to look briefly at only three figures who are of special importance for Maharashtra as a whole or for its two major divisions, Koṅkaṇ and Deś. The three figures are Agastya, Rām, and Paraśurām.

When the sage Agastya came south, bringing Brahmanical culture from northern India, the first place that he came to was Maharashtra. Told from the point of view of the Vindhya mountains, which were jealous of the cosmic mountain Meru, at the center of the world, Agastya's story is one about the shaping of the landscape (Goḍbole 1928:342):

> The god who embodies these mountains once began to say to the sun, the moon, and the others: "Move in a circle around me the way you do around Meru."
>
> They replied, "We must follow the route that the creator of the world set us in, circumambulating Meru. So we do not have any freedom in this respect."

> When he heard this, [the Vindhya mountain] began to grow, and he grew so tall that he obstructed the path of the sun and the others. So the gods and sages came to him and said, "Don't you do this." But he did not pay any attention at all. So they all went to the sage Agastya and pleaded, "The Vindhya mountain is your disciple, and he has undertaken behavior that is harmful to people. So you must instruct him that he should not do this."
>
> When the sage Agastya heard this speech of the gods and sages, he left his forest retreat and came to [the Vindhya mountain]. Then, as soon as he saw [Agastya], [Vindhya] prostrated himself. Seeing this, Agastya said to him, "Stay just like that until I get back from the south."
>
> With those words, Agastya went south, and [Vindhya] has been prostrating himself ever since.

Although Agastya is most widely known and most highly revered in Tamil Nadu (where he is credited, e.g., with having created a grammar for the Tamil language), his former presence is also invoked at many places in present-day Maharashtra. He plays a major role in the *Karavīra Māhātmya*, the Māhātmya of Kolhāpūr (Tagare 1980; Patkī 1917), the home of one of the "three-and-a-half" principal goddesses of Maharashtra (see chapter 4). He established the temple of Śiva, Viṣṇu, Brahmā, and Pārvatī at Harihareśvar in Raygad District (Parāñjpe 1946:10). His "private land" (*khājgī bhūmī*) is located in the doab between the Kṛṣṇā and Veṇṇā rivers near Gove-Limb (see chapter 1). And Nārāyaṇrāv Pavār's *Agastī Mahātma Granth* (1977:48–49) tells, along with other, more standard stories about Agastya, the story of his establishing a forest *āśram* on a hill near Pavār's village, Ainvāḍī (Khānāpūr Taluka, Sangli District).

Agastya's presence in Maharashtra highlights the fact that, in religious-geographical terms at least, Maharashtra belongs squarely to southern India.[21] The Deccan Plateau, upon which lies the larger part of Maharashtra, the Deś, is named for its southern location: the name "Deccan" derives from "*dakṣiṇa*," meaning "south" (Yule and Burnell 1903:301). Traditions in the Deś of Maharashtra, and especially in the Godāvarī valley (Marāṭhvāḍā), identify this area as the Daṇḍakāraṇya, the southern forest in which Rām, Sītā, and Lakṣmaṇ spent their years of exile. Many local stories refer to various things that these *Rāmāyaṇa* figures did as they wandered around what is now central Maharashtra, bathing, cooking, digging holes with their bows and arrows, and overturning pots of water.[22]

A story that is very popular in Maharashtra tells how Rām named various goddesses, identifying them with Pārvatī. Here is a version of the story as a schoolteacher in Jejurī told it to explain the name and identity of the goddess Jāṇāī or Jāṇubāī (see chapter 3):

> At the time when Rām went searching for Sītā, Śaṅkar and Pārvatī decided to test and see, "Is he truly faithful to his wife?" So Pārvatī took the form

> [of Sītā] and began to trick Rām. But Rām [saw through the trick, and] said, "No (*nāhī*), go away (*jā*), Mother (*āī*)." So she became Jāṇubāī.

Similarly, the schoolteacher explained, the goddess Yamāī came into being when Rām called to Pārvatī, "Come here (*ye*), Mother (*māī*)," and the goddess Tukāī came into being when Rām said to Pārvatī, "Why (*kā*) you (*tū*), Mother (*āī*)?" Devotees of the goddess Yeḍāī tell the same story to explain *her* name: in this case, Rām said to Pārvatī, "Are you crazy, Mother (*āī*)?" "*Veḍī*," the standard Marathi word for "crazy," is pronounced "*yeḍī*" in rural speech. Hence "Yeḍāī" is "Crazy Lady." This story expresses the generally (but vaguely) Śaiva character of unmarried goddesses, the connection of these goddesses with Rām (and Sītā), and also—most importantly for our purposes—the location of the goddesses in the Deccan wilderness, the Daṇḍakāraṇya.

In the case of the coastal area of Maharashtra, the Koṅkaṇ, a figure from mythological traditions known all over India not only *lived* in the region, but also *created* it. The axe-bearing incarnation of Viṣṇu, Paraśurām, brought the Koṅkaṇ into being with one of his arrows. The following version of this story comes from a Marathi pamphlet that I bought in the mid-1990s at the Paraśurām temple near Cipḷūṇ (Ratnāgiri District):[23]

> Lord Paraśurām came and stayed on the Mahendra Mountain, at what is now the village Paraśurām. However, the ocean suddenly took on a ferocious form and began to pound against Mahendra Mountain. Paraśurām told the ocean to move back, but the ocean wasn't prepared to recede. Finally Paraśurām once again put an arrow to his bow. When the earth realized the power of that arrow, she began to tremble, and the ocean, for its part, realizing that it was now going to be completely dry, surrendered to Paraśurām. In granting an assurance of safety to the ocean, which had surrendered to him, Paraśurām said, "Once I have put an arrow to the bow I cannot take it back. However, now you'll have to go back to the limit marked by the place where this arrow falls." In this way, Paraśurām shot the arrow, and the ocean moved back to the place where the arrow had fallen. This is the ocean-land (*sāgarbhūmi*) created by Paraśurām. This land extends from Baḍoc in Gujarat all the way to Kanyākumārī.

Another story about Paraśurām and the Koṅkaṇ tells of his creation of the Koṅkaṇastha Brāhmaṇs, the Maharashtrian Brāhmaṇs who are named for the Koṅkaṇ. This story also gives an etymology for the Koṅkaṇasthas' other name, "Citpāvan," and an explanation of the anomaly that the family goddess of many Citpāvan Koṅkaṇastha Brāhmaṇs is Jogāī (or Yogeśvarī) of Āmbejogāī, a place far inland on the Deś (Kāḷegāṃvkar

1963:14, citing Jogaḷekar 1952):[24]

> One day, when Paraśurām was staying in the Koṅkaṇ area, he saw the corpses of fourteen men who had been washed along by the ocean's current. Paraśurām pulled them out and brought those dead young men to life. The news had spread widely that these young men had died and that they had been put onto a funeral pyre (*cit*), and so no one was willing to give a daughter to these Citpāvans. Searching desperately for wives, these people finally came, along with Paraśurām, to the holy place that was the town of Āmbā. They expressed their wishes to the citizens of this place. The people of the place agreed to give them their daughters on one condition. The one, simple condition was that the young couples and their descendants should consider the goddess Yogeśvarī their family goddess. As soon as they had agreed to the condition, the weddings took place. The people who had come returned triumphantly to their homes in the Koṅkaṇ. And since then the goddess Yogeśvarī has been the family goddess of the Citpāvan community.

Plan of the Book

Like the connection between Āmbejogāī on the Deccan Plateau and the coastal home of the Koṅkaṇastha Brāhmaṇs, connections between places based on religious concepts, narratives, and/or practices form the basic theme of this book. Each of the chapters that follow examines a different way in which people in Maharashtra connect places, either physically, by traveling between them, or mentally, in their own imaginations. The first chapter, which focuses on rivers, adheres most closely to physical geography. Rivers are elements of the landscape that themselves most obviously connect places and form the cores of geographical regions. We will look at ways in which people in Maharashtra, reflecting on rivers or experiencing rivers' ability to form regions, have created stories, texts, concepts, and pilgrimage rituals that express the image of a river valley (or a doab or a delta) as a region. We will also look at some ways in which people have interacted in a similarly creative fashion with rivers' power to divide regions, to act as obstacles separating one place from another. The second chapter provides an extended example of one of the kinds of pilgrimages associated with rivers, and shows the nested series of regions that this particular pilgrimage enacts.

The third chapter examines stories, pilgrimages, and religious-geographical concepts in which it is deities themselves, and not only their devotees, who travel. In each of the cases that we will look at in detail, the deity who travels is a goddess. The goddesses include two who travel to be nearer to their devotees, one who travels in order to kill a demon, and one who travels toward her intended husband's home for her wedding. In all four cases, I will quote or summarize an oral or printed story about the goddess's trip, and in the first three cases I will describe in some detail a pilgrimage festival in which people retrace (or reverse) the goddess's route. Finally, I will suggest that the goddess's marriage journey throws light on an important and widespread motif in Hindu religious geography: the idea that certain goddesses whose principal temples are in different places are one another's sisters.

Chapter 4 examines a phenomenon found on the level of all of India as well as within Maharashtra: the grouping of places that are distant from one another as numbered sets of places. The sets of places discussed in chapter 4 are connected in a much more abstract way than those in chapters 1–3, and yet I will argue that even a number can serve to connect places in people's minds. In some cases, people go on pilgrimage to all the places in one of these numbered sets, but, more importantly for our purposes, the sets also provide people with conceptual tools for *thinking* about the regions throughout which the places are distributed.

If chapter 4 appears to have to do with arithmetic, chapter 5 looks at times like an exercise in algebra. This chapter, which explores the common practice of asserting identities, equivalences, and other connections between places in Maharashtra and places outside of Maharashtra (especially ones to Maharashtra's north), points out the contrast between Maharashtra and North India that this practice implies. Chapter 6 too refers to a felt contrast between Maharashtra as a whole and other parts of India. This chapter focuses on the traditions of the Mahānubhāvs, a sect whose thirteenth-century founder commanded his followers to "stay in Maharashtra" and explicitly forbade them to go to the lands immediately to Maharashtra's south. After examining the intimate connection between biography and geography among the Mahānubhāvs, this chapter shows how subsequent generations of Mahānubhāvs transformed their founder's command through pilgrimage traditions and theological and literary elaboration, including even rhetoric of the kind analyzed in its non-Mahānubhāv forms in chapter 5.

Thus, while the first four chapters and part of the sixth have to do primarily with religious ways in which Maharashtrians form regions within or overlapping with Maharashtra, chapter 5 and (in part) chapter 6 have to do with the conceptualization and religious valuation of Maharashtra as a whole in contrast to other parts of India. The conclusion suggests that pilgrimage and religious-geographical conceptions may have played a role in the founding of the State of Maharashtra in 1960. More importantly, the conclusion points out that many of the kind of religiously sanctioned regions discussed in the book have *not* in fact become political or administrative units or given rise to movements aimed at making them such. The fact that religious-geographical ideas and pilgrimage practices can contribute to the viability of a political entity does not mean that they suffice to bring about a separatist movement aiming to create such an independent or autonomous entity. Most of the ideas, rituals, and regions studied in this book enrich the lives of the people who hold, practice, or live in them, but they enrich these people's lives in mostly nonpolitical ways.

Chapter 1

Rivers and Regional Consciousness

In the course of their forest exile, the Pāṇḍava brothers, the heroes of the *Mahābhārata* epic, decided to perform a sacrifice at a place called Pāṇḍeśvar that is now located on the Karhā river. At that time the river did not exist, and there was no water at Pāṇḍeśvar. Searching for the water that they needed for the sacrifice, two of the Pāṇḍava brothers, Arjun and Nakul, found an ascetic Brāhmaṇ sage meditating on a nearby mountaintop. The brothers knocked over the ascetic's water pot (his *karhā*), and the water from the pot flowed down the mountainside and across the plateau toward Pāṇḍeśvar. With the furious ascetic hot on their heels, the two brothers ran downstream along the route that the water was taking. Each time the ascetic came too close, they would toss a grain of rice behind them. The grain of rice would turn into a Śivaliṅga, and the ascetic would stop to worship it. Thus were founded the Śiva temples of the many villages along the upper reaches of the Karhā river.[1]

This story, which is widely told in Purandar Taluka of Puṇe District, Maharashtra, is a story about the founding of a region. The story shows how a set of places came to be connected to one another. The connection among these places came into being because the two brothers ran from one of the places to another, connecting them by physically moving between them. In another sense, the places came to be connected because each of them has a Śivaliṅga that the brothers installed and that the ascetic sage was the first to worship. Most fundamentally, though, what connected the places was not the fact that the Pāṇḍavas ran from one of them to another, not the fact that the ascetic chased the brothers, and not the fact that they installed and he worshipped the Śivaliṅgas, but rather the fact that the water flowed from one of the places to another. Ultimately, the story is based on the physical-geographical fact that the Karhā river itself connects the places along its banks for the 100 or so kilometers that it flows down the gentle slope of the Deccan Plateau.

Rivers are a particularly good means of connecting places. Rivers are the only element of the landscape that themselves move. As they flow from one place to another, they connect the places that they move between. Rivers themselves are places too: moving, ever-changing places.[2] Because they move, providing a physical link among places, rivers allow people to bring spatially separated places together in their imaginations. A river allows people to conceptualize as a whole the land across which it flows, and to give that land religious value. The story of the origin of the Karhā river is but one example of the many religious ways in which people in Maharashtra use rivers to imagine, conceptualize, or experience regions. Besides oral stories like this one, people in Maharashtra have created religious texts, abstract concepts, and concrete images through which they bring various places along a river together in their minds and imaginations. In addition, people participate in very concrete rituals in which they reinforce the connections among the places that a river brings together. They do this by moving their own bodies from place to place: by traveling on pilgrimages. Such pilgrimages enable people to experience for themselves the region created by the river.

This first chapter will provide a survey of important ways in which Maharashtrians use rivers to conceptualize and experience regions. Starting with traditional texts and abstract concepts, the chapter will move on to discuss more concrete images and other stories besides the one about the Karhā river and the Pāṇḍavas. These are all ways in which people in Maharashtra connect riverside places and thereby make river valleys into regions in their minds and imaginations. Next we will look at ways in which people enact regions with their bodies, moving along a river or between a river and nearby villages in pilgrimages that dramatize and highlight the region that the river forms. The chapter will conclude by examining a number of stories and rituals that emphasize a seemingly opposite function of rivers: their role as boundaries and obstacles. Here too, we will find that at least some of the stories and rituals ultimately bring to the fore rivers' power to unite even more than their power to divide.

Images of Nuclearity

The Māhātmyas of the major rivers of Maharashtra provide a clear image of rivers as linking spatially separated places. A Māhātmya is a type of traditional verse text that glorifies something. Generally a Māhātmya glorifies a particular holy place, but there are also Māhātmyas that praise a particular ritual practice, a certain month of the religious year, or—most importantly for our purposes—a river. I have found and read Marathi Māhātmyas of the Narmadā, Tāpī, Pūrṇā, Godāvarī, Bhīmā, and Kṛṣṇā rivers (map 0.1), and Sanskrit Māhātmyas of the Godāvarī and the Kṛṣṇā.[3] Each of the Māhātmyas begins with an account of the origin of its river and then proceeds to name, to tell stories connected with, and to recite the benefits of visiting, of performing various rituals at, or even sometimes just of thinking about a series of places along the river's banks. With the exception of the *Narmadā Māhātmya* (a special case that I will discuss later), all of the river Māhātmyas I have read begin their series at the source of the river and end at the point at which the river empties into the ocean or another river. Thus, by the mute facts of their existence and their overall structure, these river Māhātmyas affirm that the various holy places strung out along a single river all belong to one set.

Sometimes there are more articulate statements of such a conception. The *Tāpī Māhātmya*, for instance, states that the Tāpī "paraded like a line of *dharma*" (*TM* 3.8), and the *Kṛṣṇā Māhātmya* asserts that the Kṛṣṇā river is holy throughout its length.[4] In the *Godāvarī Māhātmya* Śiva promises that there will be holy places (*tīrthas*) every two arm's-lengths along the Godāvarī river, and that he will be in every one of them (*GM*.Skt. 7.24). Some Māhātmyas pick out a few of the places on a river and identify them as the principal, most important, or best places along it. For example, the *Tāpī Māhātmya* lists four places along the Tāpī that are especially rare and precious.[5] The *Kṛṣṇā Māhātmya* lists four such places along its river,[6] and the *Payoṣṇī Māhātmya* gives two different lists of the three most special places along the Pūrṇā (or Payoṣṇī) river.[7] Finally, the Marathi *Godāvarī Māhātmya* (25.94–96) names three principal *tīrthas* along the Godāvarī (Tryambakeśvar, Nāndeḍ, and Rājamahendrī) as places that should all be visited during Siṃhastha, the 13-month period once every 12 years when the planet Jupiter is in the constellation Leo.[8]

One device that texts sometimes use to pick out and link a number of different places along a river also serves to express quite vividly the unity of the river as a whole. The device is that of designating various *tīrthas* as body parts of the river, thereby implicitly viewing the river as a (human) body. The *Payoṣṇī Māhātmya* (30.16), for example, names a place called Kṛṣṇakrīdan *tīrtha* the "heart" of the Payoṣṇī, and the *Narmadā Māhātmya* (22.7) calls Siddheśvar at Nemāvar the Narmadā's "navel."[9] The most elaborate example of such imagery that I have found appears in the Marathi *Godāvarī Māhātmya* by Dāsagaṇū (31.83–85). This text identifies eight "organs" or "limbs" (*aṣṭāṅga*) of the Godāvarī (see map 1.1): Brahmagiri (at Tryambakeśvar) is the Godāvarī's head; Puṇtāmbeṃ is its mouth or face; and Purī, "near the holy area (*kṣetra*) of Paiṭhaṇ," is the river's neck. The heart of the Godāvarī is Mañjarath, the navel is Śaṅkha *tīrtha* (at Nāndeḍ),

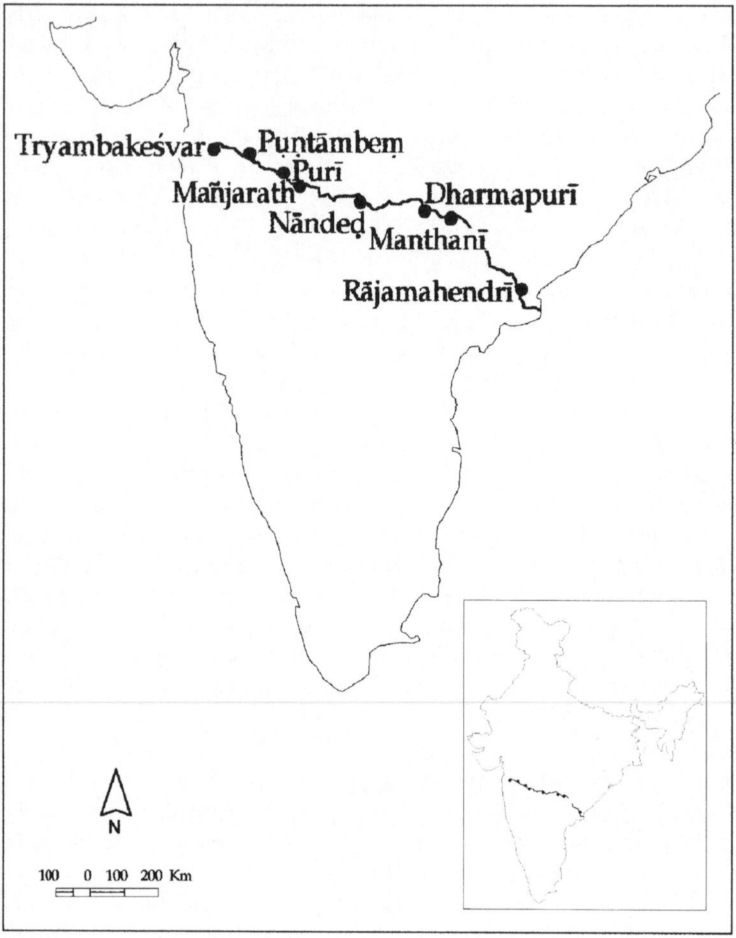

Map 1.1 The eight limbs of the Godāvarī

Manthan (Manthanī) is the hips, and Dharmapurī the knees, while Rājamahendrī is the eighth limb, the feet.[10]

A Brāhmaṇ resident of Paiṭhaṇ who was aware of this image of Dāsagaṇū's pointed out its similarity to the Puruṣasūkta of the Ṛgveda (10.90), the hymn that portrays the strata of society and of the natural world as deriving from the parts of the sacrificed cosmic giant, Puruṣa. In Doniger's translation (O'Flaherty 1981:31), the relevant part of this hymn reads as follows:

> When they divided the Man [Puruṣa], into how many parts did they apportion him? What do they call his mouth, his two arms and thighs and feet? His mouth became the Brahmin; his arms were made into the Warrior, his thighs the People, and from his feet the Servants were born. The moon was born from his mind; from his eye the sun was born. Indra and Agni came from his mouth, and from his vital breath the Wind was born. From his navel the middle realm of space arose; from his head the sky evolved. From his two feet came the earth, and the quarters of the sky from his ear. Thus they set the worlds in order. (Ṛgveda 10.90.11–14.)

Such an identification of a river as a humn body presents a powerful cosmological image. This image implies that the river is organic and that it is human. To identify the body with the Vedic Puruṣa implies in addition that the river is the stuff out of which the universe is made. By comparison, my point here seems almost prosaic: in the process of making these ambitious cosmological claims, the imagery *also* serves to bring together various places along the river in a conceptual unity.

Such unity is also implied in the idea of a *mahānadī* ("great river"), a river that flows all the way to the ocean. People who use the concept of a *mahānadī* do so to emphasize the superiority of such a river. For instance, a Brāhmaṇ temple priest in Sangli defined the term *mahānadī* as follows, applying it to the Kṛṣṇā:

> The Kṛṣṇā is a *mahānadī*, a big river . . . . A river that has the same name all the way from its source until it flows into the ocean is a big river, a *mahānadī*. And the ones that flow into it don't keep their names afterwards. So they count as small rivers.

Other people I have spoken with who have used this concept seem to place less emphasis on the fact that the name of the great river does not change than on the fact that it maintains its identity and independence. Many rivers flow into a *mahānadī*, but it does not flow into any other river.

So compelling is the prestige of the *mahānadī* concept that it appears even in the Māhātmyas of the two rivers of Maharashtra that have Māhātmyas but that flow into another river instead of into the ocean. The Māhātmyas of both these rivers take great pains to explain that their rivers really *do*, in fact, flow directly into the ocean. The Māhātmya of the Bhīmā river, which flows into the Kṛṣṇā, claims that one of the two mouths with which the Kṛṣṇā enters the ocean is really the Bhīmā (*BM* 42.26–27). The *Payoṣṇī Māhātmya* goes through even more complex contortions in order to show that the Pūrṇā river, rather than merging into the Tāpī, as it appears to do, in fact flows into the ocean. According to the last chapter of this Māhātmya (*PM* 41), when the Pūrṇā reached what appears to be its confluence with the Tāpī, it did not flow into that river, but instead split the earth and sped down into the Underworld. From there the Pūrṇā returned to earth as the Kāverī river of South India, then went to the Narmadā, in central India, first cutting across this river and then flowing into it. Next the Pūrṇā jumped upward and split the heavens. It returned to earth as the Kṣiprā river at Ujjain, then went underground again. There the Pūrṇā became the underground river Sarasvatī, pervaded the whole earth, and made an appearance at Prabhās, in Gujarat,[11] before finally transforming itself into the Gomatī at Dvārkā and flowing into the ocean there. The outcome of this complex narrative is an assertion that the Pūrṇā river, far from losing its identity in the Tāpī, in fact eventually flows into the ocean. The fact that it does so under another name seems not to matter.

In this story, the ocean greets the Pūrṇā river as his granddaughter, and she in turn calls him her grandfather (*PM.* 41.52).[12] More often, however, the relationship between the ocean and the rivers that flow into it is seen as one between husband and wife.[13] Whether viewed as a marriage or not, the union of a river and the ocean presents a powerful image of fulfillment: of reaching a goal, on the part of the river, and of replenishment, on the part of the ocean. More importantly for our purposes, even though the concept of a *mahānadī* focuses primarily on the endpoint of the river's course, it also implicitly draws attention to the river as a whole. To think of a river as a *mahānadī* is to imagine it traversing the land—generally in a more prosaic manner and via a more direct route than that in the *Payoṣṇī Māhātmya*—and emerging at the place where the land meets the ocean. Thinking of a river as a *mahānadī*, then, provides another way of thinking about the land through which the river passes.

Yet another concept that people sometimes invoke with respect to a river is even more explicitly regional. This is the concept of *pañcakrośī*. The notion of *pañcakrośī* is used most often with respect to holy *places*. The *pañcakrośī* of a holy place is the area within a radius of five *krośa*s (or kos)—approximately ten miles—that comprises the place's holy field. The best-known *pañcakrośī* is that of Kāśī (Vārāṇasī, Banaras),[14] but there are many other holy places that have a *pañcakrośī* as well.[15] In Maharashtra, the concept of *pañcakrośī* is invoked not only with respect to particular places along a river but also, in some cases, with respect to the river itself as a whole. The *Tāpī Māhātmya* uses this concept most freely, naming the rewards to be obtained within the *pañcakrośī* of the Tāpī (*TM* 60.41; 61.68–69) and identifying various places as being located within five *krośa*s of the river (*TM* 61.51; 63.27–28). The Marathi version of the *Godāvarī*

Māhātmya, in narrating the story of Rām's father, Daśarath, relates that Daśarath was freed from bondage in the world of Yama as soon as Rām came within five *krośas* of the Godāvarī (*GM*.Mar. 19.100); the Sanskrit version of the same Māhātmya (*GM*.Skt. 53.122–38) puts the distance at five *yojanas*. A *yojana*, like a *krośa*, is a measure of varying length, but it is most often said to be equivalent to four *krośas*. When the *Kṛṣṇā Māhātmya* proclaims that the land (*kṣetra*) for a *yojana* on each side of the Kṛṣṇā from the Sahyādri mountain(s) to the ocean gives liberation,[16] the text is perhaps literally claiming only four-fifths as much as if it had used the term *pañcakrośī*, but it is using an idea that is for our purposes the same. This is the idea that not just the river itself, but the land all along it, is holy: the river valley is a holy land.

Stories of Riverine Holy Lands

Besides the story of the origin of the Karhā river, there are a number of other cases in which a story links several different places along one river and provides a sense of the river valley as a holy land. Some of these stories, like that of the Karhā, link various places along a river with an account of the river's origin; others focus on places farther downstream, including doabs and deltas. One of the origin stories is told in connection with the Pūrṇā river. This river's other name, Payoṣṇī, means "Warm Milk." According to its Māhātmya,[17] the Payoṣṇī river originated when 70 million ascetic Brahmans (*ṛṣis*) tested the hospitality of an extremely generous king by demanding milk from him during the hot season. Śiva gave the king the moon's daughter, the sliver of the moon on Śiva's head, and she served each of the ascetics hundreds of cupfuls of milk, much more than they could drink. Stuffed, bloated, and short of breath, the ascetics poked holes in the bottoms of their leaf cups. Still, the milk overflowed their cups, the ascetics began to vomit what they had drunk, and milk started to flood the earth. The moon's daughter came to flow on earth as warm milk: the Payoṣṇī river.

Some people I met who live along this river and are aware of this Māhātmya story know more geographical details. According to these people, some of the ascetic Brahmans washed down in the flood of milk came to rest at various places along the river, giving the places their names. Nīlkaṇṭheśvar *ṛṣi*, at Nirūḷ Gaṅgāmāī (Bhātkulī Taluka, Amravati District), is the only one people mentioned to me whose name sounds anything like that of the place where he landed. Other *ṛṣis* I learned about are Mudgaleśvar, at Ṛṇmocan; Śukleśvar, near Vāṭhoḍā; Rāmeśvar, at Vāramtīr; and Dādājī, of Dādājīcī Bhūmī ("Dādājī's land"), at Belkuṇḍ, near Vijhulī.[18] Except for Dādājī, which is a respectful term that literally means "Elder Brother" and could apply to almost any male god or hero, the names of all these ascetics indicate that their temples are in fact temples of Śiva.

As in the story of the origin of the Karhā river, a sacrifice is central to the origin story of the five rivers that flow from the Pañcakṛṣṇā temple at Mahābaḷeśvar. This sacrifice, which was performed by the god Brahmā with the assistance of his wives Sāvitrī and Gāyatrī,[19] is said to have been completed at Harihareśvar, a place in the Koṅkaṇ; the Śivaliṅga at Harihareśvar counts as the last in a series of 12 along the banks of the Sāvitrī river between Mahābaḷeśvar and the ocean (Phaḍke 1931:230).

In addition to stories that connect places along rivers with the origin places of the rivers, other stories bring together sets of places downstream from a river's source. The goddess Sarasvatī has a temple at Bāsar, on the Godāvarī, near the point where that river flows from Maharashtra into Andhra Pradesh. Some people who live along this part of the river explain that Sarasvatī moved to Bāsar from Dharmapurī, a town downstream from Bāsar on the Godāvarī; the collapsed walls and roof of her abandoned temple in Dharmapurī can still be seen on the riverbank there. Sarasvatī moved, the people who told me about this said, because she was disappointed with the behavior of the (Brāhmaṇ) residents of Dharmapurī, but no one I talked with could tell me what it was that the people of Dharmapurī had done to offend the goddess.[20]

Further upstream in the Godāvarī valley is a set of places whose story I have been able to learn somewhat more about (map 1.2). When Mohinī (the seductive female form of Viṣṇu) killed the demon Rāhu at Nevāse, the demon's head fell at Rāhurī, upstream on the Muḷā river (a river that flows into the Pravarā above Nevāse),[21] and his body at Kāygāv ("Body-ville"), near the Pravarā's confluence with the Godāvarī. According to a priest in the Mohinīrāj temple in Nevāse, two drops of the nectar that the demon had drunk fell on Mahiṣāsur mountain in far-away Akola District; according to both the Godāvarī Māhātmya (*GM*.Skt. 36; *GM*.Mar. 15) and oral versions of the story, the rest of the nectar, the best (*pravara*) substance in the demon's body, flowed out of him as the Pravarā river. A retired civil engineer who used to work at the Rāhurī sugar factory narrated this story as follows:

> It's like this, Madam: In the past, they churned the ocean. And, at the time of the churning of the ocean, after the gods and demons had churned it, nectar emerged. After they had gotten the nectar, Viṣṇu took the nectar himself, he took the pot. And he was to serve that pot to everyone. Then the two rivers Muḷā and Pravarā came together in Nevāse Taluka. And, on the bank of the Muḷā, the whole company of gods sat in a row, in a row to eat.

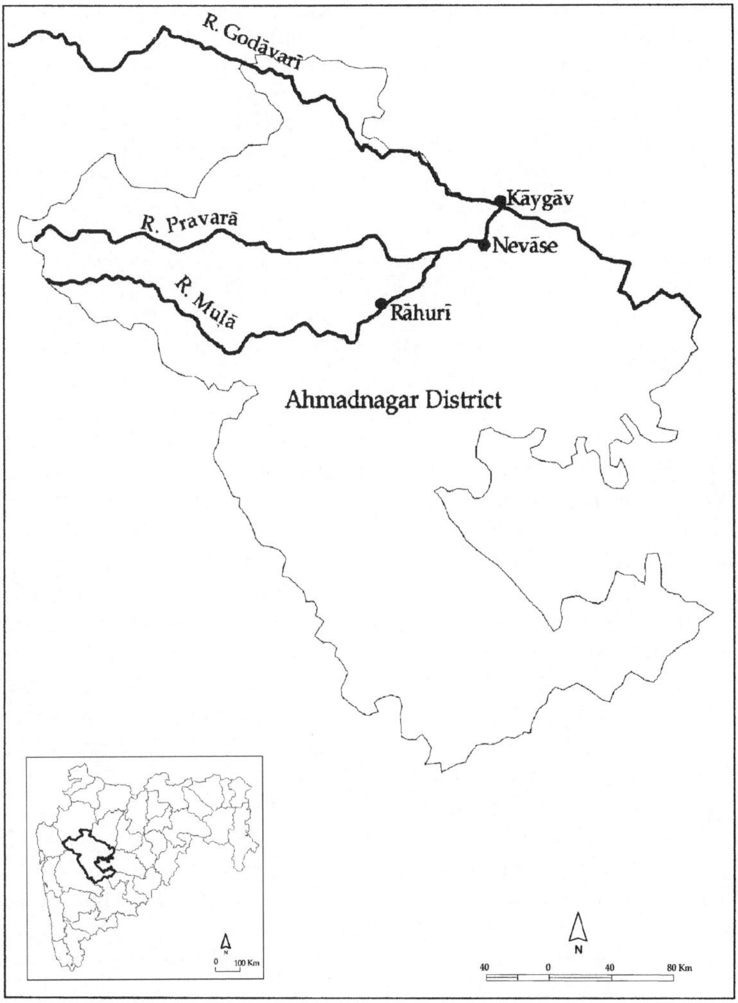

Map 1.2 The Rāhurī demon story

After I repeated the name, "Muḷā," the narrator continued:

> Yes, the Muḷā river—I mean, it's this one [at Rāhurī]. And . . . the river that is at Śrīrāmpūr or Belāpūr is the Pravarā river. That is where the demons sat. That is, the company of demons sat there, they sat on that side . . . . And then, as they were doing all this, Viṣṇu realized that, even though the gods and demons were sitting there, they [the demons] had to be tricked there.

> If the demons got any of the nectar, then their life would become permanent. And they would give trouble to humans on earth. So, if possible, they were not to be given nectar. Instead, they were to be given alcohol. And [the gods] were to be given nectar to drink. That's how it was.
>
> Then, in that way, they sat in those rows. And then Viṣṇu took the form of Mohinī. And after she had danced and done all those other things, she began to serve them. Over here, she was giving alcohol to the demons, and she was giving nectar to the gods.
>
> Among the demons were two named Rāhū and Ketū. Those demons were suspicious. They were very clever. They got up suddenly, silently, and went and sat in the gods' row. And immediately Śaṅkarjī [Śiva] realized this. And then Śaṅkar gave an order to shoot them right away. So Rāhū was shot. And his . . . head came here and fell in Rāhurī. That's why . . . this village's name is Rāhurī.

The narrator of this story also drew a map to explain the geography involved in the narrative, making it clear that for him, the story takes place in a two-dimensional area. This distinguishes this version of the Rāhurī story from the story of the origin of the Karhā, from the story of the origin of the Pūrṇā, and from the story of the goddess Sarasvatī moving from one place to another along the Godāvarī. Although these other stories do serve to bring together into single sets places that are otherwise separate, joined only by the river that runs through them, each set of places remains more or less one-dimensional. It is a line or a string of places rather than a two-dimensional area. By contrast, a doab, the land between two rivers that eventually join each other at a confluence, like the doab between the Pravarā and Muḷā rivers, forms a two-dimensional space that lends itself even better to conceptualization as a region.

Another such doab is found in the upper valley of the Kṛṣṇā river. The Veṇṇā and the Kṛṣṇā, which are both understood to originate at Mahābaḷeśvar, come together at Saṅgam Māhulī, about 50 kilometers downstream. A Brāhmaṇ man in Limb, upstream on the Kṛṣṇā from Māhulī, told me that this whole doab, all the land between the Kṛṣṇā and the Veṇṇā from Mahābaḷeśvar to Saṅgam Māhulī, is "Paraśurām's private land (*khājgī bhūmī*)." When I asked how it got to be Paraśurām's land, the man explained that Agastya gave it to him. The man named five places within this area that have temples dedicated to Paraśurām.[22]

Deltas too, areas defined by the branches of rivers that split into several streams to meet the ocean, provide images that are more two-dimensional than the line formed by a single river joining the places along it. If the beginning of the Kṛṣṇā river is a good example of a doab endowed with religious meanings, the end of the Godāvarī river provides a good example of a delta region to which people attach religious significance. To form its delta, the Godāvarī divides into several mouths that flow separately into the ocean. Given that rivers, which are generally feminine, are in some sense married to the ocean, which is masculine (see Feldhaus 1995:43, 54), we might expect to find sexual or marital imagery in the *Godāvarī Māhātmya*'s description of the meeting between the Godāvarī and the ocean. However, neither the Sanskrit nor the Marathi version of the *Godāvarī Māhātmya* employs such imagery.[23] Rather, in these texts, the ocean greets the river respectfully, confesses that he is not as great as she, and asks her to divide into several streams before coming to enter him. Although modern maps show three main streams in which the river meets the ocean, the *Godāvarī Māhātmya* explains (and oral traditions agree) that there are seven streams, one named for each of the seven sages.

The seven mouths of the Godāvarī make its delta analogous to the sets of seven rivers mentioned in Vedic and subsequent literature[24] and cause the delta to resonate with associations to numerous other seven-membered sets connected with rivers (see Feldhaus 1995). In addition, by virtue of being related to the seven sages, the delta becomes an earthly replica of the heavenly constellation Ursa Major (the Big Dipper), which in India is called the Saptarṣi, "the Seven Sages."[25] Once again, a story provides the medium through which an area of land defined by a river can come to be thought of as a coherent, meaningful, religiously sanctioned region.

River Pilgrimages

Besides such stories, images, and abstract concepts as those we have examined so far, Maharashtrians also participate in rituals that provide occasions for—and evidence of—their conceptualization of the land around a river as a region. The rituals I have in mind are pilgrimages: rituals in which people physically move across or around in an area. The idea that physically moving around in an area can make that area into a region fits well with the ideas of the philosopher Edward Casey, whom I quoted briefly in the Introduction. Casey (1993:53) sees the living human body as central to the notion of region:

> When the range of the here includes not just the place through which I am now moving (and which therefore reflects my immediate bodily movement) but all of the places to which I can effectively move, I experience a properly regional here . . . . I take myself to be *here* in this house or block or neighborhood, in this state or nation, whenever I am convinced that . . . . I can in principle move (in person or by proxy) to any part of this region, however far-flung this part might be.

Casey's point about bodily movement refers to something like what Burton Stein (1977; cf. Markovits, Pouchepadass, and Subrahmanyam 2003) meant when he used the term "circulation" to discuss varieties of movement through the Tamil-language region of India. Examining the "circulation" of different kinds of people (scribes, poet-saints, bards, ritual specialists, pilgrims, soldiers, merchants, agriculturalists, politicians, and so on) in various historical periods, Stein was particularly interested to understand the relationship of such people's movements to cognitive regions. Passing through an area with one's body, or imagining oneself—or someone else—doing so, gives one a sense of the area as a region. In most pilgrimages in South Asia, the pilgrims enact their conviction that they *can* move through a region by in fact *doing* so. At the same time, they reinforce the same conviction for those who, though they remain at home, are aware of the pilgrims' journeys. Movement through an area with one's own body, or a clear realization of the possibility of such movement, is a condition for being able to image the area as a region in *any* coherent sense.

A number of pilgrimages associated with rivers serve to dramatize regions watered by the rivers, making the regions into circulatory and thus also, at least potentially, conceptual units. Here I will examine three kinds of river pilgrimages: first, the practice of circumambulating a river; second, pilgrimage rituals in which people carry village gods to a river to be bathed; and, third, pilgrimage rituals in which people fetch water from a river to bathe a village or pilgrimage god. Chapter 2 will present an extensive description and analysis of one pilgrimage of the third type.

Circumambulation, or *pradakṣiṇā*, is the ritual gesture of walking around something (or someone) with one's right (*dakṣiṇ*) side toward it (or him or her)—that is, in a clockwise direction—as a way of showing respect. People in India regularly perform *pradakṣiṇā* toward deities, temples, saints' shrines, and holy cities and towns.[26] Sometimes people perform *pradakṣiṇā* to a river as well. Such a *pradakṣiṇā* provides a ritual expression of the unity of the river; it makes the river a circulatory and conceptual unit.

The best known and most often performed *pradakṣiṇā* of a river is that of the Narmadā. This *pradakṣiṇā* is usually referred to as the Narmadā *parikrama*. According to the *Imperial Gazetteer of India* (1909: Volume 1, p. 178), at the beginning of the twentieth century "300 or more" people set out to perform *pradakṣiṇā* of the Narmadā each year. I am not sure how this number was arrived at or what the corresponding number would be today. Many people I have talked with among the educated elite in Maharashtra seem to be at least aware of the Narmadā *parikrama*, and some have even heard of someone who has performed it. The best-known Maharashtrian pilgrim to travel to and around the Narmadā in the twentieth century was Gopāl Nīlkaṇṭh Dāṇḍekar (d. 1998), whose novel *Kuṇā*

Ekācī Brahmaṇgāthā ("The Account of Someone's Wanderings," 1957) has as its principal character a man who is performing the Narmadā *parikrama*.[27]

According to Kāgalkar (1969:17–18), the Narmadā *parikrama* may be performed in any one of three ways: (1) starting at the source and not ever crossing the river, one proceeds along the south bank to the mouth and back to the source, and then walks to the mouth and back to the source along the north bank;[28] (2) starting at the source, one goes downstream on the south bank and returns on the north bank, crossing the river by boat at the mouth; or (3) starting anywhere along the river, one makes a complete circuit of it, keeping it always on one's right and crossing it at the mouth.

Except at the mouth, the pilgrim should never cross the river—not even an old bed left behind after the river has changed its course[29]—and one should not swim anywhere in the river. The pilgrimage is to be performed entirely on foot, in bare feet. The pilgrims should bring along no money,[30] should sleep on a blanket on the ground, and should cook and eat only foodstuffs obtained by begging. During the pilgrimage, the pilgrims should not cut their hair or nails. Furthermore, except during Cāturmās (the four-month rainy season, a traditional period of retreat for wandering ascetics and mendicants in India), when the *parikrama* is to be suspended, the pilgrim should stay no more than three days in any one place (Kāgalkar 1969:19–21). The 1700-mile journey (twice that if one goes up *and* down both banks without crossing at the mouth) is quite difficult[31] and can take years to perform.[32]

Although extremely rare, something like the Narmadā *parikrama* is not unheard of in connection with the rivers that flow through Maharashtra. People in the village of Niruḷ Gaṅgāmāī, on the left bank of the Pūrṇā river, told my companions and me that a group (*diṇḍī*) circumambulating the Pūrṇā had stopped overnight in Niruḷ Gaṅgāmāī in 1987; one person—a middle-aged man, I believe—said that this was the third or fourth such group he had seen in his lifetime. The pilgrims had started from the source of the Pūrṇā; they were planning to travel as far as Cāṅgdev, at the Pūrṇā's confluence with the Tāpī, to cross the Pūrṇā there, and to return along the other side of the river.

Ritual circumambulation of the Godāvarī seems to be somewhat more common than that of the Pūrṇā. People I talked with at Paiṭhaṇ, Rākṣasbhuvan, Dhanorā (near Parat Gaṅgā) and Dharmapurī (in Andhra Pradesh) reported seeing pilgrims engaged in *pradakṣiṇā* of the Godāvarī. The sixteenth-century poet-saint Eknāth, who lived at Paiṭhaṇ, refers to the Godāvarī *pradakṣiṇā* in one of his song-poems (*abhaṅgas*).[33] In more recent times, Dāsagaṇū states in his Marathi *Godāvarī Māhātmya*, published in 1921, that he performed *pradakṣiṇā* of the Godāvarī along with a party of 35 men and women, many of whom he names (*GM*. Mar. 31.188–92).

At Paiṭhaṇ I learned of a man who circumambulates the Godāvarī every year, of another who had circumambulated *both* the Narmadā and the Godāvarī, and of a third who had circumambulated *four* rivers: the Godāvarī, the Narmadā, the Tāpī, and the Pravarā.

Pradakṣiṇā of the Godāvarī is performed most widely during the Siṃhastha period, when the planet Jupiter is in the constellation Leo (Siṃha, the lion).[34] The ritual often involves circumambulating only *part* of the river. Many pilgrims perform *pradakṣiṇā* of the Godāvarī between Tryambakeśvar and Śaṅkha *tīrtha*, the "navel" of the Godāvarī (see earlier), near Nāndeḍ:[35] Kāgalkar (1969:17) calls this *nābhipradakṣiṇā*, "Navel Circumambulation." A pilgrim at Māhūr who came from Limb in Pātharī Taluka, Parbhaṇī District, reported that people from his village perform *pradakṣiṇā* of the Godāvarī by walking up the south bank of the river to Paiṭhaṇ,[36] crossing there, and returning along the north bank. People who circumambulate the whole of the Godāvarī use one of three methods: they travel as far as Rājamahendrī and turn back,[37] they choose the principal one of the "seven" mouths of the river[38] and follow it until it meets the ocean at Antarvedī,[39] or they include the whole delta in their *pradakṣiṇā*, traveling by boat across all of the river's mouths.[40]

The *Parikramāsahit Narmadāpañcāṅg*, a Hindi book from the year 1919, includes brief descriptions of 236 places on the south bank (Caitanya 1919:97–176) and 237 places on the north bank (Caitanya 1919:177–254) of the Narmadā, along with information, instructions for the pilgrim, and summaries of stories about the places from the *Revā Khaṇḍ*, a Māhātmya-like text that claims to belong to the *Skanda Purāṇa*. The book also gives similar information in tabular form (Caitanya 1919:11–37): the distance between one place and another, the number of *tīrtha*s at each place, the names of the rivers that flow into the Narmadā, the sites of their confluences, the locations of post offices and train stations, the characteristics of the landscape along the way (how thick the jungle is and so on), and the numbers of the chapters of the *Revā Khaṇḍ* that contain stories connected with the various places. This book makes it abundantly clear that the Narmadā *parikrama*—and, by extension, the practice of circumambulating other rivers as well—is a ritual way of paying honor not just to the river as a whole in the abstract, but to the river as consisting of all the different places along it. The pilgrim connects these places by walking from one of them to another, just as the river connects them by flowing past them all.

Again, as with the concept of *mahānadī*, and as with stories, images, and lists that bring together a series of places along the banks of a single river, the region defined by the ritual of circumambulating a river is extremely long and thin. Another set of rituals covers somewhat broader areas and expresses even more clearly the nuclearity of a river to the region through which it flows. These rituals are ones in which either the gods of nearby villages are brought to a river or water from a river is carried to nearby village and pilgrimage gods. When people bring gods from nearby villages to a river to be bathed, the people most often carry the gods in a palanquin; both the palanquin and the palanquin procession are called "*pālkhī*" in Marathi.

Carrying a god somewhere in a *pālkhī* is a normal way to pay the god honor; it is a ritual that people perform for many temple gods on a regular basis: in some places every day; in others, weekly or monthly; and, at most pilgrimage temples, at least during annual festivals. Often the palanquin simply makes a circuit of the temple courtyard; sometimes it travels around in the village or town, or leaves to go somewhere else; and occasionally people use a palanquin to carry a god to a local river or lake to be bathed. In the kind of ritual I am interested in here, a number of village gods, almost all of them gods of purely local importance, travel in palanquins to one place along a river so that they can all be bathed at the same time.

One such ritual takes place in Dauṇḍ, a railway junction and taluka headquarters on the Bhīmā river in eastern Pune District, on the eleventh day of the bright half[41] of the month of Āṣāḍh (June–July). This is the day known as Āṣāḍhī Ekādaśī, the culminating day of the Vārkarīs' pilgrimage to Paṇḍharpūr,[42] the largest, best-known pilgrimage in this part of the world. On this day in 1998, 12 palanquins from different villages in Dauṇḍ Taluka and neighboring Bārāmatī Taluka (map 1.3) formed a procession at the far side of the railway tracks, away from the river (figure 1.1). The palanquins held brass masks or other portable images of goddesses[43] and Śaiva gods.[44] Leading the procession was a company of Ārādhinīs, women dedicated to the worship of goddesses who take possession of them and cause them to dance in ecstatic trance. Interspersed throughout the procession were groups of dancers who had accompanied the palanquins from their home villages; each of these groups consisted of young men dressed in a uniform way who danced in energetic unison, using the jangling, tambourine-like sticks typical of the *lejhīm* form of dance. Several of the groups also carried beautifully decorated parasols and standards (*abdagiris*) near their palanquins; one group[45] had a flag as well, and set off fireworks from time to time as the procession moved along. The procession traveled slowly through the underpass beneath the railway lines, onto the main street of Dauṇḍ, down that street past the main square and into the market area, and finally to the river. There the people accompanying each of the palanquins removed the god from their palanquin, washed the god, took baths in the river, and performed *pūjā* to the god before setting off to return home.

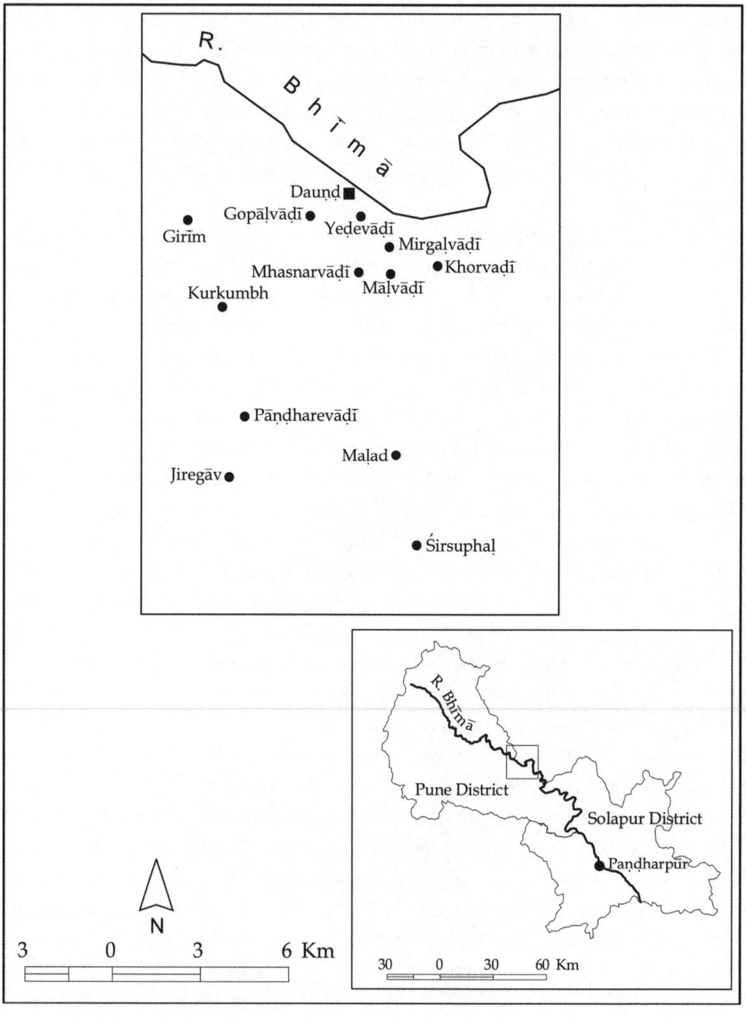

Map 1.3 The Dauṇḍ pilgrimage

As my companions and I returned to Pune later that day, we stopped in Kurukumbh, one of the places whose goddess (Phiraṅgāī) had been carried to the river at Dauṇḍ. We noticed that the festival image, a brass mask of the goddess's face that is normally in the main temple at Kurukumbh, was not there. When we asked a Gurav priest about it, she replied, "It's been carried off in the palanquin." Then she explained further, "They take the goddess's palanquin to the Bhīmā river at Dauṇḍ, give her a bath, and

Figure 1.1 Palanquins form a procession to the Bhīmā river at Dauṇḍ on Āṣāḍhī Ekādaśī.

bring her back." When we asked if this is done on the eleventh (Ekādaśī) of every fortnight, the woman explained: "No. This is the main Ekādaśī of the year, isn't it? That's why. The Bhīmā river is at Dauṇḍ, and this same river is the Candrabhāgā at Paṇḍharpūr. So because of the river we get the joy of having the sight of Pāṇḍuraṅg (the god of Paṇḍharpūr). That's why they take the goddess to Dauṇḍ in the palanquin for a bath." Earlier, a Muslim man sitting with his young son on the steps of the railway walkover at Dauṇḍ had watched along with me as the procession started out. This man too explained the timing and location of the ritual in terms of the course of the Bhīmā river and the date of the Paṇḍharpūr pilgrimage. He reminded me that Āṣāḍhī Ekādaśī is the day of the Paṇḍharpūr pilgrimage, and that "at Paṇḍharpūr they call this same Bhīmā river the Candrabhāgā."

Thus, even though the deities in the various palanquins that came to Dauṇḍ that year for the procession and bath in the river are all goddesses or forms of Śiva, these interpreters of the festival understood it in terms of the cult of the god Viṭhobā of Paṇḍharpūr, a god usually identified with Kṛṣṇa or Viṣṇu. More importantly for us, the interpreters see the Bhīmā river as linking Dauṇḍ with Paṇḍharpūr. Flowing past Dauṇḍ to Viṭhobā's distant town, a town that is the goal of hundreds of thousands of pilgrims on the eleventh day of Āṣāḍh, the river enables the villagers and gods who come to Dauṇḍ to participate in the "joy" of the larger pilgrimage that reaches Paṇḍharpūr on the same day. In addition, the Dauṇḍ pilgrimage has another religious-geographical function. It dramatizes the small region constituted by the places from which the gods in the palanquins come to Dauṇḍ. The procession of the palanquins from the various places brings together important gods of the places as well as representative citizens from the places, the men and women who have brought the gods. The procession of the people carrying the gods in the palanquins makes the region they all come from visible, both to the participants and to observers. No one but me, as far as I know, has designed a map like map 1.3, but the palanquin procession to the river forms a map of a different sort. It represents the region not on paper but by means of the images of the gods and the bodies of the people who come from the places it brings together.

On the last Monday of the month of Śrāvaṇ (July–August), a similar but more elaborate palanquin pilgrimage is held at a number of places along the Kṛṣṇā river. The place to which the most palanquins come on this day is Karāḍ, but the festival is also held at Saṅgam Māhulī, at Koṭeśvar (in the river between Gove and Limb), and at other places along the Kṛṣṇā (map 1.4). At Karāḍ, a few of the palanquins come to the beach at the foot of the main approach to the river, downstream from the confluence, but most come to the area of the confluence itself. They come either to the Karāḍ side or to the Sāīdāpūr side of the Kṛṣṇā river, but not to the third side, across the Koynā from Karāḍ and across the Kṛṣṇā from Sāīdāpūr. People numbering from just a few to large groups of 150 or 200 accompany each palanquin to the river from their home village. Sometimes there is a small band of musicians. Some villages bring more than one palanquin or more than one god in a single palanquin. Some of the groups that bring palanquins travel on foot, while others hire a tractor-trailer or a truck for the occasion. Of those traveling on foot, some come from places close enough that they can reach the river in a couple of hours' walking, while others must spend a night each way on the road.

At the river, each group carries out what is generally a fairly simple ritual: they carry the god—usually represented by a brass face mask (*mukhavaṭā*) or a brass festival image—into the water or to the water's edge and bathe it; often the people accompanying the god bathe too; a leader performs *pūjā* to the god by smearing the image with various colored powders and pastes, by offering it food and perhaps flowers, and by arranging it decoratively in the palanquin; the people sing a rhythmic song (*āratī*), clapping out the beat with their hands and in some cases with drums, while one member of the group waves tiny lighted oil lamps or bits of burning camphor; the people eat a meal; and then the group leaves.

In addition, many of the groups put their palanquins into the ferry boat at the confluence of the Kṛṣṇā and Koynā rivers (figure 1.2). The boatsmen pole the ferry out into the middle of the confluence and turn it around in

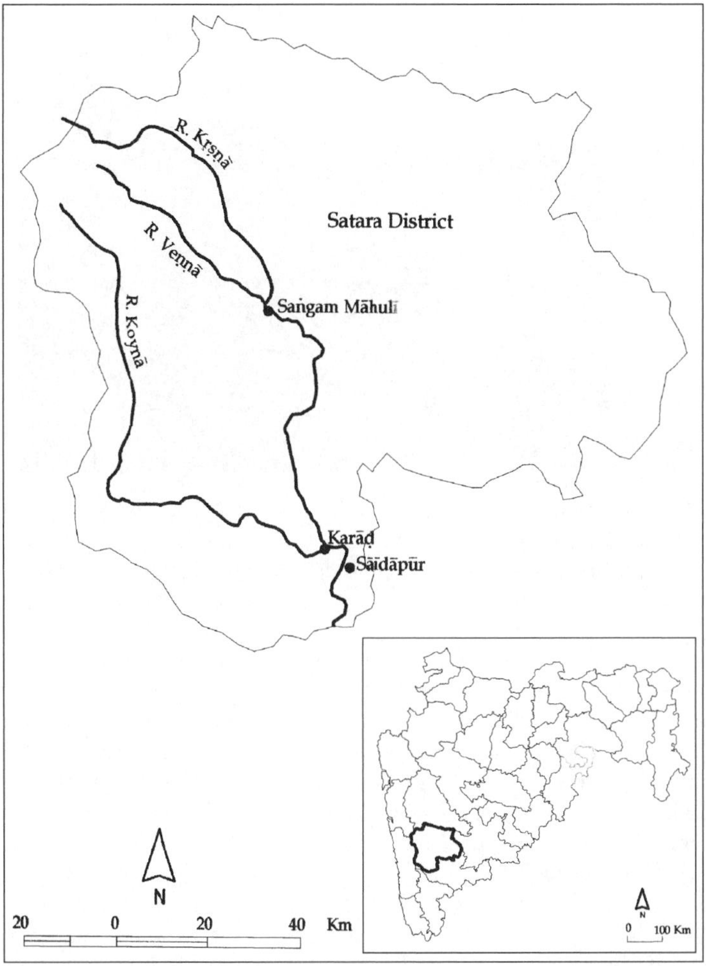

Map 1.4 Gods carried to the Kṛṣṇā river

a circle a couple of times before bringing it back to shore. The pilgrims must pay the boatsmen a rather generous fee for this trip, and so generally only the larger and more affluent groups take their gods for a ride in the boat. If there is a band accompanying the palanquin, the band gets into the boat too and serenades the god during the ride. Some of the groups with gods in palanquins also collect water to take back with them. At least some of them collect the water during the boat ride, from the midpoint of the

Figure 1.2 Palanquins and pilgrims in the ferry boat at the confluence of the Kṛṣṇā and Koynā rivers at Karāḍ. The Koynā river comes from the left and meets the Kṛṣṇā head-on, the combined river flowing off to the right as the Kṛṣṇā.

confluence. One group I talked with who had come a considerable distance said that they would use the water they had taken from the river to bathe their god the next morning, on the journey home. Groups that consist primarily or exclusively of Dhangars (members of the principal shepherd caste of Maharashtra) sometimes hold a session of *huīk* or *bhāganūk* on the beach: a man called a *bhagat* becomes possessed by the god and utters prophecies about the rainfall and other such matters for the coming year.[46]

At Karāḍ, in addition to the groups who come with village gods in palanquins, many other people also take part in the festival on the last Monday of Śrāvaṇ. Numerous devotees of the goddess Yellammā are to be seen, women or male transvestites carrying small brass masks of the goddess in an enormous basket on their heads; and other people come with their own humble collections of household gods. Some people travel to the river simply to bathe, and perhaps also to fetch water to take back to the gods at home. There is a fair with stalls where vendors sell trinkets and prepared foods, and an amusement-park area with a ferris wheel, a merry-go-round, and other rides and games.

One distinctive group at the Karāḍ festival is composed of Muslims from Sāīdāpūr, the village across the Kṛṣṇā river from Karāḍ. Bearing green flags, these people cross the river in the boat—which is owned and operated by Sāīdāpūr Muslims—and go to the shrine of the *pīr* Jāphar Mahammad Sāhab Bābā. This *pīr*'s shrine is located about 100 meters upstream from the confluence next to a cliff on the Karāḍ side of the Koynā. One year I accompanied the party of Muslims to the shrine. They performed ritual prayers to the *pīr*, stood silently for a while, chanted a prayer, and distributed *prasād*; one man went quietly into a state of possession, and others consulted him about their problems. One woman asked, "He's been gone for four or five months; there's been no letter, nothing. He's gone off, leaving wife and children behind . . . . Should I go to Bombay? Will I find him there?" Another woman worried, "My son has no job."—"Don't be afraid," came the answer.

There is no single central rite of the festival at Karāḍ, no common procession, like that at Dauṇḍ, in which all take part, no one god whom all attempt to see or to whom all make offerings. The 1961 census volume *Fairs and Festivals in Maharashtra* (Census of India 1969:381) calls this a festival in honor of Kṛṣṇābāī, the goddess who embodies the Kṛṣṇā river (Feldhaus 1995) and whose temple at Karāḍ is one of several along the main approach to the river there. However, this characterization is misleading. Some palanquins, and some other groups and individuals, stop at the Kṛṣṇābāī temple on their way back from the river, but by no means does everyone do this. People who came with palanquins did not, by and large, mention Kṛṣṇābāī when my companions and I asked them what they were doing and why.[47] Instead, they would answer in terms of the Kṛṣṇā river, or in terms of the confluence, saying that they had come to bathe their god there. The various groups who had come to bathe their gods did so individually, separately, not cooperatively or jointly.

And yet they all did it next to one another, on the same day. They bathed their gods on the same beach as one another, or on the beach across the river from one another, or—at Karāḍ, Saṅgam Māhulī, Koṭeśvar, and the other places where the festival is held—on different beaches along the same river as one another. For each group individually, the point may be that *their* god, the god of *their* village, gets a bath at the Kṛṣṇā river. But, for the sake of their several baths, the gods of many different places come together at one place—or, rather, at several places along one river. The connection with one another of the places the gods come from is thereby dramatically, if mutely, expressed, as is the fact that what brings about the connection is the river. The festival enacts the unity of the region and the centrality of the river to it.

At Karāḍ and Saṅgam Māhulī the imagery of unity and centrality is reinforced by the fact that the festival takes place at the confluence of two rivers: the Kṛṣṇā and the Koynā at Karāḍ, and the Kṛṣṇā and the Veṇṇā at Saṅgam Māhulī. At Karāḍ, when people take their palanquins by boat to the very middle of the confluence and have them circled around before bringing them back to shore, this boat trip highlights the location at the confluence. At Māhulī, the water is usually not deep enough for a boat to be used. Lee Schlesinger noticed, however, when he attended the festival at Saṅgam Māhulī in 1987,[48] that a number of groups carried their palanquins out to a small island of sand that had formed in the middle of the confluence, and that the pilgrims bathed and worshipped the god there. In both cases, the use of the midpoint of the confluence seems to express very clearly, though tacitly, that the ritual as a whole is a confluence—a coming together—of people and gods from places that are otherwise separate.

The converse of rituals in which people carry gods from a region to a river to be bathed are those in which people carry river water to pour on the gods of a region. In chapter 2 I will describe and analyze one such ritual in some detail: the pilgrimage festival in which people carry water to the temple of Śiva at Śiṅgṇāpūr in the month of Caitra (March–April). Aside from this major festival, the rituals in which people carry water to gods are most often found in connection with the Godāvarī river and during the month of Śrāvaṇ.[49] When, as happens at the Godāvarī during Śrāvaṇ, people from different places come to take water from the same river, that river is the central core along which they come together. Their ritual expresses the river's importance for villages of the surrounding region: not only the economic and physical dependence of the region on the river's water but also the way that the river sanctifies the region.

The temple of Vṛddheśvar, for instance, to which men carry *kāvaḍ*s of water from the Godāvarī at Śivarātrī as well as on the third Monday of Śrāvaṇ (see Feldhaus 1995:30), lies on the mountain range that separates the Godāvarī valley from the valley of the Bhīmā river. Rather than being perched on a peak of these mountains, Vṛddheśvar is situated well down one side—the side toward the Godāvarī valley. When men carry *kāvaḍ*s of Godāvarī water to this god, they are carrying water from the Godāvarī river to the furthest southern edge of the Godāvarī valley. The water of the river travels ritually throughout the breadth (or, rather, one half of the breadth, from one bank of the river to one edge of the valley) of the region that the river waters and drains. Not only does the region *get* its water *from* the river; it also *sends* its water *to* the river, in whatever few small streams and rivulets it can produce. By fetching the river's water and pouring it onto the gods of villages throughout the full extent of the river valley, people of those villages make the region imaginatively visible.

Rivers as Boundaries and Obstacles

The concepts, images, stories, and rituals examined in this chapter so far illustrate the variety of ways in which people in Maharashtra use rivers to connect places. The repeated emphasis we have seen on rivers' centrality to regions fits well with the historians' views that regions in traditional India are better understood in terms of nuclear or core areas than in terms of boundaries (Embree 1977) and that rivers have often formed the nucleus or core of a historical region (Stein 1969, 1980). But rivers can also keep places apart.[50] The Narmadā river joins the Vindhya mountains in separating North India from South,[51] and several other rivers form boundaries between political and administrative units within Maharashtra.[52] At Kāmbaḷeśvar, where the goddess Bhivāī (see Feldhaus 1995) has temples on two sides of the Nirā river, one in Pune District and the other in Satara District, a priest on the Satara District side once remarked to me: "This is a boundary deity." The word he used for "boundary," *bāndh*, as he pointed out, refers to the raised line of earth that often separates two fields in the South Asian countryside. Such explicit recognition of the function of rivers as boundaries between modern political units is not unusual. Where rivers form a political or administrative boundary, they were first a natural obstacle. In religious contexts too, rivers are sometimes pictured as obstacles, to be crossed by means of a ford, a bridge, or a ferry, or by swimming. The term "*tīrtha*," now commonly used for riverside pilgrimage places, for other holy places, and for holy human beings, referred originally to a ford, a place where a river can be crossed. A number of scholars have pointed out the metaphorical character of the term's extended meanings: a *tīrtha* is a place where the river of existence can be crossed, or where one can get from this world to the other.[53]

But rivers are not only metaphors. They are real obstacles to be gotten across, and crossing a river also has nonmetaphorical religious dimensions. These are found in a variety of narratives and rituals connected with rivers and riverside places. Stories about a number of pastoralist deities and their legendary devotees, for example, tell of difficulties encountered and overcome in trying to get across rivers.[54] One such story is told about the god Mhaskobā of Vīr. Mhaskobā is Kāḷbhairav of Kāśī (Banāras), who was brought to Vīr by Kamaḷājī, a Dhangar shepherd.[55] The god followed Kamaḷājī to Vīr on horseback, on condition that Kamaḷājī not look back at him.[56] When they had reached the bank of the Nīrā river, just outside of Vīr, Kamaḷājī was worried about how they would get across. Told to go ahead and cross the river on his own, Kamaḷājī swam to the other side, then glanced back to check on the god. The horse, which had just leaped into the air to jump with its divine rider across the river, fell to the ground. People still point out the marks of the horse's hooves on the rocky bank, at a place called Ghoḍe Udān ("Where the Horse Jumped"). This is the original cult place in Vīr.[57]

A steep, dramatic gorge in the Godāvarī river near Manthanī in Andhra Pradesh is named in Telugu "The Adultress's Canyon"; caverns in the cliff on the north bank of the river are called "The Adultress's Caves." A fisherman I met at this place told a story about a love affair between a woman of the Golla shepherd caste who lived on the south bank of the river and a man of a higher caste, a Kāpū, who lived on the north bank. They used to hold their trysts on the north bank, the woman crossing the river in a fired clay pot. Her husband, learning of the affair, substituted an unbaked pot for her usual one; part way across the river the pot disintegrated, and she drowned.[58]

Folk tale and myth, then, portray the crossing of rivers as a difficult and dangerous undertaking. Whether for this reason or for some other, there are traditional restrictions on the crossing of rivers,[59] and ferrymen and their passengers must observe a number of purity and pollution rules with respect to boats.[60] There are also more elaborate ritual ways of marking rivers as boundaries. These include processions in which gods cross rivers, overcoming the rivers' power to keep places apart. The most impressive such river-crossing ritual I have seen is the marriage of the god Khaṇḍobā at Pālī (or Pāl), a village halfway between Karāḍ and Sātārā. The village consists of settlements on both sides of the Tārаḷī river, an affluent of the Kṛṣṇā. At the festival, which tens if not hundreds of thousands of people attend,[61] the god's brass mask (*mukhavaṭā*) travels in a royal procession—complete with elephants, huge parasols made out of marigolds, and enormous clouds of golden-yellow turmeric powder—across the river to the place where the wedding is performed.[62] The marriage reinforces the union achieved when the god breaks through the riverine boundary between the two halves of the village.

Other festivals appear to express more directly an *opposition* between two villages that lie across a river from each other. The 1884 *Gazetteer of the Bombay Presidency* for Ahmadnagar District describes one such ritual that used to take place at Kopargāv, on the Godāvarī river: "According to an old custom in the village on the bright third of Vaishâkh or April–May the village boys fight with slings and stones with the youngsters of the village of Samvatsar across the Godâvarî."[63] In the mid-1980s an article in the Marathi newspaper *Sakāḷ* described another ritual battle of this type held at another place in Ahmadnagar District, this one on the Sīnā river.[64] The battle is held on the evening of the first day of the bright half of the month of Bhādrapad (August–September), in connection with the Gaurāī festival. In this battle, women of Śeṇḍī and Pokharḍī, two villages across the Sīnā river from each other, hold a sort of human tug-of-war. A line is drawn in the riverbed between the villages. (The river, it seems, is dry at this time.) The women of each of the villages form a chain on either side of this line, with an especially strong woman from each side in front. When drums sound the signal to begin, the women of each of the villages try to pull the front woman of the other village over to their side.

In 1984, the year when this ritual was described, the contest was declared a draw. However, the article explained, if the women of one side *do* succeed in pulling the other village's first woman over to their side of the river, they take her to the house of their village headman (*pāṭīl*). There she gets treated not as a captive prisoner, but as a married girl who has returned to her natal home from her in-laws' house for a visit. The next day her hosts feed her a special meal, give her a sari and a blouse piece, and send her back with honor. The story connected with this ritual tells of the origin of the Sīnā river and of the division between the villages, and plays on the notions of opposition and complementarity:

> In the Dvāpara Age,[65] Śaṅkar [Śiva] and Pārvatī came in the course of their wanderings to the woods at Śeṇḍī. Śaṅkar spent his time practicing meditation, coming to the aid of his devotees, and playing parcheesi (*sārīpāt*) with Pārvatī. The month of Śrāvaṇ began, and devotees came to pay homage to Śiva. No one paid any attention to Pārvatī (also called Gaurāī). That hurt her pride, and she began to argue, "I am better than Śiva." The two of them decided to compare their powers.
>
> Pārvatī created the Sīnā river out of her sweat, and with the help of the river she divided the village into two and brought into being the two villages of Śeṇḍī and Pokharḍī. Afterwards, through her power, Pārvatī put into the mind of the headman of Pokharḍī the thought, "You've given your daughter to the son of the headman of Śeṇḍī. He won't send her home for the festival. So somehow you must bring her home. Don't celebrate the festival unless she comes." Meanwhile, Śaṅkar put into the mind of the headman of Śeṇḍī the thought that *his* daughter had been given to the family of the headman of Pokharḍī, and told him to bring her home for the festival.
>
> With that, the Pāṭīls of each of the villages assigned the women of their village the task of stealing away the daughters. The women of the two villages who had set out on this errand met one another in the bed of the Sīnā river.
>
> Now, seeing that a difficult situation was in the making, Nārada muni came running to Śiva and Pārvatī; he stood before them with folded hands and said, "Because of your wounded pride, you are unjustly sacrificing your simple devotees. In reality, you are Śiva and Śakti, both together the supreme Soul." Śiva and Pārvatī understood their mistake.
>
> But by then the women of Śeṇḍī had carried off the daughter-in-law of the Pāṭīl of Pokharḍī. Nārada came quickly to Śeṇḍī. He said, "Treat the daughter-in-law of the Pāṭīl of Pokharḍī as if she were your own daughter. Behave respectfully toward her. Fill her lap[66] with a blouse piece and a coconut, and send her off ceremoniously."
>
> This fight takes place as a reminder of this event.

In the story, then, as in the associated ritual, enmity gives way to friendliness, opposition to complementarity and harmonious unity. The same pattern is found, at the other end of the cultural spectrum, in a story included in the *Māhātmya* of the Godāvarī river. This story tells of a war between two birds who live on opposite banks of the river. One of the birds, a dove, gets as his weapon the noose of Yama, the god of death, while the other, an owl, gets the fire weapon of Agni, the god of fire. After their battle has raged for some time, the birds' wives intervene, each praying to the patron god of her husband's enemy. In the end, the two male birds become friends (*GM*.Skt. 55; *GM*.Mar. 20.30–37).

In this story too, as in the ritual battles across rivers, the river serves—initially, at least—as a barrier across which opposition is expressed. And yet, significantly, both in this story and in the myth and ritual from Śeṇḍī and Pokharḍī, the opposition eventually dissolves. For, while rivers do act as obstacles, while they do create divisions and are used to express opposition, and while, for this reason, they do sometimes mark the boundaries of regions, this is not their most important role in the conceptualization of regions. More than acting as dividing lines that separate places and regions from one another, rivers serve as connecting lines that flow from one place to another, or as central lines that bring otherwise disparate places together to form regions. Although some stories, texts, rituals, and statements relating to rivers in Maharashtra do present rivers as boundaries or obstacles to be crossed, these kinds of materials much more often present an explicit or implicit recognition of the nuclearity of a river to a region.

Rivers and Maharashtra

In closing this chapter, let me reiterate an important caveat. In no case is the region delineated by any of the concepts, stories, or rituals examined in this chapter coextensive with Maharashtra. The regions that people in Maharashtra connect by means of rivers cover a smaller area than Maharashtra or overlap only partially with it. The regions dramatized by rituals in which village gods are carried to a river or the water of a river is carried to them, like the regions delineated by stories that connect various places along a river, are but subregions within Maharashtra. Moreover, the sets composed of places scattered along the whole length of a major river, like the rituals, verbal conceptions, and images that convey a sense of a major river valley as a whole, include much more, and much less, than Maharashtra.

For Maharashtra is not coterminous with any one river valley. The very fact that Maharashtra's central rivers—the Godāvarī, the Kṛṣṇā, and the Bhīmā—flow *out* of Maharashtra means that they are not the *primary* factors in the formation of the region. They cut through the southern border of the present state, where language has been more influential than riverine nuclearity in determining modern and traditional boundaries. In chapter 6 we will see hints that "Maharashtra" may at one time have been identified with the upper Godāvarī river valley, but these hints are not conclusive. Rather, the regions that focus on rivers in Maharashtra do not individually constitute or collectively add up to a single region called "Maharashtra." The set of holy places along the whole length of a river is only one among several regions that may overlap but are not fully congruent; others include the area where Marathi is spoken, the area of the modern state of Maharashtra, and areas given the traditional designation "Maharashtra" at various historical periods. This same caveat applies not only to the regions formed by the pilgrimage described in chapter 2 of this book,[67] but also to almost all of the regions we will examine in chapters 3 and 4. Only in chapters 5 and 6 and in the conclusion of the book will I attempt to turn the reader's attention to Maharashtra as a whole.

Chapter 2

The Pilgrimage to Śiṅgṇāpūr

The most elaborate example in Maharashtra of a festival in which people carry water from home to pour on a god is the annual pilgrimage to Śiṅgṇāpūr in the month of Caitra (March–April). This chapter explores the multiple layers of meaning of the festival and examines its implications for the regional consciousness of its participants. After describing the Śiṅgṇāpūr festival, I will examine the Śaiva imagery involved in it, the tradition of Śaiva *bhakti* it continues, the marriage that forms its basic, forgotten meaning, and the ways in which it brings together disparate places in and parts of Maharashtra.

Śiṅgṇāpūr is located in the Mahādev mountains, about 35 kilometers southeast of the town of Phalṭaṇ. The Mahādev range is presumably named for the god of Śiṅgṇāpūr, Śiva, who here is generally called Mahādev, Śambhu, or Śambhu Mahādev. The range is a spur of the Sahyādrīs (the Western Ghats) that runs from northwest to southeast along the northern edge of Māṇ Taluka (Solapur District) and the southern edges of Phalṭaṇ and Māḷśīras Talukas in Satara District (map 2.1). Śiṅgṇāpūr is also called Śikhar Śiṅgṇāpūr, "Pinnacle" Śiṅgṇāpūr, for the tall peak on which it perches.[1] Visible for a great distance in all directions, the temple at Śiṅgṇāpūr is arguably the most prominent religious landmark in Satara District, important also for the southeastern half of Pune District and for many people in Solapur District and beyond. In stories told by Dhangar shepherds and other rural residents of this region, Śiṅgṇāpūr takes the role that the heaven Kailās has in Purāṇic traditions: it is the place from which Śiva watches and rules over the world, the place where he lives with his wife Pārvatī, and the place where they play dice or parcheesi and quarrel with each other.

The temple complex at Śiṅgṇāpūr includes two main Śiva temples. Both are said to have been built by Siṅghaṇa, the early-thirteenth-century Yādava

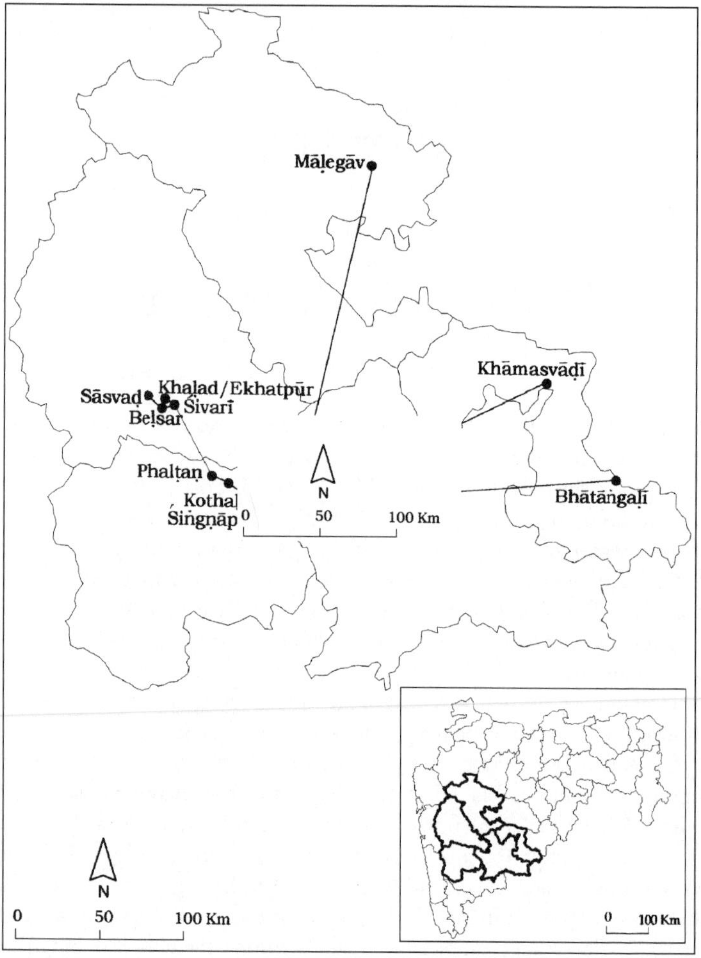

Map 2.1 The pilgrimage to Śiṅgṇāpūr

king for whom Śiṅgṇāpūr is named. The principal temple is at the very top of the mountain; this temple, which was rebuilt during the time of the seventeenth-century Marāṭhā ruler Śivājī, is quite elaborate and majestic, with beautiful stone carvings on its walls, ceiling, and columns and a large outer courtyard adorned with stone lamp pillars and surrounded by a tall, thick compound wall. The other main temple, called "Baḷī's temple,"[2] is situated slightly downhill, to the north of the first; it can be approached from below or by climbing down a flight of stone steps accessible through a large archway in the upper temple's compound wall. Baḷī's temple is built in the "Hemāḍpantī" style of the Yādava period. Below Baḷī's temple, down a road that now makes the whole temple complex accessible to vehicular traffic, lies the Śaiva monastery headed by Śiplāgirī Mahārāj. Higher up the hill, approached through a narrow passage in the north wall of the upper temple compound, is a Vīraśaiva (Liṅgāyat) monastery. A large archway, on the eastern side of the upper temple's compound wall, gives access to a long, stone staircase of more than 300 steps and then a paved path; the steps and path lead past a cluster of priests' houses, through a grove of trees, and eventually to a broad, level area on which are found the bus station, the police headquarters, the village government offices, and the rest of the village of Śiṅgṇāpūr. Also on this level is an enormous reservoir (almost never, as far as I can tell, completely full of water), which was built by Śivājī's grandfather Māḷojī. People generally refer to this body of water simply as "the tank" (*taḷeṃ*).

The most prominent feature of the pilgrimage to Śiṅgṇāpūr during Caitra is the fact that people carry water there in *kāvaḍ*s to pour on the god Śambhu Mahādev. At its most basic, a *kāvaḍ* consists of a pole slung over the shoulder with a water vessel—a bucket, a metal pot, a gourd, a tin can, or a plastic bottle with its top cut off—hanging from each end; even at their most elaborate, as at Śiṅgṇāpūr, *kāvaḍ*s are still contraptions for carrying water. The *kāvaḍ* festival at Śiṅgṇāpūr is extremely popular: it drew as many as 50,000 pilgrims in the nineteenth century (*GBP*, Satara 1885:586) and an estimated 500,000 annually in the mid-1990s. The festival is also, it seems, very old: literary evidence takes it back to at least the seventeenth century.[3]

One morning in Caitra 1994, as my companions and I were returning to Pune from a different festival, we noticed a small *kāvaḍ* set up in front of a house on the outskirts of the town of Tāsgāv, a Taluka headquarters in Sangli District. We stopped and talked with a woman who was performing *pūjā* to the *kāvaḍ*. The *kāvaḍ* was a four-legged trestle about three feet high with a horizontal beam about three feet long. A pole extended several feet upward from one end of the beam. Affixed to the top of the pole were a bunch of neem leaves and a piece of ochre-colored cloth that stretched down and was attached to the other end of the beam; the cloth thus formed the hypotenuse of a triangle whose other two sides were the horizontal beam and the pole. On each end of the beam rested a small brass image of a Śivaliṅga[4] and Nandī, Śiva's bull. Beneath the beam hung a small metal pot, which the woman referred to as a "*ghaḍū*."

The wood, the woman told us, had come from an udumbar tree (Ficus Glomerata) and had been fashioned into a *kāvaḍ* by a carpenter in Tāsgāv.

The *kāvaḍ* appeared to be fairly new; it had been made recently, the woman explained, to replace an older one that someone had burned.[5] The family had set up the *kāvaḍ* on the first day of the month of Caitra, a New Year's festival called Guḍhī Pāḍvā, and every day since then she had performed *pūjā* to it. She described her *pūjā* as follows: "We take out the old water, put in fresh, put flowers on it, put turmeric powder and red powder (*kuṅkūṃ*) on it, put ashes on it, and do *āratī*[6]. . . . And we make a food offering. We prostrate ourselves to it. That's all." The woman would perform this simple *pūjā* to the *kāvaḍ* every day, she said, until the twelfth lunar day of the month, Caitra Bāras. On that day, her eldest son would get on an S. T. (State Transport) bus, putting the *kāvaḍ* onto the roof of the bus as checked luggage. He would travel to Śiṅgṇāpūr along with other pilgrims from the village, some of whom would also have *kāvaḍs* while others went "empty-handed" (*mokaḷaṃ*). Once there, the mother explained, her son would have to

> take it by way of the reservoir, set it up and fill it, and then carry it up the hill. Climb the hill, pour a stream of water [on the *liṅga* in the temple] there, circumambulate [the temple], and then break a coconut and come back home . . . . And then, after getting back, set it up at the Gurav's house here. After setting it up, make a food offering and come home.

The men of her nuclear family, this woman said, had been carrying a *kāvaḍ* to Śiṅgṇāpūr for the past 20 years. Previously, her parents-in-law had had a *kāvaḍ* that went to Śiṅgṇāpūr, but it was the one that had gotten burned; after her eldest son was born, she and her husband had started setting up the new *kāvaḍ* on their own, "independently" (*svatantra*).

The vast majority of the hundreds of *kāvaḍs* that come the Śiṅgṇāpūr festival during Caitra probably do so as simply and in as low-key a manner as this one. In some cases, it is not just a single family or an individual but a whole village or all the members of one caste in a village that set up a small *kāvaḍ* and then bring it to Śiṅgṇāpūr. People bringing *kāvaḍs* to Śiṅgṇāpūr travel by public bus, by jeep, by bullock cart, by bicycle, or on foot. They generally get their *kāvaḍ* out of storage and set it up on Guḍhī Pāḍvā, the first day of Caitra, and they generally hold some sort of ceremony, including a meal (*bhaṇḍārā*) or some distribution of holy food (*prasād*), upon their return home. There, in most cases, the *kāvaḍ* remains on display until the full-moon day of Caitra or until the village's annual festival (*jatrā*). Many village festivals take place at or around the full-moon day of Caitra, the birthday of the village god Hanumān or Māruti.

Many of the pilgrims remain at Śiṅgṇāpūr overnight, some for two or more nights, while many others come and go in a single day. Of those my companions and I have interviewed, most, like the son of the woman outside Tāsgāv, take their *kāvaḍ* to Śiṅgṇāpūr in time to be there on Caitra Bāras, the twelfth lunar day (*bāras*) of the "bright" half of the month of Caitra. There they fill the pots of their *kāvaḍ* at the reservoir or—as in 1995, a drought year—from a "tanker," a water truck provided by the government. They carry the *kāvaḍ* up the hill to the main temple and circumambulate the temple several (ideally, five) times. Then some of the men enter the temple and pour the water over the Śivaliṅga inside. Some groups also pour water over the Śivaliṅga in the Amṛteśvar (Baḷī) temple, and a few go to pour water on the *liṅga* at a place called Guptaliṅg, two or three kilometers east of Śiṅgṇāpūr on the plateau. Most groups have a meal while they are at Śiṅgṇāpūr, and many go to meet the larger *kāvaḍ*s that form the principal attraction of the festival.

Many large *kāvaḍ*s come to Śiṅgṇāpūr for the festival. Six of them, considered especially important, have a *mān*, or special ritual role, in the pilgrimage. These six are the last *kāvaḍ*s to be carried up an extremely steep cliff on the northwest face of the mountain on the afternoon of Caitra Bāras. The cliff is called Muṅgī Ghāṭ. All six of these *kāvaḍ*s come from the northwest of Śiṅgṇāpūr, four of them from Purandar Taluka in Pune District.

The *most* important *kāvaḍ*, almost everyone agrees, is that of Bhutojī (or Bhutyā or Bhute) Telī from Sāsvaḍ, the headquarters town of Purandar Taluka (Pune District); this *kāvaḍ* has the privilege of being the very last one to climb Muṅgī Ghāṭ and the very last one to have its water poured over the god in the temple, at midnight on the twelfth day of Caitra. The second-most-important *kāvaḍ* is a rival of this one, in that the men who carry it claim to have even closer connections than the Sāsvaḍ group's to the original Bhutojī Telī. This rival *kāvaḍ* comes from a group of five villages near Sāsvaḍ that collectively call themselves "Pañcakrośī"; others tend to name the *kāvaḍ* for Khaḷad, one of the five villages. The third- and fourth-most-important *kāvaḍ*s come from the villages of Śivarī and Beḷsar, respectively, both in Purandar Taluka. And, finally, two other *kāvaḍ*s that join these four at the end of the procession come from the village of Guṇavare (Phalṭaṇ Taluka, Satara District), not far from Śiṅgṇāpūr. Each of these two *kāvaḍ*s, which are brought by Mahārs (Untouchables) named Āḍhāv, serves as the "guide" (*vāṭāḍyā*) for one of the rival Bhutojī Telī *kāvaḍ*s from Sāsvaḍ and the Pañcakrośī villages.

Each of the principal *kāvaḍ*s is composed of a heavy wooden frame made of large, square beams[7] of udumbar wood resting on four wooden legs, with two enormous copper, brass, or bronze water pots (called *haṇḍī*) that rest in bamboo slings suspended from the frame. Each *kāvaḍ* has a tall pole (called *āḍband* or, more commonly, *śīḍ*) that extends upward ten feet or so from one end of the frame. Attached to the top of the pole is a large piece of cloth called a *pharārā* ("flutterer"), which stretches, loosely rolled up, to the back of the *kāvaḍ*, where it is tied to a short, stubby wooden pole. The cloth thus forms the hypotenuse of a triangle whose other two sides are the frame and the pole. The cloth can be loosened to look—and act—like a sail.[8] Tokens of the *kāvaḍs*' privileged status in the festival (their *mān*) also hang from the top of their *śīḍ*-poles. Such tokens include a clump of long black hair—called *goṇḍā* ("pompon"), *sāj* ("decoration"), or *gāṅgvaṇ*—that ideally comes from the tail of a wild cow (*vangāī*), and a two-pointed flag, called a *savāī*, that has little pompons (*goṇḍīs*) on its points.[9]

Sometime before the pilgrimage begins, men from Sāsvaḍ, Śivarī, Beḷsar, and the Pañcakrośī villages get out the large *kāvaḍs* and spruce them up for the trip. The men wash their *kāvaḍ*. They summon a carpenter to fix anything that needs fixing. They paint the wood of the *kāvaḍ* with umber, or with oil paint the color of red-lead. They polish the metal pots and the silver or brass decorations. They tighten the ropes or bamboo slings that hold the pots. They affix the *śīḍ*-pole to the frame of the *kāvaḍ*, and attach the *pharārā* cloth, along with any clump of hair or *savāī*-flag they may be entitled to display, to the top of the *śīḍ*. They hold a meeting to go over their route and to discuss arrangements for food, water, and other provisions along the way.

All four of the principal *kāvaḍs* get set up on the first day of Caitra, Guḍhī Pāḍvā; on that day, men carry them in procession through all or part of their home village or town. The *kāvaḍs* then remain on display until Caitra Aṣṭamī or Navamī, the eighth or ninth lunar day of the month. Although all four *kāvaḍs* actually leave their village or town on the evening of the Navamī, both Sāsvaḍ and Ekhatpūr hold "setting out" (*prasthān*) processions on the evening of the Aṣṭamī. In these processions, men carry the *kāvaḍs* through their respective villages to the accompaniment of brass bands, troops of drummers playing huge barrel-drums (*ḍhoḷs*), and companies of young men dancing in unison the rhythmic stick-cymbal dance called *lejhīm*.

The departures and subsequent schedules of all four of the principal *kāvaḍs* are coordinated in such a way that the one from Sāsvaḍ always brings up the rear. The men (and a few women) who travel with the *kāvaḍs* walk or ride in bullock carts day and night, pausing for a few hours' sleep here and there and accepting meals, tea, and snacks from the same people who host them every year. In each village they pass through, the large *kāvaḍs* must be taken out of their bullock carts and carried in procession through the village. In addition, the major *kāvaḍs*, along with some others, meet up and interact from time to time on their way to Śiṅgṇāpūr.

The largest meeting, with the greatest number of *kāvaḍ*s participating and the largest crowd of spectators, takes place in the town of Phalṭaṇ on the Ekādaśī day, the eleventh day of the bright half of Caitra. Beginning early in the morning, large and small *kāvaḍ*s from Beḷsar, Śivarī, Sāsvaḍ, Pisarve, Pimprī, the Pañcakrośī villages, and several other places form a procession that cuts through the edge of Phalṭaṇ. Some of the *kāvaḍ*s enter the procession with only the relatively small group of pilgrims who accompany them all along the way, but the Sāsvaḍ and Pañcakrośī *kāvaḍ*s are preceded by elaborate retinues, including dancers, drummers,[10] and the *kāvaḍ*s' respective Buvās. In the bed of the Bāṇgaṅgā, a small and frequently dry river that separates two parts of Phalṭaṇ,[11] the Sāsvaḍ and Pañcakrośī *kāvaḍ*s perform a ritual called "Right-and-Left" (*ujvī-ḍāvī*). When they reach the river, the Pañcakrośī *kāvaḍ* and its retinue leave the road and go off to the right, or west, side of the river. Then, when the Sāsvaḍ *kāvaḍ* comes along, it goes off to the left, or east, side of the river.[12] The two *kāvaḍ*s hold these positions briefly, then rejoin the procession.

At Baraḍ, the two "guide-*kāvaḍ*s" (*vāṭāḍyā*) from Guṇavare join the pilgrimage. Then the *kāvaḍ*s cut southward and travel cross-country through the night, on an unpaved, rocky track, until they meet the Phalṭan–Śiṅgṇāpūr road near Kothaḷe. During that night, at four or five in the morning of the twelfth day of Caitra, several of the *kāvaḍ*s go to a place called Raṇkhiḷā.[13] There is a flat, circular mound of rocks here, called a *khiḷā*, with a *kār* tree in the center of the mound and another tree (a *nepaṭī*) growing out of the rocks at the side. Nearby there is a small shrine of Mahādev with a simple Śivaliṅga and, behind the shrine, a wall of rocks arranged to form a kind of bunker. The men accompanying each *kāvaḍ* perform *āratī* at the Mahādev temple, then carry their *kāvaḍ* around the mound of rocks, circumambulating it five times in a clockwise direction (*pradakṣiṇā*). In making their circumambulations, Sāsvaḍ's and the Pañcakrośī villages' *kāvaḍ*s follow their respective "guides," the two *kāvaḍ*s from the village of Guṇavare. Sāsvaḍ's *kāvaḍ* is the last to make its circumambulation.

The next afternoon, on the twelfth day (the Bāras) of Caitra, the climax of the *kāvaḍ*s' pilgrimage approaches. All of the *kāvaḍ*s that are going to climb the steep cliff known as Muṅgī Ghāṭ gather in the village of Kothaḷe. Kothaḷe, while not exactly at the foot of the Śiṅgṇāpūr mountain, is the last village before Muṅgī Ghāṭ. At Kothaḷe, the two principal *kāvaḍ*s "meet" certain other *kāvaḍ*s.[14] The meetings that I have observed are rather dramatic, and they require a good deal of athleticism. One young man stands on the frame of each of the two *kāvaḍ*s that are meeting, each young man holding onto his *kāvaḍ*'s *śīḍ*-pole. The men on whose heads the *kāvaḍ*s rest ram them swiftly toward each other through the thick crowd that has gathered to watch. As the *kāvaḍs* come close to each other, the young men standing on them embrace briefly and hand each other garlands of coconuts.[15]

As the "meetings" are going on, the other *kāvaḍs* line up in an assigned order to precede Sāsvaḍ's in the parade to Muṅgī Ghāṭ. The parade passes first down a ravine at the western edge of Kothaḷe, then through the village and across the plain to the foot of the mountain. In Kothaḷe the parade moves extremely slowly, creating a very dense crowd. The hot air reverberates with the sound of the many huge *ḍhoḷ* drums that accompany each of the major *kāvaḍs*. Large groups of enthusiastic young men dance *lejhīm* to the rhythm of the drums. As the *kāvaḍs* pass beyond the village, the pace quickens, the crowd thins out, and the men prepare for the serious business of climbing Muṅgī Ghāṭ.

At the foot of Muṅgī Ghāṭ is a level area where most of the *kāvaḍs* stop. The men carrying the *kāvaḍs* perform *āratī* here, waving lighted oil lamps or burning camphor in a circular motion while they sing and clap to a rhythmic song. In addition, the men from Sāsvaḍ pour on the ground a bit of the water from the Karhā river that they have brought in a small pot that they call a *cambū*.[16] Part way up the hill is a small, roofed shrine to a young man named Kolte who died at that spot. The men with the *kāvaḍs* stop briefly at this shrine. After they pass the shrine, the climb becomes steeper and even more difficult. To get the heavier *kāvaḍs* up the cliff, the young, strong men who carry them struggle and strain, slipping and scrabbling all the way (figure 2.1). Some men form human chains, pulling one another and their *kāvaḍs* up the hill. Others climb ahead and toss down ropes, then pull up the *kāvaḍs* from above. The Sāsvaḍ *kāvaḍ*, the last one to climb the mountain, reaches the top without the help of ropes. Instead, each of the men struggling to lift it up the cliff pushes with his head on the buttocks of the man above him.[17] By the time this last *kāvaḍ* reaches the top, it is late afternoon. A large crowd has gathered at the top of the cliff, watching through the hottest part of the day as the *kāvaḍs* have climbed the Ghāṭ. The crowd cheers at the arrival of the Sāsvaḍ *kāvaḍ*. Dignitaries from the village and temple of Śiṅgṇāpūr greet the principal *kāvaḍs* as they emerge from their climb.

Once the *kāvaḍs* reach the top of Muṅgī Ghāṭ, the men who have carried them retire to their traditional camping places in the grove or the (mostly dry) reservoir near the village at Śiṅgṇāpūr. Some begin to climb up the steps to the temples right away. Each of the groups of men with the large *kāvaḍs* visits Baḷī's temple, pouring some water on the *liṅga* there. Then they circumambulate the upper temple five times and enter that temple to pour water on the *liṅga*. The *kāvaḍs* "dance" as they proceed up the steps and around the courtyard of the upper temple. And, although the

Figure 2.1 Men pulling a *kāvaḍ* up Muṅgī Ghāṭ at Śiṅgṇāpūr.

kāvaḍs themselves do not enter the sanctuaries of the temples, the men make the *śīḍ*-pole of their *kāvaḍ* touch the upper frame of the entrance to the temple. As a man in Pisarve explained to me, "We make the *kāvaḍ* dance, don't we? As we're making the *kāvaḍ* dance, we rest the *śīḍ* against the entry gate of the god. That means that the god has met the god." The procession of the *kāvaḍs* is coordinated so that the men accompanying the *kāvaḍ* from Sāsvaḍ enter the main temple last, at or before midnight on Caitra Bāras.

The rest of the time that the men accompanying these major *kāvaḍs* spend at Śiṅgṇāpūr passes in very much the same way as the simpler visits of the people who bring smaller *kāvaḍs*: baths in the reservoir for the *kāvaḍs* and the men who carry them, visits to one another's camping places, large communal meals, and trips to Guptaliṅg. The large *kāvaḍs* generally leave Śiṅgṇāpūr two days after they arrive, on the fourteenth day of the bright half of Caitra. In most cases, they return by more or less the same routes as those by which they traveled to Śiṅgṇāpūr, reaching home on or after the full-moon day of Caitra.

As the men who bring these *kāvaḍs* are climbing up Muṅgī Ghāṭ on Caitra Bāras, other groups of pilgrims, many of them also carrying *kāvaḍs*, are already leaving. Most of these pilgrims come from the east and northeast of Śiṅgṇāpūr, from various places in Marāṭhvāḍā. These people arrive and leave by a different route, the road that leads northeast from Śiṅgṇāpūr to Nātepute and Māḷśiras.[18] These other pilgrims, who leave on (or before) the Bāras, include three groups and individuals who have especially important ritual roles in the festival. These three are a weaver who hangs a long cloth called a "*dhaj*," a horseman called "Kāḷ Gāvḍā," and the men who bring a tall pole (*kāṭhī*) that plays the role of Śiva's bride. Before the *kāvaḍs* that climb Muṅgī Ghāṭ arrive, all these men have already played their roles in the festival.

On the eighth day (Aṣṭamī) of Caitra, a weaver (Sālī) from Khāmasvāḍī (Kaḷamb Taluka, Usmanabad District) ties an extremely long, narrow cloth, called a *dhaj*,[19] from the pinnacle of the Mahādev temple to that of Baḷī's temple, a distance of several hundred feet. The weaver has worked every Monday, all year long, weaving the *dhaj*. On the first day of Caitra, Guḍhī Pāḍvā, he sets out from Khāmasvāḍī accompanied by a band and a tall pole.[20] He walks to Śiṅgṇāpūr, carrying the *dhaj* on his head all the way. After it has been raised on Caitra Aṣṭamī, the *dhaj* can be seen from a great distance, glimmering high in the air between the temples. A man in Beḷsar described this part of the pilgrimage ritual as follows:

> There's a weaver (Sālī) in Vidarbha[21]. . . .What he does is, every Monday of the year—it's called a *dhaj*; it's a narrow strip of cloth, like this—every Monday, without taking any food[22] at all—he's a great devotee; this is still going on today. It has been going on for generations. On Monday he's not to take any food; he's to fast completely. And on that day he is to weave it. He's supposed to weave that strip of cloth all year long in this way. It's called a *dhaj*.
>
> And Baḷī's temple is to the north, and Śiva's temple is to the south. There is a distance of a thousand or 1500 feet between the two temples. There's nothing in between for climbing up that temple, or for leaning something on. Still, at night, he ties one end of the *dhaj* to Baḷī's temple, and the other end to Śiva's temple. And no one at all sees it getting tied.

In fact, the *dhaj* is raised in full daylight, in the presence of a large crowd of enthusiastic witnesses, and the weaver himself is not the one who ties it between the two temples. After circumambulating the main temple at Śiṅgṇāpūr five times and placing the *dhaj* briefly on top of the *liṅgas* in the main temple at Śiṅgṇāpūr,[23] the weaver hands the huge bundle over to local Koḷīs. Some young Koḷī men climb to the pinnacle of the main temple's dome, from where they use ropes and pulleys to hoist up one end of the *dhaj*. The rest of the bundle is then unrolled, passing down over the courtyard wall of the upper temple, over the roofs of the Liṅgāyat monastery and some other buildings, over the heads and outstretched arms of the crowd of onlookers, and over the courtyard wall of Baḷī's temple below. There more Koḷī men use pulleys and ropes to pull the other end of the *dhaj* up to the top of that temple. Finally it hangs free, suspended between the pinnacles of the two temples.

More mysterious than the *dhaj* weaver's role in the festival is that of Kāḷ Gāvḍā. Unlike the *dhaj*-weaver, the results of whose year of labor everyone can see, Kāḷ Gāvḍā is a man whom few people know much about. Those who do know about him say that he is related somehow to the royal house of Indore. All agree that he has an extremely unusual ritual role in the festival. On the eleventh day of Caitra, the Ekādaśī day, the day before the *kāvaḍs* from Sāsvaḍ and vicinity arrive, Kāḷ Gāvḍā bathes in the tank, has his head shaved, and rides on a horse up the steps to the main temple at Śiṅgṇāpūr. Once there, he enters the temple without removing his footwear.[24] This is something that would be extremely disrespectful—indeed, unheard of—in normal circumstances, and that everyone who knows about Kāḷ Gāvḍā's role in the festival finds extraordinarily strange. Inside the temple, Kāḷ Gāvḍā makes offerings with his footwear on.

The most important of the groups that come to Śiṅgṇāpūr from the east and leave on the twelfth day[25] of Caitra is the group that brings the "Mhātār Kāṭhī" from Bhātāṅgaḷī (Umargā Taluka, Usmanabad District). This *kāṭhī* is a 40 foot-tall bamboo pole. It is by no means the only pole that comes to the festival,[26] but it is the one that has by far the most important role. For it plays the part of Pārvatī as she marries Śiva in a ceremony in Nātepute on the eighth day (Aṣṭamī) of Caitra.[27]

The preparations for the wedding go on for months beforehand. On the first Monday of the month of Pauṣ (January–February), three months before the Śiṅgṇāpūr festival, men from Bhātāṅgaḷī go out from the village to select an appropriate bamboo plant. They cut it down, perform *pūjā* to it, and bring it back to the village.[28] There it lies horizontal until the first day of Caitra. On that day, the New Year's day Guḍhī Pāḍvā, the men raise the pole. They tie to the top a clump of long fibers of the *ambāḍā* plant that have been stripped like jute to form a white, hair-like plume, and they decorate the pole with colorful cloth and silver ornaments. The jewelry consists of bands called "*kaṭs*" that encircle the lower end of the pole. The pole starts out from Bhātāṅgaḷī with several of these bands affixed to it, and people in the villages it passes through offer more and more of them along the way.[29] Toward the bottom of the pole a small crossbar is affixed to it;

this serves as a handle, resting on the shoulder of whoever is carrying the pole. The crossbar also provides a platform on which is set a silver image of Śiva's bull, Nandī.

When my companions and I visited Bhātāṅgaḷī in 1995, leading men of the village described their pilgrimage to us in some detail. After they set up and decorate the pole on the Guḍhī Pāḍvā day, they told us, it remains for three days at the Mahādev temple in Bhātāṅgaḷī. On the fourth day, it sets out for Śiṅgṇāpūr. Four or five thousand men and a few women accompany the pole on its six-day journey to Śiṅgṇāpūr. Several of the men are *mānkarīs*, men with special ritual privileges.[30] A specially dedicated bull[31] carries the *mānkarīs*' luggage. During the rest of the year, this bull is allowed to run loose; it is pressed into service only for the pilgrimage to Śiṅgṇāpūr. Three small *kāvaḍs*[32] also travel along with the pole.

As the pole proceeds toward Śiṅgṇāpūr, men accompanying it take turns carrying it on their shoulders. The group travels 40 or 50 kilometers a day, much of the distance on dirt roads and byways. Unlike the men who make the journey with the large *kāvaḍs* from Sāsvaḍ and its vicinity, the men who accompany the pole travel primarily during the day. The men in Bhātāṅgaḷī who told us about their trip stressed that they are supposed to carry the pole upright "all day long," and that only one man at a time ought to carry it.[33] In fact, at night the pole may be rested horizontally, and when the men are out in the countryside between villages, several men at a time sometimes carry the pole—horizontally. But, as one man explained, "when we come to a village, it's upright. People have to take its *darśan*. And we pass through and far beyond the village, and again make it horizontal." Another man broke in, saying, "That is, it is [horizontal] for a *very* short time."

As with the major *kāvaḍs*, the Bhātāṅgaḷī pole's route is set in advance, and the men make their numerous halts for meals, tea, and overnight stays at the same places where they have stopped in previous years: "The stops are always the same. The places where we spend the night are always the same. That is, whether it is a small place or a large place, we *have* to go there."[34] By evening on the eighth day of Caitra, the pole reaches Nātepute. There the marriage festivities take place at a very old Śiva temple at the edge of the town. The men from Bhātāṅgaḷī circumambulate the temple with the pole, and they cause the pole to "meet" the temple.[35] They are given a meal, and the two headmen (Māḷī Pāṭīl and Police Pāṭīl) of Bhātāṅgaḷī receive gifts that are referred to as "*rukhvat*," a term used for certain wedding presentations.[36] The—or *a*—wedding takes place at midnight in the courtyard of the temple at Nātepute, on the same day that the *dhaj* gets hung between the pinnacles of the two principal temples at Śiṅgṇāpūr.[37]

The next day, the ninth day of Caitra, the men with the pole proceed to Śiṅgṇāpūr, stopping to rest during the heat of the day at the Umbareśvar or Umbardev temple at the foot of the mountain on the Nātepute side. Reaching Śiṅgṇāpūr in the evening, they proceed directly to the main temple, carrying the pole erect up the mountain road and the hundreds of steps to the temple courtyard.[38] Once there, the men perform multiple circumambulations, carrying the pole around the upper temple five times and around Baḷī's temple once. On the morning of the twelfth day of Caitra, the group from Bhātāṅgaḷī departs, leaving Śiṅgṇāpūr before the *kāvaḍs* from Sāsvaḍ and other places climb Muṅgī Ghāṭ. The pole returns home by a different route from the one it followed coming to Śiṅgṇāpūr, and the trip lasts five days instead of the six it took to reach there. The last major stop before Bhātāṅgaḷī is Tuḷjāpūr, and Bhavānī's temple there is the last widely known temple that the pilgrims visit. When the *kāṭhī* returns home, there is a huge festival, with great celebration, a thousand torches burning, men drinking alcohol, and "this and that."

Devotion to Śiva

The Caitra festival at Śiṅgṇāpūr is a complex, multifaceted pilgrimage whose meaning can be found on several different levels. In its most basic, most clearly articulated significance, the festival expresses a kind of fierce, athletic, ascetic devotion (*bhakti*) to Śiva. This can be seen in the place itself, Śiṅgṇāpūr, and its history; it can be seen in the paraphernalia and oral history of the festival; and it can be seen in the actions, statements, and attitudes of the present-day participants.

There are several important analogies and connections between Śiṅgṇāpūr and the even more famous pilgrimage place to its east-southeast, Paṇḍharpūr.[39] But there is also an important difference. In Paṇḍharpūr, the Vārkarī poet-saints and their present-day followers have largely succeeded in applying a thick Vaiṣṇava veneer to a god and cult that were once primarily Śaiva—or, at least, pastoralist in origin and thus ambivalently *both* Vaiṣṇava *and* Śaiva (Ḍhere 1984; Vaudeville 1987). At Śiṅgṇāpūr, by contrast, the Śaiva roots and pastoralist heritage are straightforwardly evident. Śiṅgṇāpūr lies in one of the dry areas of the Deccan, in a landscape still strongly marked by the monsoon camps and pastures of Dhangar shepherds.[40] According to Ḍhere, the cult at Śiṅgṇāpūr was founded by a cowherd—a Gauḷī or Gavaḷī—named Baḷiyāppā or Baḷī, who brought the god with him from Soraṭī (Saurāṣṭra), in Gujarat. As we have seen, the second-most-important temple at Śiṅgṇāpūr is called Baḷī's temple, or Baḷī Mahādev. Ḍhere traces the Baḷī that this temple was named for to a story that Cakradhar narrates in the thirteenth-century Mahānubhāv[41] text

Līḷācaritra (Kolte 1982b, "Pūrvārdha" 460). According to Cakradhar's story, Baḷipa the Gauḷī was a friend of a Koḷī named Hīvañja, who was an incarnation of Mahādev. The two used to go hunting together; they ate together, despite their difference in caste; and eventually they came to be worshipped next to each other as *liṅgas*.[42] Koḷīs claim to have once been the principal priests at Śiṅgṇāpūr (Sontheimer 1989a:75), and they retain important roles in the rituals there.

Besides its connections with Koḷīs and (predominantly Śaiva) pastoralists, the temple at Śiṅgṇāpūr also has long-standing associations with Liṅgāyats. The Liṅgāyat *bhakti* movement, a movement of devotion to Śiva that was founded in Karnataka in the twelfth century and is still most prevelant there, has also had over the centuries a number of followers in southern Maharashtra, and Liṅgāyat literature includes some works in Marathi.[43] The sparsely populated but nonetheless surviving monastery at Śiṅgṇāpūr is one of a few examples of Liṅgāyat presence in the area.[44] The Liṅgāyats are known for their "heroic" and fierce devotion to Śiva—their other name, "Vīraśaiva," *means* "heroic devotee of Śiva."

The men who transport the *kāvaḍs* and poles to Śiṅgṇāpūr are not Liṅgāyats, but they do see themselves as maintaining a strong tradition of fierce Śaiva devotion. They smear their foreheads with white ash, and the leaders wear strings of Rudrākṣa beads. Both the ash and the beads are marks of Śaiva identity. The men make free use of other Śaiva imagery as well.[45] Śiva's bull, Nandī, for instance, is especially prominent in the Caitra festival. The men further weigh down their already-heavy *kāvaḍs* and poles with brass or silver images of Nandī. The pole that comes from Bhātāṅgaḷī travels in the company of Nandī's live representative, a bull who is allowed to graze freely, without working, during the rest of the year. The Mahādev temple at Bhātāṅgaḷī displays several additional brass images of Nandī like the one that travels on the pole. In this temple there are also a great number of smaller brass Nandīs that women use in a rather unusual way to make *navas*-vows. In making a vow, a woman will steal one of the small Nandīs; when she has gotten what she wants (most typically, a child), she brings back the Nandī she stole, along with a second one. In Śiṅgṇāpūr itself, as well, Nandī is quite prominent: the main temple there has not just one, but five large stone Nandīs opposite the door that leads into the sanctuary; each Nandī is decorated with an ornate brass cover.

But the Śaiva devotion involved in the Śiṅgṇāpūr festival is not merely a matter of the Śaiva iconography of the temples and ritual paraphernalia, nor of the Śaiva decorations the men put on their bodies. It is also to be seen in human actions and attitudes. The man who plays the role of Kāḷ Gāvḍā, for example, explains his role in the festival as deriving from a kind of angry *bhakti* on the part of his ancestor, the first Kāḷ Gāvḍā. This man was a shepherd who was a resolute devotee of Śiva, so much so that Śiva followed him from Śiṅgṇāpūr to his home at Māḷegāv (Śevgāv Taluka, Ahmadnagar District).[46] But when it was time for Śiva's wedding (see the next section of this chapter), Śiva forgot to invite this devotee:

> Mahādev and Pārvatī's wedding was set. . .. They invited all the gods. No one at all gave an invitation to Kāḷ Gāvḍā. Not even God remembered who this Kāḷ Gāvḍā was, or that he had pleased him, or that he himself had gone to the man's home. After all, it was God's wedding. Later, after Kāḷ Gāvḍā had had some kind of vision, he thought that God's wedding was taking place, that God had made a mistake, but that he wanted to go to the wedding without an invitation . . . .
>
> When he had set out, the whole court, with all the gods, was full. God's body was covered with turmeric paste. Somehow or other God suddenly looked at him. And he said, "Kāḷ Gāvḍā has come without an invitation."
>
> But he was furious. "He invited all the gods," he said. "Why didn't he give me an invitation?" His eyes were red.
>
> God was ashamed. He shut his eyes. He took refuge with all the gods, and what did he say? "Kāḷ Gāvḍā," he said, "don't be angry. Don't be angry," he said. "I forgot you in this wedding ceremony. And, even though I forgot you, even if you do my *pujā* with your shoes on, I won't get angry."
>
> This is true in the present. The *pujā* that I do now, these days, I do with my shoes on. I come from that noble family. This custom has been going on since that time.

The fierce, ascetic quality of the Śaiva devotion expressed in this festival comes most clearly to the fore in the traditions associated with Bhutojī Telī, the man for whom the *kāvaḍ* from Sāsvaḍ is named and whose tradition the men who accompany the *kāvaḍ* from the Pañcakrośī villages also claim to follow. The original Bhutojī Telī lived "four or five" generations ago, in Ekhatpūr. The Pañcakrośī *kāvaḍ* circumambulates the temple built over his memorial monument (*samādhi*) five times before setting out for Śiṅgṇāpūr. The *samādhi* lies near the cremation ground of Ekhatpūr. Men in Ekhatpūr who told me about Bhutojī Telī connected the *samādhi*'s location with the fact that Bhutojī was a devotee of Śiva, the god who by preference lives in cremation grounds.[47] As one of these men explained, this fact makes Ekhatpūr analogous to Śiṅgṇāpūr: just as in Śiṅgṇāpūr Śiva lives on a mountaintop, one of his favorite kinds of abodes, so in Ekhatpūr his devotee's *samādhi* temple is in the cremation ground, another of his preferred places. Thus, the man explained, using a fancy Sanskrit word, "Śiṅgṇāpūr is a center (*vyāspīṭh*) of devotion to Śiva; and, in the very same way, Ekhatpūr too is a center (*vyāspīṭh*) of devotion to Śiva."

Ekhatpūr is also the site of Bhutojī's house. The house has fallen down, but parts of its walls are still there,[48] and there are the remains of a stone oil mill (*ghāṇā*) in the front yard. The mill was one of the bullock-powered type that Telīs (Oilmen), members of Bhutojī's caste, traditionally used to extract oil from seeds. People in the Pañcakrośī villages and beyond refer to this place as "the Burning House," because of a story that they frequently tell to illustrate both the strength of Bhutojī's devotion and the extent of his detachment from the world. A man in Beḷsar began the story this way: "Bhutojī used to practice *bhakti*. And the way Bhutojī went [to Śiṅgṇāpūr] was that, when he left with the *kāvaḍ*, he would put a match to his house." Another man interjected, "He would burn up his whole estate, and then leave." Then the first narrator resumed: "And he had so much faith in God that he would not look back. And when he returned, his house would have remained just the same as it had been before." A man traveling with the Sāsvaḍ *kāvaḍ* told a slightly different version, when my companions and I met him in 1994 at the last resting place before Kothaḷe. This man's version extends the story from the individual, Bhutojī Telī, to his fellow pilgrims:

> My father used to tell the history of the times before this . . . . In the past, when the *kāvaḍ* was setting out from Sāsvaḍ, they used to burn their houses behind them. They would burn the house[s]. And, after they set out on the road, . . . Mahādev would test them: Are they coming back to put out the fire in their houses, or not? . . . So, in the past, people would not come back to put out the fire in the houses. And if they came back [another] day and looked, the houses would be there. The burned houses would be standing right in their place, [unharmed].

A third version of the story, like most, restricts the house-burning to Bhutojī Telī, but this version adds a further miraculous element: not only would the burned house be restored automatically, but it would also catch fire on its own. A man from Muñjavaḍī, one of the Pañcakrośī villages, told us this version at the side of the road near Ekhatpūr:

> The history was that, at the time when this *kāvaḍ* would set out from here to Śiṅgṇāpūr, on the Navamī day,[49] that Telī Bhute [Bhutojī Telī]—that is, a devotee (*bhakta*); he was a good *bhakta*—his house would catch fire on its own. That is, it would burn up. What's more, as he left, he was not to look behind him. And, after he came back, the house would be in its place as [it had been before]. That's the history of it . . . . After Bhutyā Telī died, this did not happen any more.

Finally, a man in Ekhatpūr related Bhutojī Telī's yearly deed to a *tradition* of Śaiva devotion, linking Bhutojī—and Ekhatpūr—to the more famous poet-devotees of Viṭhobā of Paṇḍharpūr:

> Ekhatpūr counts in the tradition of saints that has been received here in Maharashtra, from the point of view of Śiva *bhakti* in Maharashtra . . . . At

> the time of Jñāneśvar, which was also the time of Nāmdev, at that very time there lived Bhutojī Mahārāj, who was a great practitioner of Śiva *bhakti*. So, when he used to go from here in Ekhatpūr to Śiṅgṇāpūr, at that time, whatever estate or property he had, from the point of view of a saint, he was to give all this up. And so, after he had set out for Śiṅgṇāpūr, he wouldn't look back again at all, until he had gone directly to see the god. After the program at Śiṅgṇāpūr was over, when he got back to Ekhatpūr, Parameśvar, Śiva, Śaṅkar would put his whole house, or the estate he had, there again, completely restored.

A Telī, as we have seen, is a member of an oil-presser and -seller caste. This Telī's name, "Bhutojī," "Bhutyā," or "Bhute," derives from "*bhūt*," "ghost"; the suffix "*jī*" is an honorific. Men who travel with the Bhutojī Telī *kāvaḍ* connected this name with the uncanny—downright ghostly—ability of Bhutojī and his present-day followers to get their heavy *kāvaḍ* up the cliff at Muṅgī Ghāṭ. To this day, these men explained, the Sāsvaḍ *kāvaḍ* climbs the Ghāṭ without being pulled up by ropes. This makes people wonder, " 'How does this *kāvaḍ* go? Because these folk are people like *bhūts*. These people are like *bhūts*, and that is why the *kāvaḍ* comes up as if by the wind, as if the wind were swinging the *kāvaḍ*.' And that's why it got the name Bhutojībuvā . . . Bhutyā Telī."

The original Bhutyā Telī, many say, used to carry the *kāvaḍ* up Muṅgī Ghāṭ alone. What is more, whereas now the *kāvaḍ* goes up the hill empty, even though several dozen men are carrying it, the original Bhutyā Telī used to carry it up full. And, finally, what it would be full of was not water but sand. This feat of strength is another reason that Bhutojī was given his name. In 1994, one of the men with the Sāsvaḍ *kāvaḍ* explained, "They filled the water pot with sand and, all alone, with nobody else touching it, in such a state, he climbed up that cliff like a ghost (*bhutāsārkhā*). Because of that he got the name Bhutojībuvā."

When I asked why people would put sand into a *kāvaḍ*, which is meant for carrying water, men with the Sāsvaḍ *kāvaḍ* explained that people in "former times" wanted to "make a name for themselves," that they wanted to get a reputation "for making extreme efforts," that it had become too routine just to carry water, and so they wanted to exhibit something "strange" (*vicitra*). A Dhangar shepherd from near Śiṅgṇāpūr made explicit the notion that the sand-filled *kāvaḍ* was a test: "The point of the sand *kāvaḍ* was to test the integrity (*tatthya/tathya*) of Buvā. It makes it heavy. One man took it by himself up through Muṅgī Ghāṭ to the god. It seemed light to him. That's how much integrity he had."[50]

A final story about Bhutojī Telī—about some Bhutojī Telī, at least, several generations ago—shows him to have been not only a man of physical strength and religious integrity, but also a politically effective leader. For the story is that he led a successful tax resistance against the British. When the British imposed a pilgrim tax on the festival at Śiṅgṇāpūr, the man who was Bhutojī at that time refused to carry his *kāvaḍ* up Muṅgī Ghāṭ. Instead, he and his followers came as far as the foot of the hill and remained there. In the words of one modern-day pilgrim:

> During the British period, they levied a pilgrimage tax on the people. At that time, what did Bhutojī Buvā say? "We're not going to pay the tax. If there's a tax to be paid, we're not going to come up to the pilgrimage festival. If Mahādev wants to answer our prayers, if Mahādev wants to come, then he should come down to the foot of Muṅgī Ghāṭ. He should give his *darśan* directly. Otherwise we have no need." . . . So, . . . for a couple of years, they held the festival down below.

Accounts differ as to what happened next, but most agree that some sort of miracle occurred. According to some of the men I talked with, when Bhutojī tossed some ashes on the ground at the foot of the Ghāṭ a stream of water gushed forth. According to another man, God met Bhutojī there in the form of a snake, Nāgobā. And, according to the man whose version of the beginning of the tax story is quoted here, "When the sun was shining full blast, when it wasn't even the rainy season, lightning struck. And, as it struck, one side of the hill came slipping down and fell all the way to the bottom. As it fell to the bottom, it turned into pebbles (*peṇḍhī*)." Indeed, gravel still covers much of the lower slopes of the hill, at the foot of Muṅgī Ghāṭ.

Whatever the miracle, it sufficed to complete the men's pilgrimage at the foot of Muṅgī Ghāṭ, without their having to climb up the hill to Śiṅgṇāpūr. Eventually the boycott worked, the British withdrew the tax, and the pilgrims began climbing up to Śiṅgṇāpūr again for the festival:

> After some time, after the pilgrimage festival had been shut down, the government's tax proved a failure. Some time later, after the tax had failed, they said, "We'll give you a concession." And they gave a concession. After that the festival began to take place again. Then, after that, the *kāvaḍs* began to go [up again], then they began to go up to Śiṅgṇāpūr.

For the men who accompany the Bhutojī Telī *kāvaḍ* today, these events elucidate some otherwise unexplained rituals in the festival. In memory of the miracle at the foot of the hill, for instance, the Buvā of the Sāsvaḍ *kāvaḍ* pours out a first small stream of Karhā water from his *cambū* at the foot of Muṅgī Ghāṭ. More importantly, as at least one of Bhutojī Buvā's present-day followers explained, Bhutojī's successful resistance to the tax, his staying down at the foot of the Ghāṭ, is the reason that his *kāvaḍ*'s traditional privilege is not, as might be expected, to go *first* up the hill, but rather to go last:

> So the privilege (*mān*) of Bhutojī Buvā's *kāvaḍ* was decided at that time: that [it would go] last, that all the other *kāvaḍs* would go up, and only this one would stay below, [at the foot of] the Ghāṭ . . . . Now, in the past, what would happen was that having a privilege meant going first, having the first privilege. That one would be the one with the privilege (the *mānkarī*). So how did the *mānkarī* get to be last? Because, in this way, not paying the tax, by remaining behind as the last one, the last one got to be the *mānkarī*.

The men who play Bhutojī Telī's role today, the "Buvās" of the Sāsvaḍ and Pañcakrośī *kāvaḍs*,[51] are not seen as having miraculous powers or superhuman strength, nor are they the leaders of any resistance movement. They do, however, practice rather severe asceticism during their journey, and this is an important aspect of their Śaiva devotion. Both men fast[52] from the first day of Caitra, Guḍhī Pāḍvā, until they have reached Śiṅgṇāpūr and have poured water from their *cambūs* onto the *liṅga* in the main temple there. Both men, in addition, walk the whole way in their bare feet. The trip is an extremely difficult one for *anyone* who makes it, but especially so for someone who walks barefoot on the scorchingly hot pavement in Caitra (the hottest month of the year), or for someone who is weakened by fasting (figure 2.2). By the time they reach Kothaḷe, the Buvās are so exhausted and their feet so blistered that they can sometimes barely walk; their followers have to hold them up.[53]

In addition to the Buvās, others too practice some form of asceticism, generally less rigorous than that required of the leaders. The wife of the Pañcakrośī *kāvaḍ*'s Buvā, for instance, whom I met along the road near Phalṭaṇ during the pilgrimage in 1995, was walking barefoot, as were the women traveling with her. She was not, however, fasting. The small pot (*cambū*) of Karhā water that travels with each of the principal *kāvaḍs* is not allowed to touch the ground, and so it gets passed around among a number of the men who accompany the *kāvaḍ*; since no one wearing shoes or sandals may carry the *cambū*, several other men besides the Buvā travel in their bare feet. And, although most people do not fast during the pilgrimage festival, there seems to be a general rule that no one (not even those who remain at home in the large *kāvaḍs*' villages) should eat meat while the pilgrimage is underway. From the first day of Caitra, even people who are normally nonvegetarians refrain from eating meat until their village's *kāvaḍ* returns home—or at least until the twelfth day of Caitra, when pilgrims pour water over the *liṅga* in the Mahādev temple at Śiṅgṇāpūr.

Figure 2.2 Bhutojī Telī from Sāsvaḍ during the pilgrimage to Śiṅgṇāpūr. He stands barefoot, wearing three necklaces of *rudrākṣa* beads, and helps his companion hold the *cambū* filled with water from the Karhā river.

For those who climb Muṅgī Ghāṭ, the most difficult part of the pilgrimage is the Ghāṭ itself. The men's preparations in Kothaḷe include tightening the ropes that hold their *kāvaḍ* together (*kāvaḍ āvaḷūn 'pack' kartāt*). They tighten these ropes so that the *kāvaḍ* will not fall apart as it gets jostled around, as it slams to the ground, and as it slips back down the hill while they slowly make their way up the Ghāṭ. The name "Muṅgī Ghāṭ" means "Ant Pass." The most common explanation of this name is that from a distance—either from above or from below—the people climbing through the Ghāṭ look as small as ants. But men I spoke with in the village government office at Śiṅgṇāpūr during the festival in 1994 cited a different etymology, one that relates the name of the Ghāṭ to the difficulty of climbing it: "A place that not even an ant could climb is called 'Muṅgī Ghāṭ,'" said one of these men. What makes Muṅgī Ghāṭ important, they explained, is the very fact that it is difficult to climb.

The shrine part way up the Ghāṭ bears graphic witness not only to the Ghāṭ's difficulty but also to its potential deadliness. The shrine is a memorial to Dattātreya Nāmdev Kolte from Pisarve (Purandar Tālukā, Pune District). He was a young man, "twenty-five or thirty" years old, who died climbing the Ghāṭ during the festival one year in the early 1970s. Men familiar with the story of his death narrate it quite undramatically. A man who was tending the shrine during the festival in 1995 said simply, "He was a young boy. As the *kāvaḍ* was coming up, he passed away here. I mean, he died." A man named Kolte in Pisarve elaborated only slightly more:

> He was from this village. His name was Dattātreya Nāmdev Kolte. He had gone to the god there. It is our custom—every year we go to the god, our *kāvaḍ* goes. In that way, he had gone too. When he was climbing up, he had a little trouble. His stomach started hurting. After he sat down there, he died.

A man from Āmboḍī, a village near Sāsvaḍ, who was traveling with the Sāsvaḍ *kāvaḍ* used more religious, but nevertheless still quite simple terminology to describe the young man's death: "God knows what happened to him, but he was in good health. And, as he was just sitting there, he went into a permanent trance (*samādhi*), so we built a small temple."

The priest of the shrine, who is from Pisarve, is also named Kolte and is related to the young man—as are, it seems, many other people in Pisarve. The shrine has some income from a land-grant (*inām*), which provides modest funds for the upkeep of the shrine. In the mid-1990s people from Pisarve put a roof on the shrine, and they plan to make further "improvements" in the future.

As the *kāvaḍs* climb the Ghāṭ on the twelfth day of Caitra, most of the men with them stop briefly at the shrine to pay their respects and perhaps to offer a coin or two. The group of men with the *kāvaḍ* from Pisarve stops for a longer time. They perform *āratī* (i.e., they wave a tray of small, lighted oil lamps or bits of burning camphor and sing a rhythmic song of praise) and sit around at the shrine for several hours before proceeding on up the hill. For the men from Pisarve, the shrine provides a way for their dead companion—a man who is now, a generation later, nearly an ancestor figure—to continue to take part with them in the pilgrimage. Women (and, in at least one case, a married couple) who have had trouble conceiving children make *navas*-vows at the shrine, promising to carry a gunny sack full of other pilgrims' sandals up the hill each year for three years. In addition, not only for the men with the Pisarve *kāvaḍ* but also for everyone else who climbs up past the shrine, it serves as a reminder of the real danger of the athletic feat they have undertaken.

Thus, the *bhakti* involved in the pilgrimage to Śiṅgṇāpūr calls for heroic, athletic, dangerous, even life-threatening actions on the part of those who undertake it. In this sense, the pilgrimage is typically Śaiva in character. But, as is the case with *bhakti* generally, whether Śaiva or Vaiṣṇava, the participants do not understand their devotion to involve them in a one-sided relationship. God also plays an active role, taking an interest in his devotees and protecting them as they exert themselves in his honor. Men traveling with the Sāsvaḍ *kāvaḍ* asserted that pebbles loosened by the feet of pilgrims higher up in the Ghāṭ move harmlessly to the side, without touching the pilgrims below them. Such a pebble, explained one man, "goes off to the side, just like a vehicle. In the same way as we move our vehicle over to the side [of the road] and then proceed, that stone goes over to the side. It doesn't hurt anyone." Men in Ekhatpūr, talking about climbing the Ghāṭ, agreed with this, and then expanded: "Huge rocks break loose. Even if a rock breaks loose, it doesn't hit anyone or anything. It goes off to the side. That stone will pass between your legs, but it won't hit you."

Furthermore, these men said, the pathway up the hill is only ten feet wide in spots, with 100- or 200-foot precipices on each side. Even so, no one gets hurt. The reason for this is that Mahādev protects the pilgrims. Men traveling with the Sāsvaḍ *kāvaḍ* ascribed Mahādev's protection to his *tattva*, the power of his truth. Prompted by one man, another explained that none of these men has ever gotten badly hurt:

> Because of god's *tattva* . . . , it has never happened to us. And in the future too he is not going to allow it to happen . . . to this *kāvaḍ*, to Bhutojībuvā's *kāvaḍ*. In [all of] this Maharashtra, this privilege (*mān*), this is the privileged *kāvaḍ* of Sāsvaḍ, Purandar Taluka. Mahādev will never allow it to come to harm . . . . And he will never allow the "public" that comes with it to come to harm either. Not just Buvā, but all these people—he is not going to let anything happen to these people who are exerting themselves so hard.

Besides protecting them from danger, God also provides positive help to the pilgrims who struggle to get the heavy *kāvaḍ*s up the steep hill. Although some people talk of Śiva's shouldering a *kāvaḍ* himself, or of his helping in some other, less clearly specified way, the most common form that this idea of Śiva's assistance takes is in relation to the *pharārā*-cloth, the pennant or "sail" of the *kāvaḍ*s. As the men climb the Ghāṭ, they unfurl the *pharārā* and let it catch the wind, so that it can help propel the *kāvaḍ* to the top. God, they say, provides the wind. Some men in Ekhatpūr explained this idea as follows:

> Now, that *pharārā*. When we begin to climb the Ghāṭ at Śiṅgṇāpūr, there's nothing against saying that, at that time, opportunely, Parameśvar is

behind us. So, whatever direction the wind that comes [normally] blows from, at that time the wind will blow only from north to south [that is, up the Ghāṭ], on that day. And then, at that time, we loosen the *pharārā*. And then, with the strength of the people who have gathered and also with the strength of the wind—together we make it all the way through the Ghāṭ.

There is even a tradition that Śiva, either alone or accompanied by Pārvatī, leaves his temple while the *kāvaḍ*s are coming up Muṅgī Ghāṭ. According to one version, expressed by a shepherd who lives near Śiṅgṇāpūr, Śaṅkar leaves Pārvatī alone in the temple and comes to help the men get the *kāvaḍ*s up the cliff. A man in Beḷsar expressed another version of this tradition: people in Śiṅgṇāpūr sense that the temple is dismally empty (*udās*) while the *kāvaḍ*s are climbing Muṅgī Ghāṭ; the reason people get this feeling is that Śiva and Pārvatī have *both* left the temple at this time; they are sitting on the edge of the cliff, watching the *kāvaḍ*s make their way to the top. Thus, whether he helps actively or not, Śiva takes a great interest in what his devotees are doing.

Śiva's Wedding

But what is it, exactly, that these devotees are doing? Elsewhere (Feldhaus 1995:34–36) I have pointed out the parallel between the Śiṅgṇāpūr festival and the story of the descent of the Ganges (Gaṅgā) river. In the *Brahmapurāṇa*'s version of this story (*GM*.Skt. 4.64–65), the river flowed from heaven first onto the top of the cosmic mountain and from there to the head of Śiva. The Śiṅgṇāpūr pilgrims invert the image of the cosmic mountain, making the water travel *up* the mountain instead of flowing *down* it. By bringing the water of various rivers to the top of the mountain, the pilgrims also recreate the image of Śiva with the Ganges on his head. In this context, the mountain stands for Śiva, the god of mountains, and the water in the *kāvaḍ*s represents the Ganges, the first of rivers. By carrying water from home in their *kāvaḍ*s, the pilgrims physically transport their local rivers to the top of Śiva's head.[54]

That the men who carry *kāvaḍ*s to Śiṅgṇāpūr are implicitly bringing rivers to the mountaintop god, then, is clear. That they thereby recreate the image of Śiva with the Ganges on his head may well be a further meaning of the festival. However, even if this *is* implied in what the men who bring the *kāvaḍ*s do, it is not a meaning that any of them has ever explicitly articulated to me. The story that participants and observers more readily articulate—to the small extent that they tell any story at all—is that of

Śiva and Pārvatī's wedding. The *Bhāratīya Saṃskṛtikoś* (Jośī 1962–1979, Volume 9, p. 276) summarizes this story as follows:

> Śiva and Pārvatī were playing parcheesi on [Mount] Kailās. Śiva was losing each game that they played. Seeing that, Nārada made Śiva get angry. Śiva did get angry, and he came down from Kailās and hid in the hill at Śiṅgṇāpūr. Searching for him in the form of a tribal (Bhil) woman, Pārvatī came there. The two of them met on the fifth day of the bright half of the month of Caitra. Then the couple got married again.

In the context of this story, the reason that the *kāvaḍ*s come to Śiṅgṇāpūr is to celebrate the god's wedding. As we have seen, the wedding takes place on the Aṣṭamī, the eighth day of the month of Caitra.[55] This is the day when the *dhaj* appears, hung between the pinnacles of the two main temples at Śiṅgṇāpūr, and it is the same day that the principal *kāvaḍ*s "set out" in the evening from Sāsvaḍ and the Pañcakrośī villages. Men in the Umbareśvar temple who told us about the wedding explained that the *dhaj* is the turban of the bridegroom, Śiva. Another man called it the god's wedding crown (*bāśiṅg*); it gets attached to the uppermost part of the temple instead of being tied onto Śiva's own head. The pole that comes from Bhātāṅgaḷī is the bride, Pārvatī. And the *kāvaḍ*s that get carried up Muṅgī Ghāṭ from Sāsvaḍ and the other places are the procession, the *varāt*, after the wedding.

Men in Bhātāṅgaḷī who explained to us the festival and their role in it were quite explicit in describing the pole as a bride. In the course of our conversation, one of the men told us, "The wedding *must* take place on the Aṣṭamī, . . . at Nātepute." —"*Whose* wedding?" I asked, still unsure who plays the role of bride. "With whom?" In a chorus, a couple of the men answered, "Mahādev and Pārvatī's!" Then another man explained:

> Mahādev and Pārvatī. The meaning behind it is that . . . originally Mahādev was at Nātepute. This all continues on that assumption. So, when the pole goes there, the pole means Pārvatī. And the one who is there is Mahādev. The wedding of those two takes place there. That's how it is.

The word for "pole," "*kāṭhī*," is a feminine noun, this man pointed out. But the imagery extends well beyond grammar. Wrapped in cloth, decorated with jewelry, and crowned with a shock of white hair, the pole arrives in Nātepute dressed up like a bride for her wedding. Although the men we spoke with in Bhātāṅgaḷī rejected my interpretation of the silver bands (*kaṭ*s) on the pole as bangles (an indispensable item in a bride's trousseau), they did insist that the pole is the bride in the wedding, and they pointed out again and again that their village is her *māher*, her parental home.

The two Pāṭīls of Bhātāṅgaḷī receive at Nātepute wedding presents that are called "*rukhvat*"—a term that the men from Bhātāṅgaḷī take, in this context, to refer to gifts presented to the family of the bride.[56] Moreover, the pole itself, like any young bride, displays some reluctance to travel to her in-laws' home, her *sāsar*, at Śiṅgṇāpūr, and a clear enthusiasm to return to her parental home at Bhātāṅgaḷī. Chuckling fondly, the men in Bhātāṅgaḷī pointed out that, whereas their trip to Śiṅgṇāpūr lasts six days, the trip back to Bhātāṅgaḷī takes only five. The reason, they explained, is that there's a "pull" (*oḍh*) to the parental home. On the way to the in-laws' home, by contrast, the pole displays a tendency to dawdle:

> When she starts going to her in-laws' home, she goes a little bit tortuously. She takes an extra day. It's trouble to go. [She wants to stay in] her parental home. [She] doesn't want [to go to] her in-laws' home. But it's the same distance. The pole gets [back] in five days. It takes six days to go. No matter how fast we decide to carry it, still it won't go. But, on the way back, it comes running in five days. This is the fun in it. Because the same distance should take the same six days to cover. It doesn't happen that way. It comes back in five days.

By the time the *kāvaḍ*s that climb Muṅgī Ghāṭ reach Śiṅgṇāpūr, the wedding has been over for four days, and the pole has already left for Bhātāṅgaḷī. Besides, the wedding in which it plays a role is held, as we have seen, in Nātepute, a place some distance away from Śiṅgṇāpūr[57] and not on the Sāsvaḍ *kāvaḍs*' route. Indeed, Nātepute lies on a different side of the mountain (the northeast) from the side on which these *kāvaḍ*s climb up (the northwest). Thus, people from the Muṅgī Ghāṭ side are not particularly aware of the pole from Bhātāṅgaḷī or of its role in the festival. Some of the men who accompany the *kāvaḍ*s from Sāsvaḍ, the Pañcakrośī villages, and so on *are* aware, though, that the festival celebrates Śiva's wedding with Pārvatī; the Pañcakrośī villages' flyer mentions the wedding: "This pilgrimage festival celebrates the wedding of Śiva and Pārvatī. The turmeric ceremony is on the 5th, the flag-raising [i.e., the tying of the *dhaj*-turban][58] is on the 8th, and the wedding takes place that evening."

In fact, aside from the men we talked to in Bhātāṅgaḷī, very few people mentioned the wedding in their interpretations of the festival. One of the few exceptions were two men from Śivarī, the home of one of the four principal *kāvaḍ*s from Purandar Taluka. When I asked these men about the wedding that takes place before their *kāvaḍ*s reach Śiṅgṇāpūr, they at first said that they did not know anything about it, then contradicted this statement by adding: "Beforehand there's the turmeric ceremony, the wedding, and all that." Then one of these men proceeded to give a different version of the story of Śiva and Pārvatī's reunion at Śiṅgṇāpūr, and his own interpretation of the wedding imagery involved in the festival:

> People tell a folk tale (*dantakathā*)—I don't know if it's true—that, once upon a time, Śaṅkar and Pārvatī had a quarrel, in the Himālayas. And Śaṅkar sat there [at Śiṅgṇāpūr], sulking. There was jungle there, in front [of the temple at Śiṅgṇāpūr]. And then, as Pārvatī searched and searched on that hill of Śaṅkar's, where Śaṅkar has now taken that [incarnation], around that temple, she would see Śaṅkar. And when Pārvatī would reach the place [where she had seen him], Śaṅkar would again go ahead.
>
> In that way, around that hill, two miles apart from one another, there are temples of Śaṅkar on all sides. You take a look and see: there's a temple in Kothaḷe . . . .[59] All around, as many villages as there are, there must be fifteen or twenty temples . . . . In this way they made a circle. And . . . they climbed up by way of the cliff. Then, up there, [she saw him] in Baḷī's temple; then she saw him [where the main] temple is. And then they met there.

This story explains the several temples of Śiva that are to be found on and around the mountain at Śiṅgṇāpūr—each temple marking one of the spots where Śiva appeared briefly, then disappeared again as Pārvatī caught up with him.[60] The story also provides an explanation of the route that the *kāvaḍs* from the northwest take as they climb Muṅgī Ghāṭ. For later the narrator clarified what he had meant when he said, "They climbed up by way of the cliff": by "the cliff" he meant Muṅgī Ghāṭ. In this view, it is the *kāvaḍs* that play the role of Pārvatī in the festival. "The *kāvaḍ* is an *avatār* of Pārvatī," this man stated, and pointed out that the term "*kāvaḍ*" is a feminine noun. A man who was with him connected the *kāvaḍ*'s femininity with the clump of hair (*goṇḍā/sāj/gāṅgvaṇ*) atop some *kāvaḍs*' poles: "Pārvatī has hair," this man declared; "that's why the *kāvaḍ* has hair."[61] Yet another man made the connection with the story explicit: "The *kāvaḍs* go up by that hill because that was the road she took when she was searching. And what do we people say now? 'Why do we carry them up the hill?' But Pārvatī went by that hill." Then, addressing me, the principal narrator explained: "At that time, Tāī,[62] there was none of this; there were no roads or anything then. It must have been a jungle. Now, though, there are no trees."—"Oh!" I exclaimed, finally catching on. "She went through Muṅgī Ghāṭ!"—"She went through Muṅgī Ghāṭ," he repeated. And then another man added, "That's why the *kāvaḍs* go that way."

It is not only at Śiṅgṇāpūr, and not only as it climbs Muṅgī Ghāṭ, that the *kāvaḍ* is Pārvatī, on these men's understanding, but also after the pilgrims return home to Śivarī. Here, though, things become more complicated. For the *kāvaḍ* is not the only one who is Pārvatī: Yamāī, the goddess for whom the village of Śivarī is best known, is also Pārvatī. On the evening of the second day of the dark half of Caitra, these men said, the night after its return from Śiṅgṇāpūr, the *kāvaḍ* parades through the village "all night long—until 4 a.m.," to the accompaniment of a band playing music. This parade, which ends up in the village's Mahādev temple, is the wedding procession (*varāt*) of the *kāvaḍ*, the procession in which the bride and groom return to his home. But Śivarī is not only the home of Śiva, whose temple is in the village settlement area. It is also the home of Pārvatī, here called Yamāī, whose temple stands a couple of kilometers north of the village settlement, near the main road.[63] Six days after the *varāt* procession, on the dark Eighth (Aṣṭamī) of Caitra, the *kāvaḍ* travels in procession throughout the village once again, ending up this time at the temple of Yamāī. The men carry the *kāvaḍ* around this temple five times in a clockwise circumambulation (*pradakṣiṇā*), then pour a stream of water (*dhār*) over the goddess inside. The next evening, the *kāvaḍ* returns to the village settlement. A month later, the men put it away in the Māruti temple, where it stays for the rest of the year.

Enactment of Regions

Thus, participants in the pilgrimage to Śiṅgṇāpūr interpret the Caitra festival there in terms of Śaiva *bhakti* and, to some extent, wedding imagery. At the same time, the festival also provides them an opportunity to dramatize various geographical units, and to express and strengthen their own identification with some of these units. The large *kāvaḍ*s and poles serve, first of all, as a focal point for bringing together the villages and towns that they come from. In addition, through various kinds of intensive interactions, the journeys of these large *kāvaḍ*s and poles bring the places they come from together with the places they pass through. The Pañcakrośī *kāvaḍ* unites the five Pañcakrośī villages into a small region, and the rivalry between adherents of this *kāvaḍ* and adherents of the one from Sāsvaḍ expresses the unity, however contentious, of a greater Sāsvaḍ region. In a similar way, the marriage imagery of the festival and the timing that separates two groups of pilgrims express, on the one hand, the opposition between two regions (the region of origin of the *kāvaḍ*s that climb Muṅgī Ghāṭ and the region of origin of the *kāvaḍ*s and large *kāṭhī* that approach Śiṅgṇāpūr by the eastern road, Bhavānī Ghāṭ) and, on the other hand, these two regions' ultimate unity. Finally, the pilgrimage as a whole enacts the unity of a region that many of the participants identify as "Maharashtra."

Village Projects

Although many small *kāvaḍs* come to Śiṅgṇāpūr as expressions of the devotion of an individual or a family or to fulfil a private *navas*-vow, sending a large *kāvaḍ* or pole to Śiṅgṇāpūr is always a collective enterprise. In part, this is a matter of economic arrangements. In Beḷsar, for example, the home of one of the four principal *kāvaḍs*, the men who talked with my companions and me on the eighth day (Aṣṭamī) of the bright half of Caitra in 1995 did so in the village government (Grām Pañcāyat) office, in the presence of an enormous heap of grain that people kept adding to as we talked. On the first day of the month of Caitra (Guḍhī Pāḍhvā, a week before the day on which we held our conversation), the men explained, when the *kāvaḍ* is taken out of storage and set up in the village, there takes place a meeting of "the whole village" to decide what each family's (*kuṭumba*'s) contribution is to be. That year, each family was to contribute either three *pāylīs* (approximately 17 kilograms) of grain or 75 rupees.[64] The grain is used to feed the men who accompany the *kāvaḍ* on the pilgrimage, and the money buys more food or other necessities. Anyone who accompanies the *kāvaḍ*, including in-laws who live in other villages and people who have migrated out of Beḷsar but return to make the pilgrimage, receives a share of the food.[65]

To the extent possible, it seems, men from many different households in a village travel with the village's *kāvaḍ* or pole to Śiṅgṇāpūr, but there is no overt compulsion to do so. In Beḷsar, after the men had told us about collecting grain for the pilgrims, I asked if each family must also send a man with the *kāvaḍ* to Śiṅgṇāpūr. One man answered this way:

> No, not send. He goes of his own accord. That is, the—on the basis of the faith (*śraddhā*), the faith that he has in the god, a man from each and every household certainly goes. From some households, one man will go; four members of some households go; two members of other households go; sometimes, from some households, no one goes. No one has to tell [anyone to go], but as far as possible one man from each household goes on the pilgrimage.

Other contributions, too, are voluntary and individual. There is a Khāṭīk (butcher) who lives in Pune, for instance, who brings (vegetarian) food from there to Śiṅgṇāpūr on the twelfth day of Caitra each year; he brings the food then so that the Buvā from Sāsvaḍ can eat it to break his fast. According to men traveling with the Sāsvaḍ *kāvaḍ*, the Khāṭīk also brings enough food for "a hundred or two hundred" of the people accompanying the Buvā as well. In 1995, a drought year, we learned before the festival that the owners of "all twenty-two or twenty-three" trucks and tractors in the five Pañcakrośī villages had volunteered their vehicles, as well as their services as drivers, to carry water from wherever they could get it to Śiṅgṇāpūr to help meet the needs of the pilgrims. Whereas these men's contribution to the festival was described as disinterested "service" (*sevā*),[66] others' donations and service, on a regular or occasional basis, are made in fulfilment of a vow (*navas*). Some women, as we have seen, carry other pilgrims' sandals up Muṅgī Ghāṭ to fulfil a vow they have made at the shrine of Dattātreya Nāmdev Kolte, the young man who died there. Similarly, a man from a village near Bhātāṅgaḷī provides two barrels of cooking oil to light the thousand or so torches that burn to celebrate the *kāvaḍ*'s return to Bhātāṅgaḷī from Śiṅgṇāpūr each year; this man donates the oil for this festival in fulfillment of a vow he once made.

The various contributions that people make and services that they perform provide them an opportunity to be intensively involved in a local community project. There are also several ritual elements that seem to enact a connection between a *kāvaḍ* or pole and its home village as a whole. Either before setting out for Śiṅgṇāpūr or upon returning home, or both, each large *kāvaḍ* or pole travels in a festive procession throughout what the men describing it generally identify as its "whole" village or town.[67] People greet the *kāvaḍ* on their own doorsteps as it moves through the areas they live in; people living in outlying hamlets or in houses in the fields come in to the village center to pay their respects. As a man in Ekhatpūr explained, even simply displaying the *kāvaḍ* after it has returned from Śiṅgṇāpūr provides an opportunity for those who did *not* travel along to connect themselves with the pilgrimage: "All of our womenfolk, or the people of our village, they all—because we have come back from Śiṅgṇāpūr, the people living in the fields and pastures round about come for a sight of the *kāvaḍ*. There's a procession here again for an hour or two. [Women] do the lap-filling rite (*oṭī bharaṇ*)[68] of the *kāvaḍ* after it gets back. . .."

In many places to which a *kāvaḍ* or pole returns, there is a communal meal, usually called *bhaṇḍārā*, to which "everyone" in the village is invited. In addition, many villages time their village festival, or *jatrā*, to coincide with their *kāvaḍ*'s return from Śiṅgṇāpūr. The month of Caitra is the most popular season for such village *jatrās*. They provide an opportunity for residents of the village to celebrate their village and its principal god, and they provide an occasion for those who have moved out, whether to marry or to find employment, to return home. In villages that collectively send a *kāvaḍ* or pole to Śiṅgṇāpūr, its return to the village adds to the festivities, whether or not the village god is Śiva.

In Bhātāṅgaḷī, the pole provides a particular ritual means of enacting the unity of the village. Men in Bhātāṅgaḷī who talked with us emphasized the significance of the fact that the pole is first erected on the Guḍhī Pāḍvā day. On this New Year's festival, the first day of the first month (Caitra) of the Hindu year, people generally set up, outside the front door of their homes, a four- or five-foot-long stick or pole decorated with a piece of cloth and some leaves and crowned with an upside-down pot. The stick or pole is called a "*guḍhī*." In Bhātāṅgaḷī, however, instead of each household having its own *guḍhī*, the 40-foot-tall *kāṭhī* that will later go to Śiṅgṇāpūr serves as the one and only *guḍhī*—an extraordinarily large one—for the whole village. As one man explained, three different groups in the village perform their *pūjā*-worship of this *guḍhī* on three successive days. On the first day "everybody" does *pūjā*, and then Vāṇīs (Liṅgāyats) and "Harijans" (Untouchables, Dalits) do their *pūjā* on subsequent days. These are two groups of people who are quite likely to have been excluded from the "everybody" of the first day:[69]

> [The pole] belongs to the whole village on the Pāḍvā day. There's only one *guḍhī*, one *guḍhī* for the village. On the Pāḍvā day, what do we all do? . . . The bath, *sandhyā*,[70] clothes, jewelry—on the Pāḍhvā day, the whole village comes together to do this. We gather all the musicians and musical instruments at that place, at five o'clock. We eat a meal and make a food offering and the whole village does a single *āratī*[71] together. The whole village. Just one. We clean up the whole village, and at five o'clock we do *āratī*. We do worship (*pūjā*) and this and that and everything in the proper way . . . . And this is what comes first, at the beginning. And the next morning, when we get up, there's the Vāṇīs', Liṅgāyats' *āratī*. They do everything properly, the worship (*pūjā-arcā*) and everything properly—theirs is on the next day. And on the third day, the Harijans, the people of the "backwards classes," do their *āratī*, worship, and everything in a proper manner. It stays here for three days, here . . . in Mahādev's temple.

The Pañcakrośī Region

The *kāvaḍ* that I have been referring to as "the Pañcakrośī *kāvaḍ*" does not come from just a single village; rather, five villages cooperate in sending it. Together, in relation to the *kāvaḍ* festival if in no other context, these villages form a region whose residents speak and think of it as such, and whose residents' actions and arrangements during the festival serve to highlight the region's cohesion.

The five villages are contiguous to one another. They cluster along the banks of the Karhā river, downstream from Sāsvaḍ. The largest of the villages, Khaḷad,[72] lies on the south bank of the river, and its land adjoins that of Sāsvaḍ. The other four villages—Kumbhārvaḷaṇ, Ekhatpūr, Muñjavaḍī, and Khānavaḍī—lie in that order, from west to east (upstream to downstream), on the north bank of the river. Two of the villages, Ekhatpūr and Muñjavaḍī, share a common village council (*grām pañcāyat*),[73] but the others have separate councils. As far as I can tell, the five villages form a single, exclusive unit only in relation to the *kāvaḍ* festival. Men in Ekhatpūr, who understand Ekhatpūr to be the *kāvaḍ*'s principal home, explained the cooperative arrangement as a result of economic necessity:

> The *kāvaḍ* belongs to all five villages, doesn't it? In fact, the *kāvaḍ* belongs to only one village, but because one village cannot bear the burden, we take [the others] for help—five villages came to be [involved]. That's how it is. . .. We have taken them to help, so we say it's the *kāvaḍ* of all five villages.

Later in our conversation, when I asked the men in Ekhatpūr if Khaḷad has a separate *kāvaḍ*, one of the men said, "No. *This* is Khaḷad's, this *kāvaḍ*." —"*This* one is Khaḷad's," I said. "All right." And the man elaborated: "Really this *kāvaḍ* is Ekhatpūr's, but, because we don't have enough people to help, we say, 'Make it the *kāvaḍ* of all five villages. Make it collective.'"

Although the men of the Pañcakrośī villages thus perceive their association in the *kāvaḍ* festival as contingent upon each village's need for the others' assistance, they also understand the arrangement as one that has been going on for centuries. When I asked how long the five villages have been carrying on the festival together, the men gave me estimates ranging from 500 to 1700 years. However old the arrangement may be, the Pañcakrośī comes into being as a region in the context of the *kāvaḍ* festival. Each year one of the five villages takes its turn to host the *kāvaḍ* in the days before and after the pilgrimage. Groups of men from each of the villages dance in the *kāvaḍ*'s ceremonial departure procession. On the next day, the day of the actual departure for Śiṅgṇāpūr, a Māṅg (a member of the low-status Rope-Maker caste) from each of the five villages brings a rope that will be tied around the *kāvaḍ* in Kothaḷe, to reinforce it for the climb up Muṅgī Ghāṭ. And, finally, upon the *kāvaḍ*'s return home, it attends the village festivals of each of the five villages: Khānavaḍī's on the dark fifth day (Pañcamī) of Caitra, Kumbhārvaḷaṇ's on the dark sixth day (Ṣaṣṭhī), Muñjavaḍī's on the dark tenth day (Daśamī), Ekhatpūr's on the dark twelfth day (Bāras), and Khaḷad's on the first Monday after Akṣayya Tṛtīya (the third day of the next lunar month, Vaiśākh).

Between these festivals and after the last of them, the *kāvaḍ* returns to Ekhatpūr, where it spends the rest of the year in the Bahirobā temple. Men we talked with in Ekhatpūr made much of this fact, calling Ekhatpūr the "*māher*," or parental home, of the *kāvaḍ* and claiming that "trouble" will afflict any other of the villages that tries to have the *kāvaḍ* stay in it: "Even though this *kāvaḍ* belongs to the [whole] Pañcakrośī," these men said, "still it resides only in Ekhatpūr. If it is left in another village for even one or two nights, it immediately—they have trouble. That village has trouble." When I asked what kind of "trouble" that village would have, one of the men answered, "People get sick," and another said, "If they have a good ox, a Khilārī, it will die . . . . The next day they quietly bring the *kāvaḍ* and put it here." Then the first man summarized: "If one of the [other] villages would say, 'Why should it be kept only in your Ekhatpūr? We'll put it in our village,' the *kāvaḍ* won't be able to stay [there]." The other man chimed in, invoking the kind of bridal imagery that the men in Bhātāṅgaḷī used for their pole: "Ekhatpūr is its parental-home village (*māher-gāv*)."

Besides being the "parental-home village" of the *kāvaḍ*, Ekhatpūr is the site of Bhutyā Telī's "Burning House," as well as of the *samādhis* of the original Bhutyā Telī and his mother and father. Ekhatpūr has other characteristics too that make the men we talked to there especially proud.[74] Prominent among these characteristics is Ekhatpūr's connection with Śiṅgṇāpūr. Although the connection consists primarily in Ekhatpūr's *kāvaḍ*'s important role in the Śiṅgṇāpūr festival, this role also leads these men to see what they consider significant parallels between Ekhatpūr and Śiṅgṇāpūr. The *kāvaḍs*' water is poured at Śiṅgṇāpūr on the bright twelfth day ("the first Bāras") of Caitra, and the village festival of Ekhatpūr takes place on the dark twelfth day ("the second Bāras"), after the *kāvaḍ* has returned home. And two men chimed in together to describe Ekhatpūr's location in terms of the religious geography of the region:

> At Sāsvaḍ is Sopān Mahārāj,[75] and here to the east is Maharashtra's family god (*kuldaivat*), Khaṇḍobā of Jejurī. And here in between flows this Karhā river. And on the bank of this Karhā river is this place, a holy place (*tīrthasthān*). On that very bank is Bhutyā Mahārāj's *samādhi*. You should mention that in your [book].

Except for the claim that the *kāvaḍ* must be stored in Ekhatpūr, the possessiveness that the men express in relation to it seems to be felt on behalf of all five villages in the "Pañcakrośī." In chapter 1 we saw the term "Pañcakrośī" used for the holy area within a radius of five *krośās* or *kos* of a holy place or river, and I argued that the term is a regional or proto-regional one. Many who refer to Ekhatpūr or Khaḷad and the other four villages as jointly constituting a "Pañcakrośī" seem to understand the "five" (*pañca*) in the word as referring to the number of villages involved, and not to a distance of five *kos* from a common center. Nevertheless, the Khaḷad-Ekhatpūr and so on Pañcakrośī area is clearly a conceptual region for the people who use this term for it, as well as for residents of the region who take an interest in the joint *kāvaḍ* and its pilgrimage.

Pañcakrośī and Sāsvaḍ

In relation to the Śiṅgṇāpūr *kāvaḍ* festival, then, the Pañcakrośī area constitutes a region in itself, a region based on cooperation among the villages that belong to it. But the Pañcakrośī area also forms part of another, larger region that includes Sāsvaḍ as well. This larger region is based not on cooperation but on competition—competition between Sāsvaḍ and the Pañcakrośī villages.

A good bit of the local pride of not just Ekhatpūr but the Pañcakrośī villages as a group crystallizes around the rivalry between their *kāvaḍ* and the one that is based in Sāsvaḍ. The rivalry finds ritual expression in the "*ujvī-ḍāvī*" rites (the ritual jockeying for position at certain places along the way to Śiṅgṇāpūr) as well as in the way the two *kāvaḍ*s and their Buvās generally avoid each other. One time, when the men traveling with the Pañcakrośī *kāvaḍ* had stopped to rest and Sudhir Waghmare and I were talking with some of them, they learned that the Sāsvaḍ Buvā and his *kāvaḍ* were approaching from the rear. The men jumped up and proceeded on their way, abruptly terminating the interview. In part, their haste can be explained by the ritual requirement that Sāsvaḍ's *kāvaḍ* have the last position in the procession; however, the men also seemed anxious to avoid a meeting between the two Buvās.

No one disputes the fact that the real, original Bhutyā Telī *kāvaḍ* (or its successor) is the one that goes to Śiṅgṇāpūr from Sāsvaḍ, and no one questions its right (*mān*) to go last in the procession that eventually climbs Muṅgī Ghāṭ. What the men in the Pañcakrośī villages *do* dispute is the Sāsvaḍ Buvā's right to have custody of the *kāvaḍ*. The *kāvaḍ*, they say, was originally theirs, and it should still be theirs; moreover, they contest any claim that the Sāsvaḍ Buvā is a descendant of the original Bhutyā Telī. The history of the events that led to there being two Bhutyā Telī *kāvaḍ*s is murky, especially with regard to exactly *when* the events took place—even in what century, or how many generations ago. Everyone seems to agree, though, on the broad outlines of the story:

The *kāvaḍ* and its accompanying privileges (*mān*) belonged to the descendants of Bhutojī Telī. These descendants lived in Ekhatpūr, on or near the site of the original Bhutojī Telī's "Burning House." When, in some generation or other, one of Bhutojī's male descendants died, leaving behind a widow but no children, the widow pawned the *kāvaḍ*, handing it over to someone in Sāsvaḍ as security for a loan that she did not repay.[76] Outsiders refer to the two *kāvaḍ*s, Sāsvaḍ's and the Pañcakrośī villages', as, respectively, the "brother-in-law's" (*dīrācī*, husband's brother's) and the "sister-in-law's" (*bhāvjāīcī*, brother's wife's), implying that the person in Sāsvaḍ to whom the widow gave the *kāvaḍ* was her husband's brother—a man who might be supposed to be her husband's legitimate successor if her husband had no sons.

Some men in the Pañcakrośī villages become infuriated, however, upon even hearing the words "brother-in-law" and "sister-in-law." In Ekhatpūr, when I asked, "What is this about a sister-in-law and so on?" one man replied, rather calmly, "It's all a hoax (*labāḍī*)." Another man became quite worked up. "It's a hoax," he repeated. "It's all false . . . . It's a fabrication." And then he launched into an elaborate argument intended to show that the man in Sāsvaḍ could not possibly have been the brother-in-law of the widow in Ekhatpūr.[77] Eventually the other men became embarrassed at the vehemence of their companion's statements, and they urged him to change the subject. But he did get in one last plea to me:

> Now, you must put a very important word in that book:[78] Bhutojī Mahārāj was originally from Ekhatpūr—or Muñj . . . . If you say Ekhatpūr-Muñjavaḍī, that will do. Bhutojī is originally from [this] village. This much is proven. You must make this [known] through your writings.

In a separate conversation, at a calmer moment, a man from Muñjavaḍī told us the name of the man to whom, he claimed, the widow had pawned the *kāvaḍ*. This man (or his descendants) now lives in Phalṭaṇ, and is not even a Telī, a member of Bhutojī's oil-presser and -seller caste. But he gave the *kāvaḍ* to a Teḷī in Sāsvaḍ to keep it going, and, according to the man from Muñjavaḍī, it is this man and his descendants who have become the Buvās of Sāsvaḍ.

Meanwhile, in whatever way the *kāvaḍ* came to be in the custody of the Sāsvaḍ Buvā, people in the Pañcakrośī villages were distressed at its loss. Unable to get it back, they had a new *kāvaḍ* made, and they adopted a Telī man from Sātārā to be its Buvā. They gave him some land in Ekhatpūr-Muñjavaḍī, "so he could eat, . . . so he could support himself." It is possible that all of this happened as recently as one generation ago. The Buvā who was adopted died recently and is buried near the Bhutojī Telī temple, along with his parents; it is his son who is the present Buvā of the Pañcakrośī *kāvaḍ*; this son lives in Sāsvaḍ, though he also has a house in Khaḷad, and the people of the Pañcakrośī give him some grain and other donations to help support him. The present *kāvaḍ*, with an inscription dating it to March 27, 1990,[79] is a new one, replacing the *kāvaḍ* that the Pañcakrośī villages made after they lost theirs to Sāsvaḍ.

So the situation is quite ambiguous, and there is a considerable amount of tension, expressed in rituals as well as in words. Sāsvaḍ has the original *kāvaḍ* (or, more likely, its replacement), but Ekhatpūr has the *samādhi* of

Bhutojī Telī, as well as his original, "burning" house. Both the Sāsvaḍ *kāvaḍ* and the one from the Pañcakrośī villages carry on the top of their *śīḍ*-poles a *savāī*, the clump of black hair indicating their honorary right, or *mān*, in the festival. But the men in Ekhatpūr claim to have the copper-plate inscriptions and documents, issued by kings of Sātārā, that undergird the Pañcakrośī villages' right to place the *savāī* on their *kāvaḍ*.[80] For the 1992 ceremony dedicating the new temple over Bhutojī Telī's *samādhi*, Ekhatpūr hosted a huge assembly and feast, at which the chief guests were members of the royal house of Satara,[81] the descendants of Śivājī who are still the private owners of the Śambhu Mahādev temple at Śiṅgṇāpūr. Sāsvaḍ, for its part, has no need of such inscriptions, documents, or royal support: its *kāvaḍ* is the one that *does* hold the position of honor in the pilgrimage festival. Still, the fact that there are two rival Bhutojī Telī *kāvaḍ*s brings the Pañcakrośī villages together with Sāsvaḍ in a tense, but also intense, relationship.

Purandar Taluka

A slightly larger region, less tense perhaps but recognized as a region by at least some of its residents as well as by outsiders, includes not only the homes of the two Bhutojī Telī *kāvaḍ*s but all four of the places in Purandar Taluka from which the principal *kāvaḍ*s travel to Śiṅgṇāpūr. In Beḷsar, when people told me that their ancestors used to carry their *kāvaḍ* to Śiṅgṇāpūr filled with water, I asked what water they carried in the *kāvaḍ*. The man I was speaking with began talking about all four of the principal *kāvaḍ*s:

> Now, this Karhā river that flows here at our place, they used to fill [the *kāvaḍ*] with water from this river. Now, the Karhā river flows at Sāsvaḍ too. They also take water from the Karhā. From Khaḷad too. The Karhā is there. They too used to take water from the Karhā. At Beḷsar, Beḷsar too, it's water of the Karhā. All of these *kāvaḍ*s were carrying water of the Karhā. So there was no difference in the water. All of the four *kāvaḍ*s' people used to carry water from the Karhā.

"Śivarī too," I prompted him, and he agreed: "Śivarī also. Yes, yes, yes, yes, yes, yes. What's more, everyone's river is the same. The water is the same." Then, using words suggested by another man, he said, "The faith (*śraddhā*) is the same. Yes. Just the villages are different." Then, with some more prompting by one of his companions, the man elaborated a bit further: "The water pots (*haṇḍī*s) are different," he explained. "Otherwise, the people of the four villages have the water of the same Karhā [river]. That's how it is. There is not different water. The water is the same. The water is the same."

And All the Places Along the Way

In the conception of this man and the others he was speaking for, the unity of the four places from which the principal *kāvaḍs* come consists both in the fact that they all take water from the same river to Śiṅgṇāpūr—that they all lie, that is, in the same river valley—and in their common "faith" (*śraddhā*), the attitude or consciousness that they share by virtue of their participation in the festival. In a broader sense, all the *kāvaḍs* that climb Muṅgī Ghāṭ bring together by their final, joint procession all the places that they come from, as well as all the places that they have passed through along their way.

By the time the *kāvaḍs* line up in Kothaḷe to climb Muṅgī Ghāṭ, each of them has passed through and stopped in a number of other places. Indeed, this is true of *all* the large *kāvaḍs* and poles that reach Śiṅgṇāpūr in bullock carts or carried by men on foot. The trips of all these *kāvaḍs* and poles are arranged so as to maximize their interaction, and that of the men who accompany them, with residents of villages along the way. This interaction takes two principal forms: processions of the *kāvaḍs* and poles in the villages they pass through, and stops in which the pilgrims accept meals, tea, and other forms of hospitality from residents of these villages.

As a man in Ekhatpūr explained, "We have to take the *kāvaḍ* out [of the bullock cart] in each village. We have to take it out, hold a procession, make it dance a little while." As a *kāvaḍ* or pole processes through a village or town, people make offerings to it of grain, colored powders, and other normal *pūjā*-offerings. People tie garlands of coconuts to the *kāvaḍs*, stringing five coconuts together and hanging them from the *śīḍ*-pole. People offer silver bands (*kaṭs*) to the Bhātāṅgaḷī pole. In several places, parents lay their children on the ground like railroad ties across the path of a *kāvaḍ* or pole, in fulfillment of vows the parents made for the children's birth. And people offer significant amounts of money, tying garlands of notes, like the garlands of coconuts, to the *śīḍ*-pole of a *kāvaḍ*. About one of the places on their route, men in Ekhatpūr boasted: "We collect almost 1000 rupees in that Jogavaḍī within two hours or so. People offer 10[-rupee] or 20[-rupee] or 100[-rupee] notes."

In addition, the men accompanying the major *kāvaḍs* and poles receive numerous meals and snacks and cups of tea at the many places where they stop along their way. The stops are always in the same places, and the hosts are the same every year—until a host dies without leaving an heir who is willing and able to continue the tradition, or until a personal friendship or other influence leads to a new stop being added.[82] The groups from Sāsvaḍ and the Pañcakrośī villages include in their printed programs the schedules of their meals and other stops along the way, but the other large *kāvaḍ*s and poles also have strictly planned schedules, which the men who travel with them know well and adhere to carefully. A man in Bhātāṅgaḷī explained the sense of duty that the pilgrims feel toward their hosts:

> The stops are always the same. The places where we spend the night are always the same. I mean, whether it's small or large, we *have* to go there. Why? What does this mean? The people prepare by making food offerings (*naivedya*), provisions for a meal, cooking, and *āratī*. We *have* to go there at that time. And how is it for us? Even if we're an hour or so late some time, they wait for us. They're not satisfied unless we come. [They know] we'll always come. Why? The whole village has cooked [for us]! So? Is it a joke to feed a meal to 5000 people?

"And there's a meal in each of these places?" I asked, referring to the list he and the other men we were talking with had given us of their stops along the way. "Yes," he replied, "there's a meal in each village, going and coming." Then, prompted by another man, he added: "There are meals in the villages in between [too]. Of course there are [meals] in these places. There are [meals] where we spend the night, other ones in the morning, still others in the afternoon, still others in the evening. We have to eat a meal at least ten times a day." When I expressed astonishment, he said, "That's how it is. It's the *rule*! A meal in each village."

When the *kāvaḍ*s and poles arrive at Śiṅgṇāpūr, then, the journey they have been through has maximized their interaction with residents of the places along the way. Each *kāvaḍ* or pole arrives as the joint project or collective missive of the places it has come from and the places it has passed through. It brings together all those places through their residents' interactions with it and with the pilgrims who accompany it. Thus, when the various *kāvaḍ*s and poles come together at Śiṅgṇāpūr for the festival, they bring with them all the places that each of them has come from and passed through. They make those places into a region: the region that sends *kāvaḍ*s and poles to Śiṅgṇāpūr.

This same region is also enacted outside of and prior to the ritual context, in organizational meetings designed to coordinate the pilgrimage festival. Officials of the administrative units of this region put a good deal of work into making sure that the festival runs smoothly. In order to assure that all will go peacefully and safely, government officials call two meetings in advance of the festival. The first meeting is held three weeks beforehand, in Dahīvaḍī, the headquarters town of the taluka in which Śiṅgṇāpūr is located. The second meeting is held in Śiṅgṇāpūr itself, about ten days before the *kāvaḍ*s are due to climb up Muṅgī Ghāṭ. Among those invited are officials in charge of public health, public works, electricity, and development (the Block Development Officer) in Dahīvaḍī Taluka; officials of the State Transport bus system centers in Dahīvaḍī, Phalṭaṇ, and "Puṇe (Sāsvaḍ)"; the Sarpañc, Police Pāṭīl, and other officials of Śiṅgṇāpūr; men responsible for bringing the *dhaj* from Khāmasvāḍī; and the leaders of approximately 20 of the principal *kāvaḍ*s and *kāṭhī*s from Pune, Satara, Solapur, and Usmanabad Districts. These meetings serve to work out the transportation, water, public health, and security arrangements for the festival, and to coordinate the principal *kāvaḍs*' routes and schedules so as to avoid conflicts between them.[83] A man in Ekhatpūr who had been to at least one of these meetings described as follows the kinds of things that get discussed at them:

> So that there may not be any grounds for conflict, the government places some responsibility on us, you see . . . . Which *kāvaḍ* should proceed at what distance? At what time should which *kāvaḍ* arrive at what place? We have schedules [for] this, from the government. We have to act according to them . . . . What should we do on the day of the festival? How will the water be supplied? What should the doctor do? What should the police department do?

These meetings provide a preview of the festival itself, in that representatives of many of the principal places that send *kāvaḍ*s come together at the meetings, as their *kāvaḍ*s will come together at the festival. In this context too, then, a context that might be called a "meta-ritual" one, the whole region covered by the festival becomes visible. It is displayed in the gathering of the region's ritual leaders, as it will later become visible in the festival itself, in the gathering of the pilgrims, with their *kāvaḍ*s and poles.

Śiva's Side and Śakti's Side

Some people who have reflected on the Śiṅgṇāpūr festival point to an important distinction between two groups that come to it and between the two regions from which they come. For such interpreters, the *kāvaḍ*s that climb Muṅgī Ghāṭ are distinct from the ones that come up Bhavānī Ghāṭ, to the east. Indeed, these two groups are not supposed to meet. When Ramdas Atkar asked the men in Bhātāṅgaḷī if they climb up Muṅgī Ghāṭ, one of them replied, "No," and then explained: "The *kāvaḍ* from Sāsvaḍ[84] comes to Muṅgī Ghāṭ. And, the thing is, we and it are not supposed to meet . . . . They call us the pole. The pole. They say, 'Old Lady Pole' (*mhātār kāṭhī*). The Old Lady Pole and the *kāvaḍ* must not meet." Why this is so, the man could not explain,[85] but when I asked him what measures he and his companions take to prevent the two from meeting, he said: "They climb up here, and we climb down the hill, over here . . . at Nātepute, over here. They come from the west, and we are on the east. We come [down] on the east side, and the *kāvaḍ* climbs up from the west,[86] through Muṅgī Ghāṭ." Their paths, that is, do not cross.

Men we talked with in the Umbareśvar temple, at the foot of Bhavānī Ghāṭ, distinguished not so much between the main *kāvaḍ* (from Sāsvaḍ) and the main pole (from Bhātāṅgaḷī) as between two groups of *kāvaḍs* coming from two different areas at two different times. Speaking with these men on Caitra Śuddha Ekādaśī, the day before the *kāvaḍs* from Sāsvaḍ and environs climb up Muṅgī Ghāṭ, I asked if a large number of pilgrims had come to the Umbareśvar temple that day. "They come from the Pāḍhvā [the first day of the month of Caitra] onwards," said one of the men. "It starts on the Pāḍhvā day. It goes on just like this until the full-moon day." Then the other man specified this, saying: "Those who come on the eighth day (the Aṣṭamī) to toss rice during the wedding, the ones on the eighth day are different." The first man then repeated his own point, relating it to what his companion had said:

> Some come on the ninth day [of Caitra] (the Navamī), some come on the tenth day (the Daśamī), some on the eleventh day (the Ekādaśī), on the twelfth day (the Bāras), on the thirteenth day (the Teras)—Śambhū Mahādev's pilgrimage festival goes on for ten or fifteen days. Mahādev is the family god (*kuldaivat*) of Maharashtra.

"So tomorrow's not the main day or anything," I said, surprised that the all-important Bāras would occur in an undifferentiated list along with the other, less eventful days. Then one of the men explained the correspondence between the geography and the chronology of the festival. He started with a rhetorical question:

> What do you mean, "main day"? From the Pāḍhvā on is the main day. Now, what will happen tomorrow? These *kāvaḍs* of ours, from Marāṭhvāḍā, from Usmānābād, from the land of Varhāḍ (*varāḍdeś*), will turn around and come back here tomorrow. And Puṇe, Pune District. . .. Puṇe, Sindhudurg, the Koṅkaṇ area—tomorrow the ones from these places will come. That part there, Nagar—the eastern part, the western part, and all of Pune District, Satara District. And Kolhāpūr, Sāṅglī, Miraj—tomorrow the pilgrims from there will come. And the pilgrims from this part (*bhāg*) will

> come down tomorrow at twelve noon. These pilgrims climb up, the *kāvaḍs* that climb up at Muṅgī Ghāṭ, from there, the one called Bhutojī Buvā, from Pune District, Khaḷad, Khānavaḍī, Beḷsar, the *kāvaḍs* with an honorary right from that part (*bhāg*) climb up from there.

The difference between the two groups of *kāvaḍs*, in these men's view, is not simply that the *kāvaḍs* come from different areas, and not even simply that they reach the top of the hill at Śiṅgṇāpūr by different routes. The two groups of *kāvaḍs* also differ from each other by representing the two parties to the wedding that the festival celebrates, the wedding of Mahādev and Pārvatī, or Śiva and Śakti. The first man explained it this way:

> Those are on Śiva's side, and these are on Śakti's side. That's why they shouldn't meet one another . . . . Śiva and Śakti . . . . The ones from that part are the ones on Śiva's side, and the ones from this part are the ones on Śakti's side. That is, from Tuḷjāpūr, from the east, from east of Tuḷjāpūr—what they call Tuḷjāpūr, Ambāvārī. That's Śakti's . . . . They'll come here. And Śiva's are the ones that come from . . . the Pune area. They're going to arrive tomorrow. So, because they're arriving tomorrow, all these come down today, the ones from this side. That means, they don't meet one another . . . . ŚivāŚakti.

That the *kāvaḍs* that climb up Muṅgī Ghāṭ, those that come from Sāsvaḍ and other places to the west, should be identified as the ones forming the groom's party, those on "Śiva's side," fits well with the fierce Śaiva loyalty of the men who bring them to Śiṅgṇāpūr. That the *kāvaḍs* from the east should form the bride's party, those on "Śakti's side," fits with the fact that the Bhātāṅgaḷī *kāṭhī*, which some hold to be Pārvatī in the wedding at Nātepute, comes from that side. The designation "Śakti's side" also fits with the fact that the major goddess temple at Tuḷjāpūr, the temple of the goddess Bhavānī, lies to the east of Śiṅgṇāpūr. Indeed, as we have seen, the road leading eastward from Śiṅgṇāpūr is called "Bhavānī Ghāṭ," and Tuḷjāpūr is one of the places that the Bhātāṅgaḷī *kāṭhī* visits on its journey home.

The notion that the ebb and flow of the pilgrims at Śiṅgṇāpūr corresponds to the bride's and groom's sides of a wedding party is another example of an opposition that is at the same time a powerful image of and occasion for unity. Like the rival Bhutojī Telī *kāvaḍs* of Sāsvaḍ and the Pañcakrośī villages, and like the story and tug-of-rope ritual at Śeṇḍī and Pokharḍī,[87] the "Śiva's side" and "Śakti's side" pilgrims at Śiṅgṇāpūr constitute the poles of an opposition that is contained within a higher unity. "Śiva's side" and "Śakti's side," as the bride's and groom's parties in the wedding, present an especially clear image of the union of such polar opposites. On the level of theology, Śiva and Śakti, though opposed, are interdependent and complementary. On the level of social relations, weddings bring together two families that are, by definition, previously *not* related to each other. Indeed, bringing two unrelated families together is the very point of a wedding, as well as the source of much of the tension it involves. On the level of geography, the idea that people come from two different "sides," Śiva's and Śakti's, means that at Śiṅgṇāpūr two regions come together in a unity that encompasses them both.

Maharashtra

The wedding festival celebrated at Śiṅgṇāpūr brings together two regions and points to their inclusion in a broader, unified whole. For most participants who think about the festival, the name of that whole is simply "Maharashtra." This is so despite the fact that the actual "pilgrim field" (Bhardwaj 1973) of the festival appears to be confined to the southwestern districts of the Deś of Maharashtra.[88] A man in Beḷsar, for instance, explained as follows the procession up Muṅgī Ghāṭ (which he understood to include *all* the *kāvaḍ*s that take part in the festival, and not merely those from places to the northwest of Śiṅgṇāpūr): "As many *kāvaḍ*s as there are, from that part (*bhāg*), from that whole part, come together in Kothaḷe. Because that is the one route for climbing up. As many *kāvaḍ*s as there are in all of Maharashtra gather in that village, in Kothaḷe."[89]

The Pañcakrośī *kāvaḍ*'s 1995 flyer also speaks of *kāvaḍ*s that "come to Śiṅgṇāpūr from all over Maharashtra,"[90] and many participants in and interpreters of the festival echo these words. Such people (and also the flyer) tend to relate the festival historically not to the thirteenth-century Yādava king Śiṅghaṇa, for whom the temple at Śiṅgṇāpūr is ostensibly named, but rather to the seventeenth-century Śivājī and other Marāṭhā rulers. People who reflect on such things tend to be aware of the Śiṅgṇāpūr temple's connection with Śivājī and his ancestors—and with his descendants, the royal family of Satara, still to this day. Some people know that the Satara royal family still owns the Śiṅgṇāpūr temple, and that the temple, unlike many other major pilgrimage temples in Maharashtra, has *not* yet been made into a public trust. In addition, some people know of specific ritual connections between the Śiṅgṇāpūr festival and the surviving Marāṭhā royal houses at Satara and Kolhāpūr. They know that the royal family in Satara sends a representative to the wedding in Nātepute, for example, or that, immediately after the wedding, special messengers carry sprigs of the fragrant *davanā* plant to the temple of another Marāṭhā god, Jotibā, whose temple stands on a mountain near Kolhāpūr.

When I asked some men in Pisarve what the point (*artha*) of the festival at Śiṅgṇāpūr is, why people participate in it, what their reason for going there is, one of the men replied in terms of the pilgrims' sense of Marāṭhā tradition: "This *kāvaḍ* that goes [there] has been going since the time of King Śivājī. They were all devotees of Śiva. The Marāṭhā kingdom were devotees of Śiva. And the Marāṭhās' special god is King Śambhū. That's why people go there every year. I mean, everyone from our Purandar Taluka goes. Our honorary right (*mān*) is there." When I pushed harder, asking why the Marāṭhā kingdom's connection with Śiṅgṇāpūr means that people now should carry *kāvaḍs* on the pilgrimage, one of the men answered in terms of the *kāvaḍ* festival being a particular one that takes place at a certain time, one of many festivals throughout the year. The first speaker, though, interspersing his remarks with this man's, continued to stress the traditional character of the festival. "It's traditional," he said. "It has come down in our family." And then, "It has come from the past, so we keep it going, from before." And then, again, he pointed to the Marāṭhā character of the festival: "He's the Marāṭhās', the Marāṭhās' god, so this devotion for God, for Śambhū, that our ancestors kept going from the past, the Marāṭhās, that is what we are to do . . . . It is our custom that has come down to us until now."

Still not satisfied, I tried to explain my question: "We're trying to find out *why* your ancestors decided on this. Why *this*?" This way of phrasing what I wanted to ask finally pushed the man to identify one particular aspect of Marāṭhā tradition, its military character. It also led him to use (or quote) a cry to Śiva, "Har Har Mahādev." This cry is one that has been adopted as a slogan by the Śiv Senā, a right-wing political party with active branches in many villages throughout Maharashtra. "*This* is what the ancestors . . .," he started to say, and then interrupted himself: "The Marāṭhās' god. Śambhū, Mahādev, Har Har Mahādev, Marāṭhā—he's Mahādev . . . Har Har Mahādev . . . . And that," he concluded, "is why all our Marāṭhās went to war from the beginning." —"For Mahādev?" I asked. —"Yes. He's Mahādev, Har Har. I mean, *that* is where [why?] we go."

The Pāṭīl of Ekhatpūr keeps in a small metal trunk in his house an article clipped from a 1994 issue of *Sāmanā*,[91] the newspaper of Bal Thackeray, the most famous leader of the Śiv Senā party. The article, which the Pāṭīl showed us because it supports the claim of Ekhatpūr's *kāvaḍ* to primacy in the festival, begins by referring to "the famous Śiva temple 'Śikhar Śiṅgṇā pūr,' the temple before which, the lord before which the common people not only in Maharashtra but also in neighboring Andhra and Karnataka bow as the family god (*kuldaivat*) of all of Maharashtra." The article goes on to describe the festival as reaching all over Maharashtra (and even a bit beyond[92]) and bringing together the water of rivers throughout this area:

> On the very day of the eighth day of the bright half of Caitra, *kāvaḍs* come from many villages in all corners of Maharashtra. These *kāvaḍs* bring holy

> water of their respective areas. It gets sprinkled in the temple on the twelfth day of the month. Śambhū Mahādev gets sprinkled with this holy water. This is probably the custom of bringing auspicious water pots for a wedding . . . . The *kāvaḍs* bring holy water from all the rivers from the Tuṅgabhadrā to the Narmadā.

In explaining the distinction between the *kāvaḍs* from "Śiva's side" and those from "Śakti's side" in the wedding at Śiṅgṇāpūr, one of the men I have quoted said, "Mahādev is the family god of Maharashtra." Although these men see the wedding festival as being organized in such a way as to keep pilgrims from two different parts of Maharashtra separated, this statement hints at another aspect of their understanding. They also realize that the festival brings those two different parts of Maharashtra together: it brings pilgrims from both of the parts to the same place, at *close* to the same time, to celebrate a wedding, a festival of unity.

Thus, the Caitra festival at Śiṅgṇāpūr expresses the fierce Śaiva devotion of its participants and celebrates the wedding of the god of Śiṅgṇāpūr and his wife. At the same time, in part at least through this very devotion and this very wedding, the festival enacts the unity of a region that many of its participants call "Maharashtra."

Chapter 3

Traveling Goddesses

Goddesses link people to places. Throughout India, goddesses serve as village protector deities, grounding a village and connecting its people to it. Goddesses also serve as family deities, binding people to a distant place with special significance for their family. Typically people travel to their family goddess's temple only infrequently, but most think that they should make the trip at least whenever a new bride or baby is added to the family, to present the new member to the goddess. Tuḷjā Bhavānī, as the patron goddess of Śivājī, is becoming, increasingly, the goddess of Maharashtra as a whole, and the recently invented goddess Bhārat Mātā (McKean 1996:144–63) is coming increasingly to personify India as a whole.

Goddesses also link places to each other. We have seen some evidence of this already. In chapter 1, we saw ways that rivers, which are often goddesses, bring together the places they flow between, and we examined a variety of ritual, narrative, and abstract conceptual forms by means of which people draw attention to the connections that rivers create. In chapter 2, we saw how the Bhātāṅgaḷī pole, by virtue of its wedding with Śiva, brings together places to the east of Śiṅgṇāpūr (those on "Śakti's side") with places to the north and west (those on "Śiva's side") from which people bring the *kāvaḍs* that climb Muṅgī Ghāṭ. In each of these cases, I have argued, the places the goddesses link form regions.

The present chapter will point out yet another way in which goddesses form regions. Here we will look at stories of goddesses who themselves travel, and at pilgrimages in which people retrace the steps of goddesses who have moved from one place to another. We will first study two cases in which a story of a goddess traveling to the home of a devoted or kindly man is mirrored in a pilgrimage in which descendants of the man, along with other pilgrims, journey back to the goddess's original place. Next we will look at a trip that a goddess makes when she comes to

Maharashtra to kill demons, and at a pilgrimage that retraces the goddess's steps. We will then examine a journey that a goddess makes as a bride; and finally, we will explore the implications of the frequent claim that goddesses in different places are sisters: I will suggest that the goddesses have traveled to those places in order to marry.

In all of these cases, the travels of the goddesses connect places. The stories, images, and pilgrimages bring together, both conceptually and through the bodies of the pilgrims, the places between which the goddesses travel. They hold together these places, and the places that lie between them, in a patchwork of distinct but often overlapping regions.

The Goddess Travels to the Home of Her Faithful Devotee

First I will discuss two pilgrimage festivals that are like the Caitra Śiṅgṇāpūr pilgrimage in certain important respects. In each of these pilgrimages, as in the one to Śiṅgṇāpūr, a group of people travel together at a particular time of year. In these pilgrimages too, as in Śiṅgṇāpūr's, the pilgrims carry with them large, heavy ritual objects—though in neither of these two cases is the object the pilgrims carry a *kāvaḍ*. In making their trip, the pilgrims in these two journeys, like those who travel to Śiṅgṇāpūr in the month of Caitra, are imitating a founding ancestor—someone who first made the trip in the hoary past. The devotional love (*bhakti*) of the founding ancestor is an important theme in both of these pilgrimages, as the *bhakti* of Bhutojī Telī is in the pilgrimage to Śiṅgṇāpūr. And finally, in each case, a descendant of the original devotee (*bhakta*) is the leader of the pilgrims who now make the trip, as the two rival descendants of Bhutojī Telī are the most important figures in the pilgrimage to Śiṅgṇāpūr.

However, there is also an important difference: the two pilgrimages I will discuss here retrace the steps not only of an original devotee but also of the deity to whom he was devoted. Unlike Śiṅgṇāpūr, where the god remains in place and the devotees come to him, each of these pilgrimages has a story central to it in which the goddess *herself* travels to the original devotee's home. Hence, these two pilgrimages connect places not only by means of the physical movement of the pilgrims and the objects they carry but also through the story of the goddess's travel between her original place and the founding devotee's home. Even more fundamentally, what connects the places in these two pilgrimages is love: the love of the founding devotee for the goddess, and the love of the goddess for her devotee.

The term "*bhakti*" covers both these kinds of love. In carrying on the pilgrimage in the present, contemporary devotees imitate the founding ancestor's love for the goddess, and they also respond to the goddess's love for him. In all these respects, then, it is love that holds the two places—the starting point and the goal of the pilgrimage—together.

The stories that underlie these two pilgrimages exemplify a kind of story that is very commonly told about gods and goddesses in Maharashtra. Most often, when these gods and goddesses are remembered to have traveled from one place to another, they are thought to have done so in order to be in a location more convenient for a devoted worshipper. In such a story, the goddess generally follows the faithful devotee back from her usual, best-known temple to his home village because he[1] has become too old and feeble to make the trip to the more famous place. This kind of story generally follows one of two patterns.

In the first pattern, a god or goddess in a mountainous place follows a devotee downhill so as to be more easily accessible. In this form, the story is found at many places where the god's "original" site is located on a hill high above a lower temple that more pilgrims and local devotees visit. One of the most famous examples of this form of the story is told about Khaṇḍobā at Jejurī. Khaṇḍobā's original temple is located high above the town of Jejurī, on a mountain called Karhe Paṭhār. Khaṇḍobā came down from the upper temple to a lower part of the mountain—one that is nevertheless still "nine hundred thousand steps" above the town—because of one of his devotees. After climbing the hill every day for many years, this man finally became too old to do so any more. For the convenience of this ardent devotee, Khaṇḍobā appeared at the site of what is now his principal temple.[2]

In the second pattern, a god or goddess from a distant holy place follows home a devotee who for many years has traveled the whole distance every day to visit him or her.[3] This pattern is the most common way of expressing the fact that the god or goddess of a place in Maharashtra replicates another, more famous one at a distant place. The god Dhuḷobā, for instance, whose temple is in Vidanī, a small village outside the town of Phalṭaṇ (Feldhaus 1995:56–57), is in fact the great god Mahākāl (Mhaṅkāl) of Ujjain, one of the Twelve Jyotirliṅgas of all of India (see chapter 4). For 12 years, this god's faithful shepherd devotee Kamaḷū Śinde, who was childless, traveled every night from Vidanī to Ujjain to perform his humble *pūjā* in Mahākāl's temple there. Finally, the god of Ujjain followed Kamaḷū Śinde home to Vidanī. There the god appeared as a baby in the ashes (*dhuḷ*) of the fire that Kamaḷū Śinde and his wife had lit to celebrate the Hoḷī festival (Sontheimer 1982).[4]

Within Maharashtra, this second kind of replication is most common with respect to the "three-and-a half" (i.e., four) principal goddesses of

Maharashtra (see chapter 4): the devotees of *many* other pilgrimage goddesses claim that their goddess is one or another of the famous three-and-a-half, and that she has arrived at her current location by following an ardent devotee of the past. In almost every case, the devotee, contrary to the goddess's instructions, turned around before making it all the way home, to see if she was really following him.[5] Stark-Wild (1997) has documented a number of such replicas of the goddess Reṇukā of Māhūr, temples of Reṇukā in places to which she followed one of her devotees home. Similar sets of replicas could be found for each of the other three principal Maharashtrian goddesses.[6]

While stories like these are quite common, pilgrimage festivals that replicate them are relatively rare. The two I will discuss here are the only ones I have found so far. In the first of the two pilgrimages, the one from Jejurī to Navkhaṇ around the time of the festival of Hoḷī, pilgrims carry the goddess Jāṇāī back to her original place for a visit. In the other pilgrimage, devotees of the goddess Bhavānī carry an empty bedstead and an empty palanquin to Tuḷjāpūr for the festival of Dasarā. Here too the pilgrims understand their journey to replicate one that their goddess and one of her devotees first made.

Jāṇāī

Jāṇāī has a temple in the town of Jejurī, downhill from both the upper and the lower temples of Khaṇḍobā. Many people call Jāṇāī Khaṇḍobā's sister, but this seems to mean primarily that she lives near him but is not his wife.[7] The sibling relationship, at any rate, is an honorary one and does not mean that Khaṇḍobā and Jāṇāī share common parents. Jāṇāī's most important temple is located about 100 kilometers to the south of Jejurī, in Navkhaṇ, in Pāṭaṇ Taluka, Satara District (map 3.1). The man who is said to have brought her from there to Jejurī was Nāgo Māḷī, a member of the Gardener (Māḷī) caste. Nāgo Māḷī's descendants still live in Jejurī.

Some people tell the story of Nāgo Māḷī as a version of the first form of the "old devotee" story: the goddess at Navkhaṇ came there from her original place at Saḷve, about 20 kilometers[8] south of Navkhaṇ through mountainous terrain. More frequently, though, people tell the story as a version of the second form of the "old *bhakta*" story. Mahādu Jhagaḍe, a fourth-generation descendant of Nāgo Māḷī, combines the two forms in his version of the story. He says that the goddess first came down from Saḷve to Navkhaṇ and then appeared in Jejurī, both times moving for the sake of Nāgo Māḷī.[9] Here is Mr. Jhagaḍe's account of Jāṇāī's move from Navkhaṇ

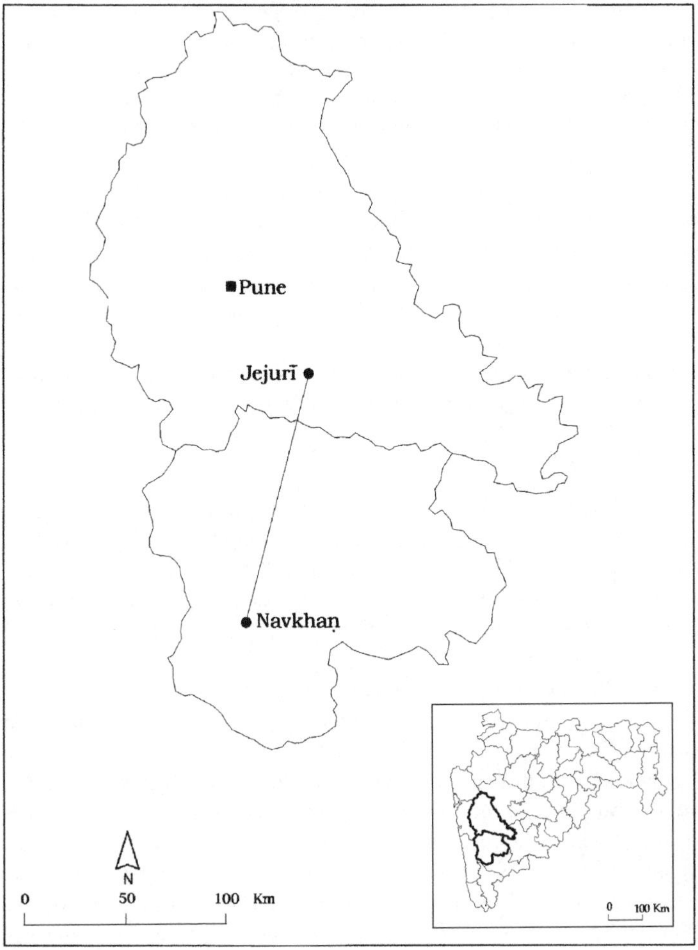

Map 3.1 Jāṇāī's pilgrimage

to Jejurī:[10]

> By the strength of his bhakti, Nāgo Māḷī brought the goddess from there to here, to Jejurī. He was god-crazy, and so he would go there. All he would say was, "My mother, Jānubāī." Nothing else. For fifty years or so he went back and forth. Finally, he got old. After he got old, he said, "Now what can I do?" She said, "You go ahead. I will follow you."
>
> Now, she had said, "I'll come," but where to look for her? So she said, "Go to such-and-such a place in the pool. I am manifest in that place," she said.

> Afterwards, when he had gone to that pool, he found three rounded stones there. So he was delighted. He began to cry out to people. He said, "Hey, the goddess has met me! The goddess has met me!" People teased him maliciously. And they grabbed the rounded stones from him and tossed them into the water. Only one was left. That stone is still there in Jānubāī's temple.

The story of Nāgo Māḷī explains not only Jāṇāī's presence in Jejurī, but also the annual pilgrimage festival in which residents of Jejurī carry the goddess in a palanquin *back* to Navkhaṇ. The pilgrimage, which began with Nāgo Māḷī carrying the goddess back once a year to Navkhaṇ in a basket on his head, has grown over the years to become larger and more elaborate:

> He would put the goddess in a basket and go along walking, all alone, slowly, slowly, slowly, slowly. So people asked, "Bābā, where are you going?"
>
> He said, "I am going to Navkhaṇ."
>
> "May we come along?"
>
> "Come on, if you want to."
>
> Then one person told another, who told ten others. Eventually 500 people knew. As people began to go, their wishes began to be fulfilled, and other people started flowing after them. People said, "Let's make a palanquin." So they made a palanquin. Then they would carry the palanquin on their shoulders. That custom continues to this day.

A schoolteacher in Jejurī explained in simple terms the basic point of the old *bhakta* story and the pilgrimage festival of Jāṇāī: "Jāṇāī's original place is there [at Navkhaṇ], and she came here from there because of *bhakti*. . . . That Jāṇubāī is from there . . . . And that goddess truly came from there to here. But once a year, on the ninth day of the month, on Phālgun Śuddha Navamī, people go to meet her."

Jāṇāī's pilgrimage festival involves a series of events spread over several weeks preceding and following the springtime festival of Hoḷī (the full-moon day of the month of Phālgun, February–March). The pilgrimage starts in Jejurī, at the Jhagaḍes' house on the main street leading uphill toward the Khaṇḍobā temple. Women bring brass masks (*mukhavaṭās*) of the goddess to the Jhagaḍes' house. These masks, along with others kept in a shrine in an inner room of the Jhagaḍes' house, get placed in a palanquin and carried in a procession around the town. In the procession, two tall poles (*kāṭhīs*) precede the palanquin, and musicians play cymbals and at least four different kinds of drums. Mahādū Jhagaḍe brings up the rear. The palanquin travels up the main street from the Jhagaḍes' house, then quickly up and back down the hundreds of steps leading to the Khaṇḍobā temple. It then circles in a clockwise direction through the western part of the town, stopping at a temple of Jāṇāī and at Jejurī's principal Māruti temple. Finally the palanquin returns to the foot of the steps that lead to the Khaṇḍobā temple. There it turns eastward, toward the largish courtyard house[11] where it will spend the next three nights. As the procession makes its way along its route, the crowd of people following it grows from a couple of dozen women and a few men to a much larger group, with more and more women possessed by the goddess dancing to the rhythm of the drums.

Three days later, the palanquin sets out for Navkhaṇ. Nāgo Māḷī's descendant Mahādū Jhagaḍe and his wife accompany it on foot, along with a small group of other citizens of Jejurī. These people travel by a direct route, overland; many others make the journey in jeeps, meeting the palanquin five days later, when it arrives in Navkhaṇ. For the next two days, a series of palanquin processions takes place, with loud drumming, firecrackers, men dancing rhythmic *lejhīm* dances in unison,[12] and women dancing wildly, possessed by the goddess. There is also a series of food offerings, culminating in a meal of mutton.[13] The festival reaches its climax at midday on the ninth day of the month of Phālgun, when two male sheep get decapitated simultaneously and huge gunny-sack parcels of unbroken coconuts, collectively called *cauk*, are set up in the courtyard of the goddess's temple. Both these events are accompanied by loud drumming, wild dancing, and the shouts of men and women possessed by the goddess. Afterward, several more sheep get killed, and women cook the mutton for their families' evening meal; the men (even those who otherwise never indulge) drink alcohol that night. Before setting out the next day to return to Jejurī, pilgrims retrieve from the *cauk* as many coconuts as they have contributed to it.

On the afternoon of Hoḷī, the palanquin completes its return trip to Jejurī. People from Jejurī wait at an intersection at the southern end of the town; they greet Mahādū Jhagaḍe by pouring water over his feet and putting colored powder on his toes. They also perform *pūjā* to the palanquin, breaking before it the coconuts they have retrieved from the *cauk* at Navkhaṇ. They make food offerings to the goddess in the palanquin, touch their babies' heads to it, and line up their children on the ground like railroad ties for the palanquin to be carried over (figure 3.1). Again there is drumming, and again women and a few men become possessed. Only after the palanquin has reached Jejurī, people say, may Hoḷī fires be lit in the town. After processing through the town again, the palanquin returns to the Jhagaḍes' house, where it is set up in an outer room open to the street.

Five days later, on Raṅgapañcamī, there takes place another sheep sacrifice, a meal of mutton for hundreds of townspeople, and a Gondhaḷ, a kind of song-and-dance performance held in honor of goddesses.[14] The sheep sacrifice is performed very simply and nearly privately. A small party of men, including Mr. Jhagaḍe and a Maulānī (a Muslim butcher), leads the

Figure 3.1 As Jāṇāī's palanquin returns to Jejurī, children (and one woman) line up on the ground like railroad ties in the palanquin's path.

sheep to the temple of Jāṇāī. The Maulānī kills the sheep there and the men carry it back to the Jhagaḍes' house. While the meat is cooking, the palanquin, preceded by one of the *kāṭhī*-poles, makes one last, relatively perfunctory procession through the town. After circling through the western side of town, stopping at the temple of Jāṇāī and circumambulating the Māruti temple, the palanquin returns to the Jhagaḍes' house. There it gets decorated with strings of small electric lights that are woven into a net on top of its canopy. Townspeople begin coming in a steady stream to the Jhagaḍes' house to perform *pūjā* to the masks in the palanquin. When the meal is ready, Mr. Jhagaḍe and a few other men carry the food-offering (*naivedya*) to Jāṇāī's temple, then place more offerings of mutton, *ghugryā*,[15] and millet bread (*bhākrī*) before the palanquin and in seven small, flat baskets in front of the permanent shrine in the inner room.

In the evening a troupe of Gondhaḷīs, performers of the Gondhaḷ, arrive. They play and sing first inside the Jhagaḍes' house, in the room with the permanent shrine. The Jhagaḍe family gathers in that room, along with friends and neighbors who have been actively involved in the pilgrimage. The Gondhaḷīs play and sing an *āratī* and other songs. Mrs. Jhagaḍe and several of the other women become possessed, convulsing their bodies, dancing, and answering questions that the Gondhaḷīs put to them. The session lasts about 20 minutes.

Meanwhile, outside the house, in the street that leads to the steps to the Khaṇḍobā temple, dozens of townspeople seat themselves on the ground in two rows facing each other. They have brought their own plates and, when the *āratī* is over, the Jhagaḍes and some helpers serve them a meal of the mutton. After the guests have eaten, the Gondhaḷ proper starts. It is held in the front room of the house: the porch-like room, open to the street, in which the palanquin rests. For the next couple of hours, the Gondhaḷīs sing, play musical instruments, and tell stories about a number of goddesses, including Jāṇāī. While the Gondhaḷīs sing and play, several women and a few men become possessed, swaying, rolling on the floor, dancing in either a wild or a relatively restrained manner, and in some cases holding a lighted torch (*pot*) as they dance. Mrs. Jhagaḍe is the most prominent among the dancers; sometimes she dances holding the lighted torch or, in both hands, a whip. The Gondhaḷ continues until about midnight, and then another man sings, accompanied by a harmonium, two percussion instruments, and a drone (*tuntun*), until early the next morning.

The final event of the pilgrimage takes place a few nights later. It is held not in the Jhagaḍes' house in Jejurī but far outside of town, in an area called Davaṇe Maḷā where the Jhagaḍes have another house and some fields. This event is called "Nāgo Māḷī's Boḷavaṇ," the "send-off" for Nāgo Māḷī. This time the group of participants is smaller and more intimate than on the previous occasions. Once again there is a meal (vegetarian this time), once again Gondhaḷīs perform, and once again people become possessed. The meal, the Gondhaḷ, and the possession all take place in a field, in front of a row of small shrines that include shrines to Nāgo Māḷī and his wife and to the goddess Marīāī.

As the evening begins, Mr. Jhagaḍe wraps a small red cloth around his hand, fashioning a turban for Nāgo Māḷī. He takes a piece of white cloth and wraps it as a shawl over Nāgo Māḷī's shoulders. Then Mrs. Jhagaḍe wraps a green sari on Nāgo Māḷī's wife and puts a blue cloth at her feet. On the cloth Mrs. Jhagaḍe places a coconut, a handful of grain, some turmeric powder, and a number of green glass bangles. These offerings are typical ones used in *oṭī bharaṇeṃ*, a ritual gesture performed to married or marriageable women as an expression of good wishes for their fecundity and well-being.[16] Mrs. Jhagaḍe also wraps a green cloth (as a sari) around the stone of Marīāī, hangs a garland over the cloth, and performs *oṭī bharaṇeṃ* to

Marīāī as well. Then, after the principal Gondhaḷī has done *pūjā* at Nāgo Māḷī's shrine, Mr. Jhagaḍe and five other men set out across the fields to make offerings and perform an *āratī* at Marīāī's "original place," waving lighted bits of camphor in a circular motion to the rhythm of a drum. They also make offerings to the stones marking "guardians" (*rakṣak*) of Jāṇāī and Marīāī, and at several other places in the fields around the shrine. Finally, Mr. Jhagaḍe presents a food offering to Nāgo Māḷī and to the nearby gods and goddesses, a Gondhaḷī plays and sings another *aratī* song, and a meal is served to multiple sittings of guests.[17]

In 1995, the Gondhaḷ started after ten o'clock at night. The Gondhaḷīs first performed a long *āratī*, then played and sang a song about their principal goddess, Bhavānī of Tuḷjāpūr. As the Gondhaḷīs continued their performance, Mrs. Jhagaḍe became possessed, in turn, by Jāṇāī, by Kāḷubāī, and by Nāgo Māḷī. Other women and men also became possessed. Those who danced in possession included a young woman who, people said, had been getting possessed by Jāṇāī since the age of six and whose initiation (*thāpaṇūk*) as a medium had not yet been performed; the young woman's husband; and another woman, who became possessed successively by the goddess of Kolhāpūr, the goddess Lakṣmīāī (in this context called Gāḍyāvarlī Āī), and Khaṇḍobā (called Sadānanda).

Each time another deity entered one of the possessed people, the person called out the deity's name; the other people would listen for these names, and the drummers would change their rhythm to one appropriate for the new possessing deity. When Mrs. Jhagaḍe was possessed by goddesses, she put on necklaces of cowrie shells and sometimes held a cloth torch (*pot*); when Nāgo Māḷī possessed her, she removed the cowrie shells and took a whip in her hands. Several times, others asked questions of the possessed persons.[18]

At one point, after two in the morning, the young woman who had not yet had her initiation as a medium went through a test of sorts. When she called out two names, Jānubāī *and* Kāḷubāī, the principal Gondhaḷī corrected her, telling her to say only one name at a time. After he gave her some more instructions, the Gondhaḷīs sang a Jānubāī (Jāṇāī) song. Then the drums stopped. The young woman dropped to her knees. Again and again, the principal Gondhaḷī urged her to speak, to say what was the matter. The dozen or more women who were still awake gathered close, watching and listening with rapt attention. When the young woman still did not speak, one of the other women told the Gondhaḷīs to sing an *āratī*. They did so. The woman danced some more, then paused, and the principal Gondhaḷī pointed out to everyone listening that the young woman was indeed subject to possession by *both* Jānubāī *and* Kāḷubāī.

The Gondhaḷīs' performance continued until four in the morning. The all-night Boḷavaṇ of Nāgo Māḷī had a quite different feel from the earlier parts of the festival. It was intimate and familial. Although others besides family members could attend, few did. The Boḷavaṇ took place in the Jhagaḍes' own fields, far outside the town of Jejurī, in the presence of their ancestors' shrine. The possession episodes were prolonged, intense, and intimate. They brought to the fore the particular significance that the pilgrimage to Navkhaṇ has for the Jhagaḍe family, and especially for Mahādū Jhagaḍe and his wife.

During the pilgrimage festival, Mahādū Jhagaḍe and his wife embody Nāgo Māḷī, and they do so in a triple sense. First, Mahādū is descended from Nāgo Māḷī, and thus related to him "by blood." Second, Mahādū and his wife imitate Nāgo Māḷī by making the trip he used to make to Navkhaṇ. And, third, in prolonged episodes of possession during the pilgrimage and especially at its end, Nāgo Māḷī takes over Mahādū's wife's body.

However, the pilgrimage to Navkhaṇ is not only a private, family one for the Jhagaḍes. Most of the people who take part in the pilgrimage do so not as relatives of Nāgo Māḷī but as citizens of Jejurī. The pilgrimage festival brings the community of Jejurī together with the distant place Navkhaṇ. Several aspects of the festival serve to create and emphasize this connection. In the first place, and most obviously, there is the fact that citizens of Jejurī participate in the pilgrimage festival in large numbers. There are some pilgrims from other places who attend the festival, but the vast majority come from Jejurī. In addition, many ritual elements of the festival indicate that it brings Jejurī and Navkhaṇ together. Of the two *kāṭhī*s, or poles, that precede the palanquin as it travels through the town of Jejurī on the first day of the festival, one accompanies the palanquin to Navkhaṇ, while the other stays behind, in the courtyard house where the first day's procession ended. The simultaneous presence of one of the poles in each of the places signifies the participation of Jejurī in the pilgrimage to Navkhaṇ.

When the palanquin from Jejurī arrives in Navkhaṇ, an official representative (*mānkarī*) from Navkhaṇ, accompanied by a band of musicians and two Gurav priests from the temple, comes to greet it. The *mānkarī* from Navkhaṇ and Mahādū Jhagaḍe embrace and hand each other coconuts, betel nuts, *pān*, black powder (*aṅgārā*), and sprigs of *davanā*, a fragrant herb. Their embrace and mutual gift-giving express the connection between the two places they represent. Finally, the coconuts that are collected for the *cauk* do not get broken open at Navkhaṇ; rather, the pilgrims carry them back to break them at home in Jejurī after the palanquin has returned. Thus, this part of the ritual offerings presented at Navkhaṇ is actually "sacrificed" in Jejurī, once again showing Jejurī's central importance to the pilgrimage to Navkhaṇ.

Many others, too, of the principal actions of the pilgrimage festival take place in Jejurī, and they provide numerous occasions for people who remain in Jejurī to participate. On the first day of the festival, long before the palanquin departs for Navkhaṇ, and also upon the palanquin's return, the palanquin, with the masks of the goddess inside, travels throughout many of the lanes of Jejurī town, stopping at doorstep after doorstep for the women of the households to perform *pūjā* to the goddess. The meal of mutton served in the street outside the Jhagaḍes' house after the return from Navkhaṇ is for *anyone*[19] from Jejurī who wants to attend, not just for those who have traveled to Navkhaṇ and back. And *no* one in Jejurī, not only those who have gone on the pilgrimage, is supposed to light a Hoḷī fire until Jāṇāī's palanquin has passed by. Thus, the pilgrimage festival expresses in many ways the connection between the town of Jejurī and the distant temple place Navkhaṇ.

For those who walk with the Jhagaḍes, the pilgrimage festival also brings together the places they pass through or stop in along the way. The pilgrims who accompany the palanquin follow a set route, which they are well aware of, and they perform set rituals at the various places where they stop. The pilgrims who travel from Jejurī to Navkhaṇ by jeep do not follow the cross-country route that those who walk take, but they do pass through other places. In both cases, the pilgrims link Jejurī not only with Navkhaṇ but also with all the places in between. In this context, then, for these pilgrims, these places constitute a set that the people bring together with their bodies, in their experience, and therefore also, whether in a verbally articulate manner or not, with their minds and imaginations. Such a set of linked places is what I am calling a region.

The region involved in the story of Nāgo Māḷī and the pilgrimage from Jejurī to Navkhaṇ is relatively one-dimensional. Like the region constituted by the holy places dotted along the banks of a river, this one resembles a line rather than a plane; it lacks the two-dimensionality of the regions constituted by places scattered throughout a whole area. And yet the story of Nāgo Māḷī and the pilgrimage from Jejurī to Navkhaṇ *do* both assert and enact a connection between places. The two principal places that they connect are, by definition, distant from one another, for the story and pilgrimage that link the places make no sense unless the places are far apart. If the distant place were nearby, it would not be difficult for Nāgo Māḷī to go there, and there would be no need for the goddess to follow him home. By the same token, if the distant place were nearby, the pilgrimage would present less of a challenge and would bring little satisfaction to the pilgrims who now make the journey.

Thus, the "region" constituted by the story of Nāgo Māḷī and by the pilgrimage that retraces his and Jāṇāī's route is most importantly a connection between two places: a local place and a distant one. For devotees at the local place—the ones for whom, after all, the story is important—the story puts their locality into a broader context and connects their home with a larger, outside world. The story creates a conceptual region, however narrow, consisting of the local place, the distant place, and all the places in between. When such a story is associated, as here, with a pilgrimage in which devotees from the "branch" temple travel to the "original" temple from which the goddess came, the conceptual region is also a circulatory one, with pilgrims' own bodies effecting the connection between the places.

Tuljāpūr Bhavānī's Palanquin and Bedstead

Burhāṇnagar, a village on the outskirts of Ahmadnagar, provides a different and more complex example of a linked story and pilgrimage connecting a "branch" temple with its original. Here too the goddess is understood to have traveled from her original place to a local temple, and here too the story told about this involves devotion, *bhakti*. The story, however, is not the typical "old *bhakta*" story found in so many other cases. Rather, the kind of *bhakti* involved here is one more often associated with devotion to the baby Kṛṣṇa. Called *vātsalya bhakti*, this sort of devotion is parental love, love for a god whom one sees as one's child. The pilgrimage takes its participants from Burhāṇnagar, Ahmadnagar, or places even father away to the goddess's original temple at Tuḷjāpūr (map 3.2). What the pilgrims carry with them is not, as in Jāṇāī's pilgrimage, an image of the goddess herself, but rather some of the heavy, wooden equipment that will be used in her festival.

The original temple in this pilgrimage is that of the goddess Bhavānī at Tuḷjāpūr. Bhavānī, generally much better known in Maharashtra than Jāṇāī, is one of the three-and-a-half principal goddesses of Maharashtra (see chapter 4). Many understand Bhavānī to have been the protector goddess of the Marāṭhā leader Śivājī, and to have been embodied in his sword, which was named "Bhavānī." Tuḷjāpūr, Bhavānī's principal pilgrimage place, attracts large numbers of pilgrims, especially at the time of the autumn festival of Navarātra and Dasarā. Of the many pilgrims who travel to Tuḷjāpūr for this festival, we will focus here on two rival, related groups. One of these groups carries an empty palanquin to Tuḷjāpūr, and the other carries an empty bedstead. Both the palanquin and the bedstead are brought to be used in the goddess's festival.

The devotee because of whom the goddess of Tuḷjāpūr is also found in Burhāṇnagar was named Jānkojī Devkar. Like Bhutojī, the principal or founding *bhakta* of the Śiṅgṇāpūr *kāvaḍ* festival, Jānkojī was a Telī, a member of the oil-presser caste. Arjun Kisan Bhagat, a descendant of Jānkojī who lives with his family at the Tuḷjā Bhavānī temple in

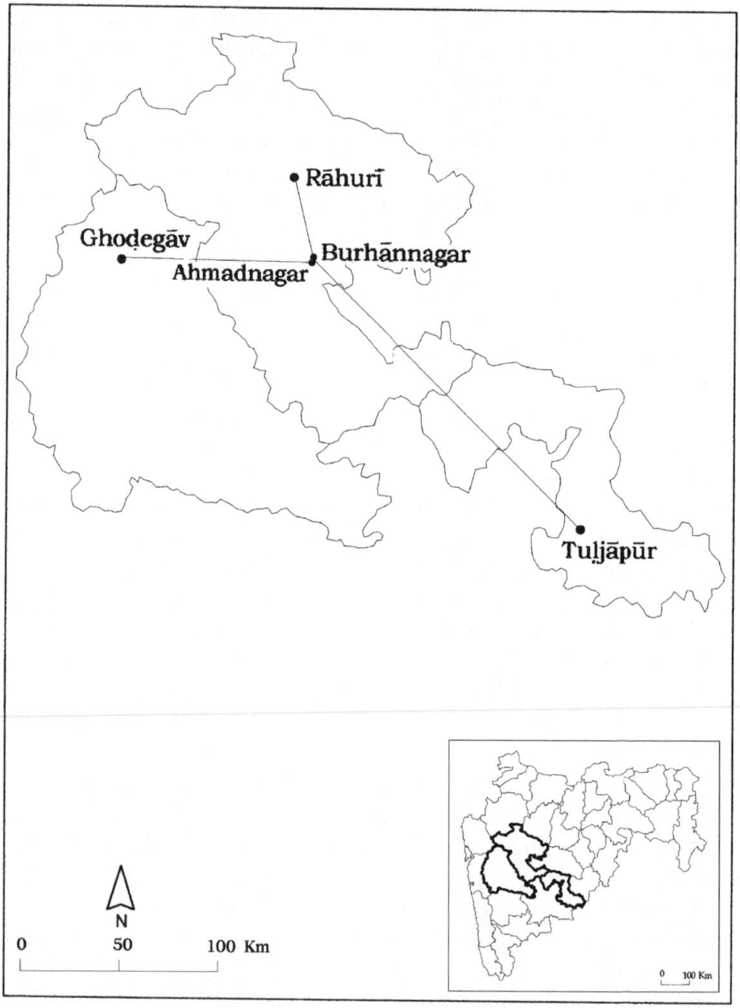

Map 3.2 The palanquin and bedstead pilgrimage to Tuḷjāpūr

Burhāṇnagar, narrated the story of Jānkojī and the goddess at much greater length than Mahādū Jhagaḍe did the story of Nāgo Māḷī and Jāṇāi. I will give an abbreviated version here:

> Our original male ancestor, Jānkojī Devkar, was a dedicated devotee of the goddess. And his home was poor. He fed himself by doing labor for people. Once, when he had gone to work, a little girl with a skin disease all over her body came wandering into the village. No one took her in, no one took care

of her. As she wandered, she came and sat on the stone platform outside [the temple here]. The girl asked an old lady who was there, "Grandma, may I sit here?"

"Sit down, my child," she said. It was in the morning, at 9 or 10 a.m. The girl sat down there then. At midday, when Jānkojī came home to eat, she was still sitting there. "Whose child is this sitting here?" he asked his wife. She replied, "That child has been sitting there since morning. I don't know whose she is."

Now, the meal was of fenugreek (*methī*) vegetable, sesame husks, and *bājrī*-millet bread. Before he put the first bite into his mouth, he thought . . . that this girl had been sitting there since morning, that a skin disease had broken out all over her body, that nobody in the village had taken her in, that she was tormented with hunger. So he got up and gave the girl some vegetables and millet bread to eat. After he had fed her, she seemed a bit refreshed and brighter.

And then he asked the girl, "My child, whose are you?" And she replied, "I am an orphan. I have no mother, no father, no one at all. I'm all alone."

And they had no children at all. So he asked the girl: "Child, will you stay here with us?" She agreed happily, because, she said, "I have no one to take care of me. I'm an orphan." And then they took her into their house, gave her a bath, and took care of her. They put ashes from the stove on her, they rubbed her with oil from the mill. And gradually her skin disease got a little better.

After she had gotten better, she said, "Bābā, why do you go away to work? Why don't you run the oil-mill in our house?"

He said, "I wouldn't mind running it, but that takes capital. It takes money. Where am I to get that kind of money?"

She said, "Don't you worry about that. After you get up in the morning, go to the money-lender in the village. He'll give you all the capital you need."

And the Mother (Āī-sāheb) appeared to the money-lender at night in a dream: "In the morning, when a laborer, a Telī, comes, you give him capital, a bullock, and whatever he needs."

"All right," he replied.

In the morning, when he got up and looked, he saw that Telī at his door. And he remembered exactly the dream he had had at night. So he said, "What do you need, Jānkojī?"

He said, "Not much, Śeṭjī. Give me a bullock, safflower seeds, and a certain amount of capital to run the oil-mill."

"Go on," he said. "Take what you need."

Then he got the oil mill that's right over there, he got his bullock, he got safflower seeds, he got the oil-mill running. And in a very short time he had such good sales that he became one of the wealthiest merchants in the village.

Now the people of the village began to view him differently. "Look where this man has gotten to! It used to be that sometimes he couldn't get enough to eat. And now he has become a famous, rich merchant." Or, "The girl that has come to his house must be good fortune, Lakṣmī." Then they said, "Why shouldn't we ask for her in marriage?" Everybody began to scramble to get her.

At that time, he had built seven large houses. He had built storerooms to keep safflower seeds and oil. On the platform in front, where the goddess's place is now, there was a large sitting room. Some prospective in-laws came and were seated in that room. They said, "Go, bring the girl to show her."

The girl was named Ambikā.[20] Jānkojī went into the house, to get his daughter and show her. When he called out, "Ambikā!" a sound came from another room. When he went to that room, the sound came from a third room. As he did this again and again, two or three hours passed, but he couldn't find the girl. He kept going from room to room.

The prospective in-laws were sitting outside. They said, "*Why* doesn't he bring out the girl and show her? This old man is intentionally making mischief. He doesn't want to show the girl, so he is wasting our time." They got angry and said, "You [won't] show us your daughter, so we'll throw you out of the caste. We'll ostracize you, that's what we'll do." And they left.[21]

In those days, putting a person out of caste was a very bad punishment. So he was very distressed. After the prospective in-laws had left, he saw the girl, and he said, "I've been looking for you for three or four hours. Why couldn't I find you? I could hear your voice. Where did you go?" Then he said, "Are you a ghost? Or a goblin? Who are you?" In his anger he began to beat his face and bang [his head] on the ground. The goddess grabbed him, and she gave him a vision. "Ask for whatever boon you want," she said. "Ask for money, ask for sovereignty, ask for wealth, or ask for fame—ask for whatever you want."

Well, he was dumbfounded. He couldn't imagine what to ask for and what not to. He just started to stare like a madman. He was so surprised and so confused, thinking—"For ten or twelve years, I have treated this girl like my own child. How could I fail to recognize her?" He was bewildered, and he started feeling that he had committed an offense.

Now, a divine being who has been pleased doesn't stay around very long. So she said, "What's behind you? Look!" He turned around and looked back, and she disappeared on the spot. He looked all over, and he began to say again and again, "She was here. Where did she go? She was here. Where did she go?" Wandering along like a madman, he reached Tuḷjāpūr.

In Tuḷjāpūr, the Mother and Bhāratī Buvā were sitting playing parcheesi.[22] There is a well there. He thought, "After these people have gotten up and left, I'll jump into that well and commit suicide. Because I've searched so much, but I haven't found her at all. And there's no point to my life." Then, as they were playing, Bhāratī Buvā said, "Mother, why are you delaying the game?"

And a money-lender called on her for help. His boat was sinking. When the goddess had helped with the boat, Jānkojī recognized her. Immediately he took hold of the goddess's feet again. "Mother, now I'm never going to let go of you," he said.

So she said, "Don't do that. Ask for whatever other boon you want."

Then he said, "Mother, what am I going to ask for? Give me just one boon: that your name and mine will continue for generation after generation. There should be no break in it. Give me that boon."

"All right," she said. "You should bring the bedstead and the palanquin to Tuḷjāpūr every year. Every year on the Dasarā day I will do the boundary-crossing rite in the palanquin you have brought. And I will stay on the bedstead for the five days until the full-moon day. On that day I'll get back onto my throne."

And from that year until today, this has been the custom.

According to Arjun Kisan Bhagat, it was 27 generations ago, or "before A.D. 1200," that this all happened. His, he said, is the twenty-eighth generation that has been following this custom. Five generations ago, the family split into those who carry the bedstead (*palaṅg*) and those who carry the palanquin. The first group, appropriately named Palaṅge, is descended from a sister, and the other group, with the surname Bhagat, is descended from her brother. The leader of the bedstead-carriers, Bāburāv Ambādās Palaṅge, lives in the city of Ahmadnagar (the city of which Burhāṇnagar is an eastern suburb), next door to another Tuḷjā Bhavānī temple, which he owns. No one explained the split in the family to me in a way that I understood, but it was clear that there is still a good deal of tension between the two branches of the family and between the two groups of pilgrims who travel with the bedstead and the palanquin.

For both the palanquin and the bedstead, the journey lasts more than a month, and in each case the route and the halting places are fixed. The bedstead starts from Ghoḍegāv, in northwest Pune District, and the palanquin from Rāhurī, in northern Ahmadnagar District. Each year a Sutār (Carpenter) in Ghoḍegāv makes[23] a new bedstead in his workshop at the orders of Telīs from Ghoḍegāv. He does *pūjā* of the bedstead, and then the Telīs carry it in procession around the town (in a *nagar-pradakṣiṇā*) and to a temple of Śani (Saturn) in Ghoḍegāv. Here it remains, the centerpiece of a festival, for "eight or ten days." Then, on or shortly after the fifth day of the bright half of the month of Bhādrapad (September–October), the Telīs carry it in procession on another circuit of the town and finally to the village gate of Ghoḍegāv.[24]

From here it gets handed on from village to village, men from each village where the bedstead stops for the night accompanying it to the next village along its route. Some volunteers also stay with it, carrying it all along the way. At each place where the bedstead stops, people come to look at it, to make offerings to it, and to perform a sort of partial circumambulation by squatting to climb under it and emerge on the other side. Some of the places hold a small festival. At the second overnight stop, at Junnar, the canopy, mattresses, and bedspread (*pāsoḍā*) are added. A couple of stops before Ahmadnagar, at Tātyāñcā Maḷā, the men who have been carrying the bedstead hand it over to Bāburāv Ambādās Palaṅge. He must get it to his home at Subjail Square in Ahmadnagar on the evening of the first day of the Navarātra festival, the day on which the pot that is typical of this festival gets installed, and then he is responsible for getting the bedstead to Tuḷjāpūr in time for Dasarā, the tenth day of the festival.

While the bedstead is carried relatively sedately, at first by four men and eventually, people said, by as many as 50, the empty palanquin gets passed along more wildly from village to village on its route. A Sutār (Carpenter) and a Lohār (Blacksmith) in Rāhurī make the palanquin. These artisans use the same long, curved bamboo pole each year and make a new wooden cradle reinforced with iron. The Burhāṇnagar Telīs bring the pole to Rāhurī on the third day of the bright half of the month of Bhādrapad, and the carpenter and the blacksmith begin work the next day (Gaṇeś Caturthī, the first day of the annual autumn Gaṇeś festival). They must have the palanquin ready to set out by the beginning of the next fortnight. The carpenter and then the blacksmith do the first *pūjā* of the completed palanquin, then men from Rāhurī carry it through the town to a new Tuljā Bhavānī[25] temple in Rāhurī. On the first day of the dark half of Bhādrapad, a meal is served in that temple in honor of the palanquin. The next day, men carry the palanquin through the town again, stopping in the town hall for officials of Rāhurī to perform *pūjā* of the palanquin and to honor the carpenter, the blacksmith, and others who perform services for it. Then the palanquin sets off on its journey.

To the sound of large *ḍhoḷ* drums and accompanied by groups of young men dancing *lejhīm*, the extremely heavy wooden palanquin proceeds sporadically from one village to the next, twisting around in circles, jumping up and down, and at times running far off in the opposite direction from its goal. Sometimes the strong young men hold it atop their upraised arms, and sometimes it rests on their shoulders. Once in 1995 I saw it fall to the ground as 20 young men tossed it around all at once. At the border of two villages, I saw two huge wrestlers, one on each end of the palanquin, fighting for control of it. As with the bedstead, in each village where the palanquin stops, people come to look at it and to make offerings to it; and some of the places hold a small festival. At Burhāṇnagar there is a larger festival. The palanquin must reach there by the third day of the bright half of the month of Āśvin (October–November), the third day of the Navarātra festival.

The palanquin and the bedstead meet at the Mārutī temple at the village gate of Bhiṅgār, a place near Burhāṇnagar on the eastern outskirts of Ahmadnagar. The pilgrims accompanying the bedstead proceed on foot from there toward Tuḷjāpūr, making no more overnight stops, while those who travel with the palanquin wait in and around Burhāṇnagar and then proceed to Tuḷjāpūr by train on the eighth day of the Navarātra festival. On the last night of Navarātra—or, rather, very early on the morning of the next day, Dasarā—the palanquin serves to carry the main image of the goddess (not any smaller, festival image such as most temples use, but the main one from the inner shrine) around the courtyard of her temple in a boundary-crossing procession called Śilaṅgaṇ (Sanskrit, Sīmollaṅghana). The goddess is then put to rest on the bedstead, where she sleeps until the full-moon day, while the extremely excited crowd in the temple courtyard hacks to pieces all but the long, curved bar of the palanquin, ripping the palanquin's cradle apart with their hands and dashing it repeatedly against the ground. (The bedstead gets saved until the following year, when it gets burned up in the Navarātra oblation fire after the new bedstead has reached Tuḷjāpūr.)

Jānkojī's descendants understand themselves to be carrying on the father–daughter relationship between their ancestor and the goddess of Tuḷjāpūr. Arjun Bhagat goes to Tuḷjāpūr to meet his daughter, the goddess, just as Jānkojī did. At the climax of the festival, on the last night of Navarātra in Tuḷjāpūr, Bhagat carries a food offering to the goddess in the sanctuary of her temple; he carries the offering over his stomach, in a cloth tied around his waist, he explained, because that is how one carries food for a child. I am not quite sure what he meant by this,[26] but his wife's parental gesture was unambiguous, when she illustrated the tender way her husband puts his hand under the goddess's head as he places her in the palanquin—another thing he gets to do during the last night of Navarātra. "Like a daughter," I said, interpreting the movements of Mrs. Bhagat's hands. "Yes," she replied, and smiled.

On the morning of Dasarā, after the goddess has processed around the courtyard in the palanquin and the crowd has subsequently torn it up in a literally riotous manner, at 7 a.m. or so the Bhagat family and those who have journeyed with them gather at Jānkojī's memorial (*samādhi*) in a residential neighborhood in Tuḷjāpūr. They sit on the platform where the palanquin rested before they carried it to the temple, and they eat[27] a sweet, thick liquid that they have brought from the temple, as well as the food offering that Arjun Bhagat wrapped around his waist to carry in for the goddess. The food consists of chapatis and a vegetable typical of Telīs: a cooked mixture of fenugreek leaves and the husks of sesame seeds from which the oil has been removed. This is the same vegetable that Jānkojī gave the little-girl-goddess in the story Arjun Bhagat narrated. Like the more dramatic possession episodes after Nāgo Māḷī's descendants' return from their pilgrimage to Jāṇāī's temple, Jānkojī's descendants' ritual meal reinforces their identification with their founding ancestor and model *bhakta*.

Like Jāṇāī's pilgrimage, the journey of the palanquin and bedstead to Tuḷjāpūr brings together other people besides the families who have the most prominent roles in the festival, and it links the goddess's original location (in this case, Tuḷjāpūr) with many other places besides her principal *bhaktas*' home (Ahmadnagar and its suburb Burhāṇnagar). Two of the places that the pilgrimage connects with Tuḷjāpūr are Ghoḍegāv and Rāhurī, the places where the bedstead and the palanquin get made. The carpenter and blacksmith from Rāhurī are invited to Burhāṇnagar, where they are honored at the festival there on the third day of Navarātra.[28] In the weeks before the pilgrimage begins, Mr. Bhagat keeps in close touch with the carpenter and blacksmith in Rāhurī who make the palanquin, and Mr. Palaṅge keeps in touch with the men who get the bedstead made in Ghoḍegāv.

Like Jāṇāī's palanquin, and also like the *kāvaḍs* and poles of the Śiṅgṇāpūr festival, Tuḷjā Bhavānī's palanquin and bedstead pass through a number of places in the course of their pilgrimage. The palanquin and bedstead bring together these places that they pass through. In each village that the palanquin or bedstead stops in along the way, from the places where they are made to the homes of the principal devotees (*bhaktas*) responsible for them, and from there to Tuḷjāpūr, residents greet the palanquin or bedstead, make offerings to it, and celebrate festively its presence in their village.

As the bedstead passes from one village to another on the way to the place where Mr. Palaṅge meets it, some volunteers remain with it, carrying it all the way. It is thus always accompanied, either by him or by them. The palanquin, by contrast, gets handed over unchaperoned from village to village until it reaches Burhāṇnagar. The pilgrimage of the palanquin, and to some extent that of the bedstead too, then, differ in an important respect from the Śiṅgṇāpūr and Jāṇāī pilgrimages. In the Tuḷjāpūr palanquin-and-bedstead pilgrimage, it is only the wooden objects, and not also the people who carry them, that cover *all* the ground from the beginning of the pilgrimage to the midpoint to the end, and that bring together the many places along the pilgrimage route. After the palanquin has reached Burhāṇnagar, and even before the bedstead reaches Ahmadnagar, the two objects come into the charge of their respective *bhaktas*, Bhagat and Palaṅge. From there on, these leaders and their companions join the objects that they carry in connecting the places they pass through.

Between the two families descended from Jānkojī, the Bhagats and the Palaṅges, there is a tension analogous to that between the groups who carry the two principal *kāvaḍs* to Śiṅgṇāpūr. There is less disagreement about the source of the Bhagat–Palaṅge split than there is between the rival groups of Śiṅgṇāpūr pilgrims about the reason for the split between the two Bhutojī Telīs. The current leaders of the bedstead-carriers and the palanquin-carriers agree that they are both descended from earlier descendants of Jānkojī: the Palaṅges from a sister and the Bhagats from a brother. Neither side told me of any particular disagreement that led to the split. However, as in the case of the Bhutojī Telīs, the leaders of the groups that take the bedstead and the palanquin from Ahmadnagar and Burhāṇnagar to Tuḷjāpūr appear to avoid each other as far as possible.

The one mandatory meeting of the bedstead and the palanquin that I witnessed, in Bhiṅgār in 1995, was very brief, and it took place extremely late. The group carrying the bedstead needed to get going in order to complete their journey to Tuḷjāpūr on foot and to stop at all the places where people were waiting expectantly for their arrival. The palanquin, traveling in its normal riotous way and not itself due to depart the neighborhood of Ahmadnagar for several more days (and scheduled then to travel by train rather than to be carried on foot), arrived at the village gate in Bhiṅgār approximately eight hours after the bedstead-carriers thought it should have been there. The meeting was extremely perfunctory, and the bedstead set off immediately, moving out rapidly away from Bhiṅgār and onto the road toward Tuḷjāpūr.

The groups that travel with the bedstead and the palanquin, then, are locked in a tense unity. It is, nonetheless, a unity, one constituted by the blood relationship between the groups' leaders as well as by the complementary roles of the bedstead and the palanquin in the Navarātra and Dasarā festival at Tuḷjāpūr. The journey of the bedstead from Ghoḍegāv to Ahmadnagar to Tuḷjāpūr and the journey of the palanquin from Rāhurī to Burhāṇnagar to Tuḷjāpūr constitute a single pilgrimage, despite the differences in their routes and programs. Because the palanquin and the bedstead start from different places and follow different routes to the midpoint of their pilgrimage (and then from there to Tuḷjāpūr), the places that they connect form a region that is more two-dimensional than the relatively one-dimensional line of Jāṇāī's pilgrimage.[29] Combined, the palanquin and bedstead bring together a region that includes places in northern Pune District, central and southern Ahmadnagar District, western Bid District, eastern Solapur District, and much of Usmanabad District.

In the pilgrimage of the bedstead and palanquin to Tuḷjāpūr, then, as in that of Jāṇāī from Jejurī to Navkhaṇ and back, pilgrims travel along routes that their goddesses took before them. The journeys of the human pilgrims—or of the heavy objects they pass along from one place to another—provide physical connections between the places on their route. Mental connections take the form of stories about the journeys of the goddesses and the ancestor-devotees in the past. In the case of Jāṇāī and Tuḷjā Bhavānī, but also in the case of other goddesses (and gods), stories about their traveling to be near a beloved devotee provide narrative tools with which the people who tell, listen to, or think about the stories bring together mentally the places that the deities start from, the ones they go to, and the ones they pass through along the way.

Maḷāī Kills the Demon

But goddesses do not travel only in order to go to their devotees' homes. In the course of my own travels in Maharashtra, I have learned about another goddess who makes a journey for the good of her devotees, and whose devotees hold an annual pilgrimage festival that retraces her steps, but the immediate purpose for whose journey is different from that of Jāṇāī or Tuḷjā Bhavānī. This goddess travels in order to kill a demon. Her name is Maḷāī (sometimes Maḷābāī or Maḷgaṅgā).

Maḷāī has temples and shrines in dozens of villages and towns in Ahmadnagar District and in the northern, Junnar Taluka of Pune District. Many of these are subsidiary shrines that have been set up by devotees, at least some of them following the pattern of the "old devotee" story. A few of the places, however, are not places where Maḷāī went (or has been installed) because of some individual's devotion, but, rather, places where she stopped in the course of her journey to kill the demon (map 3.3). As Maḷāī moved along, she created replicas of herself in a number of different places. This goddess is thus in one sense a set of goddesses, but the goddesses that form the set are all, in another sense, identical with one another. Their reason for being in the different places is the trip once made by the one goddess that they all embody.

The story of Maḷāī and the demon that she killed is narrated in the *Maḷāī Māhātmya*, a text composed and published in the 1980s by Sakhārām Bāḷājī Bhagat, a politically and socially active poet born in 1917 into a family of agricultural laborers in Ciñcolī (Pārner Taluka, Ahmadnagar District).[30] According to this Māhātmya text, the principal demon that Maḷāī came to earth to kill was Dhūmrākṣa. I will summarize his story here.

Dhūmrākṣa was the son of the water nymph Urvaśī. Banished from Indra's heaven after becoming distracted when she noticed that god Brahmā was attracted to her, Urvaśī became a mare on the bank of the Gomatī river. In this form, she became pregnant by breathing the smoke of the fire in which Śiva had burned Kāma, the god of desire. She remained pregnant for 12 years. Finally Pārvatī convinced Śiva to come to earth and relieve Urvaśī of the embryo.

Dhūmrākṣa was born in the form of a horse. Smoke (*dhūmra*) emerged from his nostrils when he snorted.[31] Dhūmrākṣa practiced asceticism and

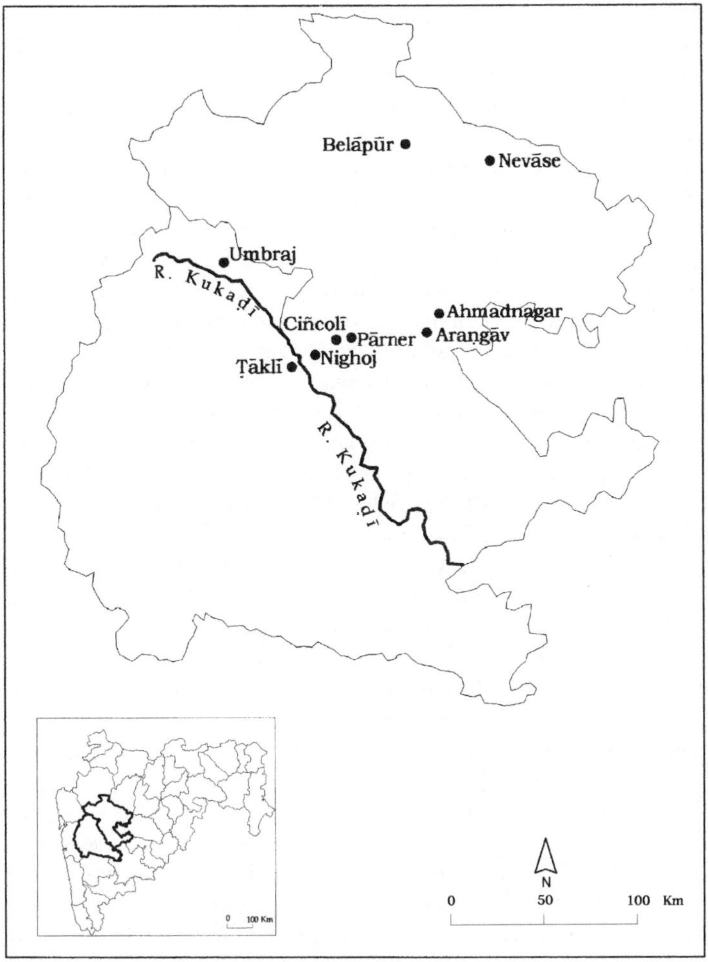

Map 3.3 Maḷāī's pilgrimage

wrangled from Śiva a boon of immortality. Śiva agreed to make him invicible to "gods, demons, humans, sages, Gaṇas, and Gandharvas," but warned him: "In the future a beautiful woman will be born . . . . She is the one who can kill you."

Harassed by Dhūmrākṣa, the gods gathered in Kāśī (Vārāṇasī, Banaras), each disguised in a particular way.[32] Conferring together, they decided to call for help to the primordial Māyā (Muḷ Māyā), the creatrix of the world.

They stood together in the water of the Ganges river and sang a hymn of praise to her. She came to the Ganges, at first invisible in a deep pool of water and eventually emerging from the water holding a pot of nectar. The goddess sprinkled nectar on the gods, and they named her "Maḷgaṅgā Devī."

Maḷgaṅgā instructed the gods to prepare for battle, and she sent them to protect people and to settle in their present locations.[33] Eventually, driven out of everywhere else, Dhūmrākṣa came to the Vindhya mountains; there, frightened off by the goddess Vindhyavāsinī, he fled into Maharashtra. In Maharashtra he saw the primordial Māyā in place after place.[34]

At Brahmagiri (the mountain at the source of the Godāvarī river), the goddess had created an illusionary city, Māyā City, full of enchantresses. Going there in disguise, Dhūmrākṣa was overcome with lust. When the primordial Māyā grabbed him by the hair, Māyā City disappeared, and he found himself alone in the forest with the goddess Maḷāī before him: a delicate, beautiful girl. Maḷāī again grabbed him by the hair and beat him. When his mother, Urvaśī, interceded, Maḷāī took him with her and traveled downhill to Bhiṅgār, just east of Ahmadnagar.[35] There she summoned all the *yoginī*s and sent them out to kill demons. Seven of the *yoginī*s went to the east and killed a demon there. His blood spilled onto the ground, giving birth to demons that continually changed their forms, becoming in turn rams, elephants, horses, lions, cocks, and skylarks. The goddess picked up a whip and herded the demons as far as Pārner, a taluka headquarters west of Ahmadnagar. There she summoned "all the gods" to keep the demons penned in, and she assigned the Apsarases and the Nine Caṇḍīs to serve as border guardians.

On the first lunar day of the month of Aśvin (the first day of the autumn Navarātra festival), the battle began. The army of the demons was 700 million strong. The goddess mounted her horse and hurled a weapon at the demons. Her army came running from all sides and began cutting off demons' heads. As the corpses began to pile up, Vetāḷ, the king of ghosts, summoned his troops. The ghosts made a snack of the corpses. Finally, his army decimated, Dhūmrākṣa took on a human form in order to fight Maḷāī himself. Before fighting him, though, she killed his six lieutenants (*sardār*s); the female ghouls Śaṅkhinī and Maṅkiṇī came in the form of hawks and ate their meat.

Dhūmrākṣa went mad. He changed into a horse and ran toward the precipice. Maḷāī chased him. At the foot of the hill, they encountered each other in battle. The heavenly gods—Viṣṇu, Gaṇeś, Śiva, and Pārvatī—came in their sky-chariots to watch. Finally the goddess killed Dhūmrākṣa. In a cave on the hill called Ḍhumyā Ḍoṅgar, Maḷāī grabbed his topknot and cut off his head. The gods showered down flowers from the sky.

They placed the goddess in a palanquin and brought her "to a peaceful spot in a tamarind grove," to Ciñcolī.

Oral traditions, besides being generally much simpler than this narrative, tend to specify more clearly the route that Maḷāī took in her journey through the Deccan. Women from one of the principal places, Umbraj (Junnar Taluka, Pune District), whom I talked with during the Maḷāī festival at another of the places, Nighoj (Pārner Taluka, Ahmadnagar District), said that the goddess came originally from the area of Kāśī (*kāśīkaṇḍ*), that she emerged on a hillside near Ciñcolī, that she went from there to the grove in Ciñcolī, then to Nighoj, and then to a pool in a deep and tortuous rock formation (called the "Kuṇḍ" or "Pool") in the Kukaḍī river near Nighoj, below a place on the rocky bank where she now has another temple. Finally the goddess went to Umbraj, their own home town. With the exception of the claim that these women's home village of Umbraj was the goddess's final stop, other people seem to agree with the most important details of this route: the goddess came originally from Kāśī, went first to a hillside near Ciñcolī that is generally called Ḍhumyā Ḍoṅgar, then to Ciñcolī proper, then to Nighoj, and from there to the pool in the river near Nighoj.

Most people seem to hold that the most important, "original" places of Maḷāī number seven.[36] A group of men from Umbraj with whom I spoke about Maḷāī at the festival in Ciñcolī said that Maḷāī came originally from "Kāśī Kṣetra." They listed her seven principal ("original," *muḷce*) places as Pārner, the Ḍhumyā Ḍoṅgar, Ciñcolī, Nighoj, the Kuṇḍ, Umbraj, and "Biṅgāv Ṭākḷī" (presumably the Ṭāklī across the Kukaḍī river from Nighoj). But these men also knew of another place where Maḷāī had stopped on her way to these places. As she was traveling southward, before she reached Pārner, she came to the Godāvarī river near Nevāse. There she found that she could not cross the river. She called to a Koḷī, a fisherman or boatsman, from Nevāse. He took her on his shoulders and swam her across the river, using floats tied around his waist. After carrying the goddess across the river, the men said, the Koḷī demanded that she stay with him: this demand seems to explain the presence of a Maḷāī temple in Nevāse.

Maḷāī's Pilgrimage

The pilgrimage festival of Maḷāī, which takes place at the height of the hot season, brings together a number of Maḷāī's places and follows the most important part of her route. Palanquins from Umbraj, Belāpūr, and Ciñcolī and poles from a number of places[37] gather in Ciñcolī, where they take part in a parade on the afternoon of the seventh day of the dark half of the month of Caitra.[38] Afterwards some of the pilgrims go to the Ḍhumyā Ḍoṅgar, the hill near Ciñcolī. That evening or the next day, the Umbraj and Belāpūr palanquins proceed to Nighoj along with the pilgrims who have accompanied them. There, on the eighth day of the dark half of Caitra, people fulfil *navas*-vows,[39] the people of Nighoj provide a free evening meal (*prasād*) for the pilgrims, and a nighttime parade (*chabinā*) climaxes in the miraculous emergence of a water pot (*ghāgar*) from a step-well in the village.[40]

On the next day, the ninth day of the fortnight, yet another parade makes its way through Nighoj. Starting from the Maḷāī temple in Nighoj, it winds through the village, out to the main road, and then down that road the three kilometers or so to the Kuṇḍ on the Kukaḍī river. In 1994, when my companions and I watched this parade, it was quite elaborate. It started with six groups of men from different villages, each group dancing *lejhīm* to the accompaniment of its own band of huge *ḍhoḷ* drums and heavy brass cymbals.[41] These groups were followed by 14 poles (*ḍaulkāṭhīs*) and then by a group of 100 or 150 men and women who were dancing, possessed by Maḷāī, as they slowly moved forward. After this group came a band playing horns and flat drums (*kalgī-turā*). Then, flanked by two parasols and a round standard (*abdāgirī*), came a man carrying a wooden structure that at least some people referred to as a "*pālkhī*" (palanquin) but that others called "Maḷāī's honorary *kāvaḍ*." It resembled the *kāvaḍs* that people carry to Śiṅgṇāpūr, except that it had no water pots and except for the fact that in place of the Nandīs found on many of the Śiṅgṇāpūr *kāvaḍs*, this one had four small, carved, wooden horses. The man carrying it came from Araṇgāv[42] (Ahmadnagar Taluka); two light trucks ("tempos") full of people had come along with him, I was told.

Immediately following this *kāvaḍ*-palanquin came, side-by-side, three palanquins holding brass masks of Maḷāī. These palanquins came from Tilak Road in Ahmadnagar, from Belāpūr, and from Umbraj. Next came a group of women, another band, three round standards (*abdāgirīs*), and then two more palanquins. The larger of these was from Nighoj itself and contained seven brass masks of Maḷāī; the other had come from Nevāse. Finally, bringing up the rear of the parade, came a bullock cart holding a huge kettledrum. Starting in the heat of the afternoon, the parade reached the Kuṇḍ well before sunset.

Thus, although the Maḷāī of Ciñcolī does not travel to Nighoj, nor does the Maḷāī of Nighoj travel to Ciñcolī, their serially combined festivals bring together Maḷāī palanquins (and, in one case, a *kāvaḍ*) from five other places, for a total of seven. Because I am interested in the phenomenon of the seven sisters, which I will discuss shortly, I was quite concerned to figure out the exact number of goddesses and palanquins. When asked, people knowledgeable about Maḷāī say that she is—or that the Maḷāīs are—seven sisters. However, no one I talked with about Maḷāī seemed as interested as I was in the arithmetic of the festival. What is more important to those involved in this cult is, first, that other Maḷāīs come to visit the main ones, those at Ciñcolī and Nighoj, and, second, that several of these Maḷāīs, as well as the pilgrims who accompany them, follow the same route as Maḷāī does in stories about her: from Ciñcolī, sometimes via the Ḍhumyā Ḍoṅgar, to Nighoj, to the Kuṇḍ on the Kukaḍī river.

The story and pilgrimage of Maḷāī, then, connect a number of different places in several ways. They connect the places, first of all, by means of the notion that the goddesses in them are sisters. Since all of the goddesses are called Maḷāī, the places are further connected by the idea that the goddesses in them are also, in some sense, identical. The story of the goddess going from one place to another in pursuit of a demon brings the places together in a single narrative and strengthens the idea that the goddesses are identical with one another. And, finally, the journey of the story finds its replica in the journey of the pilgrims. As they move from one to another of her places, not only do these pilgrims carry the goddess's masks with them in palanquins, but many of them also embody the goddess more directly themselves, as they dance under the influence of her possession. Through their own bodies, through the palanquins that they carry, and through the masks and other concrete forms of the goddess that they carry *in* the palanquins, the pilgrims bring together physically the places that the ideas of the sisterhood and the common identity of the various Maḷāīs bring together conceptually, the same places that the story of the goddess's journey brings together in narrative form.

The Goddess as Bride: Jogāī

So far we have looked at goddesses who travel in order to be more convenient to a faithful devotee or in order to kill a demon. Such journeys, though quite appropriate for divine beings, male *or* female, are not the kind of trip that human women are very likely to make. The trips that Jāṇāī, Tuḷjā Bhavānī, and Maḷāī make have more to do with their divinity than with their femininity. Human women in Maharashtra most typically travel when they are young brides moving into their in-laws' house or returning for visits to their childhood home. As in most of India, marriage in Maharashtra is typically virilocal and households are ideally multigenerational. A new bride and groom generally live together with his parents, his unmarried sisters, and his brothers and their wives and children. Especially at the beginning of her marriage, a girl can find herself traveling fairly often, as her life oscillates between her *sāsar* and her *māher*, her in-laws' house and her parents' home.

Some goddesses too, like human women, make the journey from *māher* to *sāsar* and back. The trip that the Bhātāṅgaḷī pole makes to Śiṅgṇāpūr, for example, is one that the men who carry and accompany it think of as its wedding trip. Like any reluctant bride, the pole, which the men see as Śiva's wife Pārvatī, takes longer to reach its husband's home at Śiṅgṇāpūr than to return to Bhātāṅgaḷī, its parental home. Just as, on the human level, women travel between and thus bring together their natal villages with the villages in which they live out their adult lives, so too, on the level of religious imagery, goddesses bring places together through the trope of marriage. Some people even articulate the Bhātāṅgaḷī pole's marriage to Śiva as the union of the primordial complementary opposites Śiva and Śakti, and see the Śiṅgṇāpūr wedding festival as bringing together two regions called "Śiva's side" and "Śakti's side." In the cases to be examined in the rest of this chapter, the goddess's wedding fails to take place, or the husband is merely implied. Nevertheless, the geographical consequences are more or less the same as if there had been a wedding and a husband.

Many Citpāvan Koṅkaṇastha Brāhmaṇs (also called simply Citpāvans, or simply Koṅkaṇasthas), people whose current or ancestral home is in the Koṅkaṇ, have as their family deity (*kuldevatā*) the goddess Yogeśvarī, Jogeśvarī, or Jogāī of Āmbejogāī. Āmbejogāī lies far from the Koṅkaṇ, across the formidable barrier of the Sahyādri mountains, or Western Ghats, and well inland in the Deś, in Bid District in Marāṭhvāḍā (map 3.4). In theory, at least, each family that has Jogāī as its family goddess makes the long trip from its home to Āmbejogāī to present to the goddess each new bride and baby that gets added to the family. This very explicit but anomalous and difficult connection between these two parts of Maharashtra is one of the great puzzles of Maharashtrian religious geography.

Several different stories are told in order to explain the connection. We have seen one of these stories in the introduction to this volume. This story connects the Citpāvans with Paraśurām, the creator of the Koṅkaṇ coast. After Paraśurām had revived the Citpāvans' corpses, which he had found floating in the ocean, no one would give a daughter to the Citpāvan men; as they searched for wives, it was only at Āmbejogāī that they found girls whose parents were willing to give them to the men (Kāḷegāṃvkar 1963:14, citing Jogaḷekar 1952). In this version, then, the Citpāvan men started out in the Koṅkaṇ and found their wives at Āmbejogāī. Another version has the first Citpāvans traveling in the opposite direction: starting in the area of Āmbejogāī and moving from there to the Koṅkaṇ at

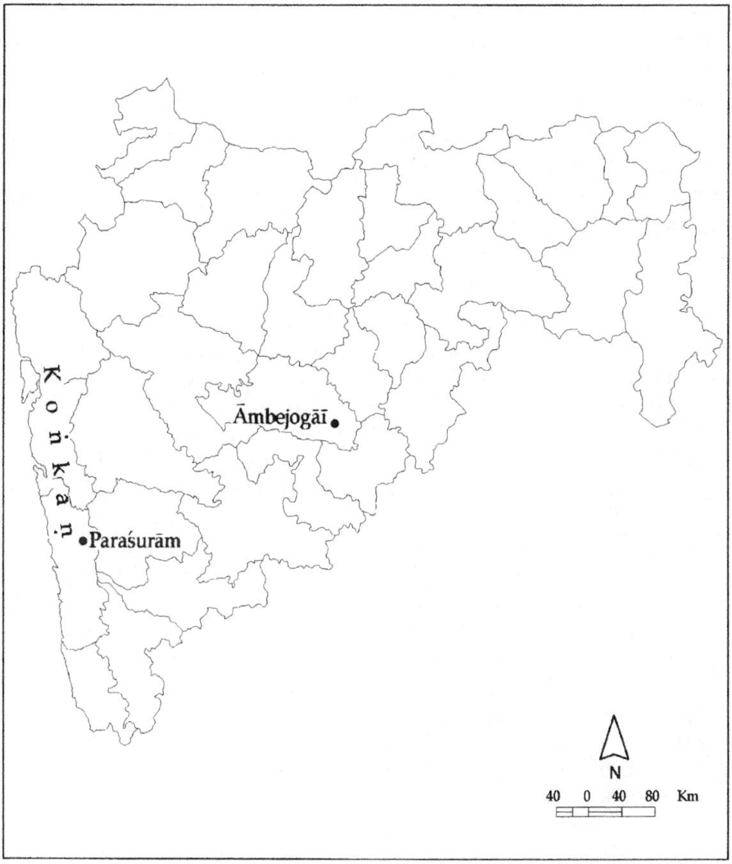

Map 3.4 Āmbejogāī and the Koṅkaṇ

Paraśurām's request (Kāḷegāṃvkar 1963:15):

> After Lord Paraśurām had caused the ocean to retreat and had made the land near the coast suitable for cultivation, he needed people to do the farming. As he wandered around searching for people, he came to Āmbejogāī. And he took sixty families from the fourteen lineages in Āmbejogāī and went to the Koṅkaṇ coast. Later that is where these families settled. When they were in Āmbejogāī, these families' family deity was Yogeśvarī Mātā. She remained there, and so Koṅkaṇasthas from the sixty families in the fourteen lineages continually come for *darśan* of their family goddess.

The most widely told story connecting Āmbejogāī and the Koṅkaṇ does not involve Paraśurām, nor does it include a journey or migration on the part of the original Citpāvan Brāhmaṇs. It does tell about a wedding, though, and it does involve a trip from the Koṅkaṇ to the Deś. This time, however, it is the goddess who travels, and it is for the purpose of her own marriage that she makes the trip. Her intended bridegroom is Śiva, in his form as Vaidyanāth of Paraḷī, a place near Āmbejogāī. Although in the end the marriage does not take place, the goddess does not return to the Koṅkaṇ but stays on at Āmbejogāī (Kāḷegāṃvkar 1963:13–14):

> As a girl, Yogeśvarī was to be married to Vaidyanāth of Paraḷī. Because Yogeśvarī lived in the Koṅkaṇ, she set out to go to Paraḷī along with the retinue of her wedding party. Staying at one place after another along the way, the day before the wedding this whole company camped on the bank of the Jayantī river near the town of Āmbejogāī, about fifteen miles from the town of Paraḷī. The moment for the wedding was at daybreak the next day. Very early in the morning, everyone in the wedding party got up and began busily to get ready to set out.
>
> Yogeśvarī, however, did not get up early. She really should have been more enthusiastic about her own wedding. But that is not the way it was. After she got up, she began to comb and braid her hair. Her coiffure would not get done quickly. And the moment was about to arrive. The people in the wedding party became anxious, but Yogeśvarī was intentionally procrastinating and making herself late. Finally the morning rooster crowed, and the moment for the wedding had been missed. The wedding did not take place. Instead of going back to the Koṅkaṇ, the goddess Yogeśvarī settled down forever right here on the bank of the Jayantī river, at the place where her temple now is.[43]

The motif of the goddess procrastinating about her own wedding and in the end preventing it from taking place is a common one, perhaps especially in South India. The most famous example of such a goddess is Kanyā Kumārī, the goddess at the southern tip of India whose very name ("Virgin Girl") brings to mind the story of her aborted marriage to Śiva of Sucindram (Shulman 1980:144–49). In Maharashtra, Mahālakṣmī, the goddess of Kolhāpūr, is supposed to marry the god Vyaṅkaṭeś of Tirupatī, far away in Andhra Pradesh, but that marriage too fails to take place. For us, though, the fact that Jogāī's wedding did not, in the end, take place is of only secondary importance to the geographical point that her story makes. For the story gives the reason for the Koṅkaṇasthas' connection with a place far inland on the Deś: the wedding trip that their goddess once made. Whether the wedding ceremony was actually held or not, the goddess's trip explains the connection between Koṅkaṇ and Deś that is enacted again and again in the lives and imaginations of Koṅkaṇastha Brāhmaṇs. As Kāḷegāṃvkar (1987:33) explains: "While the goddess Yogeśvarī was in the Koṅkaṇ, she was the family goddess of the people there (Kokaṇasthas). Now, even though she was staying in a different place, their faith did not change, and so, still today, she is the family goddess of many Kokaṇasthas." Whether the Koṅkaṇastha Brāhmaṇs make or merely contemplate the journey from their homes in the west to Āmbejogāī, their connection with that place stems from a trip that their goddess made before them.[44] By means of her wedding trip, the goddess Yogeśvarī or Jogāī of Āmbejogāī brings together the two main divisions of Maharashtra: Koṅkaṇ and Deś.

The Seven Sisters

The sisterhood of geographically separated goddesses seems to me to constitute another kind of connection between places that depends on the idea of the goddesses' being married women. Imagining places as connected not just in terms of any human social relationship but in terms of the relationship of sisterhood in particular is an extremely effective way of expressing both the separation of the places and the ties that bind them together. It is a very good way of thinking about a region. As we will see, the ties among the places are based on an implicit notion that the goddesses have left their common parental home and have traveled as brides to their present locations, where they live in their respective husbands' homes.

Most often the number of such divine sisters is said to be seven. Sets of seven sister goddesses are found throughout South Asia, with enormous variation as to which goddesses, from which places, are included in the sets. From the seven major pilgrimage goddesses of the "greater Panjab area" of northern India (Erndl 1993:37–60) to the seven village goddesses of South India,[45] there are many different sets, each set usually confined to a relatively small area. Thus, the seven sister goddesses present an array of regional variations on a widespread theme.

In Maharashtra, saying that goddesses are one another's sisters is perhaps the most common way of relating them to one another. In some cases, the goddesses who are said to be related as sisters are found together. In the shrine of Saṭvāī in Kolṭāvaḍe (Āmbegāv Taluka, Pune District), for example, there are two other goddesses, Mesāī and Rāṇbāī, as well as Saṭvāī. People I talked with at the shrine called the other two goddesses Saṭvāī's sisters. Many people use such terminology for goddesses who appear as subsidiary deities in one another's shrines or temples. Another place where one goddess appears in another's temple is Rāśīn (Karjat Taluka, Ahmadnagar

District). The temple of the goddess Yamāī in Rāśīn has an image of Tukāī (the goddess Bhavānī of Tuḷjāpūr, under another name) next to that of Yamāī in the main shrine. Gurav priests in Rāśīn explain that the reason that Tukāī stands to Yamāī's right (i.e., on the side of honor) is that Tukāī is Yamāī's elder sister.

Most often when sister goddesses appear *together* they are found in groups of seven. One such group is the Seven (Sātī) Āsarā. These water goddesses, who are basically invisible, are represented by seven pebbles placed in a row on a riverbank, by seven (or more) daubs of red-lead painted on a stone surface (a boulder, steps leading down to a river, or the side of a well), or by a plaque (*ṭāk*) or small brass statue (*mūrti*) showing seven women standing next to one another.[46] The seven Āsarā sisters live together, it seems, in the places where they are active. Similarly, Lakṣmīāī, the goddess of both disease and wealth, appears as a set of several—often but not always seven—stones daubed with red-lead at the edge of a village, or even occasionally as seven female figures standing next to one another in a shrine (figure 3.2). Bhivāī, or the Seven Bhivayyā, a river goddess with a highly developed cult—several kinds of priests, an elaborate pilgrimage festival, and an extensive oral literature—is at once one goddess and seven sisters (Feldhaus 1995:48–50, 55–57). Near her principal temple, at a place on the boulders that form the south bank of the Nīrā River at Kāmbaḷeśvar (in Phalṭaṇ Taluka, Satara District), Bhivāī has fourteen footprints, lined up in pairs; the "self-formed" (*svayambhū*) image in the nearby temple is a

Figure 3.2 Lakṣmīāī at Rāhurī.

single stone composed of seven humps (Feldhaus 1995, illustration after p. 64). Carved and painted images generally portray Bhivāī as seven women standing next to one another. Marathi stories about Bhivāī oscillate back and forth between singular and plural forms of her name (Bhivāī or Bhiubāī in the singular, Bhivayyā in the plural), of pronouns used to refer to her, and of verbs used to express her actions.

Besides such sets of sisters who are found together in one place—either as subsidiary goddesses in one another's shrines or as beings who stay together because they are fundamentally identical with one another—goddesses also get grouped in another form of sisterhood, one that is more significant for understanding regions. In this form of sisterhood, goddesses located at *different* places are understood to be one another's sisters. Placing an image of one of the sisters in a temple dedicated primarily to another of the sisters, as in Rāśīn, is one way of expressing such a connection. So is the practice of painting on the walls of a goddess's temple pictures of other goddesses in specific, distant places. Most often, though, the sisterhood of distant goddesses is a concept or verbal image; it takes the form of a list of goddesses said to be one another's sisters.

Such lists can include any number of goddesses. There seems to be a widespread understanding, though, that the number of sisters is seven—even if the person listing them cannot remember all seven members of the list. Most significantly, the identity and location of those that people do remember vary greatly, depending on where (and whom) one asks. Such lists provide revealing glimpses into the mental maps of those who make them. Major, distant goddesses often find themselves next to local goddesses who might not appear on lists from other places, and the many different lists together present a rich variety of conceptual regions.

For example, people at Deuḷgāv Uṅgaḷe or Deuḷgāv Devī (Jāphrābād Taluka, Jalna District) named the following goddesses as the sisters of the goddess of Deuḷgāv: Mahākāliṅkā (Mahākālī), the goddess of another place in Jāphrābād Taluka; three goddesses from neighboring Cikhalī Taluka (in Buldhana District); and the three more distant, more famous goddesses of Māhūr, Tuḷjāpūr, and Kolhāpūr. In the temple of the goddess Reṇukā at Godrī, one of the places in Cikhalī Taluka that appear on the list from Deuḷgāv Uṅgaḷe, the outside wall of the sanctuary is decorated with oil paintings of seven goddesses. Three of these—Ambā Mātā, Gāyatrī, and Durgā Devī (seated on a lion)—are not identified by location, unless "Ambā Mātā" (a name that means "Mother Mother") is taken as referring to Ambābāī or Mahālakṣmī of Kolhāpūr, in southern Maharashtra. Three others of the seven are the other three of Maharashtra's four principal goddesses: Tuḷjāpūr Bhavānī; Reṇukā Mātā, pictured as she appears at Māhūr; and Saptaśṛṅgī.[47] The seventh goddess is only half female: the Ardhanārī ("Half-Woman") form of Śiva, which people at Godrī told me is located at Pañcavaṭī in Nāsik.

At Vuruḍ Budruk, part way between Deuḷgāv and Godrī, I heard yet another list of seven sisters: besides the goddesses of Māhūr and Tuḷjāpūr, this included the goddesses of nearby Deuḷgāv; of Vāghrūḷ and Kokaraśaṃ, two other places in Jālnā Taluka; of "Reṇukā's Pimpaḷgāv" (presumably Pimpaḷgāv Reṇukrāī, in Bhokardan Taluka, Jalna District); and of Śendalaṃ, in Mehkar Taluka, Buldhana District. A priest of the goddess Piṅgaḷāī at Ner Piṅgaḷāī in Amravati District drew one member of his list of seven goddesses from even farther away than the people at Deuḷgāv did theirs. Along with Piṅgaḷāī, his list included three other goddesses from Amravati District and Reṇukā of Māhūr, the nearest of Maharashtra's four principal goddesses[48] to Ner Piṅgaḷāī. But he also put on his list the goddess Kālī of far-distant Calcutta.

At Kelāpūr, in Yavatmal District, a priest mentioned a story that the goddess of Kelāpūr, Bhavānī, travels by an underground route to far-distant Candrapūr to visit the goddess Mahākālī there. When I asked what the relationship between the two goddesses is, the priest answered, "Now, take them as sisters," and he began to name other sister goddesses. After listing Reṇukā of Māhūr and the goddesses of Tuḷjāpūr and Kolhāpūr, the priest had to struggle a while before coming up with Lakhamāī of Pāthroḍ, his own family goddess. Finally he gave up: there are seven sisters, he said, but he could not remember the name of the seventh.

A farmer in Kurkumbh (Yavat Taluka, Pune District) told my companions and me that there are nine sisters, but his list included fewer than that number of goddesses. Besides Phiraṅgāī of Kurkumbh, he said, the sisters include the goddesses of Rāśīn and Tuḷjāpūr, as well as Kāḷubāī, Jāṇāī, Bolhāī, and Tukāī. Tukāī he identified as the goddess of Tuḷjāpūr, making her identical with the goddess he had earlier identified by place-name. When I asked him what other goddesses should be on the list, he was unsure. "Yamāī, probably," he said naming a goddess found, among other places, in Rāśīn, and thus perhaps another duplicate.

Even further south, a Brāhmaṇ priest of the goddess Śākambharī or Baṇśaṅkarī at Badāmī in Karnataka said that there are five places of Śaktī. He could name four of these places. Three of them—Badāmī, Yallamāguḍḍi (i.e., Saundattī, the principal pilgrimage place of the goddess Yelammā or Yallamā), and Ciñclī, the place of the goddess "Mahāmāyā" (Māyavvā)—are in northern Karnataka, while the fourth, Kolhāpūr, is nearby, in southern Maharashtra. Far to the north, in Khāndeś, a Brāhmaṇ in Khāpar (Akkalkuvā Taluka, Dhule District) also included Kolhāpūr in his list, while the other goddesses and places he mentioned—Ekvīrā of Dhuḷe, Nāsik (he did not name a particular goddess here, but perhaps he meant to refer to Saptaśṛṅgī, whose principal pilgrimage place lies to the north of Nāsik), Kālikāmātā of Akkalkuvā, Hedambā of Rojhvā, and Khāpar itself—are all in Khāndeś.

Finally, the goddess of Lāsūr (Gāṇgāpūr Taluka, Aurangabad District) appears on lists of seven sisters that I collected at Māñjrī (also in Gāṇgāpūr Taluka) and Mhaismāḷ (Kultābād Taluka, Aurangabad District), while neither of these places appears on the list that a Brāhmaṇ in Lāsūr gave me. Although this man said that there are a total of seven sisters, he could think of only five in addition to Dākṣāyaṇī, the goddess of Lāsūr. Besides the standard, most important goddesses (Saptaśṛṅgī, Māhūr, Tuḷjā Bhavānī, and Mahālakṣmī of Kolhāpūr), the five included Mohaṭā Devī (Pātharḍī Taluka, Ahmadnagar District), a goddess who has recently become quite prominent and whose temple Indira Gandhi visited.

Some goddesses' sisterhood is expressed more elaborately than by simply listing the goddesses verbally or painting pictures of them next to one another on a wall. In some cases, people indicate that one of the sisters is senior to the others. We have already seen that Tukāī, identified as the goddess of Tuḷjāpūr, is the elder sister of Yamāī in Rāśīn. The goddess of Tuḷjāpūr is also the elder sister of Yeḍāī, the goddess of Yermāḷā. Yeḍāī's temple stands on a hill three kilometers south of Yermāḷā, in Usmanabad District. Several of my friends and I attended Yeḍāī's pilgrimage festival at the full moon of Caitra (March–April) in 1995. Pilgrims at the festival explained that Yeḍāī was a young woman whose marriage had been arranged and was to be performed in the town of Yermāḷā. She did not want the marriage, and so she went, sulking (*rusūn*), to the hill south of town where her temple now is. At least one person said that Yeḍāī disappeared at the site of the marriage ceremony and then reappeared on the hilltop as a goddess. In any case, Yeḍāī—like Jogāī, Kanyā Kumārī, and the others—managed to escape her own wedding. This is one reason for her name: Yeḍāī is glossed as *yeḍī āī* or *veḍī āī*, "Crazy Lady."[49]

During the annual festival at Yeḍāī's temple near Yermāḷā, the nighttime parade (*chabinā*) that some people called the goddess's wedding procession goes not to a wedding hall but to a cliff at the southern edge of the goddess's hill. There, at a small temple of Bhavānī of Tuḷjāpūr, people sing and clap to the rhythm of an *āratī*,[50] and then the palanquin returns to the temple. When we attended the festival, we saw that many pilgrims remained standing—before, during, and for some time after the *āratī*—staring south, over the cliff and into the distance. There, some of them explained, if you are lucky, you can see a flame reach up into the sky. The flame comes from the main temple of Bhavānī, at Tuḷjāpūr, about 50 kilometers to the south, and it indicates Bhavānī's greetings to her younger sister Yeḍāī, who has come to see her.

What does it mean to say that goddesses in different locations are one another's sisters? In the case of Maḷāī, what is sometimes called the "sisterhood" of the various Maḷāīs seems to mean that they are fundamentally identical with one another, or that they represent different moments in a single narrative of a battle with a demon. In the case of the other sets of sisters that people listed for me, there is no such story of a struggle with a demon, and no such clear notion of the goddesses' common identity.[51] So what is implied when people say that seven different goddesses are one another's sisters? The 1961 Census volume *Fairs and Festivals in Maharashtra* (1969:78) presents a relatively elaborate story that names seven sister goddesses. The story links the locations of the seven goddesses in relation to a journey or set of journeys that they took. I think this story can give us a clue:

> Seven sisters by name (i) Mahalakshmi, (ii) Mahakali, (iii) Vajrabai, (iv) Gangadevi, (v) Renuka, (vi) Kalika and (vii) Gauri Saraswati are said to have started from Kolhapur about 7 to 8 generations back and [gone] to different places. Vajrabai went to Vajreshwari in Bhivandi Taluka of Thana district, Gangadevi went to a village in Umbergaon Taluka in Surat district (Gujarat State), Renuka went to Wani village in Kolaba district, Kalika went to Pawagad in Gujarat and Gauri Saraswati and Mahakali remained with their sister Mahalakshmi at Viwalwedhe.

The story as the Census volume narrates it does not state the reason for the sisters' journey. Generally, however, and quite likely in this case as well, the idea that goddesses located in different places are one another's sisters implies that they are married women who have left their common maternal home (*māher*) to live in their respective in-laws' houses (*sāsar*).[52] A woman who lives next-door to the Lakṣmīāī at the side of the road in Rāhurī (figure 3.2) made this point more explicit. After telling me that that particular Lakṣmīāī has an elder sister with a big festival at a place to the west of Rāhurī, the woman explained: just as "among us,[53] one sister is given in marriage in this place, another sister is given in that place," so the goddesses have their places (*ṭhāṇe*) "here and there."

Just as women, by marrying, link their parental homes and villages to the in-laws' homes and villages that they move into, so do these goddesses, by being sisters and by living in a variety of places, link those places by virtue of their implied common childhood. To say that the goddesses of different places are one another's sisters is to imply that they have traveled to their present locations from a common parental home. Each of the goddesses, that is, has at some point, as a bride, left that common home and come to live in her in-laws' place. The intensity of the married sisters' ties to one another derives in part from their long separations and the infrequency of their meetings, but its basis is the companionship, the shared fun and love, of their life together before marriage, in their *māher*.[54] When goddesses located in a single place are called one another's sisters, the implication is that the place *is* their *māher*, and they are presumably unmarried girls. The imagery that calls goddesses of *different* locations one another's sisters portrays the goddesses as adult women, not as children; but the basis of their connection with one another is their shared childhood in their parental home.

At Karāḍ, where the Kṛṣṇā and Koynā rivers come rushing directly toward each other and then turn aside (figure 1.2), their confluence (*saṅgam*), which forms a perfect "T," is called "Prītisaṅgam," "Love Saṅgam." Some outsiders to Karāḍ think that the term "Prītisaṅgam" refers to the union of two lovers, one of whom is male and the other female. Citizens of Karāḍ, however, know that the Kṛṣṇā and the Koynā are one another's sisters. A song that the recording artist Lata Mangeshkar made popular relates the Prītisaṅgam to the love of married sisters for one another and for their maternal home. Images of the Koynā and the Kṛṣṇā in separate temples—located, respectively, upstream and downstream from the confluence—represent the two rivers as women, each with her neck bent at an unusual angle. People in Karāḍ explain the images as those of the two sisters, Kṛṣṇā and Koynā, each peering toward their meeting place and waiting expectantly for the other to arrive. Goddesses who are not rivers do not physically flow together, but their sisterhood nevertheless implies a strong emotional pull toward one another and toward their common parental home.

The sisterhood of goddesses located in different places, then, presents an emotionally powerful image of a region. The sisters, separated from one another by the demands of virilocal marriage, are linked by bonds of memory and longing. The places, too, though separated by the facts of geographical extension, come together in a poignant unity when people understand the goddesses who reside in them to be sisters.[55] Separate location combined with emotional connection characterizes, after all, not only adult, married sisterhood but also a region. A region involves both separation and unity of places. In a region, places that are distinct from one another—places that are not the same place and not *in* the same place—are nevertheless brought together and sensed to belong together. The area within which they come together, the area throughout which they are scattered, is a region. Although the places are not identical, and also *because* they are not identical, they are nevertheless connected.

The goddesses we have considered in this chapter connect places by traveling from one of them to another. Ultimately, though, the glue by which these goddesses hold places together is love. Jāṇāī, Bhavānī, and other goddesses (and gods) who travel in order to be near a faithful or kindly devotee act out of love for that devotee and for others who might follow him; subsequent generations of devotees keep the love alive by retracing the goddess's steps in an annual pilgrimage festival. Maḷāī kills the demon out of love for her devotees; they in turn maintain an annual festival that follows her route and connects some of the places where she went. The trope of the goddess traveling to get married implies a kind of love, even when the bride is unwilling and the wedding does not in the end take place. And, finally, the sisters who have traveled to the homes of their implied husbands bring these places together through a kind of love-in-separation for one another and for their implied *māher*. The kinds of love vary greatly, and yet, in each case we have examined in this chapter, it is love that forms the basis of the connection between places.

Chapter 4

The Arithmetic of Place: Numbered Sets of Places

Love may form the common link among the sets of places discussed in chapter 3. However, in the case of the sets of sister goddesses described at the end of that chapter, it is not only emotional bonds that bring each set together but also the number seven. The present chapter moves beyond the kinds of emotional connections examined in chapter 3—the love between god and devotee, the love between husband and wife, or the love among married sisters—to study sets of places connected only or primarily by numbers. I will argue that even when the device that brings separate places together is not an emotionally powerful bond but rather just a number, the mere numbering of the places makes them collectively a region. In this case, too, as in that of the seven sisters, the places are distinct from one another and are spread throughout an area, but now the main thing that brings them together is not a personal relationship but something much more abstract: a number. The mental act of counting the places together, of listing them as distinct members of a single set with a joint name, gives a particular coherence to the area within which they are found. It makes of that area a large place in which several different places are brought together into an arithmetically defined set. It makes the area into a region.

Numbered sets of places are found on the level of all of India as well as on the regional level, including within Maharashtra. Unlike in the case of the many, varied sets of sister goddesses that I listed in chapter 3, almost everyone agrees which places belong to each of the sets we will look at here. Numbered sets bringing together places found throughout India include the seven liberating cities (Saptapurī), the 12 Jyotirliṅgas, the four sites of the Kumbh Melā, the 108 or 51 Śakti (or Satī) Pīṭhs, and the four Dhāms. Let us look first at these India-wide sets, before proceeding to examine sets found on other levels.

The Saptapurī are seven cities pilgrimage to any one of which provides liberation from rebirth. The seven places, indicated with triangles on map 4.1, are Mathurā, Dvārkā, Ayodhyā, Hardvār,[1] Kāñcīpuram (Kāñcī),[2] Ujjain, and Vārāṇasī. Vārāṇasī (Kāśī, Banaras) is the most important of the seven places (Eck 1982:284), but any of them can fulfill the set's defining function. In this respect, the members of the set are identical to one another, except that they are in different places. I have not been able to find any story that links all seven of the places, telling of some one thing that happened at all of them or some series of things, one of which happened at each of them. However, a Sanskrit verse "known to practically every literate brahmin" names all of them as "liberating" (*mokṣada*; Eck 1982:36).

The 12 Jyotirliṅgas (indicated with dots on map 4.1), a set of 12 major pilgrimage places of Śiva,[3] are linked by not just a verse but a story: all of these places are associated with the story of Śiva's miraculous "*liṅga* of light" (*jyotirliṅga*). The "*liṅga* of light" is the form in which Śiva emerged from the earth to illustrate his superiority to Brahmā and Viṣṇu when these two gods were competing with each other as to which of them was better (Eck 1982:107–09). Most stories about the Jyotirliṅgas do not explain why there are more than one of them. The following version, though, *does* account for the multiplicity of Jyotirliṅgas. As far as I can tell, this story, found in a Marathi pamphlet about Tryambakeśvar (Pāṭaṇkar 1984:16–17), is *not* very widely known:

> Once upon a time, when Śiva and Pārvatī were making love, they began to doubt each other's capacity, and they began to struggle. However large Śaṅkar [Śiva] made himself, Bhavānī [Pārvatī] made herself grow just as large. Finally, when Pārvatī set her mind on Viṣṇu, Viṣṇu entered Pārvatī's body and kept the struggle going. Later, seeing the struggle, which caused torment to all beings, moving and stationary, all the troops of gods became terrified. Viṣṇu called out to Śaṅkar. Immediately Lord Śaṅkar regained consciousness, and he felt a bit ashamed.
>
> At that time, God Brahmā praised Śaṅkar greatly. This made Mahādev [Śiva] happy, and he said that Viṣṇu should divide the *liṅga* joined with the *yoni*[4] into twelve parts, so that the whole universe could benefit by worshipping it.
>
> Accordingly, Viṣṇu divided the *liṅga* joined with the *yoni* into twelve parts. As he was dividing it, lights (*jyoti*) came into being. Because of that, these twelve parts began to be called Jyotirliṅgas.

Another version of the origin of the 12 Jyotirliṅgas relates them to Viṣṇu's form as the seductress Mohinī. Mohinī is the form that Viṣṇu took in order to distract the demons and trick them out of the nectar that had emerged when the ocean of milk was churned. Although this story is widely known, the episode that connects it with the Jyotirliṅgas is less well known: as Śiva, aroused, chased Mohinī around, the Jyotirliṅgas sprang up at the places where his semen fell to the ground. Thus, both these stories show the 12 places to be identical with one another. They are identical either because, in the story of the divided *liṅga* and *yoni*, they are the sites of 12 parts of one conjugally joined entity, or because the same event (according to one version of the story, the contest between Brahmā and Viṣṇu; according to another version, an ejaculation of Śiva's semen) happened at each of them. Both Tryambakeśvar (Pāṭaṇkar 1984:14–16) and Vārāṇasī (Eck 1982:109) claim that their Jyotirliṅga is the principal one. But, aside from the primacy of one or another place, the only thing that distinguishes the 12 Jyotirliṅgas from one another is their separate locations.[5]

The four sites of India's most famous and most elaborate pilgrimage, the Kumbha Melā, form another set of places; for this set there is not only a story but also a coordinated cycle of pilgrimages. The four places are Hardvār, Allāhabād (Prayāg), Ujjain, and (jointly, it seems) Nāsik and Tryambakeśvar (these places are marked with squares on map 4.1). The Kumbha Melā takes place at one of these places every three years in a cycle of 12 years, strictly regulated by astrological calculations based on the movements of the sun and Jupiter through the zodiac.[6] A story connects the places, explaining their power at the particular times specified for the Melā. The following version of the story is taken from a Marathi pamphlet about one of the places, Tryambakeśvar (Bhujaṅg n.d.:19):

> In the Satya Yuga, the gods and demons churned the ocean. At that time, they acquired fourteen gems . . . . After they had received nectar, the fourteenth gem, the gods were worried: "If, when the fourteen gems are being distributed, the demons get the nectar, they will constantly trouble us, because nectar has the power to restore life." For fear of this, they told Indra's son Jayant to run away with the pot of nectar. The demons did battle for twelve days to get the pot of nectar, and, in the course of that battle, some drops from the pot of nectar fell to earth. The places [where the drops fell] were Hardvār,[7] Prayāg [Allāhabād], Ujjain, and Tryambakeśvar. In order to protect that nectar, the gods come together every twelve years in the form of holy men and ascetics to guard it. The Kumbha Melā is held in those four places.

Here again, the story connects the places, but it does not distinguish among them.

In the case of the 108 (or 51)[8] Śakti Pīṭhs, the story that brings the places together also differentiates them from one another. The word "*pīṭh*" means "seat," and "*śakti*" is a term for feminine divine energy. The Śakti Pīṭhs are the places where parts of the corpse of Śiva's wife Satī fell as he

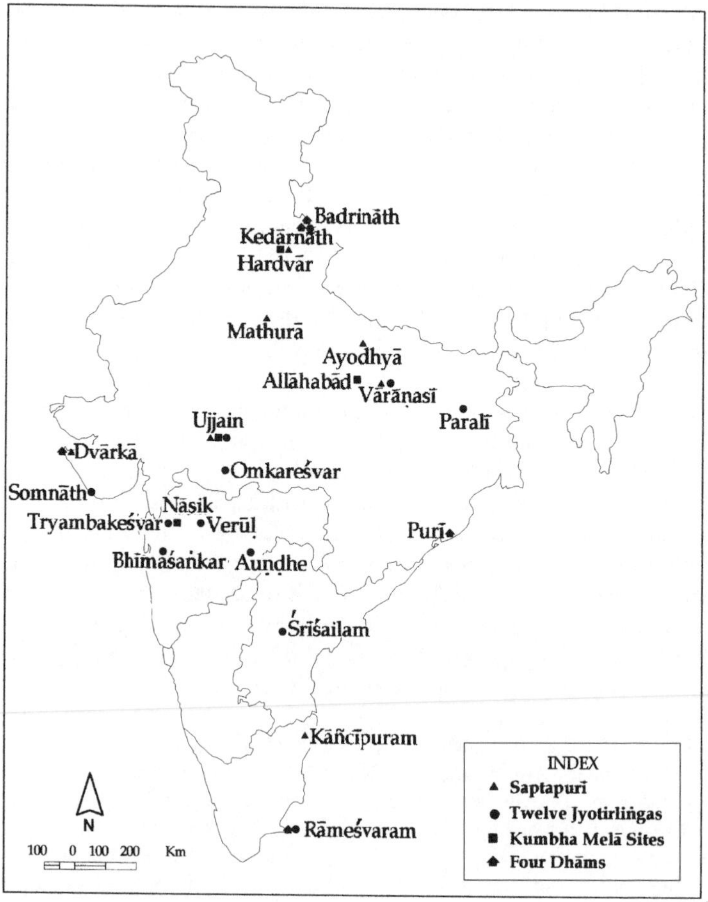

Map 4.1 Sets of pilgrimage places throughout India

wandered around, griefstricken, carrying her body over his shoulder. The places are therefore sometimes also called Satī Pīṭhs. In theory, each of the 108 (or 51) Śakti Pīṭhs marks the spot where a different part of Satī's body fell. A Marathi pamphlet about the goddess Mahālakṣmī of Kolhāpūr summarizes as follows the version of the story found in a text called *Tantracuḍāmaṇī* (Govaṇḍe 1981:3):

> Once Prajāpatī Dakṣa held a sacrifice. He invited all the gods and sages to the sacrifice, but he did not invite his son-in-law, Lord Śaṅkar [Śiva]. Even

> so, Satī went to the sacrifice that her father was performing. Dakṣa insulted Śaṅkar in front of her. Because of that, Satī, enraged, jumped into the sacrificial fire pit. As soon as Śaṅkar learned of this, he became furious. He destroyed Dakṣa along with the sacrifice. Then, taking Satī's corpse from the fire pit and carrying it over his shoulder, he began to wander around in the three worlds.[9] In order to stop this mad wandering of Śaṅkar's, Viṣṇu let fly his Sudarśan discus and cut the corpse to bits. At each of the places where fifty-one of the pieces fell to the earth, a Śaktī Pīṭh came into being.

Sanskrit textual traditions identify the places where the various parts of the goddess's body fell. Some texts also give the name of the goddess at each of the places, add the name of the Bhairava (a form of Śiva) associated with the place, and identify the part of the goddess's body that fell there.[10] Sircar, who has studied these textual traditions in painstaking detail (1948, 1973), finds little consistency among the lists that different texts give, or sometimes even within a single text. He states (1948:32): "There was apparently little influence on these writers of something like a recognized tradition about the number of the Pīṭhas, the names of the deities worshipped at them, and their association with particular limbs of the mother-goddess."

Local, oral traditions in Maharashtra are characterized by a similar lack of systematization or uniformity. Except for Kolhāpūr, which knowledgeable people identify as the place where the goddess's three eyes fell, oral traditions in Maharashtra do not reveal much awareness of the textual lists.[11] Not only do local claims that a place is a Śakti Pīṭh appear not to be bound by textual traditions, such claims also do not seem to be subject to any kind of pressure for consensus or to be regulated by any other kind of authority. Nearly everyone in Maharashtra who knows in any detail about the Śakti Pīṭhs agrees that the goddess's genitals, her *yoni*, fell at Kāmākhyā in Assam.[12] Beyond that, however, there seems to be no agreement, nor any particular concern to reach agreement. Like the splinters of the holy cross—which, if they were taken from their reliquaries in various parts of the Christian world and all glued together, would add up to many more crosses than one—the parts of the goddess held to have fallen at all the places that claim to be Śakti Pīṭhs would probably, if put together, add up to much more than one body. At the same time, they would probably not add up to one *whole* body, either: some parts would be duplicated in many different places, and others would be missing altogether.

Nevertheless, such lack of systematization with respect to the details does not detract from the power of the overall idea. For the *idea* is that each of the places received a different part of the goddess's body, and that taken together the parts that fell make up the whole body of the goddess. This idea both *differentiates* the places from one another and at the same time *links* them to one another. It brings them together in a kind of unity that can best be called organic: the kind of unity that holds together a human—or, in this case, divine—body.

Finally, there is one set of places that demarcates the full extent of India. The four Dhāms, or "abodes [of God]" (marked with small houses on map 4.1), are four major pilgrimage places that are brought together and differentiated from one another in terms of the cardinal directions: Dvārkā lies in the west of India, Purī in the east, Badrināth (for worshippers of Viṣṇu) or Kedārnāth (for worshippers of Śiva) in the north, and Rāmeśvaram in the south.[13] Well-known places, located at the four cardinal points of the Indian subcontinent, the four Dhāms are otherwise, as far as I know, not linked by any one common theme unique to them, and I know of no story that brings all four of them together. Dvārkā, Purī, and Badrināth are primarily (if not exclusively) Vaiṣṇava places, while Kedārnāth and Rāmeśvaram are places of Śiva. Rāmeśvaram and Kedārnāth are two of the 12 Jyotirliṅgas and Dvārkā is one of the Saptapurī, but Purī and Badrināth belong to neither of these sets. The set of four Dhāms partially overlaps with the set of the four seats (*pīṭhs*) of the Śaṅkarācāryas, heads of India's most prominent orders of ascetics,[14] but, again, the congruence is not complete.

David Sopher (1980a:315) described the four Dhāms, along with other holy places on the periphery of India, as "boundary markers of sacred space," whose placement "on the periphery of the religious-cultural ecumene" is "deliberate."[15] The four Dhāms serve to "outline," according to Sopher, "the shape of Hindu India." They also clearly fit Victor Turner's description of the "pilgrims' goal" as a "center out there," a peripheral place whose religious importance stems from its very remoteness (Turner 1973). For centuries, the feet of pilgrims have linked the four Dhāms,[16] and in the present era, the wheels of "four Dhām" buses carry increasing numbers of pilgrim-tourists the entire distance to all of the places, around the circumference of India. But the four places are also brought together, much more easily and rapidly, by the verbal formula "four Dhāms" and by the images in the minds of all the pilgrims, tourists, and sedentary people who have *thought* about the four Dhāms as a set.

Unlike the Dhāms, sets of places like the Jyotirliṅgas and the Śakti Pīṭhs do not outline India. However, by virtue of being spread throughout it, they serve to unify it in several important ways. Individually, as places with broad pilgrim "fields" (Bhardwaj 1973:6–7, 97–115), they provide an opportunity for people from all over the Indian subcontinent to meet. As *sets*, they provide an occasion for people to travel not just from their homes in various places to some one place, but *throughout* the subcontinent.

In addition to these mechanisms, which may be said to be based on *circulation* (Stein 1977; Markovits, Pouchepadass, and Subrahmanyam 2003; cf. chapter 1 in this book), on people actually moving around among the different places, such sets of pilgrimage places also serve to give India a *conceptual* unity. They provide an occasion and a means for people to *think* about India as a whole. As the four Dhāms represent all of India by marking its boundaries, so do the 12 Jyotirliṅgas, the 51 Śakti Pīṭhs, and so on represent all of India by being distributed throughout it and by being brought together, mentally and verbally, into a single set. "The whole of India," states Diana Eck (1996:142, referring especially to the Śakti Pīṭhs), "adds up to a body-cosmos." A large map of India placed near a statue of "Mother India" on the ground floor of the Bhārat Mātā temple in Hardwar suggests this image too. The map is clearly meant to be a cartographic version of the goddesses. According to McKean (1996:157), the map is

> mounted on a raised platform in the center of this ground floor shrine. On it are marked mountains and rivers, major centers of Hindu pilgrimage, and "all important centers of culture."[17] Thus the map represents the political boundaries of the Indian state while inscribing its topographic features in terms of Hindu cosmography.

Some scholars have noted the power of pilgrimage places to unite India. In discussing the 12 Jyotirliṅgas, for instance, the *Bhāratīya Saṃskṛtikoś* (*BSK*, Volume 3, p. 686) states: "For centuries, pilgrims have considered these twelve principal places of Śiva, scattered throughout all of India, from the Himālayas to Setubandha,[18] to be extremely holy places. These places play a special part in the cultural unity of India." The erudite scholar of classical Hindu law (*dharmaśāstra*) P. V. Kane (1973:553) elaborates on this point and makes it more general:

> In ancient and medieval India pilgrimages brought many advantages to the community as well as to the pilgrims themselves. Though India was divided into many kingdoms and the people of India followed several cults and subcults, pilgrimages tended to foster the idea of the essential and fundamental unity of Indian culture and of India also. Benaras and Rāmeśvara were held sacred by all Hindus, whether they hailed from the north of India or from the peninsula. Though the Hindu community was broken up into numerous castes and suffered from caste exclusiveness, pilgrimages tended to level up [*sic*] all men by bringing them together to the same holy rivers or shrines.

In fact, not "all men" in India are included in the community of those who travel on pilgrimage to these Hindu holy places or hold them to be sacred. The inclusiveness with respect to caste, sectarian, linguistic, and other differences among Hindus that such religious geography and pilgrimage can foster has as its shadow the exclusion of Indians who do not consider themselves Hindu. Finding in Hindu religious geography an analogy to the "theology of politics and . . . symbology of otherness" that Pollock (1993:286, quoted by Duara) shows some medieval Hindus to have found in the *Rāmāyaṇa*, Duara points out (1995:63):

> Pilgrimage is perhaps the privileged means by which a religious community is both ritually and spatially delimited. In India, pilgrimage centers marked an interlinked, subcontinental-wide territory not simply as a sacred space, but in the face of a demonized Other living in this territory, as the sacred space of Hindus.

In some of its extreme forms, such an idea requires those who hold it to equate the categories "Hindu" and "Indian," denying full Indian-ness to members of non-Hindu religious communities, or redefining those communities as Hindu.[19] V. D. Savarkar, for example, found in the sacrality of India for Hindus one of the strongest arguments for the brand of Hindu nationalism he espoused. In his 1924 work *Hindutva*, Savarkar argued as follows (de Bary ed. 1958:331–32):

> the tie of common holyland has at times proved stronger than the chains of a Motherland. Look at the Mohamedans. Mecca to them is a sterner reality than Delhi or Agra. Some of them do not make any secret of being bound to sacrifice all India if that be to the glory of Islam or [if it] could save the city of their prophet. Look at the Jews. Neither centuries of prosperity nor [a] sense of gratitude for the shelter they found can make them more attached or even equally attached to the several countries they inhabit. Their love is, and must necessarily be, divided between the land of their birth and the land of their prophets. . . .
>
> The ideal conditions, therefore, under which a nation can attain perfect solidarity and cohesion would, other things being equal, be found in the case of those people who inhabit the land they adore, the land of whose forefathers is also the land of their Gods and Angels, of Seers and Prophets; the scenes of whose history are also the scenes of their mythology.
>
> The Hindus are about the only people who are blessed with these ideal conditions that are at the same time incentive to national solidarity, cohesion, and greatness. Not even the Chinese are blessed thus. Only Arabia and Palestine—if ever the Jews can succeed in founding their state there—can be said to possess this unique advantage.

The power of such ideas is undeniable, and echoes of these words are still to be heard today. However, not only do non-Hindus also attach religious meanings to the landscape of India,[20] but the territorially monolithic India that statements like Savarkar's assume is also counterbalanced to some extent by the multiplicity of regions that Hindus sacralize.

Numbered sets of holy places similar to the 12 Jyotirliṅgas, the 51 Śakti Pīṭhs, the four Dhāms, and so on are found on regional and subregional levels as well as on the level of all of India. The Gaḍhvāl region in the Himalayas has a four-Dhām pilgrimage to Badrināth, Kedārnāth, Gaṅgotrī (the source of the Ganges river), and Yamunotrī (the source of the Yamunā river) that, in that region, supercedes the four Dhāms of all of India in importance (Ghāṇekar 1993:33; cf. Mahājan 1994). Another north Indian set consists of Prayāg (Allāhabād), Kāśī (Vārāṇasī, Banāras), and Gayā, three major pilgrimage places along the Ganges river that are together referred to as "Tristhalī." These three places form the subject matter of a voluminous sixteenth-century Sanskrit pilgrimage manual called the *Tristhalīsetu* (Salomon 1985), and they are the joint goals of a pilgrimage that is generally performed each winter (Kulkarṇī 1972:1).

South India has one set of five Śivaliṅgas, located in Tamil Nadu and Andhra Pradesh, in which each *liṅga* represents one of the five elements (Ramesan 1969:70),[21] and another set of five Śivaliṅgas, confined to four districts of Andhra Pradesh, in which each *liṅga* is understood to be part of an original one that was broken up (Ramesan 1969:114). Fred Clothey (1972; 1978:116–17) discusses yet another such South Indian set, the holy places of the god Murukaṉ in Tamil Nadu. Clothey makes this set's cosmological function abundantly clear (1972:87):

> The six sites, like the god's six faces[,] connote the totality of divinity. They suggest that divinity in its fullness has been enshrined in Tamil Nadu, and that Tamil Nadu has become the sacred domain of the god. But the number six takes on other significance as well. Six also is used to symbolize the fullness of the cosmos. The god himself, by virtue of his being six in one, is homologized in myth and speculation with the cosmos, which is also depicted as being six-in-one. Thus, the world's six directions—North, South, East, West, up, and down—are said to be encompassed by the god's six faces. The five elements plus the whole are pervaded by the god's presence . . . .
>
> The fact that there are six pilgrimage centers in Tamil Nadu seems to suggest then, at least for some Murukaṉ devotees, no less than that the region in which the six centers are set is sacralized and cosmicized. Tamil Nadu becomes a microcosm with six *cakras*, even as the human frame is a microcosm in the symbol-system of yoga and the temple is a microcosm in the symbol-system associated with temple ritual.

The Deccan Plateau is home in whole or in part to several sets of holy places analogous to the six places of Murukaṉ in Tamil Nadu and to the Saptapurī, the 12 Jyotirliṅgas, the 51 Śakti Pīṭhs, and the four Dhāms in India as a whole. One such set is made up of pilgrimage places that lie along the Nallamalai hills in Andhra Pradesh: the hills are seen as an embodiment (or resting place) of the cosmic serpent Śeṣa, with Śrīśailam as his tail, Ahobalam as his curving body, and Tirupatī as his head, the seven hills around Tirupatī forming his seven hoods (Ramesan 1969:29, 58; Bhaṇḍārī 1992:57). Overlapping Andhra, Karnataka, and three other states is the set of five Vīraśaiva *pīṭhs* or *maṭhs*, the five most important religious centers for the sect: according to Padoux (1987:12), these are Kedārnāth, Śrīśailam, Balehalli, Ujjain, and Vārāṇasī.[22] And, finally, a set of four major places of the god Dattātreya (Datta) brings together three places in Maharashtra with one in North India under the rubric of the god's daily routine. According to a Marathi verse recited by the Brāhmaṇ proprietor of an eating place in Māhūr,[23] Datta has his morning bath at Prayāg (at the confluence of the Ganges and Yamunā rivers, the place now called Allāhabād), performs his morning religious observances (*anuṣṭhān*) at Pāñcāleśvar (on the Godāvarī river), begs for his food at midday in Kolhāpūr, and rests from noon to sunset on the mountain called Datta Śikhar at Māhūr.[24]

In addition to sets like the four places of Dattātreya, which overlap the Marathi-language area and some other area or areas, there are also numbered sets of pilgrimage places found within the boundaries of what is now Maharashtra. The next sections of this chapter will examine three such sets: a set consisting of the four (more precisely, three-and-a-half) principal goddesses of Maharashtra; a set of eight temples of Gaṇeś (or Gaṇapati), the elephant-headed god; and a set of 11 temples of Māruti or Hanumān, the monkey god. In each case, I will argue, the main thing that holds the set together is the number that appears in its name. Despite the abstractness of this kind of link, it serves in each case to demarcate a coherent region that is conceptual as well as circulatory.

The Three-and-a-Half Śakti Pīṭhs

India's 108 (or 51) Śakti Pīṭhs include a set of four places in Maharashtra. Though people identify four places as belonging to the set, they invariably call the set the "three-and-a-half" Śakti Pīṭhs of Maharashtra. The four places most often named as belonging to this set are Māhūr, Tuḷjāpūr, Kolhāpūr, and Saptaśṛṅgī (map 4.2).[25] Māhūr is a hilly, heavily forested pilgrimage center in Kinvaṭ Taluka, Nanded District; the goddess there is Reṇukā. Tuḷjāpūr, a Tālukā headquarters town in Usmanabad District, is home to the goddess Bhavānī. The goddess of Kolhāpūr, the capital of the southernmost district on the Deś of Maharashtra, is named Ambābāī or Mahālakṣmī. And the goddess of Saptaśṛṅgī or Saptaśṛṅga Gaḍ, a mountain in Diṇḍorī Taluka, north of Nāsik, is named for her mountain: she is called Saptaśṛṅganivāsinī ("She Who Resides on the Seven-Peaked Mountain") or, more often, simply Saptaśṛṅgī ("She of the Seven-Peaked Mountain").

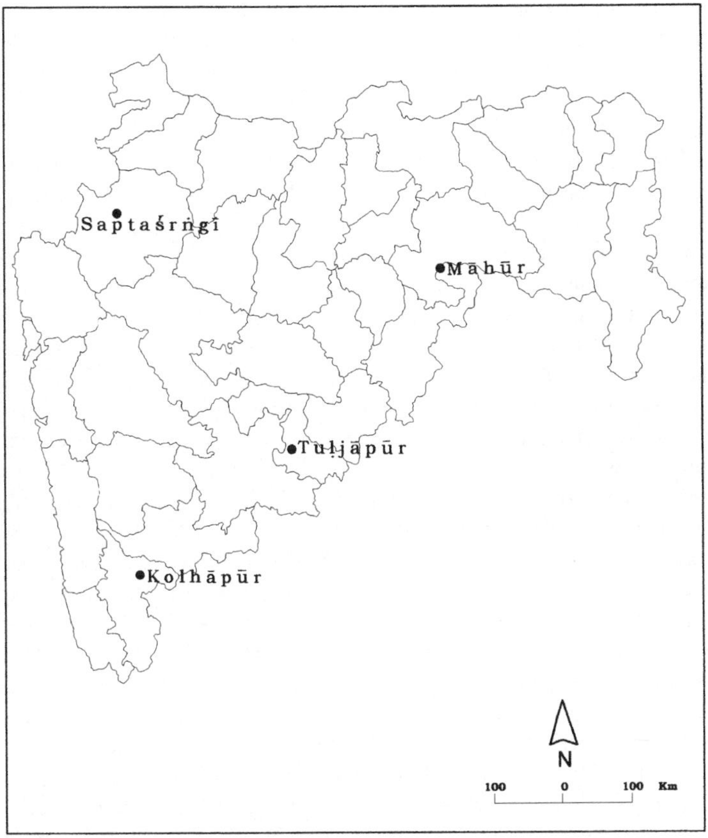

Map 4.2 The three-and-a-half Śakti Pīṭhs

As a subset of the 51 or 108 Śakti Pīṭhs, the four goddesses are connected with the story of Śiva's wife Satī. Individually, however, their identities are tied more closely to those of other goddesses with other stories. Saptaśṛṅgī is Mahiṣāsuramardinī, the goddess who slew the Buffalo Demon, Mahiṣa; she came to the seven-peaked mountain to rest after the exertion of killing Mahiṣa and other demons.[26] Bhavānī of Tuḷjāpūr, sometimes called (as we have seen) Tukāī, is also a demon-killing goddess. Whereas the main image in her temple portrays her as Mahiṣāsuramardinī (Cendavaṇkar 1964a:20), a story that explains an etymology of the place-name Tuḷjāpūr tells of her killing a different demon, Kukūr (Cendavaṇkar 1964a:12–14). Her more important connections are with Rām, whom she blessed[27] and who gave her the name Tukāī,[28] and with the seventeenth-century Marāṭhā warrior-king Śivājī (Jansen 1995:99–133). The goddess of Kolhāpūr is yet another demon-killing goddess, with the demon Kolāsur or Kolhāsur her principal victim (Desāī 1969:68). But she is also—at least, according to one tradition[29]—Lakṣmī, the wife of Viṣṇu, come to Kolhāpūr after a tiff with her husband, who himself went to Veṅkaṭagiri at Tirupatī in southern Andhra Pradesh.[30] The goddess of Māhūr, Reṇukā, also known as Ekvīrā and Yellammā, was the wife of the irascible sage Jamadagni. Jamadagni commanded their son Paraśurām to cut off Reṇukā's head, and then, at Paraśurām's request, brought her back to life. Later, Paraśurām came to Māhūr to perform his parents' funeral rites under the tutelage of Dattātreya, who was already established at Māhūr and who still has a temple there on a hill near Reṇukā's.

The number of these goddess places, three-and-a-half, may seem strange in most languages; it is fairly common, however, in Marathi. Marathi has a single word for three-and-a-half, *auṭ*,[31] which people of at least the older generations know (it is one of the numbers whose multiplication table elementary-school students used to memorize), and which occurs as the number not only of the three-and-a-half Śakti Pīṭhs but also of other sets: types of musical instruments (Haṇamante 1964:54), auspicious times of the year,[32] the mores (*mātrās*) in the syllable *oṃ* (Dāte et al. 1932–1938:499), the "wise men" (*śahāṇe*, a term generally used with at least a little irony) of the Peśvā period (Haṇamante 1964:54), and so on.[33] As the number of the set of goddess places, three-and-a-half also serves to rank the places among themselves, with Saptaśṛṅgī most often the inferior, half, place.[34]

People refer to the four goddesses together as "the three-and-a-half goddesses," or even as Maharashtra's "three-and-a-half Śakti Pīṭhs," without making much explicit mention of the story of Satī. Kolhāpūr, which may be the oldest of the four places,[35] is the only one of them that seems to be assigned a specific role in the story of the dismembering of Satī and the distribution of the parts of her body:[36] according to the Sanskrit textual sources and oral traditions about the Śakti Pīṭhs,[37] it was in Kolhāpūr, as we have seen, that the goddess's three eyes fell to earth. No one seems especially concerned to discover what parts of Satī's body fell in the other three places in Maharashtra.

Those attempting to systematize the relationships among the goddesses tend to relate them, rather, to other well-known sets of entities or beings. Mahādevśāstrī Jośī (1951, Volume 2, p. 20), for example, writing about Mahālakṣmī of Kolhāpūr, connects three of the four principal Maharashtrian goddesses with the three *guṇa*s ("qualities" or "strands" of nature: *tama*s [darkness], *raja*s [passion], and *sattva* [purity]) of Sāṃkhya philosophy and with the wives of the three principal Purāṇic gods, Brahmā, Viṣṇu, and

Śiva. Jośī also connects two of the Maharashtrian goddesses with goddesses in North India:[38]

> Of the three-and-a-half *pīṭhs* of the Mother of the World, Kolhāpūr is known as the principal *pīṭh*. The one single, primordial Śakti displays herself according to the distinctions of the *guṇas*. Mahākālī, characterized by the *guṇa tamas*, stays in Calcutta and, in the south, on the Māhūr hill-fort (Māhūrgaḍ). Mahāsarasvatī, characterized by the *guṇa rajas*, has selected the Himālaya mountains in the north[39] and Tuḷjāpūr in the south. And Mahālakṣmī, "pre-eminently characterized by *sattva* (*sattvāgaḷī*)," has settled in Kolhāpūr.

Although Jośī mentions that there are three-and-a-half Śakti Pīṭhs, the correspondences he presents in this passage are to sets (of *guṇas* and goddesses) with three, rather than three-and-a-half, members. As a result, his systematic listing ignores the fourth Maharashtrian goddess. In a book about that fourth, "half" goddess, Saptaśṛṅgī, the one who is presumably inferior to the others, Nerkar manages not only to include her in a scheme of correspondences similar to Jośī's, but to do so by claiming that far from being inferior to the other three goddesses, she includes and is thus superior to them.[40]

Despite such esoteric systems of correlations between the Maharashtrian goddesses and other important sets, and despite the organic unity implied by the story of the parts of Satī's body being scattered across the landscape of India, the trope that most often connects the Maharashtrian goddesses, and therefore also their places, is no elaborate imagery but rather simply their *number*, three-and-a-half. Individually, the goddesses are most often referred to in terms of their places—Bhavānī *of* Tuḷjāpūr, Mahālakṣmī *of* Kolhāpūr, Reṇukā *of* Māhūr, and Saptaśṛṅgī, the goddess of the seven-peaked mountain. Indeed, the names of the places frequently serve as substitutes for the names of the goddesses. Marathi speakers say "the goddess of Tuḷjāpūr," or "the [feminine] one of Kolhāpūr," or even quite simply "Māhūr" quite normally to refer to the goddesses of these places, and Saptaśṛṅgī's name *is* that of her place. The locations of the goddesses are of basic importance to their individual identities, as the number three-and-a-half is to their collective identity.

The three-and-a-half Maharashtrian goddesses stand near the borders of, and thereby serve to demarcate, the Marathi region very much the way the four Dhāms do India as a whole. Rather than being located in the four cardinal directions, however, as the four Dhāms are in relation to India, the four Maharashtrian goddess places form a triangle, with Saptaśṛṅgī in the northwest and Kolhāpūr, Tuḷjāpūr, and Māhūr ranged in that order from southwest to northeast along Maharashtra's southern border. It is tempting to see these latter three as boundary guardians, especially because they stand along the southern side of Maharashtra, where there is no obvious physical-geographical separation between Maharashtra to the north and Karnataka and Andhra Pradesh to the south.[41] The early Mahānubhāv literature provides some evidence that Kolhāpūr and Māhūr may have served some such border-guarding function in the thirteenth century, but the evidence is not conclusive.[42]

In any case, whether or not all or any of the three-and-a-half goddess places have ever served to demarcate the borders of Maharashtra, the fact that the places are seen as being three-and-a-half out of a total of 108 (or 51) Śakti Pīṭhs *does* assert a relationship between Maharashtra and the rest of India. The number three-and-a-half—the one constant link among the places—also relates them, and hence Maharashtra as well, to the total list of Śakti Pīṭhs, and thus to India as a whole. This assertion, that Maharashtra is 3-1/2 108ths—or even 3-1/2 51sts—of India, is relatively modest in comparison to some of the claims to be examined in chapter 5 of this book. Nevertheless, the assertion demarcates Maharashtra as a distinctive *portion* of the implied organic whole of India.

Finally, the number three-and-a-half is half of seven. As the number of a set of goddesses, it may thus also echo the many sets of seven sisters discussed at the end of chapter 3. It can at least serve to remind *us* of them and of the affective bonds that link the separate places that make up a region. And yet, when people refer to the three-and-a-half goddesses as a set, I sense that the notion of sisterhood is generally overshadowed by the simpler, more abstract number as the factor that brings the goddesses together.

The Aṣṭavināyak

The other two Maharashtrian sets of places to be discussed in this chapter are not, like the three-and-a-half goddesses, subsets of any set of places spread throughout all of India. Neither do these two sets cover as broad an area as the three-and-a-half goddesses; each set is, rather, confined to a few neighboring districts in western Maharashtra. The region that each of these two sets defines is therefore relatively tightly focused, and in each case it corresponds with an important political order or movement in the history of Maharashtra. The two sets are, first, the eight places known as the Aṣṭavināyak and, second, an analogous set called the Eleven Mārutis. In these cases too, as with the three-and-a-half goddesses, the number, though usually unexplained, proves basic to the deities' identity as a set.

The Aṣṭavināyak is a set of eight temples all located within 100 kilometers of Pune and dedicated to Gaṇapati or Gaṇeś, the son of Śiva who is also called Vināyak.[43] "*Aṣṭa*" is a Sanskrit word for "eight." The eight

Map 4.3 The Aṣṭavināyak

Vināyak places are arrayed in an irregular circle around the city of Pune (map 4.3). Most of them are found in Pune District, but two lie on the eastern edge of Raygad District and one on the western edge of Ahmadnagar District. The two in Raygad District are Pālī and Mahaḍ (or Maḍh). Pālī is located west of Pune, and Mahaḍ west-northwest of Pune; both lie on the western side of the Western Ghats, at the eastern edge of the

Koṅkaṇ coastal area. Leṇyādri and Ojhar are found to the north-northwest and north of Pune, respectively, in Junnar Taluka of Pune District. Rāñjaṇgāv (Śirūr Taluka, Pune District) lies directly northeast of Pune, on the road to Ahmadnagar. Theūr (Havelī Taluka, Pune District) and Siddhaṭek (Karjat Taluka, Ahmadnagar District) are both located to the east of Pune, Siddhaṭek beyond Theūr. Finally, Morgāv, in Bārāmatī Taluka, Pune District, is east-southeast of Pune.

How old the eight places are is not clear, nor is it clear when they were brought together as a set. All eight appear to have been preexisting holy places that became prominent in the seventeenth and eighteenth centuries. One of the places, Leṇyādri, is apparently quite old as a place, although probably not as a Gaṇeś temple: the present temple is in what was clearly one of a group of Buddhist caves (Govaṇḍe 1995:55) and is therefore approximately 1,900 years old as a carved-out building (L. Preston 1980:108). Aside from this temple at Leṇyādri, only one of the Aṣṭavināyak temples appears to predate the seventeenth century. This is the temple at Rāñjaṇgāv, where in the nineteenth century some remains of a "Hemāḍpantī" temple (one, i.e., built in the massive, mortarless style associated with the thirteenth-century Yādava minister Hemādri or Hemāḍpant) could still be found.[44]

A number of the Aṣṭavināyak places, particularly Morgāv, were connected with the seventeenth-century Deśastha Brāhmaṇ holy man Morobā Gosāvī (1610–1659) of Ciñcvaḍ. Ciñcvaḍ was a village (and is now an industrial suburb) near Pune on the Bombay–Pune Road. Until the line died out in 1809, Morobā Gosāvī and six generations of his descendants were considered incarnations of Gaṇeś and were therefore called "Dev" ("God"). Morobā Gosāvī, and later the Devs, regularly traveled on pilgrimage to Morgāv from Ciñcvaḍ, and the family played an important role in the finances and administration of several of the Aṣṭavināyak temples, even building some of them. Other rulers, including the prodigious temple-builder Ahilyābāī Hoḷkar of Indore,[45] built and endowed other Aṣṭavināyak temples. The Citpāvan Brāhmaṇ Peśvās, who ruled from Pune in the eighteenth and early nineteenth centuries, visited, built, donated land or cash to, and/or made additions to temples at several of the places, especially Morgāv and Theūr. The Peśvās had particular devotion for Gaṇeś, and they supported the festival celebrating his birthday (L. Preston 1980:119) that the nationalist leader B. G. Tilak later transformed (in 1893) into a public Hindu alternative to the widely celebrated Muslim festival of Muharram.[46]

The Aṣṭavināyak temples and the (primarily urban) Gaṇapati festival notwithstanding, and outside the small (but, of course, influential) and primarily urban world of Citpāvan Brāhmaṇs, Gaṇeś is not a particularly important family, village, or pilgrimage god.[47] Gaṇeś does not arouse the deep-seated folk piety found in the cults of goddesses or Khaṇḍobā (Gaṇeś does not, e.g., generally possess people or respond to *navas* vows[48]) or the fervent *bhakti* devotion addressed in Maharashtra primarily to Viṭhobā. Gaṇeś is, however, ubiquitous, even in the countryside, as a doorway guardian of Brāhmaṇ and middle-class houses. In addition, people invoke him when they start to perform a major agricultural task, as well as at the beginnings of Brāhmaṇical and modern rituals such as the increasingly popular Satyanārāyaṇ Pūjā.

The contemporary popularity of the Aṣṭavināyak sites and their pilgrimage is in large part a product of modern means of transportation and communication. A priest at one of the Aṣṭavināyak temples told me that the numbers of pilgrims who visit the Aṣṭavināyak places have grown greatly in recent decades, after a popular Marathi film called "Aṣṭavināyak" showed the good things that happened to its hero after he made the pilgrimage, and the bad things that happened when he failed to keep a promise to do so.

Today pilgrimage to the eight temples is most popular in the form of a middle-class outing from Pune. Many pilgrims to the Aṣṭavināyak temples travel to the eight places in private jeeps, cars, and buses. In addition to (and in competition with) private bus companies, the State Transport bus system also provides regular service to the whole set of places, covering the eight of them in two day-long trips from Pune. There is no particular pilgrimage festival, such as those examined in other chapters of this book, during which people travel *en masse* to the Aṣṭavināyak temples.[49] Thus, pilgrims can make the trip on weekends, during school holidays, and at other times convenient to an urban way of life. Crowds tend to be greater, though, during the winter and autumn Gaṇapati festivals: that is, around the fourth day of the bright half of the month of Māgh (January–February) and for ten days during the bright half of the month of Bhādrapad (September–October). There is no particular order in which one should visit the places, except that—according to priests at Morgāv, at least—it is best to start with Morgāv.[50]

In fact, it is not particularly clear what coherence the Aṣṭavināyak temples do have as a set. Each place's Gaṇapati has a different name,[51] and each place has its own story, telling about Gaṇeś's interactions with kings, gods, and/or demons.[52] Although some of the same characters appear in them, these stories, for the most part, do not seem to be coordinated with one another.[53] Nor is there an overall, systematized division of narrative motifs, a scheme of the sort found among the "six" places of Murukaṉ in Tamil Nadu (Clothey 1972), according to which the god is born in one place, kills a demon in another, marries his wife in a third, and so on.

In other respects as well, the Aṣṭavināyak temples are not particularly unified or systematically related to one another. Not all the temples, as we have seen, were built at the same time or by the same person, and they continue to be added onto and improved in an apparently uncoordinated fashion. All of the places have Brāhmaṇ priests, but some of the places also have Gurav priests,[54] and the Brāhmaṇ priests are not, as far as I know, related to one another in any formal, organized way.[55] The temples face different directions: most of them face toward the east, but not all of them do.[56] Nor do they all face toward a common center. Some, but not all, of the Gaṇeś images in the temples are "self-formed" (*svayambhū*), uncarved rocks. In one of the temple images, that at Siddhaṭek, Gaṇeś's trunk curls to his right; in the others the trunk turns to the more normal, left side. One of the temples is difficult to get to—one approaches Leṇyādri up a steep hill, by climbing 283 steps (Govaṇḍe 1995:49)—but the others are on relatively level ground. The temple at Mahaḍ especially attracts infertile couples hoping for the birth of a son (Govaṇḍe 1995:63), but the rest of the temples do not have any special attraction for such people; the temple at Pālī is generally reputed to be effective at answering petitions expressed in the form of *navas* vows (Govaṇḍe 1995:75–76), but the rest of the temples do not have this reputation.

What is it, then, that brings the Aṣṭavināyak together?

In part, it is the fact that all the places are dedicated to the same god: the one known as Gaṇeś, Gaṇapati, or Vināyak, the name that appears in their joint title "Aṣṭavināyak." But there must be hundreds of thousands, if not millions, of temples and shrines to Gaṇeś in India. Why have *these* eight been chosen to belong to the set? A further factor that brings together these particular temples is the fact that they are all located within a reasonably accessible distance of Pune. But, here too, within the area covered by the Aṣṭavināyak there must be hundreds of temples and shrines to Gaṇeś. So what is it that brings these temples together?

The answer is surprisingly simple. What brings the temples together is the number eight. Along with Gaṇeś's name Vināyak, the number eight, *aṣṭa*, also appears in their name. The number eight is what defines the set of temples. It makes the set finite, bounded, and therefore specific. And, to the extent that the numbered set is finite, bounded, and specific, the area throughout which it extends is a coherent region. In Preston's words (1989:16), "In many ways the astavinayak help to define the regional identity of Pune." The Pune region, that is, is the region within which the circumscribed set of Aṣṭavināyak temples is located.

But, if it is important only that the set of temples be finite, bounded, and specific in number, why should their number be exactly eight? With so many Gaṇeś temples and shrines within this region, the number of temples could easily have been nine, or 12, or 108. Why, then, are the places the *Aṣṭa*vināyak, and therefore eight in number? It is tempting to relate the places to the cardinal and intermediate directions, and to think of the Aṣṭavināyak as directional guardians of Pune.[57] It is certainly not unheard of for Gaṇeś to be such a guardian. The village of Lāsūr (Gāṅgāpūr Taluka, Aurangabad District), for example, forms a mandala, with the goddess Dākṣāyaṇī's temple in the middle and four Gaṇapati temples on the edges, one on each of the village's four boundaries. Vārāṇasi has seven concentric circles of eight Gaṇeś shrines each, with each of the shrines located in one of the cardinal or intermediate directions in relation to a central Gaṇeś called Dhundirāj (Eck 1982:187). Gaṇeś's frequent position as a doorway guardian—placed above, rather than to the side of, a doorway—makes the idea of the Aṣṭavināyak as directional guardians more plausible, as does the Sanskritic motif of the *dig-gajas*, the elephants in the eight corners of the sky (Sircar 1971a:331). However, as map 4.3 shows, the Aṣṭavināyak places form only a very rough circle around Pune. None of the places is located in the southern quadrant, and the places in the other three quadrants are by no means equidistant either from Pune or from one another.[58]

Because the eight places, unevenly spaced though they may be, are mostly[59] located on a perimeter surrounding Pune, it is also tempting to consider them as forming a *pradakṣiṇā* route, a route for performing the auspicious circumambulation of the city. *Pradakṣiṇā* is the "clockwise" movement around a holy person or object in which one honors it by keeping one's right (*dakṣiṇ*) side toward it. Such circumambulation is found in the case of many other holy places, and it would certainly be reasonable to look for it here. It would be especially appropriate in relation to Ciñcvaḍ. This place, which is now best known as an industrial suburb of Pune, was in the seventeenth and eighteenth centuries the seat of Morobā Gosāvī and the Devs who incarnated Gaṇeś.

However, I have not heard of anyone using—or advising pilgrims to use—the Aṣṭavināyak to perform a *pradakṣiṇā* of either Pune or Ciñcvaḍ. Indeed, people I know who have "done" the Aṣṭavināyak have followed whatever route seemed to them most convenient, and at least one of the readily available Marathi pilgrimage pamphlets about the Aṣṭavināyak (Govaṇḍe 1995:vi) seems to advise this as well. The author of the pamphlet begins by explaining that a well-known Sanskrit verse lists the Aṣṭavināyak places in a certain order: (1) Morgāv, (2) Siddhaṭek, (3) Pālī, (4) Mahaḍ, (5) Theūr, (6) Leṇyādrī, (7) Ojhar, and (8) Rāñjaṇgāv. Following this order would have the pilgrim travel from the east-southeast of Pune to the far east, to the west, back to the east, then to the north, and finally to the northeast—not a *pradakṣiṇā*, and not, more importantly to the pamphlet's author, a convenient or efficient route. As he explains, "because, if one follows the above order, the trip will take one back and forth a lot, in this book we have used another order, chosen from the point of view of the pilgrims' convenience. If one follows this route, the pilgrimage will be satisfying, and one will be able to take more time in each Gaṇapati temple for *darśan* of Gaṇeś."

The alternative order that the pamphlet follows—Morgāv, Theūr, Siddhaṭek, Rāñjaṇgāv, Ojhar, Leṇyādri, Pālī, and Mahaḍ—starts with the four temples to the east (and east-southeast and northeast) of Pune, then proceeds to those to the north, and finally arrives at those to the west (and west-northwest). This order has the pilgrim travel in a roughly counterclockwise direction, making the pilgrimage almost the exact opposite of an auspicious circumambulation of Pune. In fact, most pilgrims, rather than circumambulating Pune in *either* direction, travel repeatedly out from and back in to Pune. In informing prospective pilgrims of the rail and bus routes (and, in some cases, schedules) they can use to make the journey to each of the places, the pamphlet generally advises its readers to start from Pune. By public transportation, at least, and also to some extent in private vehicles, it is usually[60] easier to return to Pune than to cut across to the next of the Aṣṭavināyak temples on one's itinerary.

In either case, whether one follows the order in the Sanskrit verse or an order that better fits one's own convenience and the available public transportation routes, the pilgrim ends up crisscrossing the area within which the Aṣṭavināyak places are found. This is one of the ways in which the Aṣṭavināyak places serve to make this area a region. From Morobā Gosāvī's seventeenth-century travels between Ciñcvaḍ and Morgāv to the weekend outings of contemporary day-trippers, the feet and wheels of pilgrims have moved back and forth across the Pune region, connecting the Aṣṭavināyak places and bringing them together as a set. In recent decades, the Maharashtra Tourism Development Corporation, the State Transport bus system, and numerous private bus companies have facilitated and accelerated the process, turning the area around Pune into a circulatory region defined, in one respect, by travel to the Aṣṭavināyak places.

But it is not only, and not even primarily, through the mechanism of pilgrimage that the Aṣṭavināyak contribute to the formation of their region. Many more people in the Pune region are aware of the Aṣṭavināyak than have ever been to any of the places. Even most of those who have gone on pilgrimage to one or more of the Aṣṭavināyak temples have not, or not yet, managed to travel to all of them. Nevertheless, the existence of the Aṣṭavināyak as a numbered set makes possible a sense of their area as a region. Even without *traveling* to all of them, residents of this region can *think* of the eight of them as a unit by saying the name "Aṣṭavināyak" or by looking at the combined holy picture that is multiplied many times over on

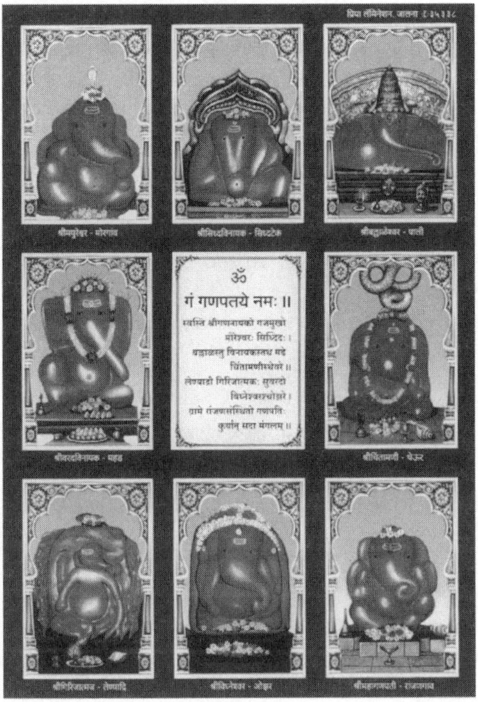

Figure 4.1 A typical Aṣṭavināyak picture.

living room walls, on refrigerator doors, and in household shrines throughout the region (figure 4.1).

This holy picture (called a "*phoṭo*" in Marathi) occurs in a number of variants, most of which schematize the set of eight places to fit a rectangular frame. The picture is generally divided into nine rectangular blocks, with the middle block reserved for the legend or for a standard, nonlocalized image of Gaṇeś. The eight blocks that form the edges of the rectangle contain more-or-less stylized but clearly differentiated depictions of the actual Gaṇeś images in the Aṣṭavināyak places, with the name of the place and the name given to Gaṇeś in that place generally printed under each image, toward the bottom of its block. The images are not arranged to correspond to the relative locations of the places—nor do they seem to be arranged according to any particular principle at all.[61] In fact, the Gaṇeś images have different positions in different versions of the holy picture.

The Aṣṭavināyak "photo," then, is not a map, not even a stylized map, of the Aṣṭavināyak places or their region. The picture does, however, represent the Aṣṭavināyak as a group, and it therefore also represents as a whole the region throughout which the Aṣṭavināyak are distributed. It serves as a reminder, to family members and to visitors in the many households in which it is displayed, of where they are and what that "where" includes. It fosters in people of the Pune region, whether they have visited the Aṣṭavināyak or only heard of them, an awareness of how their world holds together. And, when the many people who place the Aṣṭavināyak image in or near their household shrines perform *pūjā* to the image, they worship the whole set of Gaṇapatis at once. To the extent that the Aṣṭavināyak represent the region in which they are found, such people's *pūjā* of the Aṣṭavināyak image also, at the same time, pays homage to the region.

The Eleven Mārutis

Analogous to the Aṣṭavināyak but not nearly as popular is a set of places called the Akrā Māruti. The Akrā Māruti are eleven (*akrā*) temples of the monkey-god, Māruti, also known as Hanumān, the servant and companion of the epic hero Rām. Māruti is quite important in the everyday religious life of most Maharashtrians,[62] not so much because of his part in the Rāmāyaṇa story[63] as because of his role as a protector of villages. In theory, at least, people say, a temple of Māruti holds a central place in "every" village in Maharashtra.[64] However, Māruti's temples are generally of purely local importance, and his significance in such contexts is to local communities as *wholes*. Māruti does not generally serve as a family god (*kuladevatā*), nor are his temples ones to which people generally travel on pilgrimage. The 11 places of the Akrā Māruti constitute an important exception to this rule.[65] A set of shrines and temples intentionally established by a particular historical figure, they are presently being promoted as pilgrimage places analogous to the Aṣṭavināyak.

The Akrā Māruti places cluster in Satara, Sangli, and Kolhapur Districts (map 4.4). Seven of these Mārutis are found in the northern part of Karāḍ Taluka, in Satara District: two in the village of Cāphaḷ; a third on a hill just outside Cāphaḷ; a fourth at Mājgāv, only a mile and a half from Cāphaḷ; and a fifth at Umbraj, less than ten miles east of Cāphaḷ on the national highway that leads from Mumbai to Bangalore (and, in more local terms, from Sātārā to Karāḍ). The sixth and seventh Mārutis are found at Masūr and nearby Śahāpūr, about ten miles east of the highway and a bit south of Umbraj. Another two of the Eleven Mārutis, Bahe (or Bāhe, or Bahe-Borgāv) and Śirāḷā, lie in the western end of Sangli District, Bahe on an island in the Kṛṣṇā river about 22 kilometers northeast of Peṭh (a place on the national highway near Islāmpūr), and Śirāḷā about 15 kilometers

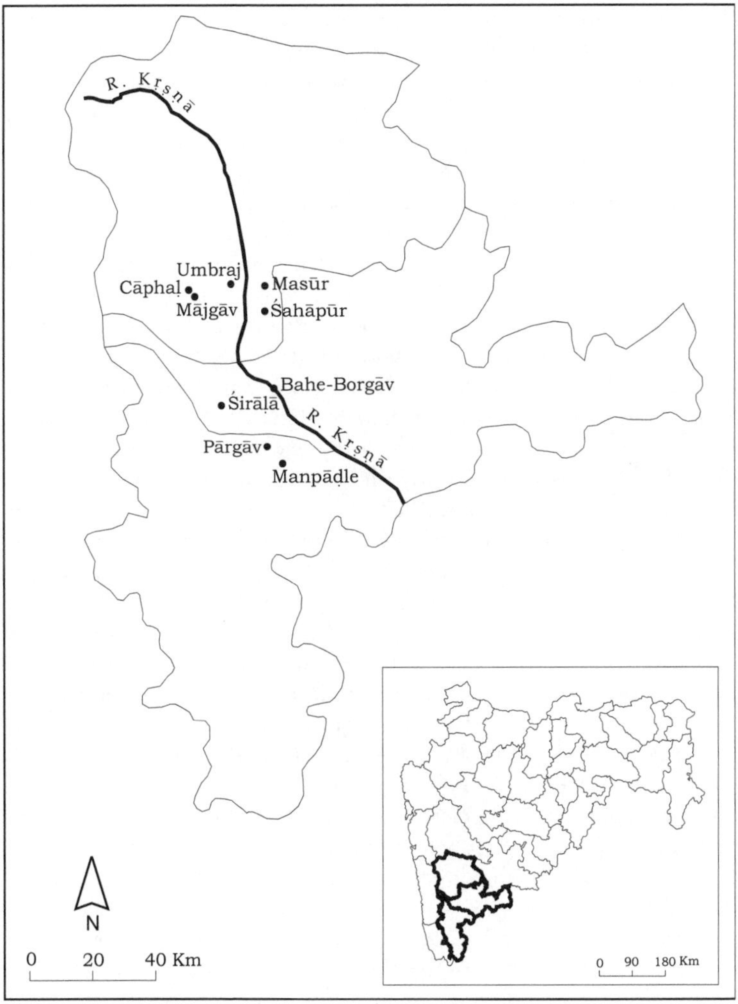

Map 4.4 The Eleven Mārutis

southwest of Peṭh. Finally, the two southernmost Mārutis of the set are located in the northern part of Kolhapur District: one in Pārgāv, at the edge of the district, and the other five miles south, in Manpāḍle.

The Akrā Māruti are supposed to have been founded by Rāmdās (1608–1681), the strong, ascetic, Brāhmaṇ guru figure associated in popular historiography with the Marāṭhā ruler and military leader Śivājī.

Rāmdās is understood to have established all 11 places within a single decade in the mid-seventeenth century, beginning with Śahāpūr in 1644 and ending with Śirāḷā in 1654. Each of the Mārutis is associated with an episode in Rāmdās's life; he is said to have lived in or visited each of the places and to have had some particular reason for establishing each Māruti. Harṣe (1983:46) speculates that proximity to the major pilgrimage temple of Jyotibā (at Vāḍī Ratnāgiri, near Kolhāpūr) may be what led Rāmdās to install the Māruti at Manpāḍle, and that proximity to the strategically important fort of Panhāḷā may be what led him to install the Māruti at Pārgāv (Harṣe 1983:47). Cāphaḷ, the site of two of the Mārutis in the set, is a place where Rāmdās lived for some time; Rām and Māruti are said to have appeared in his dreams and told him to establish their temples there (Harṣe 1983:38). While he lived at Cāphaḷ, Rāmdās used to walk to Śiṅgaṇvāḍī, on a nearby hill, to meditate (Harṣe 1983:40). He also used to go to Umbraj to bathe in the Kṛṣṇā river there, and he received some land at Umbraj as an *inām*-grant before he established the Māruti temple and later a monastery there (Harṣe 1983:41).

Some of the Mārutis were installed because of specific disciples of Rāmdās. One of these disciples, Mahādjī Sābājī Deśpāṇḍe, came from Śirāḷā, and it was at his insistence that Rāmdās established the Māruti there. Rāmdās installed the Māruti in the Brahmapurī part of the village of Masūr because a family of his disciples named Kuḷkarṇī lived in that neighborhood (Harṣe 1983:36), and he established the Māruti at Śahāpūr for the benefit of a newly converted woman disciple there, Satībāī Kuḷkarṇī (Harṣe 1983:34–36). Finally, two of the Akrā Mārutī places are directly connected with Rāmdās's most prominent disciple, Śivājī: Rāmdās and Śivājī are supposed to have met under a tree at Śiṅgaṇvāḍī, and they are also said to have met for "secret political consultations"[66] at Pārgāv. Pictures of Śivājī and Rāmdās are displayed prominently, either together or separately, at the Akrā Māruti temples.

The most elaborate story about any of the Eleven Mārutis, however, the one told about the Māruti at Bahe, an island in the Kṛṣṇā river near Borgāv, does not involve Śivājī or any other particular disciple of Rāmdās. The story has two main episodes. One of the episodes is set in the time when Rām, Sītā, Lakṣmaṇ, and Māruti were wandering around in the Deccan (see the introduction), and the other episode is set in the seventeenth century, in the lifetime of Rāmdās.[67] The first of the episodes is as follows:

> When Rām and Lakṣmaṇ were returning with Sītā after having killed Rāvaṇ, they stayed in the village of Bahe. They left Mother Sītā in the village and came to bathe in the Kṛṣṇā river. Śrī Rāmcandra took his bath and

established a Śivaliṅga there. As he was engrossed in doing *pūjā* of that Śivaliṅga, the Kṛṣṇā swelled with delight and began suddenly to flood. Lord Māruti stood behind Śrī Rāmcandra, blocked the Kṛṣṇā's current with both arms, and said to the Kṛṣṇā, "Flow on both sides." Because Māruti had blocked the Kṛṣṇā, an island was formed there and a deep pool of water was created as well. The two branches of the Kṛṣṇā that were formed because of Māruti's arms (*bāhū*) went on downstream and came together again. In this way, Māruti removed the potential obstacle to Lord Rāmcandra's concentration. Because the river flowed in streams on both sides, this place came to be called Bahe (Bāhe) [from *bāhū*, plural *bāhe* = arm].

Much later, when Rāmdās visited this place, he jumped into a deep pool of water in which people told him Māruti was staying. After staying in the water for several hours, Rāmdās brought Māruti out briefly. The image he installed in Bahe was modeled on the form of Māruti that had been in the water hole.

As this story shows for the Māruti at Bahe, the Akrā Māruti appear generally not to have been preexisting village or pilgrimage Mārutis that were taken over to be included in the set of 11 places. Most of the 11 seem, rather, to have been newly, intentionally installed. The clearest exception to this is the Māruti at Mājgāv. About this one, Harṣe (1983:43) tells the following story:

People say that, at the edge of this village, there was a huge boulder shaped something like a horse. People would worship this boulder as the village guardian Māruti. Once, when Samartha had gone to this village, the villagers showed him the boulder and entreated him, "Please re-install this Māruti with your holy hands." Seeing this faith of the villagers, Samartha carved an image of Māruti on the boulder, and in Śake 1571 (A.D. 1649) he installed the Māruti in a festive manner and built a temple there too.

Not very different from village Mārutis in the surrounding area, the Akrā Māruti images nevertheless are for the most part recognizable as related to one another. All are reliefs, and most of them resemble one another in style. None, however, is identical to any of the others. The Māruti that faces the temple of Rām at Cāphaḷ stands with his hands (or, rather, paws) folded together and his neck bent in an attitude of obeisance typical of the pose called "Dās Māruti" (i.e., "Māruti as a servant"); all the others show Māruti in one or another warrior pose: in a "Vīr" ("heroic") or "Pratāp" ("valorous") form, most often crushing a demon under his left foot. With the exception of the Mārutis at Mājgāv and Pārgav, which are carved stones, the images of the Akrā Māruti are reliefs formed of sand, lime, clay, mud, hemp fiber, cow dung, or other malleable materials.

The Māruti at Pārgāv is considerably smaller than the others. One story explaining this fact (Harṣe 1983:47) tells that Rāmdās made the images of all 11 of the Akrā Māruti in one night. Day began to break before he was finished, and so he made the last image, the one at Pārgāv, smaller than the others. A painting at Pārgāv, one of several large murals on the inner walls of the recently renovated Māruti temple there (figure 4.2),[68] portrays Rāmdās founding the Akrā Māruti; the small Māruti image from Pārgāv rests in Rāmdās's begging bag.

Although each of these stories links one of the Eleven Mārutis to Rāmdās, none of them explains why Rāmdās would establish a *set* of temples in different places. Nor do the stories, taken individually or together, explain why the images he established would be of Māruti or why there would be exactly 11 of them. According to a Marathi religious pamphlet about the Eleven Mārutis (Kālgāvkar 1973:4), Rāmdās established them in order to "awaken" (*jāgṛtī karaṇeṃ*) the area in which they are found—that is,

Figure 4.2 Mural of Rāmdās and the Eleven Mārutis, Pārgāv. In the begging bag hanging from Rāmdās's shoulder is the Māruti from Pārgāv.

in order to lend religious legitimation to the Marāṭhā kingdom and religious enthusiasm to the Marāṭhā armies' opposition to Muslim rule. Whatever the historical accuracy of this claim for the seventeenth century, it is at the very least clear that the seventeenth-century region exists for the twentieth-century author of this pamphlet.[69] Others go into more detail. Gokhale (1973:141), relying in part on another biographer of Rāmdās, explains the political-geographical significance of the Akrā Māruti in the seventeenth century as having to do with the fact that they were established "in the lion's den of the power of the Ādilśāhī," the Sultanate of Bijāpūr:

> [T]he names of the famous Eleven Mārutis were useful for the politics of that time, and so they became especially important when independence was being established. After Hirojī Pharjand had taken Panhāḷā Fort, King Śivājī went to Pārgāv from Rāygaḍ. At the same time, Rāmdās went there from Polādpūr for secret consultations about politics. The village of Masūr was a very important place between the territory of Vijāpūr [Bijāpūr] and Śivājī's land grant in the Pune region. The Māruti places Śahāpūr, Masūr, Cāphaḷ . . ., Mājgāv, Umbraj, and Śiṅgaṇvāḍī were under the Ādilśāhī center of power at Karāḍ; the Māruti places at Śirāḷā and Bahe-Borgāv were closely connected with the Ādilśāhī center at Miraj; and the Māruti places at Pārgāv and Manpāḍle watched over Ādilśāhī policies[70] at the Vāraṇā river and Panhāḷā fort.

As Harṣe (1983:26–28) points out, all 11 of the Akrā Māruti places lie in the valley of the Kṛṣṇā river. This region is the one that Rām and Māruti instructed Rāmdās to "save": appearing to Rāmdās while he was practicing asceticism, Rām and Māruti commanded him, "Save the world on the banks of the Kṛṣṇā!"

In addition to the 11 members of the Akrā Māruti set, Rāmdās established several other Mārutis—at Mahābaḷeśvar, Ṭākḷī, and other places (Gokhale 1973:141). Thus, 11 is by no means the total number of Mārutis that people understand Rāmdās to have set up. Moreover, none of the stories I have examined lay any particular stress on the exact number of Mārutis that Rāmdās *intended* to install. So where did the number 11 come from? A likely source is a set of 11 gods called the 11 Rudras. Māruti is sometimes seen as an incarnation of Rudra,[71] the Vedic form of Śiva. This connection may explain why it seemed appropriate—whether to Rāmdās himself or to some of his more influential followers—for the total number of Mārutis in the set to be 11. However, if this was the basis for choosing the number 11, no one I have talked with has said so to me, nor have I found this written in any of the books and pamphlets I have examined.

Still, even if the connection of Māruti with Rudra does explain the number of the Akrā Māruti places, it does not explain why Māruti is the god that Rāmdās installed in them. Why would he choose Māruti as the god whose images to establish? Here the answer may lie in the values that Māruti exemplified for Rāmdās. These are values in which, not coincidentally, Rāmdās closely resembled the object of his devotion.

Māruti and Rāmdās are similar in several significant ways. Rāmdās, as his name implies, was a "servant" (*dās*), or devotee, of Rām. Māruti was also Rām's servant; indeed, this is Māruti's principal role in the *Rāmāyaṇa* story. That story portrays him as celibate and as completely dedicated to the service of Rām. Rāmdās too, like Māruti, was celibate. His celibacy did not imply world renunciation, but kept him involved and active in the world. Just as Māruti is renowned for his strength, Rāmdās is portrayed as tall and strong, with a muscular body and huge thighs (figure 4.2).

In some cases, the relationship between Rāmdās and Māruti even seems to go beyond similarity, beyond devotion, to suggest a more fundamental identity. The image of Pratāp Māruti at Śahāpūr, for instance, has a moustache—because, it is said, his face resembles that of Rāmdās. An episode in Rāmdās's life that is set in Śahāpūr builds on this resemblance to assert that Rāmdās and Māruti are one. When a woman devotee who would not eat until she had had her daily sight of Rāmdās finally found him at Śahāpūr after she had gone several days without a meal, he asked her to sit down with her back toward him. She did so. She turned around, however, before he told her to, and saw not Rāmdās but in his place a brilliant (*tejasvī*) image of Māruti.[72] Elsewhere Harṣe (1983:21) states the point of this story quite baldly: "People understand Lord Samartha Rāmdās to be an incarnation of Hanumān."

As a god of strength, Māruti is particularly appropriate to inspire a heroic, politically mobilized, even militaristic attitude. This, at any rate, is the motivation that modern interpreters ascribe to Rāmdās in founding the Akrā Māruti. Harṣe (1983:26) explains as follows:

> Because Śrī Rām and Hanumān had appeared to him while he was practicing asceticism and had commanded him, "Save the world on the banks of the Kṛṣṇā," . . . he decided that he would use his powerful voice, his knowledge, his experience, and the yogic powers he had achieved to turn the Hindu people's minds to devotion to Rām and to get them out of their miserable condition . . .. At the same time, he also decided to teach people to worship the strength of Māruti, the most excellent servant of Rām who delivers his message. Realizing that in order to do this it was necessary to bring the people together and to awaken them, he wandered from village to village in Maharashtra and established Māruti in numerous places. By getting people to worship Māruti, he created among them resolve, virility, and competition with respect to gaining strength.

The editor of the Rāmdāsī magazine *Sajjangaḍ* is even more explicit (Ciñcolkar 1995:7):

> As he wandered around India, Samartha Rāmdās had a chance to see the disastrously weak and fragmented state of Hindu society. His principal intention was to make Hindu society integrated and strong by establishing, in place after place, temples of Māruti, who is the embodiment of integration and strengthening . . .. For Hindus to become a nation, Rāmdās felt, it was necessary that they become strong. And so most of the Mārutis that he established are in the heroic (*vīr*) form or the valorous (*pratāp*) form.

This late-twentieth-century author, then, ascribes to seventeenth-century Rāmdās motivations characteristic of twentieth-century Indian and Hindu nationalism.

Today, with the possible exceptions of the Mārutis at Bahe and Cāphaḷ, most of the Eleven Māruti places are relatively obscure. The temples are generally simple and unpretentious, and in some cases they are also quite run-down.[73] In my own visits to the Eleven Mārutis, I found no evidence that any but those at Cāphaḷ and Bahe attract pilgrims in significant numbers. Those pilgrims who do visit all 11 of the Akrā Māruti, it seems, are for the most part followers of the Rāmdāsī sect (Gokhale 1973:141), which is relatively restricted in numbers. However, the Brāhmaṇ ascetic saint Rāmdās seems to be achieving increasing prominence as a model and patron of middle-class, Brāhmaṇ-led, politicized Hinduism of the style associated with the Bharatiya Janata Party (BJP). He is becoming, more and more clearly, the patron saint of that party in Maharashtra, as his disciple Śivājī has become the patron saint of the Shiv Sena (the right-wing political party that has taken Śivājī's name). In these circumstances, it is quite possible that the obscure, neglected set of Akrā Māruti places will achieve greater prominence and popularity both as pilgrimage sites and as a collective image of a regional (or even national) Hindu community. Indeed, this seems to be the hope of those who write and publish pamphlets like the ones I have quoted here.

Already in the late 1990s, when I visited the Eleven Māruti places, my companions and I noticed Marathi signs printed in bright orange (the politicized Hindu color, as opposed to the more subtle burnt ochre of less politicized religious places). A Brāhmaṇ from Nāsik, we were told, had arranged to have these signs installed at each of the places. The signs do not mention either Māruti or Rāmdās. They focus, rather, on the god of whom both Māruti and Rāmdās are servant-devotees: the royal god Rām. Rām's recent prominence in India is related to the popularity of the television

"Rāmāyaṇa" series and to the tension and violence associated with the mosque that stood until 1992 on the alleged site of his birthplace in Ayodhyā. The signs at the Eleven Māruti places extol the virtues of the mantra "Śrīrām, Jayrām, Jayjayrām" ("Lord Rām; victory to Rām; victory, victory to Rām"), and announce that it will be recited 330 million times during the traditional four-month period of prayer and asceticism (Cāturmās) each year.

In the foreword to his book on the Akrā Māruti, Harṣe (1983:5) expresses hope that the pilgrimage to this set of gods will become as popular as that to the Aṣṭavināyak:

> The pilgrimage to the Aṣṭavināyak has certainly become quite popular. In the same way, I hope, the pilgrimage to the eleven Mārutīs established by Samartha will also become popular. I also hope that this book will make some contribution to that goal.

With the rise in the popularity of Rāmdās, it may well be that Harṣe's "hope" will be fulfilled.

Thus, even when the device that connects otherwise separated places is not the emotionally powerful bond of married sisterhood or the organic image of body parts strewn across a landscape, but rather just a number, the numbering of the places makes them collectively a region. In this case, too, the places are distinct from one another and are spread throughout an area, but now it is the number that provides the mental hook that brings them together. The act of counting the places together, of listing them as distinct members of a single set with a joint name—"*three-and-a-half* Śakti Pīṭhs," "*eight* Vināyaks," "*eleven* Mārutis," or the others—gives a particular coherence to the area within which the set of places is found. It makes of that area a region.

Chapter 5

The Algebra of Place: Replication of North Indian Religious Geography in Maharashtra

Up to this point, we have been examining Maharashtrians' religious-geographical imagination primarily in terms of their articulations and conceptualizations of regions within which they themselves live and move. This accords with the understanding of a region as an area throughout which people are aware that they (or their gods or ritual objects) either actually move or can move. The present chapter and part of chapter 6 draw attention to another kind of religious-geographical phenomenon and point to another element of a definition of a region. In order to have a sense of a particular region in which one lives and throughout which one moves, one must also have a sense of some other region from which one's own region differs. The other element of a sense of region, then, besides the awareness of one's ability to move around in it, is an awareness that the region one finds oneself in contrasts with another, similar region over against which it stands. In the words of Edward Casey (1993:53), the philosopher I have quoted in the introduction and in chapter 1, experiencing oneself as being in a particular region requires that one be "convinced that . . . some other more or less comparably extensive region stands opposed to my current here-region: *another* neighborhood, *another* state, over there and in relation to which I am now truly here, on *this* side (*diesseits*) of whatever boundary or difference demarcates the two regions in question."

The sense of difference between one region and another is not necessarily a matter of clear and definite boundaries.[1] However, a sense of being in a place or region does require a sense of some other place or region where one is not. In South Asia, the importance of boundaries is a modern phenomenon, one that became salient only in the colonial and postindependence periods (Embree 1977). Despite this fact, there is clear evidence that people in premodern India made distinctions between one region and another. For example, the early-twelfth-century legal compendium *Mitākṣarā* addresses as follows the question of what constitutes a "different country" (Kane 1973:285): "Where there is a large river or there is a mountain that separates (one territory from another) or where the languages differ then there is a different country (*deśāntara*). Some say that a different country means the distance of sixty *yojanas*, while others put it down at forty *yojanas* and still others at thirty *yojanas*."[2] In chapter 6, we will see how the thirteenth-century founder of the Mahānubhāv sect is understood to have differentiated Maharashtra from other lands, in particular from lands to its south.

The present chapter will approach this question of difference in another way. Here I will analyze a kind of rhetoric that Maharashtrians and others in the Deccan use to assert that their holy places and rivers are related to holy places and rivers in other parts of India, especially the North.[3] Whether by replicating those other places, by containing them, or by being physically connected with them, many Maharashtrian and other Deccan holy places acquire a good deal of their sanctity from their relationships with distant places widely acknowledged to be holy. As we will see, the vast majority of distant places in terms of which people glorify Maharashtrian ones are located in North India. The implicit meaning of Maharashtrians' repeated assertions of their places' close relationships with North Indian ones, I will argue, is an admission of Maharashtra's distance from—and felt inferiority to—the North.

Inherently paradoxical, the religious rhetoric that the present chapter investigates is quite normal—indeed, almost commonplace—in Maharashtra, and it is found in other parts of India as well. The rhetoric to be be examined here can be implicit or explicit; it is found in stories, images, analogies, and direct statements; it occurs in Māhātmyas and other texts, in paintings and three-dimensional images, and in oral traditions. I will first present at some length a catalog of the forms that this rhetoric can take. Then I will analyze what this kind of rhetoric can tell us about the regional consciousness of people who use it.[4]

Replication

One of the most common rhetorical techniques for glorifying holy places in Maharashtra is to claim that they are replicas of holy places located somewhere else. In the religious-geographical discourse of Maharashtrians, people or texts frequently express the greatness of a place in relation to some other, named place or places. The relationship can take any one of a wide variety of forms. If we call the place being praised X, and the place in terms of which the praise is expressed Y, the claim is sometimes simply that

X *is* Y.

For example, according to the *Payoṣṇī Māhātmya*, each holy place (*tīrtha*) along the Pūrṇā river *is* Kurukṣetra, the holy area near Delhi that was the site of the *Mahābhārata* war, and each confluence along the river *is* Prayāg, the site of the confluence of the Gaṅgā and Yamunā rivers at modern Allāhabād (*PM* 41.16–17).

More frequently, some particular way is specified in which the Maharashtrian place replicates or resembles the other place. For many a local temple (X), it is claimed that

X is another Y.

There is "another" temple of the goddess Saptaśṛṅgī (one of the famous three-and-a-half goddesses discussed in chapter 4) near the Godāvarī river at Nāsik, for example, for the convenience of those who want to worship the goddess but cannot make it all the way to her major temple 40 kilometers to the north.[5] In the village of Hivare, west of Sāsvaḍ, there is "another" Tryambakeśvar. A priest at this temple explained its name on the basis of a purely local phenomenon, the fact that there are three (*tri*, as in *tri-ambakeśvar*) Śivaliṅgas here. However, he also attested that in the "olden days" people in Hivare used to describe their temple as an exact replica of the Tryambakeśvar at the source of the Godāvarī, down to such minor details as the trays used for waving small oil lamps in front of the god.

Sometimes people affirm a particular modality of replication that relates the Maharashtrian place to the distant one. That

X is an *upa*-Y

(i.e., a subsidiary Y), for example, is the claim that Gaṇeś Sadāśivśāstrī Lele makes in identifying Maharashtrian replicas of the Jyotirliṅgas. Lele states that a Śivaliṅga in the middle of the Kṛṣṇā river at Bayāborgāṃv[6] is an *upaliṅga* (a subsidiary *liṅga*) of Rāmeśvaram in the far south of India (1885:157), that the god Jyotibā on a mountain near Kolhāpūr is an *upaliṅga* of Kedārnāth in the Himālayas (1885:158), and that Siddheśvar, at the confluence of the Pravarā and the Godāvarī, is an *upaliṅga* of Tryambakeśvar (1885:128). In another variation, with Prayāg perhaps as the place most often replicated, the claim is that

X is the invisible Y.

The basis of such a claim, when made to assert that a place replicates Prayāg, is the idea that the Sarasvatī river, which loses itself in the underworld when it disappears in the northwestern desert, is present in invisible or hidden (*gupta*) form as a third river that joins the Gaṅgā and the Yamunā as they flow into each other at Prayāg. Already invisible at this, the principal spot where it emerges from the underworld, the Sarasvatī "appears"—invisibly—at numerous other, less famous confluences throughout South Asia.

Sometimes a claim that a place X replicates a place Y takes a relativistic form. Adherents of X might assert, for instance, that X is the Y in some particular time or place, or for some particular group of people. The *Kṛṣṇā Māhātmya* makes a claim of this sort when it states that the confluence of the Kṛṣṇā and the Veṇṇā is the equivalent of Prayāg in the Kali Yuga.[7] Priests of the Gaṇeś at Morgāv, the most important of the Aṣṭavināyak temples discussed in chapter 4, point to a similarly relativistic kind of replication. They draw an extended analogy between Morgāv and two nearby places, on the one hand, and famous north Indian pilgrimage places, on the other. Morgāv is Kāśī (Vārāṇasī, Banaras), they told me, for devotees of Gaṇeś. Those same devotees have two Gayās: Pāṇḍeśvar, a place that lies downstream from Morgāv on the Karhā river as Gayā lies downstream from Kāśī on the Gaṅgā; and Theūr, another of the Aṣṭavināyak places, which is located on the bank of the nearby Muḷā-Muṭhā river. Pāṇḍeśvar, the priests explained, is the devotees' Pitṛgayā, the place where they make memorial riceball (*piṇḍa*) offerings for their father (*pitṛ*), while Theūr is their Mātṛgayā, the place where they make *piṇḍa* offerings for their mother (*mātṛ*).

The most common claim of this relativistic sort, at least in the Deccan Plateau,[8] takes the form

X is the southern (*dakṣiṇ*) Y.

Many places in the Deccan are called Southern Kāśī (that is, Vārāṇasī or Banaras): Alampūr, on the Kṛṣṇā in Andhra Pradesh; Dhom, on the Kṛṣṇā near Wāī; Karāḍ; Kolhāpūr; Nandikeśvar, east of Badāmī; Nevāse; Paiṭhaṇ; and Wāī,[9] to name but a few. Nāsik is called not only Southern Kāśī[10] but also sometimes Western Kāśī (Jośī 1950:10). A Brāhmaṇ funerary priest at Nānded pointed out to my companions and me that his town is the Southern Kāśī for Sikhs, whose tenth guru, Govind Singh, is buried there. Lele (1885:159) calls Narsobācī Vāḍī the Kurukṣetra of the south, and Phaḍke (1931:164–65), making a much more complicated point, not only refers to Kolhāpūr as Southern Kāśī, but also calls the confluence west of Kolhāpūr (where the Pañcagaṅgā river is formed) Southern Prayāg.[11]

Most people identifying a place X as the southern Y do not take "southern" to mean "of the underworld," as Phaḍke does, but neither do they always simply mean that place X lies geographically to the south of place Y.

When a river—most frequently the Godāvarī, but also sometimes the Kṛṣṇā[12]—is called the southern Gaṅgā, people often explain this to mean that the river flows *toward* the south, rather than that it is located *to* the south of the northern, Bhāgīrathī Gaṅgā. The Godāvarī, whose overall route takes it generally from west to east, is considered to flow southward at Paiṭhaṇ and Muṅgī, for example, and also at Nāsik. Most often the southward flow of a river seems to bring out an analogy with Kāśī, where the Ganges travels from north to south. But a Brāhmaṇ woman temple priest at Nāsik seemed to connect the Godāvarī as flowing southward there with the fact that Nāsik is considered a good place for putting the bones and ashes of a cremated corpse into the river: south is the direction of Yama, the god of death.

Short of stating that X *is* Y, there is a type of story whose point is that

X *would have been* Y, but . . .

for the fact that something occurred to prevent it from becoming Y. Typical of this sort of story is the one told to explain why Karāḍ, the town at the confluence of the Koynā and Kṛṣṇā rivers in Satara District, is *not* Kāśī. The story has to do with the goddess Reṇukā, who migrated here from the south, and whose temple lies on the outskirts of Saīdāpūr, the village across the Kṛṣṇā river from Karāḍ. In the version narrated by a Brāhmaṇ woman in Karāḍ, prompted by her husband:

> As the goddess Reṇukā was coming from the other side, her menstrual period started. After the menstrual period has started—the Kṛṣṇā river is holy (*pavitra*), isn't it? . . . So, because she shouldn't touch the water, she stayed behind on the other side of the river . . . . And if she had come here to this side, and if she and Kṛṣṇābāī[13] had met, that is, if they had lived together, . . . then Karāḍ was going to become Kāśī. Kāśī Viśveśvar.

A textual version of this kind of story is told in the *Tāpī Māhātmya*. This story explains why the Gaṅgā, or Ganges river, is more famous than the Tāpī. Repeated three times in the text,[14] the story relates that at Gaṅgā's instigation, the trouble-making sage Nārada stole the Tāpī's *māhātmya*—the Tāpī's glory, that is; or perhaps the Māhātmya text expressing that glory, the *Tāpī Māhātmya* itself.

Comparison

Less defensive than such excuse stories and less ambitious than statements of identity or equivalence are relatively simple statements that

X is *like* Y.

Phaḍke (1931:205), for instance, states that when one sees the Brāhmaṇs' morning rituals on the riverbank in Wāī,[15] "one gets the sense that one is in a religious center (*dharmapurī*) like Kāśī." Most often, statements of similarity take the form

X does what Y does

—the Godāvarī–Phenā confluence, for example, destroys sins as the confluence of the Gaṅgā and the Yamunā does—or

X has what Y has.

This latter kind of assertion is, for example, a favorite argument for calling Wāī "southern Kāśī": temples of "the" five major gods of Kāśī (Kāśī Viśveśvar, Kālbhairav, a north-facing Māruti, Bindumādhava, and Dhunḍīrāj Gaṇapati) are also found in Wāī.[16] Yet another sort of assertion of similarity takes the form

X has something analogous to what Y has.

For example, priests at Auṇḍhe, one of the Maharashtrian places that claim to belong to the all-India set of the twelve Jyotirliṅgas,[17] point out that the *piṇḍ* (*liṅga*) at the Nāganāth temple there is made of sand (*vālūcī*), like the one at Rāmeśvaram, a Jyotirliṅga whose membership in the set of 12 is undisputed. A man at the Rām temple at Kāleśvaram on the Godāvarī in Andhra Pradesh asserted that this temple has its images of Rām, Lakṣmaṇ, and Sītā positioned in the same way as these gods' images are at the more prominent Rām temple at Bhadrācalam, farther downstream. And a Koḷī at Paṇḍharpūr described the Mhasobā in a temple on the opposite bank of the Bhīmā (Candrabhāgā) river there as the Koṭvāl (the head policeman) of the god Pāṇḍuraṅg (or Viṭhobā) and of the saint Puṇḍalik of Paṇḍharpūr; in saying this, the Koḷī was making an implicit analogy to Kāśī and its Koṭvāl Kālbhairav.

Less subtly, the *Kṛṣṇā Māhātmya* states that just as there are five *liṅgas* at Kāśī composed of the five elements, there are eight *liṅga*s at the confluence of the Kṛṣṇā and Ghaṭpā (Ghaṭprabhā) rivers.[18] Since having eight *liṅga*s may be better than having five, this statement in the *Kṛṣṇā Māhātmya* may be implying not just a *similarity* between its place and Kāśī but also the *superiority* of its place to Kāśī in some respects—even though having eight *liṅga*s nullifies the parallel to the five elements. In many other cases, the claim to superiority is clearer: it is not simply that the nearby holy place has something the same as or similar to a distinctive attribute of the distant, more famous place, but rather that the nearer place is *better* than the distant place, for it has something that the distant place does not.

This kind of claim, then, takes the form,

X has something that Y does not have.

Not even Kāśī, various people have told me, has a pilgrimage festival (*jatrā*) like Vīr's,[19] a temple as large as Wāī's Kāśī Viśveśvar, a Mārjāra *kṣetra* like Mañjarath's (for expiating the sin of killing a cat), or the eight Mahādev *liṅga* shrines of the Śivāḷe tank at Ellora (Verūḷ).

More abstractly, people and texts often claim that the nearby place is simply better than the distant one:

$$X > Y.$$

The *Godāvarī Māhātmya*, for example, states variously that Kuśatarpaṇa *tīrtha* at the confluence of the Prāṇītā and the Godāvarī (*GM*.Skt. 91.77), Śukla *tīrtha* (*GM*.Mar. 21.94), Śārdūla *tīrtha* (*GM*.Skt. 58.82), and four others (*GM*.Mar. 20.94) are superior to Vārāṇasī (Banaras, Kāśī). According to the *Tāpī Māhātmya*, not even Dvārkā, Ujjain, Kāśī, or Gayā (*TM* 4.3) equals Padmakāśī on the Tāpī. The *Kṛṣṇā Māhātmya* asserts that the confluence of the Malāpahā (Malprabhā?) and the Kṛṣṇā is superior to Gaṅgā, Kurukṣetra, Gayā, and Puṣkar (*KM*.Skt. 55.49–50), and that the nearby Chāyā *kṣetra* is superior to Kurukṣetra, Prayāg, and the Naimiṣa forest.[20] A priest at Pāṇḍeśvar, the place on the Karhā river where the Pāṇḍavas performed their sacrifice (see chapter 1), said of his temple, "This temple is more excellent (*śreṣṭha*) than Kāśī." And a man at Wāī affirmed, at greater length: "Of all [the rivers] in Hindustan, in our Indian subcontinent, the Gaṅgā river, where Kāśī Viśveśvar is, in northern Hindustan, in Uttar Pradesh, the one that comes from Haridvār, that Gaṅgā river is considered the most holy (*pavitra*) of all. But the Kṛṣṇā river has even more importance (*mahattva*) than that."

Sometimes a speaker or an author *quantifies* the superiority of a local place or river to a distant, more famous place or river. Often such quantification takes the form of stating how many times better the local place or river is than the distant one: that is,

$$X = nY.$$

According to Dāsagaṇū's Marathi version of the *Godāvarī Māhātmya*, for instance, the Godāvarī is 100 times better than the (Bhāgīrathī) Gaṅgā (*GM*.Mar. 1.38); using the same factor, a Brāhmaṇ at Dharmapurī, on the Godāvarī, claimed that his town is 100 times greater than Kāśī. Others, instead of quantifying the superiority of a local place X to a distant place Y by saying how many *times* greater X is than Y, specify an *amount* of additional greatness by which X exceeds Y. In such cases, the amount by which they most often assert the local place to be greater than the distant place is a grain of barley (*jav*). That is:

X = Y+1 barleycorn.

Bhairava *tīrtha* on the Kṛsnā, for instance, is a barleycorn greater than Kāśī, according to the Sanskrit version of the *Kṛṣṇā Māḥātmya* (*KM*.Skt. 10.49); according to the Marathi version, by bathing at this *tīrtha* on the Kṛṣṇā and having *darśan* of the nearby god Kālbhairav, one gets a barleycorn's worth more merit than at Kāśī (*KM*.Mar. 10.45). The confluence of the Payosnī and the Tāpī is a barleycorn better than Kāśī (*PM* 39.56); so are Mahābaleśvar[21] and the Kadrū river (*GM*.Skt. 30.32). And performing a sprinkling ritual (*abhiṣek*) at the Payoṣṇī Mahāprācī (i.e., the Pūrṇā river) produces a barleycorn more merit than at Kāśī (*PM* 18.63).

Slightly larger than a barleycorn and two or three times as heavy is a *guñj*. This is another kind of seed that, like a barleycorn, is used as a measure. Lele (1885:170–71) reports an instance in which a *guñj* seed has been used iconographically to make an assertion of superiority. An image of Viṣṇu that Lele saw in the late nineteenth century at the Virūpākṣa (Śiva) temple at Hampi (Vijayanagara) portrays Viṣṇu resting one hand on a Śivaliṅga (presumably Virūpākṣa) and holding a *guñj* seed in his other hand; people explained the image as referring to the *Hampi Māhātmya*'s statement that the glory of this place is a *guñj*-seed greater than that of Kāśī.

Because *guñj* and barleycorn seeds are used as weights, the implicit claim of the assertions that one place is a barleycorn or a *guñj*-seed greater than another is that

X weighs more than Y.

Mandlik (1870:259) describes an image that expresses this weighing metaphor quite explicitly: "There is a temple on the banks of a small river called *Tāmraparṇā*, very near to the temple of [Gokarṇa] Mahābaleśvara dedicated to the goddess *Tāmra Gaurī*, who is represented as a human figure holding in one of her hands a pair of scales for weighing the relative sanctity of *Gokarṇa* and *Kāśī*. The scale is of course turned in favour of the former!"

Besides being heavier, another way in which a local place can be superior to a distant, more famous place is to be older. Thus, many people's claims about the superiority of a local to a distant place take the form

X is older than Y.

One example of this sort of assertion is the claim of Muṅgī, downstream and across the river from Paiṭhaṇ, to have been settled even earlier than Paiṭhaṇ: Brahmā, the creator of the world, began a sacrifice in Muṅgī, say Muṅgī's partisans, that was only later completed in Paiṭhaṇ. Also with respect to Muṅgī in relation to Paiṭhaṇ, residents of Muṅgī point out that

X's name comes before Y's.

The owner of a tea stall in Muṅgī asserted that people generally say "Muṅgī-Paiṭhaṇ" rather than "Paiṭhaṇ-Muṅgī" in referring to the two towns together, or even just to Paiṭhaṇ alone. He explained this fact by telling a story about Eknāth ("Nāth Mahārāj"), the sixteenth-century saint of Paiṭhaṇ: "Nāth Mahārāj used to live here [in Muṅgī]. People say—I don't know if it's true—that as Nāth Mahārāj was going along, some kind of ant (*muṅgī*) bit his ear and wouldn't let go. He said, 'Let me go.' It said, 'I won't let go. Give me a place before you.' So Nāth Mahārāj gave a rule: 'First your name, then my name.' As a result, it's 'first Muṅgī, then Paiṭhaṇ.'"

Perhaps the most frequent strategy that people use in praising one place in terms of another is to compare the benefits to be obtained at the one place with those to be obtained at the other. The simplest form of such a comparison asserts that

going to X = going to Y.[22]

More ambitiously, people and texts often claim that their local place or river gives *greater* benefits than a particular distant place or river—that is, that

going to X > going to Y.

A number of stories found in river Māhātmyas imply this latter sort of claim. The *Payoṣṇī Māhātmya*, for instance, includes a version of the story of the sin of brahminicide that Indra incurred when he killed the demon Vṛtra (who was not only a demon but also a Brāhmaṇ). In this version, Naimiṣa and other holy places, and Gaṅgā and other rivers, all hide when Indra approaches them with Vṛtra's skull in his hand. Only at Mocanakapāla *tīrtha* on the Pūrṇā does Indra finally get freed from his sin; the skull falls onto the riverbank there (*PM* 13.20–14.31).[23] In another story, this one in the *Tāpī Māhātmya*, five ascetics are on their way to Rām *kṣetra* on the Tāpī, *instead of* to the Naimiṣa forest, Kurukṣetra, Puṣkara, Dvārkā, Ayodhyā, Vārāṇasī, Prayāg, the Gaṅgā or (again) the Naimiṣa forest (*TM* 3.82 ff.); presumably they find the otherwise obscure Rām *kṣetra* more effective than these more famous places. And in yet another, very graphic story—again from the *Tāpī Māhātmya*—King Gajadhvaja of Vārāṇasī, who has unwittingly killed a cow, is afflicted with leprosy, and worms crawl on his body at night. He does not get freed from these ill effects at Gayā or the Naimiṣa forest, at the Gaṅgā or the Revā (Narmadā), or at any of "all great *liṅga*s," nor by spending four months at Prayāg, six months at Puṣkar, or a year in Kedārnāth. Finally, in despair, he sets off to commit suicide at Śrīśailam. En route, he comes to the Tāpī, washes his feet and face at a place there called Gupteśvar, and immediately loses the effects of his sin (*TM* 53.54–61).

Sometimes such a claim of superiority is quantified, in that going to the local place is asserted to be a particular number of *times* more beneficial than going to the distant place—a claim that in its simplest form follows the formula,

going to X = *n*(going to Y).[24]

In other cases, a text states that going to or seeing a local place is equivalent to performing some particular rite at a distant place—that is, that

going to X = doing ritual R at Y.[25]

In another variation, a text sometimes claims that going to a local place at any time is as effective as going to a distant, more famous place at some special time—that is, that

going to X = going to Y at time T—

or that going to the local place is several times as effective as going to the distant one at the special time:

going to X = *n*(going to Y at time T).[26]

Somewhat more modest than these assertions is the claim that doing some particular rite at a local place or river is as effective as simply *going to* a distant, more famous place:

doing ritual R at X = going to Y.

The story of the Brāhmaṇ Yauvanāśva in the *Bhīmā Māhātmya* illustrates this kind of claim. When Yauvanāśva's ancestors complain that they have not gotten liberation (*mokṣa*), Yauvanāśva replies that he has gone to Prayāg and to other holy places. His ancestors then say, "Child, Kāśī Vārāṇasī is not necessary. If you bathe once at Bhīmaśaṅkar, you get unlimited merit" (*BM* 41.22–23). The *Tāpī Māhātmya* makes a variant form of this claim—

doing ritual R at X = *n*(going to Y)—

when it states that bathing at Karaka *tīrtha* on the full-moon day of the month of Phālgun gives the reward of 12 pilgrimages to Kāśī (*TM* 11.20).

Claims that performing a ritual at a nearby holy place has the same result as performing the same ritual at a distant, more famous one—that is, that

doing ritual R at X = doing ritual R at Y—

assert equality between the places.[27] But sometimes the claim is the more ambitious one that performing a ritual at a nearby place or river is *more* beneficial than performing the same ritual at a distant, more famous place or river:

doing ritual R at X > doing ritual R at Y.[28]

Sometimes such claims of the greater benefits to be obtained at the local place or river are stated in relatively precise terms, with an assertion either that performing a particular ritual there produces the same merit as performing the ritual a certain number of times at the distant, more famous place, or (which is, for all practical purposes, the same thing) that performing the ritual at the local place or river produces a certain number of times as much merit as performing the ritual once at the distant place:

doing R at X = doing *n*R at Y

or

doing R at X = *n*(doing R at Y).[29]

A particular case of the two equations is the claim that

staying briefly at X = staying longer at Y;

a rather dramatic example of this kind of claim is the *Tāpī Māhātmya*'s that the reward of staying at (*sevan*) Prayāg for 12 years is obtained by being at the Tāpī's confluence with the ocean for only half a moment (*TM* 78.33).

A further set of variations is found in claims that doing one kind of ritual at a nearby place is equivalent to doing another kind at a distant, more famous place—that is, that

doing ritual R at X = doing ritual R′ at Y—

where R′ is often a ritual for which the distant place Y is famous. For instance, according to the *Tāpī Māhātmya*, by bathing at Koṭī *tīrtha* on the Tāpī, one gets the merit obtained by dying at Prayāg (*TM* 32.54), and by bathing at Kurukṣetra *tīrtha* on the Tāpī, one gets a reward equal to that of giving away a load of gold (*hema bhār*) at the northern Kurukṣetra (*TM* 55.30). Prayāg is the north Indian pilgrimage spot best known as the place to commit religious suicide,[30] and Kurukṣetra is renowned as a place for giving alms (*dāna*). There are also claims that compare the benefits of performing some particular ritual at a nearby place with going to or performing a ritual (the same one or another) at a distant, more famous place at a particularly auspicious time. Such claims can be formulated as

doing ritual R at X = going to Y at special time T,
doing ritual R at X = doing ritual R at Y at special time T,
doing ritual R at X = doing ritual R′ at Y at special time T,[31]
doing ritual R at X at time T = doing ritual R′ at Y at time T′,

and so on, or as

doing ritual R at X > doing ritual R′ at Y,

and variants of this formula. At the furthest extreme of this series of statements praising a nearby place by comparing the benefits to be obtained through it to those obtained by performing specific rituals at a distant, more famous place is a statement of the form

thinking about X = *n*(doing ritual R at Y)

or

hearing about X = *n*(doing ritual R at Y).[32]

The equations we have examined so far imply that going on pilgrimage to, performing a ritual at, or thinking about or hearing the praises of some particular local holy place or river can *substitute* for a visit to or a ritual performed at a distant, more famous one. Another formula of praise, by contrast, suggests that *both* the local place and the distant one should be visited: first the distant, famous place and then the local one. For the visit to the local place *completes* a pilgrimage to the distant, famous place:

going to X completes a pilgrimage to Y.

A Gurav priest at Gopālpūr, on the outskirts of Paṇḍharpūr, said that a pilgrimage to the four Dhāms[33] becomes complete when one comes to Gopālpūr and places one's hand on Kṛṣṇa's feet there. In a similar vein, the *Tāpī Māhātmya* boasts that to go to Kedār, in the Himālayas, without having *darśan* of Gupteśvar on the Tāpī is only half a pilgrimage (*TM* 53.15–16).[34]

Going beyond formulaic praise that can be expressed in a single equation, the comparison of places can also take the form of an elaborate set of equivalences, reminiscent of the tables of measure that children memorize in parts of the world where the metric system has not yet caught on (2 cups = 1 pint, 2 pints = 1 quart, 4 quarts = 1 gallon, and so on). I have found examples of this kind of series of equivalences in several Māhātmyas. A passage in the *Payoṣṇī Māhātmya* claims that whereas one bath in Puṣkar *tīrtha* destroys the sins of ten lifetimes, one bath at Gaṅgāsāgar (the mouth of the Bhāgīrathī Gaṅgā) destroys the sins of 100 lifetimes, and one bath at the confluence of the Gaṅgā and the Yamunā (i.e., at Prayāg) destroys the sins of 100 lifetimes of a very bad sinner, a bath at the confluence of the Tāpī and the Payoṣṇī on the fourteenth of the (dark half of the) month of Kārttik destroys Brāhmaṇ murder (*PM* 41.6–9), the very worst of sins. The *Kṛṣṇā Māhātmya* creates a more quantified table of measure to compare the merit to be obtained by bathing at various kinds of water sources: bathing in a large well or pond (Skt. *vāpī*; Mar. *vihīr*) produces 100 times as much merit as bathing in a small well (Skt. *kūpa;* Mar. *āḍ*); bathing in a lake produces 1,000 times as much; bathing in a river produces 10,000 times as much; bathing in a river that goes to the ocean[35] produces an infinite amount of merit; and bathing at the confluence of two rivers produces an inexpressible amount of merit. An inexpressible amount, it would seem, is even more than an infinite amount; it is certainly more, as the text explicitly states, than the merit of bathing and giving alms at Kāśī.

Several of the river Māhātmyas include a passage comparing the power or holiness of a number of different rivers; in each case, the river in whose Māhātmya the passage occurs comes out on top. The *Tāpī Māhātmya*, for instance: whereas the Gaṅgā purifies one when one bathes in it, the Narmadā removes one's sins when one sees it, and the Sarasvatī saves one when one drinks its water, the Tāpī purifies one just by one's thinking of it (*TM* 3.7; cf. *TM* 70.26). The *Payoṣṇī Māhātmya* claims that whereas one gets purified by going to three places where the water of the Sarasvatī is to be found, or to five places along the Yamunā, but immediately by bathing (once) in the Gaṅgā, simply the sight of the Payoṣṇī (*PM* 39.82) makes one pure.[36]

Containing Other Places

A very different rhetorical strategy from the kinds of equations and tables of measure we have examined so far involves the assertion that a holy place or river *contains* other holy places, rivers, *tīrtha*s, gods, or Śivaliṅgas. Most often the other places, rivers, and so on are nameless, and usually there is a large number of them. Frequently the number is specified. Twenty-five rivers, for example, join the Godāvarī at Soma *tīrtha* at Devgiri (*GM*.Skt. 35.20–25). There are 32 *tīrtha*s at Paiṭhaṇ (Morwanchikar 1985:58–59), 100 *tīrthaliṅgas*[37] at Pāpapranāśana *tīrtha* on the Bhīmā (*BM* 41.19), 108 *liṅga*s at Bhīmasthāna on the Bhīmā (*BM* 23.52), and 108 temples in Dharmapurī on the Godāvarī in Andhra Pradesh.[38] According to one man in Wāī, there is a total of 180 *tīrtha*s along the Kṛṣṇā; according to the *Tāpī Māhātmya*, there are 30 million *liṅga*s along the Tāpī (*TM* 5.21). The *Godāvarī Māhātmya* counts three and a half crores (35,000,000) of *tīrtha*s along the Godāvarī;[39] the *Payoṣṇī Māhātmya*, three and a half crores along the Pūrṇā (*PM* 39.3–4). There are 360 *liṅga*s at Tuḷāpūr, the site of the confluence of the Bhīmā, Bhāmā, and Indrāyaṇī rivers;[40] 29 lakhs (2,900,000) of *liṅga*s at Hanumān *tīrtha* on the Bhīmā (*BM* 33.21); 33 crores of gods at Mudgal on the Godāvarī;[41] and 60 crore, 60 thousand (600,060,000) *ghāṭ*s in the Narmadā around its source at Amarakaṇṭaka.[42]

Many of these numbers appear to be simply miscellaneous, but some of them are especially significant. These include 108 (a standard holy number), 360 (the number of days in an idealized year), and three-and-a-half (another standard number, discussed in chapter 4 in relation to the three-and-a-half principal goddesses of Maharashtra), as well as 33 crores (330,000,000, one version of the total number of Hindu gods). Eight, the number of the cardinal and intermediate directions, is another significant number; riverside places that are said to have a set of eight *tīrtha*s, called Aṣṭatīrtha (literally, "eight *tīrthas*"), include Rākṣasbhuvan and Bāsar on the Godāvarī,[43] Gāṇgāpūr on the Bhīmā,[44] and Karāḍ (Gupte 1927:6) and Wāī[45] on the Kṛṣṇā. At Śivāḷe tank at Ellora, the eight *tīrtha*s are explicitly related to the eight directions (Lele 1885:127), but when the eight *tīrtha*s are at a riverside place, they are generally strung out along one side of the river rather than forming a circle. One exception is the confluence of the Tāpī and the Pūrṇā, where gods and *tīrtha*s are arrayed in the eight directions around Brahmā *tīrtha* at the confluence.[46] Here, as at Ellora, the *tīrtha*s may be seen as directional guardians,[47] but at most of the places the configuration does not encourage this interpretation.

In most cases where there is said to be some number of *tīrtha*s, *liṅga*s, or so on at a given spot, the exact number seems not to be as important as the fact that it is large. The large number cited most frequently in these contexts is a crore (Sanskrit and Marathi *koṭi*), ten million. There are a crore of *liṅga*s both at Bhairav *tīrtha* on the Bhīmā (*BM* 33.35) and within the sacred precincts (the *kṣetramaryādā*) of Mahākuṭ in Karnataka (Lele 1885:166); there are a crore of *tīrtha*s in the vicinity of Brahmā *tīrtha* on the Bhīmā (*BM* 37.9), as well as, according to an elderly man at Narsobācī Vāḍī, along the Pañcagaṅgā river from its source in the Sahyādris to its confluence with the Kṛṣṇā at Narsobācī Vāḍī. In addition, there are a number of places called Koṭitīrtha and a number of Śiva temples whose god is called Koṭīśvar. There is also a place on the Godāvarī in Andhra Pradesh called Koṭiphalli.

People explain these names in a wide variety of ways. A Koṭitīrtha near Nāsik is said to contain one crore (ten million, a *koṭi*) of the three and a half crores of *tīrthas* that originated from the sweat that Śiva worked up in his fight with the demon Andhaka (*GBP*, Nâsik 1883:523–24). The *Payoṣṇī Māhātmya* states that other *tīrthas* bathe at a Koṭitīrtha on the Pūrṇā, but the text stops short of claiming that a crore of them bathe there (*PM* 23.55, 57). A crore of *gods* bathe at a Koṭitīrtha on the Narmadā (*NM* 7.48), and a human who bathes at this place gets the reward of a crore of *tīrthas* (*NM* 7.49). The name of the Koṭitīrtha that is one of the eight *tīrthas* at Gāṇgāpūr is also explained in two ways: first, by bathing here one gets the merit obtained by bathing at all the *tīrthas* on Jambudvīpa (i.e., in India); and, second, a single act of almsgiving performed here produces the merit of a crore of acts of almsgiving anywhere else (Pujārī 1935:11). The name of Koṭiphalli, on the Godāvarī in Andhra Pradesh, receives a similar explanation: "Kothiphali is considered by the Hindus to be a very sacred place; and the name—from *koti*, 'a crore,' and *phalam*, 'fruit'—is derived from the notion that every act of devotion performed there will be repaid ten million-fold" (Morris 1878:41).

The name Koṭīśvar (or Koṭeśvar), "Lord of Crores," with the typical Śaiva ending *-īsvar(a)*, receives an even wider range of explanations than does the name Koṭitīrtha. The *Payoṣṇī Māhātmya* states that a Koṭīśvar near Kholāpur on the Pūrṇā river is so named because the place has all seven crores of *tīrtha*s that are found on earth (*PM* 23.16). The Koṭeśvar temple a few miles below Bhīmaśaṅkar, at the place where the Bhīmā first appears as a substantial, perennial stream,[48] gets its name explained in at least two ways: according to the temple's priest, Śiva took on a crore of forms here; according to a priest at Bhīmaśaṅkar, all the gods came here to bathe. And a Koṭīśvar at Mahābaleśvar is said to be named for the demon Mahābaḷ's army, which numbered a crore of soldiers (*koṭisainya*. Udās 1891:51–52).

A Koṭeśvar that is quite prominent in Sātārā District is the one in the bed of the Kṛṣṇā river between the villages of Gove and Limb. Three different men, all Brāhmaṇs, told me a story that explains this temple's name; one of these men, from Limb, narrated the story as follows:

> In the past, when Paraśurām twice rid the earth of Kṣatriyas, he suffered extreme, heartfelt remorse that he had done such a very bad deed. So he prayed a great deal to Śaṅkar and, when Śaṅkar had become pleased with him, made this request: "Free me from this sin." And [Śaṅkar] said, "You'll become free from as much of it as the number of times you bathe in the Kṛṣṇā." So, since Paraśurām was freed from a crore of sins here, it is Koṭīśvar.

Another meaning of the name Koṭeśvar at this place depends on a pun, substituting for *koṭi*, crore, the Marathi word for "false" or "untrue," *khoṭā* (m.)/*khoṭī* (f.)/*khoṭeṃ* (n.). According to the same man, a pool (*kuṇḍ*) at this Koṭeśvar temple called Koṭeśvar's Pool is renowned as a good place to take an oath: if one wants to be sure that people will keep their word, one should bring them here to take an oath, this man explained. Thus Śiva as Koṭeśvar is also understood here as the "Lord of Lies."

One step beyond calling a place Koṭitīrtha is to call it Sarvatīrtha. The word *sarva* means "all" in both Marathi and Sanskrit; a Sarvatīrtha is a *tīrtha* that includes all other *tīrtha*s. A priest at Bhīmaśaṅkar explained the name Sarvatīrtha as follows: "'Sarvatīrtha' means that the water of all *tīrtha*s is summoned and brought together in that *tīrtha*, and it is used for *pūjā* of the god. Because of this old [idea], it is called Sarvatīrtha. In short, if one bathes in that *tīrtha*, one gets the merit of having bathed in all *tīrtha*s." A Sarvatīrtha is an example of a microcosm, a unit that contains a larger whole, an epitome of the world. The identification and elaboration of microcosms is one of the delights of traditional Indian thought. The body of a yogi contains the universe, and a temple, which also replicates the human body, is based on a mandala, a model of the universe.[49] The idea of Sarvatīrtha, the idea that one river, *tīrtha*, or *kṣetra* contains all gods or all holy places, is a religious-geographical version of the microcosm idea.

At Bhīmaśaṅkar there is a pool (*kuṇḍ*) called Sarvatīrtha; at least one place in the Kṛṣṇā river is called Sarvatīrtha (*KM* 25); and there are many more places to which the *notion* of Sarvatīrtha is applied. The *Payoṣṇī Māhātmya* claims that "goddess Payoṣṇī" is composed of all *tīrtha*s and has the form of all deities.[50] The *Kṛṣṇā Māhātmya*'s chapter on Śrīśailam states that the Kṛṣṇā combines all *tīrtha*s as Śrīśailam combines all *kṣetra*s and Mallikārjun (the name of Śiva at Śrīśailam) all gods.[51] At the confluence of the Pañcagaṅgā and the Kṛṣṇā, at Narsobācī Vāḍī, there reside not only all *tīrtha*s, but also all sages (*ṛṣi*s) and all gods (Lele 1885:159, citing *KM*). And one version of the origin story of the Karhā river (see the beginning of chapter 1) states that the waterpot that overturned to form that river contained an infinite number of *tīrtha*s brought by all the gods (Phaḍke 1931:234).

Often there is some particular time at which all *tīrtha*s and/or all rivers are held to come to and/or bathe in some one river. All *tīrtha*s and all rivers come to Śiva *tīrtha* on the Tāpī during the month of Āṣāḍh (*TM* 16.2); during that same month, all (other) rivers bathe in the Tāpī (*TM* 70.25). On the fourteenth day of the month of Āśvin (October–November), all rivers and all *tīrtha*s are present at the confluence of the Tāpī and Pūrṇā rivers (*PM* 41.23), and every day at noon, all rivers join the Candrabhāgā, the Bhīmā as it flows past Paṇḍharpūr.[52] But the most prominent example of a particular time at which all rivers or *tīrtha*s are said to be present in some one river is the Siṃhastha period, the 12-yearly 13-month period when the planet Jupiter is in the constellation Leo and all *tīrtha*s reside in the Godāvarī (*GM*.Skt. 82.38 etc.). A Sanskrit verse about the Siṃhastha expresses in an unusually elaborate image what occurs during this period (Anonymous 1920:31): "The Godāvarī's water is Śambhu [Śiva] and its rocks are Janārdana [Viṣṇu]. All its grains of sand are ascetic sages (*muni*s), and all its trees are gods."[53]

Other Physical Connections Between Holy Places

The claim that large numbers of—or even *all*—holy places, rivers, *tīrtha*s, gods, or *liṅga*s are found in a single place or river is usually expressed anonymously, without naming the multitudes that are found there. Even in this verse about the Godāvarī, which identifies the river's water as Śiva and its rocks as Viṣṇu, the more striking claim, that all the grains of sand along the river are ascetic *muni*s and all the trees on its banks are gods, does not name the *muni*s or the (other) gods. Similarly, statements specifying large numbers of *tīrtha*s that are to be found at various holy places, including the assertions implied by calling a place "Koṭitīrtha" or "Sarvatīrtha," seldom name any of the myriad, distant holy places involved. Other formulas of praise, while similarly asserting that the place or river they are praising is geographically proximate to, or in some way physically linked with, a distant place or river, *name* the other place or river. The simplest claim of this sort takes the form of an assertion that a particular distant, named holy place or river (Y) is physically present at the local place being praised (X):[54]

Y is at X.

Such are, for instance, the *Tāpī Māhātmya*'s statements that the Gautamī (Godāvarī) river is present at Rudrākṣamālikā *tīrtha* (*TM* 10.5; cf. *TM* 11.1, 46.42) and that Kāsī Viśveśvar is directly visible at Viśveśvar *tīrtha* (*TM* 54.1; cf. *TM* 53.8), both on the Tāpī.[55]

A man in Wāī whose proof that Wāī is the southern Kāśī was that Wāī has temples of "the" five major gods of Kāśī[56] connected the presence of these gods in Wāī with their having come from Kāśī for Brahmā's sacrifice at nearby Mahābaḷeśvar.[57] The gods later returned to Kāśī, the man said, but each left a bit (*aṃśa*) of himself here, or stayed here in miniature (*sūkṣma* or *bārīk*) form. Thus Wāī is not a full Kāśī, but it is Kāśī in miniature (*thoḍyā rupāne*), a bit (*aṃśa*) or particle (*kaṇ*) of Kāśī. This man's claim took the form, then,

X is a piece of Y.

Sometimes people express the importance of rivers in terms of a place *toward which* they flow. As chapter 1 has shown, there is a fairly widespread view in Maharashtra that a river that makes it all the way to the ocean is better than one that does not. People mention this idea particularly frequently in connection with the Kṛṣṇā river, and on this basis they call it a *mahānadī*, a "great river." Chapter 1 has also illustrated the extraordinary lengths to which Māhātmyas can go in order to show that their river, despite appearances to the contrary, does finally reach the ocean. But the ocean is not the only place toward which people in Maharashtra like to think of their local river as flowing. Another such place is Paṇḍharpūr. In chapter 1, I quoted some people who explained the significance of the Dauṇḍ pilgrimage festival in terms of the fact that the Bhīmā river, at which the festival occurs, flows to Paṇḍharpūr. I have on occasion heard people claim that the Karhā or the Nīrā also flows to Paṇḍharpūr. Since these rivers' waters do indeed flow into the Bhīmā and hence eventually past Paṇḍharpūr, this claim makes physical-geographical sense. More difficult to justify in physical-geographical terms is the claim made by a man carrying Godāvarī water from Paiṭhaṇ to his village:[58] the Godāvarī too, according to him, flows to Paṇḍharpūr.

Quite often people claim, especially about rivers, that

Y appears periodically at X.

The Sarasvatī river is said to appear for a day once every 60 years in one of the niches in the Pañcagaṅgā temple in Mahābaḷeśvar.[59] The Gaṅgā is held to appear at irregular intervals in a Mahādev temple at Nīrā Narasiṅgpūr—three times in October 1987, for instance, after a gap of 12 years. This phenomenon is apparently of only local fame; much more widely known—especially among Brāhmaṇs—is the appearance of the Gaṅgā approximately once every three years at Rājāpūr, in the Koṅkaṇ.[60] Here a series of pools is filled by a number of springs that sometimes gush water especially plentifully; this phenomenon, known as *gaṅgā yeṇeṃ*, the "Arrival of the Gaṅgā," has been recognized for at least a couple of centuries as an appearance of the Ganges river at this place.[61]

Probably the most famous periodic appearance of the Gaṅgā in Maharashtra is its coming to the Kṛṣṇā river once every 12 years, during Kanyāgat, the 13-month period when Jupiter is in Virgo. The Gaṅgā appears as dampness or seeping water in an otherwise-dry niche in the Pañcagaṅgā temple at Mahābaḷeśvar. The Gaṅgā also appears in Wāī, in a niche in the small temple of Rāmeśvar on the riverbank. Labeled "Gaṅgotpatti" ("source of the Gaṅgā"), this niche too is otherwise dry. A man in Wāī described the appearance of the Gaṅgā as follows:

> The Kanyāgat comes once every twelve years. During Kanyāgat, the Bhāgīrathī [Ganges] comes here to meet the Kṛṣṇā river. Now, Rāmeśvar's temple is . . . right here in Rāmḍohāḷī. In that temple of Rāmeśvar there is a kind of niche that is completely dry for twelve years. But every twelve years water begins to come from it. In the same way, at the place at Kṣetra Mahābaḷeśvar where this river has its source, there's a stream on the north side. That stream is completely dry, it is completely "dry" [the English word],

it is "completely dry" [both words in English]. But during Kanyāgat, a little trickle of water begins to flow.

Another man stressed that in the Rāmeśvar temple in Wāī, as the Gaṅgā water flows from the niche, in the wall farthest from the river, to the exit point, at the foot of the wall closest to the river, the water flows over the *piṇḍ* of Mahādev (the Śivaliṅga). This is a "self-formed" *liṅga* set in a square base a foot or a foot-and-a-half deep. Here, according to yet another man, the Ganges water appears as milk,[62] which mixes with the water of the Kṛṣṇā. An old woman from Wāī explained that on the day when the Gaṅgā is due to arrive, two piles of colored powder, one of turmeric and the other of *kuṅkūṃ*,[63] are placed before the niche in the wall of the Rāmeśvar temple; "Brāhmaṇs recite *mantras*, and when the piles get damp, that means that the Bhāgīrathī [Gaṅgā] has come. Then they stop [reciting the *mantras*], and they do *pūjā* of Mahādev."

Besides the regular miracle of the Gaṅgā's physical appearance in the Rāmeśvar temple, a man whose family owns the temple reported[64] a further marvelous phenomenon that occurred at this temple in connection with the Kanyāgat that began in 1979. His story is as follows:

In 1979, at the time of Kanyāgat, the river flooded. And . . . the temple was completely filled with water, and . . . it was filled with mud . . . . What did we do? Now, it was right before the Kanyāgat. Jupiter was about to enter Virgo, so we were going to have the festival, we needed to paint and so on. So, a couple of days ahead of time, we went to the temple to clear out the mud. I myself . . . went to see how much mud there was. And on the steps there was a cobra at least seven feet long and this thick [about six inches in diameter]. And six feet long. There was a snake that long. And he was wound around the whole temple and was sitting on Mahādev's *piṇḍ*. I saw it myself.

After seeing this I came up [out of the temple] and called people and brought them there. By that time, [the cobra] had gone and was sitting in the hole in the rock from which the Bhāgīrathī [Gaṅgā] was going to emerge.

And after that we cleared out all the mud, washed the temple, made it clean, and set up the lighting. But still the beast was in that spot. Afterwards, when it was time for the Bhāgīrathī to come, the snake went back and sat on the *piṇḍ*. All the Brāhmaṇs were doing *pūjā*; they sprinkled water ritually, they recited the Mahārudra, they placed a cupful of milk as a food offering. And the next day, at twelve o'clock at night, the snake drank the milk and left the temple of its own accord.

During Kanyāgat the Gaṅgā is present throughout the whole length of the Kṛṣṇā. Most places do not exhibit the physical indications of its presence that people at Wāī and Mahābaḷeśvar report.[65] Nonetheless, all along the Kṛṣṇā, Kanyāgat is a time for special observances and for the special celebration of regular observances. The Kṛṣṇābāī festival,[66] for instance, is especially splendid (*viśeṣ thāṭāce*) during Kanyāgat (Phaḍke 1931:205), and an intercalary month that falls in Kanyāgat is even more productive of merit than otherwise.[67] But the primary significance of Kanyāgat, people who live along the Kṛṣṇā agree, lies in the fact that it proves the importance of the Kṛṣṇā. The presence of the Gaṅgā in Maharashtra is also a convenience, of course, but most people explaining the Kanyāgat stress its implied glorification of the Kṛṣṇā. In the words of a temple priest in Sāṅglī,

> The people of our older generation used to go from here to Kāśī, three or four hundred miles away, to do religious rites (*dharmik vidhī*) at the Gaṅgā. That same Gaṅgā comes to our door to visit. That is, the importance of the Kṛṣṇā is so great that even the Gaṅgā comes to meet her, every twelve years. She doesn't go anywhere to meet anyone.

Time and again, people in Wāī and elsewhere on the Kṛṣṇā repeated that what happens at Kanyāgat is that the Ganges comes to *meet* Kṛṣṇā. Gaṅgā and Kṛṣṇā are sisters, and at Kanyāgat, Gaṅgā, who is perhaps for this reason usually said to be the younger sister, comes to meet her sister Kṛṣṇā. This is in accord with the rule of hospitality that generally inferiors should visit their superiors, juniors their seniors, and seldom the reverse. In contrast to Gaṅgā, Kṛṣṇā is so important, people say, that she never goes to meet anyone; anyone who wants to see her must come to her.[68]

No one I have talked with seems to worry about the exact mechanism or route by which the Ganges appears in the Kṛṣṇā during Kanyāgat. In other cases, though, people specify the mode of physical connection between one holy place or river and another. Sometimes—most often with respect to holy waters—the claim of a physical link between one holy place and another takes the form of an idea that

Y is connected with X by an underground passage.

The routes the *Bhīmā Māhātmya* and *Payoṣṇī Māhātmya* describe to demonstrate that their rivers do in fact empty into the ocean (see chapter 1) may be taken as illustrations of this idea, as may the numerous appearances of the underground river Sarasvatī[69] at various places in Maharashtra. The idea of an underground connection also appears to be involved in a kind of miracle story in which an object dropped into the water at a distant, famous holy place shows up at a local holy place.[70] A story of this kind is told in connection with Gomukh "cow's mouth" *tīrtha* at Tuḷjāpūr. According to Mate (1962:54), the "local tale" is that "the water flowing down from the Gomukh is Ganga herself." An ascetic named Garībnāth was skeptical about this. So he traveled on foot to North India and dropped a stick and a lemon into the Ganges river there. When he returned to Tuḷjāpūr and bathed at Gomukh *tīrtha*, the stick and lemon came out of the stone cow's mouth (the Gomukh) at the *tīrtha*.

Another kind of story that establishes a particular connection between two places is one in which the god of one place moves to another, often in order to be close to a particularly faithful devotee. In the beginning of chapter 3 we examined several stories of this type, along with pilgrimages corresponding to two of them. In the present context, we must realize that such stories also generally serve to glorify a local place by showing that the god of a distant, more famous place has migrated there: that is, that

God G has followed devotee D from Y to X.

There are many more examples of this pattern besides the ones discussed in chapter 3. If we consider only stories about the 12 Jyotirliṅgas, the story that Mahākāḷ of Ujjain came to Phalṭaṇ as Dhuḷobā because of the devotion of the Dhangar shepherd Kamaḷū Śinde (chapter 3) is matched by several other stories of Jyotirliṅgas migrating to Maharashtra. Mhaskobā of Vīr (Purandar Taluka, Pune District) was brought to Vīr by another Dhangar, Kamaḷājī. Mhaskobā is originally Kāḷbhairav of Sonārī,[71] a place that Dhangars call "Kāśī" (Sontheimer 1989:179); thus, in some sense, Mhaskobā of Vīr is the Jyotirliṅga (usually called Viśveśvar) of Kāśī. The god Someśvar at Karañje, near Nīrā, is the Jyotirliṅga Somnāth of Soraṭī, who came from Saurāṣṭra at the request of a cowherd woman who had traveled there to worship him every day for 12 years (Sontheimer 1989: 169–71). In another tradition, Śambhu Mahādev too is the Jyotirliṅga Soraṭī Somnāth, brought to Śiṅgṇāpūr by his devotee Baḷī or Baḷiyāppā (Ḍhere 1992a:17–22). Finally, the god Jyotibā of Ratnāgiri mountain near Kolhāpūr is identified with the Jyotirliṅga Kedārnāth in the Himālayas. It seems likely that about Jyotibā too there would be a story of his having been brought to Kolhāpūr by a local devotee; however, I have not yet found such a story.[72]

Other stories give different reasons for gods' migrations. The story that Mahākāḷeśvar and his wife came to the Pūrṇā river when she got bored in Avantī (Ujjain) on the Kṣiprā (*PM* 22.185–204) takes the form

God G, bored in Y, comes to X.

Better known, perhaps, is the story about Śiva as Viśveśvar having to leave Kāśī when Divodās became king there. This story takes the form

God G, expelled from Y, comes to X.

Although, in the version of the story told in connection with Kāśī, Śiva cannot be satisfied elsewhere and manages eventually to return

(Eck 1982:148–57), the version told in connection with a certain Rāmtīrtha[73] indicates that in Śiva's eyes this place equalled or even surpassed Kāśī (Lele 1885:162–63):

> There is a story in the Purāṇas about Rāmtīrtha that god Brahmā gave king Divodās numerous boons and anointed him king of the holy area (*kṣetra*) of Kāśī. Afterwards that king, by the power of his asceticism, told Viśveśvar to leave Kāśī. Because there was nothing else to do, Viśveśvar abandoned Kāśī, and he went and stayed on a mountain named Mandara. There Viśveśvar was reminded over and over again of Kāśī, and could not be content . . . .
>
> Then he commanded Nandī, "Go all over the world, and if there is a place like Kāśī, quickly find it, so that we can go and stay there." Nandī set out. After he had gotten tired out going all over the world, he saw a pleasant spot; as he rested [there], he felt that the beauty and holiness of that place were special, and he was very satisfied . . . . Nandī decided that this place gives even more joy than Kāśī. Then he went to the Mandara mountain and told Viśveśvar this news. At that, Viśveśvar came there with Pārvatī, and, seeing the beauty of that mountain peak, he was deeply satisfied.
>
> Then he said to Nandī, "Anyone who gives *piṇḍa*s at this place will get the reward of doing *śrāddha* at Gayā!" When he had said this, he stayed there under the name Viśveśvar. Afterwards all the *tīrtha*s and deities in Kāśī came and stayed at this place. The Gaṅgā river at the *kṣetra* has the place Maṇikarṇikā in it.

The last paragraph invokes the praise formula "Doing ritual R at X = doing ritual R at Y,"[74] as well as the notion that the place contains all the *tīrtha*s and deities of Kāśī, with Maṇikarṇikā receiving special mention. These are, however, merely embellishments. The basic point of the story is even more dramatic: the principal god of Kāśī actually *prefers* to reside in Rāmtīrtha.

The Maharashtrian Ganges

To conclude this survey of the kinds of rhetoric used to express the identity, equivalence, or superiority of places and rivers in Maharashtra to other, more distant, more famous rivers and places, let us look at a particular case that brings together several different formulas of praise, but that does so in a particularly complex fashion. This is the identification of the Godāvarī river of Maharashtra with the Gaṅgā, the Ganges river of North India.

The word "*gaṅgā*" occurs in modern Marathi in three distinct senses (cf. Feldhaus 1995:37, n.15). Marathi-speakers use the word, first, as a name of the Ganges or Bhāgīrathī river of North India; second, as a word meaning "river"; and third, as a name of the Godāvarī river. In context, the three meanings are generally easily distinguishable from one another. The first meaning needs no further comment, as it agrees with the usage in Sanskrit and other Indian languages. The second and third meanings, however, call for some further discussion.

In rural areas and riverside towns in Maharashtra, "*gaṅgā*" is the normal and natural word for "river" or "the river." It is apparently used more regularly than either the dictionary word for "river," *nadī*, or the name of the specific river being referred to. As various Brāhmaṇs in Wāī explained to me, no one there talks about going to the *nadī* or the Kṛṣṇā to bathe: they talk about going to the *gaṅgā*. But it is difficult to tell to what extent—either etymologically or in the intentions of individual speakers—this usage points to a connection with the Bhāgīrathī Gaṅgā.

One man in Wāī explained that the usage *is* a way to connect a local river with the Bhāgīrathī: "If you go to any holy place in India, the river there, the river in that town or area, is considered to have the nature of the Gaṅgā. When we people of Wāī go to Kṛṣṇābāī[75] to bathe, or to forget our sorrows and joys, or to be alone to think, we don't say, 'I'm going to Kṛṣṇābāī.' We say, 'I'm going to the Gaṅgā.' In Nāsik they don't say, 'I'm going to the Godāvarī.' They say, 'I'm going to the Gaṅgā.'" The Gaṅgā has a higher status than other rivers, this man explained; "for this reason, any river is given the form of the Gaṅgā." In other words, in this man's view, people use the term "Gaṅgā" metaphorically for other rivers. Other people I have spoken with hold that other rivers are substantially identical with the (northern) Gaṅgā. Such was the statement, for instance, of a Mahādev Koḷī priest in the Pañcagaṅgā ("Five Rivers") temple in Mahābaḷeśvar. With respect to the water of the five rivers that originate in this temple, seeping from the back wall and flowing together into a pool,[76] this priest explained: "All of these are nothing but the Gaṅgā. There's no question about it. What difference is there between the Gaṅgā's water and other water?"

In the case of the Karhā river, some people at least give a rather complex Sanskrit folk etymology to justify using the name "Gaṅgā" to refer to their river. The Karhā flows past Morgāv, the chief of the eight Gaṇapati temples called the Aṣṭavināyak (see chapter 4). Sāsvaḍ lies upstream on the Karhā from Morgāv, and so the river flows toward Morgāv from Sāsvaḍ. A Brāhmaṇ in Sāsvaḍ used the notion of a seed syllable (a *bīja-akṣara*, a syllable that names, and in a sense contains, a god) to explain to me why people call the Karhā "Gaṅgā": "'*gaṃ*' is the seed syllable of Gaṇapati. And, according to the definition 'a river that goes (√*gam*) toward "*gaṃ*" is the Gaṃgā [i.e., Gaṅgā],' the Karhā can also be called Gaṅgā. 'One that goes toward *gaṃ* is Gaṅgā' (*gaṃ gacchati sā gaṃgā*)."

While I am certain that such intellectual gymnastics and Sanskrit wordplay are seldom involved in the everyday use of "*gaṅgā*" to refer to a local river, it is not clear to me what intellectual processes *are* involved. It seems unlikely that the ordinary person who uses the word "*gaṅgā*" is conscious of speaking metaphorically or of asserting a substantial identity. But, if asked to reflect, how often would such a speaker come up with an explanation that the local river is identical with or analogous to the Bhāgīrathī? When a Kannada-speaking boatman at the Bhīmā in Gāṇgāpūr told me in Marathi that his family deity (*kuladevatā*) is Gaṅgā, another man explained that that means "river" (*nadī*); it is a name for the river (*nadīcem̩ nāv*). Yet another member of the group that had gathered added, "Gaṅgā is the name that has been given to it. This is the Bhīmā river." If these men were thinking of the Bhāgīrathī, they certainly did not say so.

The third meaning of "Gaṅgā" is attested from the earliest period of Marathi literature: "Gaṅgātīr," "the bank(s) of the Gaṅgā," is the regular name for the Godāvarī valley in the *Līḷācaritra* and other early Mahānubhāv texts (see chapter 6). Still today, at least in districts of Maharashtra bordering on the Godāvarī, "Gaṅgā" is the simplest and most normal way of referring to that river; we have seen this (in the introduction) in Kāḷe's discussion of his fellow villagers' use of "toward the Gaṅgā" as a term of directional orientation. The mythological basis for this terminology is a story found in the *Gautamī Māhātmya*, the Sanskrit Māhātmya of the Godāvarī that forms part of the *Brahmapurāṇa* (*GM*.Skt. 2–8). According to this story,[77] the Gaṅgā is a river in heaven. It originates in Brahmā's water pot, gets poured over Viṣṇu's foot, and falls to earth via Śiva's matted hair. *Before* the river comes to earth in the Himālayas at King Bhagīratha's request and flows from there across North India as the river called Bhāgīrathī, Jāhnavī, or Gaṅgā, it *first* comes to earth at the request of the Brāhmaṇ sage Gautama on the mountain Brahmagiri at Tryambakeśvar. From there it flows across the Deccan Plateau as the river called Godāvarī, Godā, or Gautamī.

This story makes use of a variety of forms of the rhetoric of praise that we have examined in this chapter. It asserts, to begin with, that the Godāvarī is substantially identical with the Ganges river of North India. The water that flows in the Godāvarī is of the same substance as the water that flows in the Ganges. Like the Ganges, the Godāvarī river is made up of water that originated in heaven, came from Brahmā's waterpot, was poured over Viṣṇu's feet, and fell onto Śiva's matted hair.[78] But the Godāvarī is not merely identical with the Ganges; the Godāvarī is also *superior* to the Ganges. The story shows this in two ways. First, Gautama, the person who obtained from Śiva the portion of the water on his matted hair that became the Godāvarī, was of higher caste than Bhagīratha, the person who obtained the water that became the Ganges. Whereas Gautama was a Brāhmaṇ, Bhagīratha, as a king, was a Kṣatriya. Thus, the Godāvarī is called the Brāhmaṇ Gaṅgā, while the Bhāgīrathī is called the Kṣatriya Gaṅgā.[79] Second, the Godāvarī is older than the Ganges. Gautama brought the Godāvarī to earth at Brahmagiri *before* Bhagīratha brought the Ganges to earth in the Himalayas. Hence, the Godāvarī is called Vṛddhā, or "Elder," Gaṅgā. Thus, besides expressing a formula of praise of the sort

X is Y,

and meaning this in an unusually concrete way, the *Gautamī Māhātmya*'s story of the descent of the Gaṅgā/Godāvarī also involves two other claims. These claims follow the formulas

X is the higher-caste Y

and

X is older than Y.

Despite the existence of this story in the *Gautamī Māhātmya*, it is not clear how many people who regularly refer to the Godāvarī as "Gaṅgā" know the Māhātmya's story of the descent of the river or think about it as they use the name "Gaṅgā" for their river, nor is it clear what role, if any, the story has in the history of the use of "Gaṅgā" as a name of the Godāvarī. A particularly thoughtful man from a village 18 miles from Paiṭhaṇ gave a sociolinguistic explanation of the difference between calling the river "Gaṅgā" and calling it "Godāvarī." This is the same man I referred to earlier as saying that the Godāvarī flows to Paṇḍharpūr; I met him in Paiṭhaṇ when he had come there to get Godāvarī water to carry home to his village gods. Those who say "Gaṅgā," he explained, are completely uneducated people. The river looks big, so people call it Gaṅgā, he added—suggesting that to some extent he saw the use of that name as based on an analogy to the (northern) Ganges. But then he also said—and this was the context in which he stated that the Godāvarī flows to Paṇḍharpūr—that the river has different names in different places, that it changes its name as it flows along. At Nāsik the river is called Gaṅgā; at Paiṭhaṇ, Godāvarī; and at Paṇḍharpūr, Candrabhāgā: it is all one river, but the names change.[80] Thus, if the normal use of the term "Gaṅgā" to refer to the Godāvarī or to other rivers in Maharashtra is an example of the rhetoric of praise we have been examining in this chapter, it is an example in which the rhetoric is often less than fully self-conscious.

Maharashtra's Southern Identity

Almost all the claims that we have examined here imply that a visit to the place being praised—the one called X in the formulas—can replace a visit to the place in terms of which it is praised—the Y of the formulas. As the places X are generally nearer for the people who make (and hear or read) these claims, and the places Y are farther away, substituting place X for place Y can make a pilgrim's journey much easier. Usually, however, the claim is not just that the nearby place being praised is more convenient than the more distant place in terms of which it is praised, but that it is equal or superior to the distant place.

Most often, the distant places and rivers in terms of which places and rivers in Maharashtra get praised are located in North India. In the many texts and oral statements I have examined, the distant places that serve as the measure or standard of comparison, the Y's, are sometimes other places in Maharashtra (Paiṭhaṇ, Kolhāpūr, or the Godāvarī, for instance). Very occasionally they are places that lie to the south or southeast of Maharashtra (Rāmeśvaram and Śrīśailam are two such places I have found in this role). But the predominance of North Indian places is nonetheless overwhelming.

According to a rough survey of the materials I used to study the religious meanings of rivers in Maharashtra, the Ganges (the Bhāgīrathī Gaṅgā) occurs the most often as the standard of measure in the river Māhātmyas. Kāśī, Kurukṣetra, and Prayāg are found the next most frequently in those Māhātmyas, occurring almost as often as one another. Next comes Gayā, followed by the Naimiṣa forest and Puṣkar, then Kedār, Prabhās, and the Narmadā,[81] Yamunā, and Sarasvatī rivers. In oral statements, by contrast, and in modern texts based on oral traditions, people use the Ganges, and perhaps even more Kāśī, as a standard overwhelmingly more often than they do any other place or river. Ayodhyā and the Sarasvatī river also get mentioned fairly often in this role, Gayā and Prayāg less frequently, and other places hardly at all.

Imprecise though this information about frequency is,[82] it does provide a rough idea of the relative valuation of various North Indian places and rivers in some of the oral and written traditions of Maharashtra and surrounding areas. This rough idea is suggestive. For instance, the fact that Kāśī stands so much more nearly alone as the standard measure of a holy place in the oral traditions of Maharashtra than it does in the river Māhātmyas suggests that oral statements are more likely than written ones to become stereotyped; it may also continue a historical development in which Kāśī has gradually overshadowed in renown the oldest most important places of pilgrimage—Kurukṣetra, Prayāg, Gayā, and Puṣkar (Ensink 1979:111).

More importantly for our purposes, the overwhelming predominance of North Indian places as the standard for measuring the greatness of Maharashtrian ones implies something about the way people making the comparisons view Maharashtra. It suggests that they identify Maharashtra as southern. That is, Maharashtra finds its identity at least in part through its contrast and opposition to North India. People seem to feel little if any corresponding contrast to South India.[83] For all the dozens of Southern Kāśīs and the several Southern Gaṅgās in Maharashtra, there are no Northern Madurais, Northern Tirupatīs, or Northern Kāvēris to be found.[84] Although this fact is undoubtedly related to the dominance of North Indian places in the pilgrimage traditions and sacred geography of India as a whole, it also indicates that Maharashtrians define their region in contradistinction to northern, rather than southern, India.

There is a good deal of other evidence that in the religious sphere at least, Maharashtra should be counted as southern rather than northern.[85] Maharashtra lies to the south of the Vindhya mountains and the Narmadā river, the two principal dividing lines between northern and southern India. The Maharashtrian Hindu calendar follows the southern, *amānta* system, in which months end with the no-moon day (*amā* or *amāvāsyā*), rather than the northern, *pūrṇimānta* system, in which months end with the full-moon (*pūrṇimā*) day (Freed and Freed 1964). Maharashtrian Hindus date years according to the southern, Śaka era rather than the northern, Vikram era. Many Maharashtrian Brāhmaṇs have their family gods (*kuladevatās*) in Karnataka or Andhra Pradesh. And there are substantial similarities in the religion of pastoralists across the Deccan Plateau, including the fact that the Maharashtrian god Khaṇḍobā is nearly identical with Mallaṇṇa in Andhra Pradesh and Mailār in Karnataka.[86] Thus, in highlighting the southern identity of Maharashtra, the frequent assertion that a place is the "southern Kāśī" or a river the "southern Gaṅgā" fits in with other sorts of religious evidence.

But the kind of replication we have been examining in this chapter also provides further light on the subject of the regional consciousness of the Maharashtrians who use such rhetoric. For it implies a sense of inferiority with respect to North India, and at the same time a kind of defiant pride. "Our places are just as good as theirs, or even better," say these Maharashtrians stridently—as if afraid it might not be so. The very act of making this assertion, and the repetition of the assertion in different forms with respect to various places, fosters a kind of regional consciousness and identity. This consciousness and identity are analogous to those of a group of social "inferiors"—colonial people, minorities, or women—who have bought into the value system of their "superiors." To say that a local holy place is as good as Kāśī, or even better, is to concede that Kāśī is really the best, the standard or measure by which other places are to be judged. It is like an American saying that a Chevrolet is as good as a Mercedes.

Thus, even when the ostensible claim is that the nearby place being praised is equal or superior to the distant place in terms of which it is praised, the person making the claim implicitly admits that the distant place is in fact superior. For that place is the one *in terms of which* the praise is formulated. The distant place is the measure against which the nearer place is to be tested, the truly famous place whose fame the other seeks to borrow. Thus, in employing this sort of rhetoric, in praising their places and rivers in terms of North Indian places that they replicate, resemble, exceed, contain, or are otherwise connected with, many Maharashtrians not only define their region by distinguishing it from a North Indian other; they also betray their own lack of self-assurance in relation to that other.

Chapter 6

Pilgrimage and Remembrance: Biography and Geography in the Mahānubhāv Tradition

In this chapter, we turn to the history of a particular religious movement that began in the thirteenth century C.E. and is still alive today. The movement is that of the Mahānubhāvs. The Mahānubhāvs and the Vārkarīs are Maharashtra's two principal surviving medieval *bhakti* movements. Although today the Vārkarīs are much more numerous, more popular, and better known than the Mahānubhāvs, the Mahānubhāvs are nevertheless extremely important for understanding the beginnings of regional consciousness in Maharashtra. For the Mahānubhāvs were among the first to choose Marathi as a language of literary expression, and their literature was the first to ascribe religious meaning to a whole region that they called "Maharashtra." As we will see, some Mahānubhāv authors, using the kind of rhetoric that we have examined in chapter 5, praise their holy places by connecting them with more widely known ones in northern India. However, Mahānubhāv literature also preserves a tradition that goes beyond finding correspondences with places elsewhere in India and explicitly values Maharashtra as a whole in its own right, as a place that is *better* in significant respects than other places. Ironically, the value of Maharashtra to the man who started this tradition seems to have been a rather negative one: the fact that Maharashtra is inconvenient, uncomfortable, and therefore, all in all, a good place to practice asceticism.

The Mahānubhāvs are theologically extremely exclusivistic: they recognize only one supreme God (though they hold that the one God has had multiple incarnations). The sect places a high value on asceticism, and has for most of its history remained withdrawn from the world around it.

For example, although the Mahānubhāvs created a significant portion of the earliest Marathi literature, both prose and poetry, they preserved that literature in manuscripts written in secret codes.[1] Their prose texts include hagiographies of their founder, Cakradhar;[2] his guru, Guṇḍam Rāüḷ;[3] others of the sect's five principal divine incarnations;[4] and Cakradhar's successor, Nāgdev.[5] Other important Mahānubhāv prose texts are the anthology of Cakradhar's aphorisms, the *Sūtrapāṭh* ("The Text of Aphorisms"), along with its numerous commentaries and subcommentaries, and—most important for our purposes—a text called the *Sthānpothī* ("The Book of Places") that lists, locates, and describes places where the divine incarnations, especially Cakradhar and Guṇḍam Rāüḷ, lived or visited (Kolte 1976). Mahānubhāv verse texts include a number that praise one or another of these places; as in non-Mahānubhāv literature, such a text is generally called a "*Māhātmya*" ("Glorification") or "*Varṇan*" ("Praise") of the place. The hagiographies and the *Sūtrapāṭh* date from the late thirteenth century, the *Sthānpothī* from the mid-fourteenth century, and the *Sūtrapāṭh* commentaries, the *Māhātmya*s, and the *Varṇan*s from the fourteenth through the seventeenth centuries.

In keeping with the typical *bhakti* disdain for special places, as well as with an earlier tradition of ascetic renunciation,[6] Cakradhar urged his followers not only to shun holy places but to avoid attachment to any place at all. The sect's early literature portrays Cakradhar as having prescribed for his followers a life of constant, solitary wandering. The very first aphorism of the "Ācār" ("Good Conduct") section of the *Sūtrapāṭh* (XII.1) enjoins: "Renounce your attachment to your own land; renounce your attachment to your own village; renounce especially your attachment to your relatives."[7] Rather, says another *sūtra*, "Stay in places where you know no one and no one knows you" (XII.22). Still other *sūtra*s command Cakradhar's followers to avoid important places, staying away from cities and towns (XIII.20) and places of pilgrimage (XIII.19). Two *sūtra*s (XII.25 and XIII.134) name particular pilgrimage places to avoid: Mātāpur (Māhūr), Kolhāpūr, and Puruṣottamkṣetra.[8] Instead, Cakradhar's followers are to keep to "miserable little villages" (XII.36), they are to stay "on hillsides and off the road" (XII.35), and they should sleep under a tree or in an abandoned temple outside a village (XIII.66).

The most frequently repeated of Cakradhar's commands in this connection is the command to stay "at the foot of a tree at the end of the land" (XII.26, XII.72, XIII.219; cf. XIII.43). Several *sūtra*s elaborate on this command. One specifies that the tree one stays under should not bear flowers or fruits (XIII.206); another recommends a thorn bush; and a third reminds the ascetic, whose life of wandering aims at eliminating not just attachments but habits (*savay*), "Do not get used to any one tree; do not get used to any one place" (XII.37). The point, it seems, is to be nowhere in particular—and not to be there very long.

In striking contrast to this theme of detachment from any place in particular, another of Cakradhar's *sūtra*s (XII.24) commands: "Stay in Maharashtra." The primary concern of the present chapter is to elucidate this command. I will attempt to explain what Cakradhar meant by "Maharashtra" and why he wanted his followers to stay there. I will also examine what his followers have made of the command to stay in Maharashtra: the kinds of holiness they have attributed to Maharashtra and the responses they have made to that holiness. This will lead to an investigation of Mahānubhāv pilgrimage traditions and the literature associated with them.

Cakradhar's Maharashtra

When Cakradhar commanded his followers, "Stay in Maharashtra," what did he mean by "Maharashtra"? What did his followers understand him to mean? The *Sūtrapāṭh* does not answer these questions directly, but it does give a number of clues. The *sūtra* expressing the command to stay in Maharashtra follows immediately in the text upon one that begins, "Do not go to the Kannada country or the Telugu country" (XII.23). By naming the lands to the south and southeast of Maharashtra,[9] this *sūtra* implicitly defines Maharashtra in contrast to them. The text does not mention any of Maharashtra's northern neighbors, including Gujarat. This is particularly intriguing in light of the fact that Cakradhar himself came from Gujarat. For Mahānubhāvs, Cakradhar was the supreme God, Parameśvar, who had taken over the body of the son of a royal minister (*pradhān*) in the service of a Gujar king.[10]

Mahānubhāv literature does not make very much of the fact that Cakradhar was an immigrant to Maharashtra, but it does occasionally mention his outsider status. At one point in Cakradhar's biography, the *Līḷācaritra*, someone praises his fluency in speaking Marathi,[11] implying that he was not a native speaker. Earlier, the *Līḷācaritra*'s account of the pilgrimage that brought Cakradhar to Maharashtra in the first place makes it extremely clear that there was a felt contrast between the land from which Cakradhar came and the land to which he went.[12] When Cakradhar expresses his desire to travel to Rāmṭek, near present-day Nāgpūr, his father says to him, "That's a foreign land: one shouldn't go there."[13] One edition of the text makes Cakradhar's father's objection to the pilgrimage more explicitly political, or even military, referring to a state of war between the

Gujar kingdom (in Gujarat) and that of the Yādavas (in Maharashtra).[14] Thus, the failure to mention Gujarat, at least, if not other northern neighbors, in the context of the command to stay in Maharashtra and out of the Kannada and Telugu lands does not indicate any lack of contrast between Maharashtra and its northern neighbors. It does, though, suggest once again that Maharashtra's more important connections (and thus the greater temptations for Cakradhar's followers) are to the south.[15]

By naming the lands to the south of Maharashtra for the languages spoken in them, the *sūtra* about the Kannada and Telugu lands implicitly gives a linguistic definition to Maharashtra as well. Maharashtra, that is, is the land in which Marathi is spoken and Kannada and Telugu are not. A similarly linguistic definition is implied in the commentators' interpretation of the recurring phrase "the end of the land" (*deśācā śevaṭ*). According to them, "the end of the land" is an area in which people speaking Marathi and another language intermingle.[16] The periphery is understood linguistically, as a borderland between two language regions.

Another *sūtra* of the *Sūtrapāṭh* specifies not just a linguistic region but a physical-geographical one where Cakradhar's followers are to stay. *Sūtra* XIII.83 commands: "Stay on the banks of the Gaṅgā" (*gaṅgātīrīṃ asīje*)—that is, in the valley of the Godāvarī river. What neither this nor any other *sūtra* of the *Sūtrapāṭh* makes clear is whether this command is meant to be synonymous with the command to stay in Maharashtra. Did Cakradhar and his early followers understand the Godāvarī valley as coterminous with "Maharashtra"?

Mahānubhāv literature seems generally to use the term "*gaṅgātīr*," "the banks of the Gaṅgā," to refer not to the whole length of the Godāvarī river valley but only to its upper part. If this is so, the command to stay in the Godāvarī valley would be consistent with the commands to stay in Maharashtra and out of the Telugu land, even though the Godāvarī river flows out of Maharashtra and into the area where Telugu is spoken. Did Cakradhar and his immediate followers, then, restrict the use of the name "Maharashtra" to the Marathi-language part of the Godāvarī valley? Probably not.

Sources predating Cakradhar do use "Maharashtra" to refer to a much smaller area than that encompassed by modern uses of the name. R. G. Bhandarkar (1895:2) points out that "Maharashtra" once referred only to "the country watered by the upper Godavari and that lying between that river and the Krishna," as distinguished from Aparanta (northern Koṅkaṇ), Vidarbha, and the valleys of the Tāpī and Narmadā rivers. H. Raychaudhuri (1960:36), drawing, like Bhandarkar, on sources that predate Cakradhar by several centuries, concludes:

> It is obvious that early Hindu geographers used the name Mahārāshṭra in a very restricted sense. The only region in the present Marāṭha country which

> does not seem to be expressly excluded by these authorities is the *desh* or open country behind the Ghāṭs, stretching from the Pravarā or perhaps the Junnar-Ahmadnagar hills to the neighbourhood of the Kṛishṇā.

A source more nearly contemporary to the *Sūtrapāṭh*, a mid-thirteenth-century *Kāmasūtra* commentary,[17] identifies Maharashtra as being located between the Narmadā river and "Karṇāṭa" (Karnataka)—that is, in a larger area than that indicated by either Bhandarkar's or Raychaudhuri's sources. However, not even this provides conclusive evidence as to the meaning of "Maharashtra" in the *Sūtrapāṭh*.

Commentaries on the *Sūtrapāṭh* do give answers, but their answers disagree; and, as one of the commentaries currently in print is undated and the other dates from as late as the middle of the seventeenth century, it is impossible to tell how closely they reflect the usage of the *Sūtrapāṭh* itself. The undated commentary (*AMM* 166) states in a rather offhand manner that the *sūtra* commanding Cakradhar's followers to stay in the Godāvarī valley refers to Maharashtra. This commentary is primarily concerned, at this point, to contrast the Godāvarī valley, which it calls *madhya deś* ("the middle of the land" or "the central land"), with "the end of the land" (*deśācā śevaṭ*)—the preferred location for an ascetic. In order to reconcile *sūtra* XIII.83's command to stay in the Godāvarī valley with the *Sūtrapāṭh*'s more frequent command to stay "at the end of the land," this commentary says that it is men who are to go to the end of the land, while women are to stay in the Godāvarī valley. Thus, Maharashtra would include both the Godāvarī valley and "the end of the land." In a different context, the seventeenth-century commentary *Ācārband* (Kolte 1982a:18) lists the Godāvarī valley as only one of five subregions (*khaṇḍa-maṇḍalas*) that together make up Maharashtra: (a) the Marathi-speaking region south of Phalṭaṇ; (b) the region north of that, up to Bāleghāṭ; (c) the Godāvarī valley; (d) the region [from the Godāvarī valley to?] Meghaṅkar *ghāṭ*; and (e) Varhāḍ (Vidarbha). For this commentary, too, then, even more clearly than for the other, "Maharashtra" refers to a great deal more than just the Godāvarī valley.[18]

Mahānubhāv literature more closely contemporary with the *Sūtrapāṭh* seems to indicate that the early Mahānubhāvs thought of the Godāvarī valley as a region distinct from and in some sense opposed to Vidarbha.[19] Although Cakradhar's activities were centered in the Godāvarī valley, his guru, Guṇḍam Rāūḷ, lived in Ṛddhipūr, which is located in Vidarbha (Varhāḍ), and Cakradhar's disciples went to Vidarbha to stay with Guṇḍam Rāūḷ after Cakradhar's "departure."[20] In one episode related in the Mahānubhāv hagiographies from the late thirteenth and early fourteenth centuries, Guṇḍam Rāūḷ and one of the immigrant disciples have an amusing misunderstanding because of differences between their Godāvarī-valley and

Varhāḍī dialects of Marathi. Guṇḍam Rāüḷ's petulance about his food in this episode, typical of his behavior toward his servant-devotees, illustrates his divine madness:[21]

> One day Mahādāïseṃ asked the Gosāvī, "Lord, Gosāvī, I'll give you a *dhīḍareṃ* [to eat] today. Don't go out to play, Gosāvī."
>
> The Gosāvī accepted her offer. He was delighted, and said, "Oh, drop dead! She'll give me a *dhīḍareṃ*, I tell you!" He didn't go out at all to play. "Oh," he said, "she'll give me a *dhīḍareṃ*, I tell you. I should eat it . . . I shouldn't eat it, I tell you."
>
> Then Mahādāïseṃ prepared a *dhīḍareṃ* and put it onto a plate. She prepared a seat. The Gosāvī sat in the seat, and Mahādāïseṃ offered him the *dhīḍareṃ*. She poured ghee into a metal cup.
>
> Then the Gosāvī looked at the *dhīḍareṃ*. And he said, "Hey, this isn't a *dhīḍareṃ*, I tell you. This is an *āhītā*, I tell you. Come on! Bring me a *dhīḍareṃ*! Bring me one, I tell you!" And he acted angry.
>
> "Lord," said Mahādāïseṃ, "in the Gaṅgā valley,[22] where I come from, they call it a *dhīḍareṃ*. Here in your Varhāḍ they call it an *āhītā*."
>
> "Oh, bring me a *dhīḍareṃ*," he said. "Bring me one! Bring me one, I tell you!" And he acted angry.
>
> Mahādāïseṃ began to think, and suddenly she had an idea. So she put some fine wheat flour into milk. She mixed it up. She sponged some ghee onto the earthen griddle. She poured [the batter] onto it in a phallic shape. (According to some, she poured it in the shape of a conch.) On top she sprinkled powdered cardamom, black pepper, and cloves. When one side was done, she turned it over and took it off. She put it onto his plate.
>
> It looked different to him, and he said, "This is what I want. Now it's right, I tell you. Oh, It's good, I tell you." So, delighted, Mahādāïseṃ served him more.
>
> In this way the Gosāvī accepted the meal.

In two other episodes in this same text, residents of Varhāḍ identify Guṇḍam Rāüḷ as belonging to their region, and they express their resentment of the immigrant devotees. On one occasion, when Guṇḍam Rāüḷ has destroyed the arrangements for the Navarātra festival, the residents of his town, Ṛddhipūr, hold the immigrants responsible for his misbehavior.[23] On another occasion, when the devotees are about to take Guṇḍam Rāüḷ to the Godāvarī valley (here called "Gaṅgā valley" and "Sīvana"[24]), Varhāḍī bards come to dissuade him from leaving; they prostrate themselves and say,[25] "No, Lord, our Varhāḍ deity must not go to the Sīvana country. If these people from Sīvana take you away, Lord, Varhāḍ will be orphaned. The Rāüḷ is our mother. The Rāüḷ is our father. Without the Rāüḷ, everything is desolate. We are subject to calamities and afflictions, Lord. Please turn back, Gosāvī."

Two other passages in early Mahānubhāv texts contrast Vidarbha and the Godāvarī valley in a more cryptic fashion. Several commentaries interpret *Sūtrapāṭh* XI.132, "An old woman on the banks of the Gaṅgā, and a prostitute in Varhāḍ," to mean that the people of the Godāvarī valley are stingy and those of Varhāḍ generous.[26] For an ascetic mendicant, that is, Varhāḍ is easier, but it is not necessarily better, because the ascetic's life does not aim at ease.

In *Smṛtisthaḷ*, a text from the early fourteenth (Tulpule 1979:320) or the first half of the fifteenth century (Raeside 1960:499; Feldhaus and Tulpule 1992:59), Cakradhar's successor Nāgdev makes a similar point. Taking the point of view of a woman in a virilocal society, he says, "Varhāḍ is our parental home, and the Godāvarī valley our in-laws' house."[27] Even though, as I have pointed out in chapter 3, a woman may have a lifelong sentimental attachment to the home in which she grew up, and may make many pleasant visits there, it is in her in-laws' house that she really lives her life. So too the Mahānubhāv ascetics, though they may like Vidarbha more, should spend most of their time in the Godāvarī valley.[28]

Thus, some Mahānubhāv texts suggest that the *Sūtrapāṭh*'s command to stay in the Godāvarī valley reflects a preference for this region from the point of view of the ascetic life. However, none of the texts identifies the Godāvarī valley as all of Maharashtra, and so it seems unlikely that Cakradhar's command to stay in Maharashtra was felt to be equivalent to the command to stay in the Godāvarī valley. At the time of the *Sūtrapāṭh*, "Maharashtra" probably included both the Godāvarī valley and Vidarbha, and these were seen as contrasting—indeed, as competing—parts of a larger whole. How much else this whole included is not clear.

Why Stay in Maharashtra?

Whatever Cakradhar meant by Maharashtra, why did he command his followers to stay there? And how is this command to be reconciled with the command to be in no place in particular—"at the foot of a tree at the end of the land"? One important answer is that such geographical restriction is a necessary consequence of Cakradhar's (and his successor Nāgdev's) use of and insistence on Marathi, the language of Maharashtra. *Smṛtisthaḷ* reports, for instance, that Nāgdev replied angrily to two fellow disciples who asked him a question in Sanskrit: "I don't understand your '*asmāt*' and '*kasmāt*.'[29] Śrī Cakradhar taught me in Marathi. That's what you should use to question me."[30] On another occasion, when Kesobās, the Sanskrit pandit who would eventually compile the *Sūtrapāṭh*, asked Nāgdev's permission to render one of its chapters in Sanskrit verse, Nāgdev forbade him to do so. "Don't do that," Nāgdev said. "That will deprive my old ladies."[31] Women disciples, that is, would not be able to understand the scripture if it were composed in Sanskrit. As with other medieval *bhakti* movements, the Mahānubhāvs' use of the regional language made their teachings accessible to a broader range of people—to women, to members of lower castes, and to others not educated in Sanskrit—than Sanskrit traditions could reach, while at the same time restricting the teachings to a more limited geographical area. Thus, Cakradhar's command to stay in Maharashtra must be seen, at least in part, as a case of legislating the obvious, once the importance of Marathi is established.

The *Sūtrapāṭh* itself, however, does not give this rationale for the command to stay in Maharashtra. In fact, this text does not directly provide any reason for the command. Implicitly, though, a rationale can be seen in the command's context within the *Sūtrapāṭh*. The previous *sūtra*, which, as we have seen, enjoins Cakradhar's followers *not* to go to the "Kannada land or the Telugu land," *does* give a reason for *its* command. The full *sūtra* reads: "Do not go to the Kannada land or the Telugu land. Those regions are full of sense pleasure. There ascetics are honored" (XII.23). That is, the Kannada and Telugu lands present a twofold danger to the ascetic life: first, the temptations of sense pleasure; and, second, the more subtle temptation of complacency. For in the Kannada and Telugu lands those who avoid sense pleasure are given honor. The *sūtra* enjoining, "Stay in Maharashtra" follows directly upon this rationale for avoiding the Kannada and Telugu lands. By implication, then, Maharashtra is a place where sense pleasures are few and ascetics are not particularly honored. Cakradhar's preference for Maharashtra over the Kannada and Telugu lands would thus be analogous to his preference for the Godāvarī valley over Vidarbha.

The Glorification of Maharashtra

If this is indeed the reason for Cakradhar's command to stay in Maharashtra, that command is thus consistent with the command to stay "at the foot of a tree at the end of the land." Maharashtra is not recommended for any positive qualities, but because—like the side of the road, the foot of a tree, or the end of the land—it is a good place to practice asceticism. Subsequent Mahānubhāv literature values Maharashtra not for its insignificance, inconvenience, or lack of comforts, but rather for positive qualities it ascribes to the region. The two published *Sūtrapāṭh* commentaries that explain the command to stay in Maharashtra do mention the danger, in other lands, of being honored and provided with sense pleasures;[32] but the commentaries' overwhelming emphasis is on the physical and psychological benefits of living in Maharashtra, and on the moral superiority of Maharashtra to other places. Both of these commentaries are in fact subcommentaries on a text whose relevant passage is as follows:

> "Maharashtra" means "great (*mahanta*) land (*rāṣṭra*)." "Land" means "country" (*deś*), but [this one is] blissful and beneficial. Other lands are sorrowful and harmful. "Great" means "large" (*thor*). Some countries are large in land;[33] some countries are large in people;[34] some countries are large in grandeur;[35] some countries are large in power;[36] some countries are large in witchcraft and lust.[37]
>
> In some countries one gets diseases and faults. One becomes sullied. One gets the itch. In some countries one is troubled by deities (*adhidaivīk tāp*); in some countries one is troubled by the elements (*adhibhautīk tāp*); in some countries one gets trouble from oneself (*adhyātmīk tāp*).
>
> In some countries the people poison foreigners (*deśāntarīya*). In some countries they put foreigners to the sword. They sacrifice them to a deity. In some countries they take foreigners prisoner; they sell them; they make slaves of them. In some countries they give them honor; they do homage to them; they subject them to sense pleasure.
>
> In some countries the people are *rājasic*;[38] in other countries they are *tāmasic*. The soil of some countries is *rājasic*; that of other countries is *tāmasic*. Some countries' food and water, fruits, leaf vegetables, trees, temples, houses, vegetable gardens, and all their holy places (*sthānem̐*) are *rājasic*—everything, living and non-living, is *rājasic*. In some countries, everything is *tāmasic*. One's body and mind are harmed just from proximity to such things; so how much worse must it be to make use of them?
>
> Maharashtra is *sāttvic*. The living and non-living things in it are also *sāttvic*. No bodily or mental harm comes from being there. Being in Maharashtra cures bodily and mental afflictions that have arisen in other countries. Its food and water are curative. Its herbs are curative. Its wind, rainstorms, and showers are also *sāttvic* and cure all afflictions.
>
> "Great" means faultless and virtuous. Some countries are faultless but not virtuous. Maharashtra is faultless and virtuous. It is faultless and virtuous itself, and it makes others faultless and virtuous too. It is faultless because it does not do harm; it is virtuous because it does do good. When one is there, one does not think of doing wrong, and if one does think of it one doesn't get to do it. Maharashtra does no wrong itself, and it allows no one else to do wrong. Maharashtra is where *dharma* gets accomplished.

To make his point, the author of this commentary uses the traditional methods of etymology and of classification by means of the three *guṇas*—*sattva* ("purity"), the best; *tamas* ("darkness"), the worst; and *rajas* ("passion"), in between. He also uses a good bit of hyperbole. But the basic message is simple: one should stay in Maharashtra because it is good for one's health and one's morals. This is an extraordinary development from the implicit claim that Maharashtra is good because it is unpleasant and does not pay honor to ascetics.

Mahānubhāv Pilgrimage Practice and Literature

Mahānubhāv pilgrimage practices imply another, more specifically religious, kind of importance for Maharashtra. These practices find a sacrality in Maharashtra analogous to that found by Christians in "the Holy Land" and by worshippers of Kṛṣṇa in Braj. Starting in the time of Nāgdev, Mahānubhāvs have made of Maharashtra a vast network of pilgrimage places, each sanctified by the former presence of Cakradhar, Guṇḍam Rāūḷ, or another of the human incarnations of God. A good deal of Mahānubhāv literature is devoted to describing and praising such places. This literature glorifies the places not only in terms of the deeds (*līḷās*) the incarnations did at them and the power (*śakti*) they deposited in them, but also, in some cases, in terms of their pre-Mahānubhāv significance.

As we have seen, the ascetic life that Cakradhar prescribed for his followers included constant, solitary, aimless wandering.[39] Cakradhar also commanded his followers to practice *smaraṇ*, recollection, of the names, appearance, and deeds of the divine incarnations. It was Nāgdev who combined the wandering with the recollection and made the wandering goal-oriented rather than aimless. He instituted the practice of pilgrimage to places where the divine incarnations had performed their deeds. *Smṛtisthaḷ*, the account of the early development of the Mahānubhāv sect under Nāgdev's leadership, portrays him sending off one of the first Mahānubhāv pilgrims as follows:[40] "Once Bāïdevobās set out to wander. Bhaṭobās [Nāgdev] said, 'Bāïdeyā, you should direct your wandering to the holy places. You should bow to all the places.'" In this way, the wandering that Cakradhar had said should be aimless[41] becomes, at Nāgdev's direction, a journey from one holy place to another. It becomes pilgrimage.

Nāgdev himself took part in the very first Mahānubhāv pilgrimage. This pilgrimage is described earlier in *Smṛtisthaḷ* (in chapter 5 of the text). Griefstricken at the death of Guṇḍam Rāūḷ, which occurred several years after Cakradhar's departure, Nāgdev and a number of other disciples travelled from Ṛddhipūr to the valley of the Godāvarī river (map 6.1). There they bowed to the riverbank at all the holy spots from Rāvasgāv (about

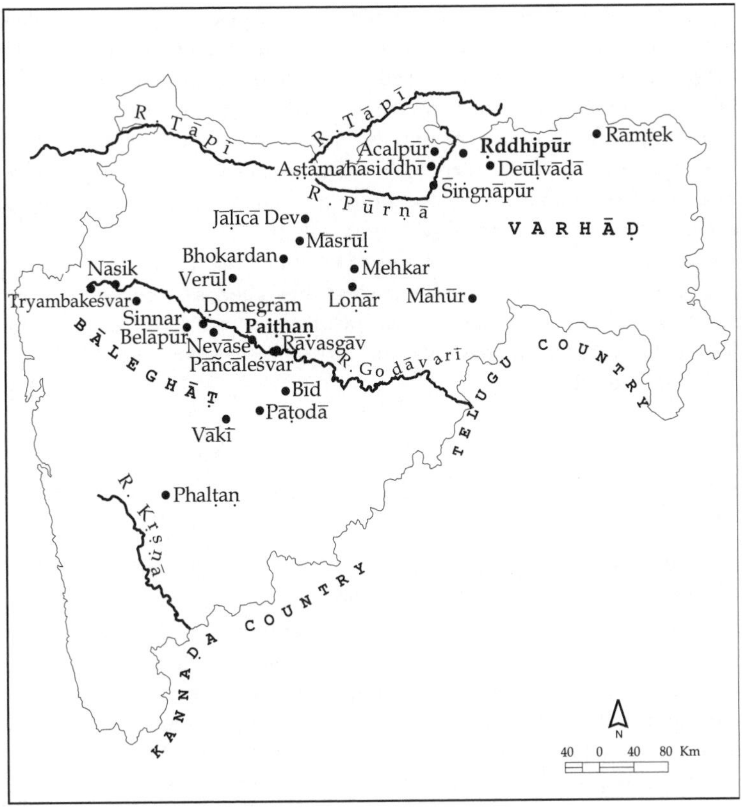

Map 6.1 Mahānubhāv holy places in Maharashtra

60 miles downstream from Paiṭhaṇ) to Ḍomegrām (about the same distance upstream from Paiṭhaṇ). The text does not say what thoughts or emotions (other than grief, *dukha*) prompted the trip or accompanied the bowing, but it appears that the pilgrimage provided a way of remembering Cakradhar, whose visits to these places was what had made them worth bowing to. In yet another passage in *Smṛtisthaḷ*, Nāgdev makes explicit the connection between pilgrimage and the recollection (*smaraṇ*) that Cakradhar had enjoined (chapter 39): "One day Bhaṭobās said, 'Go to holy places (*tīrthas*), and remember the *līḷā*s that have taken place at them. That is what you should remember there.'"

For the Mahānubhāvs, then, biography and pilgrimage are intimately linked. This can be seen elsewhere in Mahānubhāv literature as well. The biographies, which are rather cavalier about chronology, are scrupulously precise about location. They give details indicating in exactly which village a given episode occurred—as well as, in some cases, under exactly which tree or at exactly which corner of a building or courtyard. This suggests that locational information was important to the biographer and his early readers. In addition, early Mahānubhāv literature includes a text devoted to listing and describing the villages and towns that Cakradhar and Guṇḍam Rāüḷ visited and to noting the spots where they stood, sat, stayed, ate, slept, and even defecated. This text, which reveals quite clearly the biographical foundation of Mahānubhāv pilgrimage practice, is called the *Sthānpothī*, "The Book of Places."

The *Sthānpothī*

The *Sthānpothī* is something like a guidebook for Mahānubhāv pilgrims. It identifies and lists the Mahānubhāv holy places, and describes their locations in relation to temples and other landmarks in the villages and towns where the places are found. It gives information about the directional orientation of the landmarks and the holy spots, their directional relation to one another, and sometimes the distance from one to another. Frequently it gives the total number of holy places in a particular village or town. It tells about the buildings, gates, and doorways that the divine incarnations used, and refers laconically to the deeds, or *līḷās*, that they performed on the spots. However, despite the fact that the *Sthānpothī* has some of the characteristics of a guidebook, it has other characteristics that mitigate its usefulness as such, or that at least make it impractical as the pilgrim's sole *vade mecum*. These latter characteristics indicate the *Sthānpothī*'s dependence on the Mahānubhāv biographies.

The *Sthānpothī*, first of all, does not tell the pilgrim how to get from one village or town where there are Mahānubhāv holy places to another. In the absence of railroads, buses, and modern roads, this is quite natural (even in modern India, except for travel between major cities, most travel arrangements are best made, and directions best asked, locally). Beyond this, however, the *Sthānpothī* lists the places in an order that is quite often not at all convenient for a pilgrim. For example, the first town named, in the very beginning of the text, is Phaleṭhāṇ (Phalṭaṇ, in modern Satara District, Maharashtra). This is followed by Mātāpūr (Māhūr, in modern Nanded District), about 500 miles to the northeast, then by two places in Gujarat

(Dvārāvatī and Bharavas), and then by Ṛddhipūr and some other places in modern Amravati District, Maharashtra. Not only is this not the most efficient route for visiting *these* places, but later passages of the *Sthānpothī* mention many more holy places that lie between them. Moreover, the *Sthānpothī* mentions Ṛddhipūr, the Mahānubhāvs' most important pilgrimage place, several more times, most notably in a long section entitled "Ṛddhipūr Sthāneṃ."[42] Clearly, the text does not follow the order of a pilgrim's convenience.

A modern Mahānubhāv guidebook, by contrast, *Sthān-Mārga-Darśak* (Śevalīkar 1970), gives the direction and mileage from one holy place to the next, and in many cases provides instructions for proceeding from place to place by road and/or rail. In addition, *Sthān-Mārga-Darśak* follows an order that is much more practical for pilgrims than that in the *Sthānpothī*: it starts with Phalṭaṇ, moves on to a series of places in the districts Ahmadnagar, Bid, Aurangabad, and so on (in central Maharashtra), and then proceeds through places in Amravati, Vardha, Nagpur, and Bhandara Districts (in northeastern Maharashtra) to Māhūr, only at the end guiding the pilgrim to a handful of places in Gujarat and other parts of North India.

Comparison with the Mahānubhāv biographies reveals why the order of places in the *Sthānpothī* is not closer to the more convenient order in the modern guidebook. The *Sthānpothī* follows the order of the biographies. The first few places in the *Sthānpothī*—Phaleṭhāṇ, Mātāpūr, Dvārāvatī, Bharavas, Ṛddhipūr, and so on—are the scenes of the first few chapters of the early Mahānubhāv biography of Cakradhar, the *Līḷācaritra*. The places occur in the *Sthānpothī* in the order in which they are found in the *Līḷācaritra*: Phaleṭhāṇ and Mātāpūr in chapter 1 of Tulpule's edition (1972); Dvārāvatī in chapters 2, 3, and 4; "Gujarat" (exact location unspecified) in chapters 4, 5, and 6; and Ṛddhipūr (under the name Parameśvarpūr) in chapter 7. Kolte's edition of the *Līḷācaritra* includes a number of interpolated chapters,[43] but most of the places listed in the *Sthānpothī* do occur in Kolte's *Līḷācaritra* too, and they occur in the same order as in the *Sthānpothī*.

Once we accept that the *Sthānpothī* follows the order of the Mahānubhāv biographies, we can also understand its repetitions of places. Repetitions occur for places that one of the divine incarnations visited more than once, or for places that more than one of the incarnations visited. Thus, Ṛddhipūr is mentioned early in the *Sthānpothī* because Cakradhar went there early in his life, and his first visit there is related early in the *Līḷācaritra*. Ṛddhipūr recurs elsewhere in the *Sthānpothī* because Cakradhar visited there on some other occasions that the *Līḷācaritra* tells about later, and because Guṇḍam Rāūḷ spent most of his life there and it is thus the setting for most of the *Ṛddhipurcaritra*.

Not only the order of the places in the *Sthānpothī* but also the divisions of the text indicate its dependence on the Mahānubhāv biographies. In Kolte's second edition of the *Sthānpothī*, its divisions are entitled "Ekāṅka Sthāneṃ," "Pūrvārdha Sthāneṃ," "Uttarārdha Sthāneṃ," and "Ṛddhipūr Sthāneṃ." The first three of these correspond to the three sections of Tulpule's edition of the *Līḷācaritra* ("Ekāṅka," "Pūrvārdha," and "Uttarārdha"),[44] and the fourth to the *Ṛddhipurcaritra*. Thus the title "Ṛddhipūr Sthāneṃ" means not "*Sthān*s in Ṛddhipūr," as one might initially expect, but rather "*Sthān*s in the *Ṛddhipurcaritra*."[45]

More fundamentally than either the order of the places in the text or the titles of its divisions, the fact that the *Sthānpothī* assumes its readers' familiarity with the episodes narrated in the biographies indicates its dependence on them. The *Sthānpothī*'s references to the episodes, or *līḷā*s, that took place at the spots it describes are so succinct as to be, in many cases, incomprehensible without a thorough knowledge of the biographies. This illustrates the interdependence of early Mahānubhāv literature generally. The *Līḷācaritra*, the *Sūtrapāṭh*, and an anthology of Cakradhar's parables called *Dṛṣṭāntapāṭh* (Bhavāḷkar and Nene 1937) form an interlocking set of texts, with the *Līḷācaritra* and the *Sūtrapāṭh* each assuming a knowledge of the other, the *Līḷācaritra* assuming a knowledge of the *Dṛṣṭāntapāṭh*, and the *Dṛṣṭāntapāṭh* referring to *sūtra*s of the *Sūtrapāṭh*.[46] The fact that the *Sthānpothī* assumes a knowledge of the episodes of the *Līḷācaritra* and the *Ṛddhipurcaritra* provides but a further example of this interlocking character of the early Mahānubhāv texts.

As a result of its close connection with the Mahānubhāv biographies, the *Sthānpothī* can, like the pilgrimage tradition from which it stems, serve its readers as an exercise in *smaraṇ*, a way of practicing recollection of the *līḷā*s narrated in the biographies by thinking about the places where the *līḷā*s occurred. It seems likely that the *Sthānpothī* has been read—or memorized and recited—as often by Mahānubhāvs practicing sedentary *smaraṇ* as by Mahānubhāvs engaged in actual pilgrimages. This possibility fits well with the fact that the order of the places in the *Sthānpothī* is conducive to recollection, even though it is impractical for actual pilgrimage.

The possibility of *thinking* about the places without actually *going* to them can be seen even more clearly in another Mahānubhāv text, *Tīrthamālikā* (Śevalīkar 1981). This is a verse text that lists places visited by the Mahānubhāv incarnations. Sometimes the text tells how long the incarnations stayed in the places, and occasionally it refers to things they did at them. Like the *Sthānpothī*, *Tīrthamālikā* follows the order of places in the *Līḷācaritra* and the *Ṛddhipurcaritra*. Also like the *Sthānpothī*, *Tīrthamālikā* is divided into sections corresponding to the divisions of the biographies: "Pūrvārdha Tīrthamālikā," "Uttarārdha Tīrthamālikā," and "Ṛddhipūr Tīrthamālikā." *Tīrthamālikā* does not attempt to describe the places; rather, it simply gives their names, sometimes listing them in a litany-like fashion for which the text's title ("The Garland of Holy Places"[47]) is extremely apt. Such a list can serve to remind potential pilgrims of the places that they *could* visit, but it cannot be of much further help as a pilgrimage guide. *Tīrthamālikā*, then, serves much more clearly as a stimulus to recollection than as a guide for pilgrimage. This suggests that, in the case of the *Sthānpothī* as well, the pilgrimage it guides may at least as often have been mental as actual. In any case, the mental element of even an actual pilgrimage is essential: the *smaraṇ*, the recollection, of the god who once lived in the places the pilgrim visits.

Ṛddhipūr and Contemporary Mahānubhāv Pilgrimage Theory

A heavily pious version of such *smaraṇ* is illustrated in Nārobās's (Nārāyaṇ Vyās's) *Ṛddhipurvarṇan* (Deśpāṇḍe 1929). This is an early-fifteenth-century poem of 641 verses written in an ornate style. Amid long excurses on the poet's unworthiness and shorter ones on the mercy of God, each step adorned with elaborate strings of highly artificial similes, the poet describes his approach to Ṛddhipūr. He dwells in turn upon the outskirts of Ṛddhipūr; the trees, temples, and lakes on the outskirts; the entry into the town; the main street leading to the complex of three temple-monasteries where Guṇḍam Rāüḷ lived; the steps up to the main gateway of the compound; the gateway itself; the verandah of the Rājmaḍh (the Narasiṃha temple that was Guṇḍam Rāüḷ's principal residence); the dilapidated wall of the Rājmaḍh; its doorway; the Narasiṃha image inside; the spots where Guṇḍam Rāüḷ had his massage and his meals; Guṇḍam Rāüḷ's cot; and—from toes to head—the parts of his remembered body. The poem ends on a note of *viraha*, sorrow that Guṇḍam Rāüḷ is no longer there.

Modern-day visits to Mahānubhāv pilgrimage places seem less solemn than this, but they do bring the divine incarnations to mind. The village of Ṛddhipūr, for example, the most elaborate of the many Mahānubhāv places, is studded with simple, aniconic concrete blocks called *oṭā*s. These *oṭā*s mark spots where Cakradhar and Guṇḍam Rāüḷ did various things. Many of the *oṭā*s are housed in shrines or temples; more of them simply stand out in the open; several are found in monasteries and in the houses of lay people, both Mahānubhāv and non-Mahānubhāv.[48] Map 6.2 indicates the locations of a number of the *oṭā*s of Ṛddhipūr, but there are many

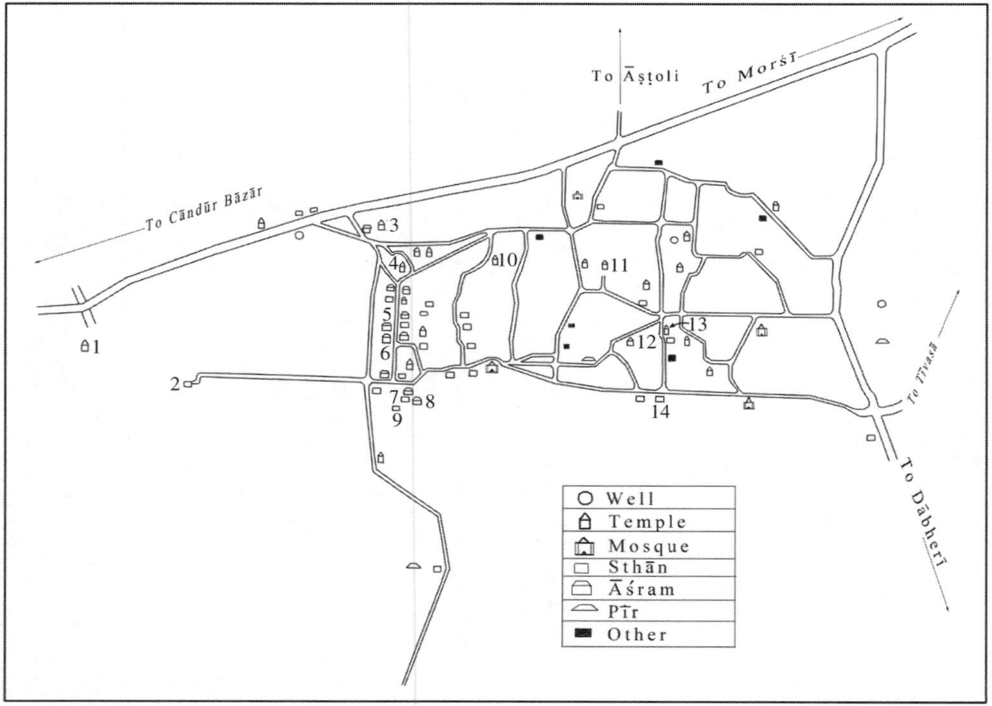

Map 6.2 Ṛddhipūr. 1, Vājeśvarī temple; 2, The Place of the Water Jars; 3, Bhairav Burūj; 4, The Twelve Horses; 5, Yakṣadev monastery; 6, Gopīrāj monastery; 7, The Thinking Rock; 8, Pāc Rāüt monastery; 9, Rājmaḍh/Jummā mosque; 10, Mahākālī temple; 11, Kolhārāī temple; 12, Measure-Breaking Gaṇapati temple; 13, Māruti temple; 14, Śeṅguḷ-Buḍaḍeṃ (first meeting of Cakradhar and Guṇḍam Rāüḷ). Map by S. Y. Waghmare. Reprinted by permission of the Centre for South Asian Studies, University of Toronto.

more. Prominent among the revered places (*sthāns*) are the Thinking Rock (Vicār Cīrā), where Guṇḍam Rāüḷ used to sit and think where to go next; the Twelve Horses (Bārā Ghoḍe), rocks he used to sit on and pretend were horses; the Measure-Breaking Gaṇapati, a Gaṇeś image on whose head Guṇḍam Rāüḷ used to break false measures from the marketplace; several places where Cakradhar and Guṇḍam Rāüḷ met (e.g., numbers 2 and 14 on map 6.2); and numerous spots in the Rājmaḍh compound.

The stories connected with the places are not illustrated on the *oṭās* or their shrines, and at only one place in Ṛddhipūr, the Rājmaḍh, are the things that happened there listed in writing nearby. But the stories are told orally, or referred to, by pilgrims to one another, or by residents of Ṛddhipūr (Mahānubhāv and non-Mahānubhāv) to pilgrims. In many cases, the *līḷās* that were done at the places give the places their names, so that merely to name the place is to bring its story to mind. Since much that Guṇḍam Rāüḷ did was crazy, odd, or funny,[49] people often refer to the stories with a chuckle and a smile. Occasionally people draw a moral from the stories and apply it to contemporary life in Ṛddhipūr. For instance, the head of one of Ṛddhipūr's monasteries told me, referring to the Measure-Breaking Gaṇapati, that people still say that Ṛddhipūr is Guṇḍam Rāüḷ's town, and so storekeepers there should not cheat.[50] Bhau Mandavkar, a literary figure, scholar, and social reformer who is not a Mahānubhāv but has a research interest in the Mahānubhāv pilgrimage places, pointed out another sort of analogy. Just as Guṇḍam Rāüḷ, although he was a Brāhmaṇ, spent a good deal of time in the houses of low-caste people and Untouchables, so the *sthāns* of Ṛddhipūr today are concentrated in low-caste and Buddhist neighborhoods.[51]

Thus the *sthāns* of Ṛddhipūr, and those of other Mahānubhāv pilgrimage places, serve as concrete reminders of the deeds of God, and the idea of remembrance, *smaraṇ*, appears to be an important element of Mahānubhāv pilgrimage practice to this day. On the other hand, many pious pilgrims and residents of Ṛddhipūr do homage to—that is, bow to and touch with their foreheads—*oṭās* marking spots that they cannot identify, spots about which, when asked, they say simply "*sthān āhe*" ("It's a *sthān*"), or "*kāhītarī keleṃ*" ("He did something-or-other"), sometimes with a tone implying that the questioner is demanding too much specificity. Such people, at such a *sthān*, are clearly not reflecting on any specific deed that was done at the place. Rather, they are simply showing reverence for the fact that a divine incarnation has been there. Moreover, in explaining the importance of the *sthāns* to an outsider, present-day Mahānubhāvs draw on other concepts more often than they use the concept of *smaraṇ*.

One of the concepts they draw on is the idea that contact with a divine incarnation causes *śakti*, power,[52] to be deposited in a place. This idea is found as early as the *Sūtrapāṭh*: *sūtra* X.171 states, "*Śakti* is deposited through contact with the Absolute." Present-day Mahānubhāvs well-educated in the tradition distinguish two kinds of *śakti*: *kṛpā śakti* and *māyā śakti*. A divine incarnation leaves *māyā śakti* automatically, they say, in everything he touches and every place he goes; *kṛpā śakti*, by contrast, must be deposited intentionally. It is *śakti* of both these kinds in the Mahānubhāv holy sites that makes pilgrimage to them effective: they help one solve practical, worldly problems, and they increase one's inner worthiness, thus helping one to transcend this world and its suffering and to attain the permanent presence of God.[53]

Related to the concept of *śakti*—but not, as far as I can tell, identical with it—is the concept of *pavitratā*. This term, which could perhaps best be translated "holiness," also has (not unlike "holiness") the sense of "purity." The *pavitratā* of a place attracts pilgrims to it, but it can also cause them to keep a respectful distance. This idea is basic to an important chapter in the oral history of Ṛddhipūr. According to several of the best-informed residents, the monasteries of Ṛddhipūr are a relatively recent development. From the death of Guṇḍam Rāūḷ until a couple of hundred years ago (estimates vary from 100 to 400 years, with 150 being a fairly standard number), Mahānubhāv monks and nuns would not stay in Ṛddhipūr. Nowadays monks and nuns not only live in Ṛddhipūr, they also urinate and defecate there, and wear there sandals made of the skin of dead animals. But this was not always the case. According to some contemporary Mahānubhāvs, the monastic establishments of Ṛddhipūr grew up only after an initial year in which a sizeable group of monks (more than a hundred, though accounts vary greatly as to the exact number) spent the four-month rainy season retreat in Ṛddhipūr, collecting their urine and feces to be carried out each morning beyond the farthest boundaries of the town. When I asked why Mahānubhāv monks and nuns avoided staying in Ṛddhipūr until such elaborate precautions had been worked out, the abbot who gave me the fullest version of this story[54] explained: "This was all *pavitra* ground. That is, this was ground that had become *pavitra* by being marked by [Guṇḍam Rāūḷ's] feet." Another monk[55] expressed the idea this way: "Since Govindprabhu was an incarnation of God, how can we put our feet where he has put his? It would be like sitting in the Collector's[56] chair!"

Prominent in such explanations of the *pavitratā* of the Mahānubhāv places—and also, to some extent, in explanations of their *śakti*—is mention of the touch of a divine incarnation's feet. This is the closest I could get, for instance, to a standardized explanation of one of the more distinctive types of Mahānubhāv holy places. These are the *pariśray sthān*s, places where Cakradhar or Guṇḍam Rāūḷ defecated. The *Sthānpothī* mentions such places quite frequently, and several of them, marked by *oṭā*s, are revered today. What makes the *pariśray sthān*s important, everyone agrees, is that *anywhere* the divine incarnations did *anything* is important. But several people suggested an explanation for the fact that the *pariśray sthān*s are singled out for special attention: where Cakradhar and Guṇḍam Rāüḷ squatted to defecate, these people explained, their feet touched the ground longer than usual at a single place. It is the prolonged touch of the feet that makes these places important.

Text, Place, and Memory[57]

The history of the identification of the Mahānubhāv holy places reveals a complex interaction among the *Sthānpothī*, the practice of pilgrimage, the practice of recollection (*smaraṇ*), and notions of the power deposited in the places themselves. However much it may have been used as an aid for sedentary recollection, the *Sthānpothī* gives evidence, in the sheer detail of its descriptions, that its author or authors had actually visited the places the text describes. Further, some of the variants included in the text of the *Sthānpothī*[58] indicate the work of a subsequent editor-scholar who visited the places and checked the *Sthānpothī*'s information, revising or supplementing it on occasion. Kolte suggests (in 1976:3–9) that the text of *Sthānpothī* is the product of a series of editings, beginning with a set of notes made by Bāïdevobās in the course of the pilgrimage reported in *Smṛtisthaḷ* 115 (mentioned earlier) and ending with the work of a fifteenth-century author named Ciḍale: according to Mahānubhāv oral tradition, Ciḍale went to the holy places, measured their distances from one another and from other landmarks, and added his measurements (in the form "*pāṇḍā 5, pāṇḍā 10*" and so on) to the text. The particular series of authors that Kolte names cannot, perhaps, be established beyond doubt,[59] but it does seem likely that the *Sthānpothī* is the product of a number of successive editions, most of them based on the editors' actual visits to the places in the text.[60]

Besides the process of revising the *Sthānpothī* in the light of evidence found at the places themselves, the converse process, that of using the *Sthānpothī* to identify the holy places, can also be seen at work in the Mahānubhāv tradition. To some extent, this converse process occurs every time a pilgrim consults the *Sthānpothī* in the course of a pilgrimage. But it also probably occurs as the decision is made where to place the *oṭā*s that mark the holy spots. It seems that such decisions have been made on many occasions in the course of the centuries.

Mahānubhāv tradition credits the fourteenth-century monk Munivyās (or Munībās) Koṭhī with having first built the *oṭā*s.[61] Of the two texts that mention Munivyās's building of the *oṭās*, neither says anything about his having used the *Sthānpothī* to identify where to put them.[62] Some present-day Mahānubhāvs hold that there has been a continuous, unbroken tradition of knowledge of the locations of the holy spots;[63] others speculate that Munivyās, as well as others who repaired or replaced the *oṭās* after him, used the *Sthānpothī* to locate the places.[64] The most elaborate account I have heard of how the places must have been rediscovered was given by an exceptionally learned, octogenarian head of a monastery in Ṛddhipūr. He told of a process that combined measurements based on the *Sthānpothī* with the practice of recollection and the experience of miracles:

> These *sthān*s were built by Koṭhī Munībās . . ., as many *sthān*s as there are—Cakradhar Svāmī's *sthān*s, Śrī Govind Prabhu's [Guṇḍam Rāüḷ's] *sthān*s, Śrī Kṛṣṇa Cakravartī's *sthān*s, Śrī Dattātreya Mahārāj's *sthān*s. Koṭhī Munībās did the building of these *sthān*s . . . .
>
> There were books (manuscripts, *pothyā*). First there was the *Sthānpothī* and the book of biographies (*caritrācī pothī*). Then Śrī Cakradhar Svāmī did such-and-such a *līḷā* in such-and-such a place . . . . That's [in] the *Sthānpothī* . . . .
>
> For instance, now, this is the Rājmaḍh.[65] To the east of this Rājmaḍh, so-and-so many *pāṇḍās*—that is, paces—away, is this childbirth (*sueracem̃*) *sthān*. It's in our monastery. *Suer* means assisting at the birth of a child.[66] . . . So, according to the *Sthānpothī*, this *sthān* is so-and-so many *pāṇḍās*—that is, paces—east of the Rājmaḍh. So, is it here, or over here? We've measured the paces. So is it in this place, or in this other place? Then we sit doing *smaraṇ* in that place.
>
> [I asked: In both places?]
>
> No, just in one place. [Koṭhī Munībās] would sit here and do his *smaraṇ*. He would pray to the Svāmī, "Where is this *sthān*? How is it?" and sit doing *smaraṇ*. As he practiced *smaraṇ*, he would come to know. Something would appear there. He would understand that this *sthān* is here, and the Svāmī did a deed (*līḷā*) in this place. And then he would mark the place and build up the *sthān*. As many *sthān*s as there are in all of Maharashtra were built in this way . . . .
>
> Now in some places a few *sthān*s have fallen into disrepair. In those places too, pious people (*sant-mahant*) do *smaraṇ*, five or ten people perform *āratī* or incense-*āratī*, and then some marvel occurs. They build the *sthān* where the marvel has occurred.
>
> In this way Koṭhī Munībās built some *sthān*s. Later they fell into disrepair. Then later some pious people rebuilt them. And it still goes on now. Pious people go on (re)building *sthān*s that have fallen into disrepair.

There is a great deal of testimony, both verbal and visual, to this ongoing process of building and rebuilding *oṭās* to mark the holy spots. Such testimony is especially plentiful in Ṛddhipūr. There several people told me about Lāndge Buvā, a pious monk of the last generation who is said to have rebuilt a number of the *sthān*s that currently stud the pathways, courtyards, doorsteps, and empty lots of the town. In addition, some of the more prominent abbots of Ṛddhipūr today are involved in projects of renovating various *oṭā*s or building domes, shrines, or temples over them. In many of these cases, it seems, a new *oṭā* simply replaces an old one on the same spot, but sometimes an *oṭā* is built where none was there before. In these cases, the *Sthānpothī* can be of help.[67]

The relationship between the *Sthānpothī* and the Mahānubhāv holy places, then, is a process of mutual correction, arising out of the living pilgrimage tradition of the Mahānubhāvs. The dependence of the *Sthānpothī* on the Mahānubhāv biographies reflects that pilgrimage tradition's basis in the practice of *smaraṇ*, recollection, of the Mahānubhāv incarnations of the one, supreme God. In the Mahānubhāv sectarian context, the *Sthānpothī* is thus significant and has value through its service to Mahānubhāv pilgrims and to other Mahānubhāvs practicing *smaraṇ* of their divine incarnations: it identifies the places where Cakradhar and the other incarnations visited, lived, and did particular things, and this is the basis of its usefulness for Mahānubhāvs.

However, the *Sthānpothī* also provides other information, incidental to the Mahānubhāv sectarian context, that reveals a good bit about the pre-Mahānubhāv and extra-Mahānubhāv religious history of Maharashtra. Many of the places where Cakradhar and the other Mahānubhāv incarnations lived, visited, and performed their deeds were places of religious significance before the Mahānubhāv incarnations went to them. Many of the places were temples and shrines of deities that Mahānubhāvs do *not* worship, deities that Mahānubhāvs see as having at best a divinity far inferior to that of the one God who was incarnated as Cakradhar and Guṇḍam Rāüḷ.[68] In many cases, the images of these deities have by now been replaced by aniconic Mahānubhāv *oṭā*s, and the temples have been transformed into Mahānubhāv temples. Sometimes no trace is left of the former resident deity, and at other times only the deity's name remains as a reminder.[69] The process by which Mahānubhāv *oṭā*s and temples replace Hindu temples and images is a gradual one, and one that is by no means complete even today. The *Sthānpothī* preserves the record of an early stage of the process. It thus provides, incidentally to its own purposes, a good deal of information about what might be called the religious archaeology of Maharashtra.[70]

Thus, the *Sthānpothī* can be of help in charting the rise and fall of cults in Maharashtra. More generally, the text's great interest in directional orientation illustrates the universal importance of the cardinal directions in Hindu architecture and religious thought.[71] As far as I know, directional orientation has no specifically Mahānubhāv significance. The reason that the *Sthānpothī* describes temples and other structures in terms of the directions their doors and gateways face and in terms of their directional relation to one another and to the village or town where they are located is not, apparently, that particular directional orientations make the *sthāns* any holier for Mahānubhāvs. It is, rather, that the most natural and informative way to describe such structures is in terms of their directional (usually cardinal) orientation. As an unintended consequence of the descriptions of the Mahānubhāv holy spots, the *Sthānpothī* provides information about the directional orientation of approximately 900 temples and other structures in medieval Maharashtra. This too is of potentially great use for studying the religious archaeology of Maharashtra.

Non-Sectarian Arguments for the Holiness of Maharashtra

The holiness of Maharashtra implicit in Mahānubhāv pilgrimage practice is based on the fact that Maharashtra is the locus of almost all the activities of the Mahānubhāv incarnations. This is the reason that Mahānubhāvs read or recite the *Sthānpothī*, and it is Mahānubhāvs' motive for locating, building, and rebuilding *oṭās*. This kind of holiness is a purely sectarian one. Just as Mahānubhāvs are theologically indifferent to the original gods of the temples that Cakradhar and the other Mahānubhāv incarnations visited, so too are non-Mahānubhāvs unlikely to see the fact of these incarnations' former presence as a significant basis for the places' holiness.[72] There is, however, one important exception to the Mahānubhāvs' sectarian exclusiveness. This is the work of the early-seventeenth-century Mahānubhāv poet Kṛṣṇamuni Kavi Ḍimbh. Kṛṣṇamuni describes the holiness of Maharashtra in terms drawn from and relevant to the wider Indian tradition. To praise both Maharashtra as a whole and particular Mahānubhāv holy places within it, Kṛṣṇamuni employs the same kind of rhetoric that we saw non-Mahānubhāvs using in the previous chapter.

For instance, in a passage in his *Ṛddhipūr Māhātmya*, Kṛṣṇamuni explains the greatness of Maharashtra as follows:

> 307. Brahmā said to Nārada, "I'll tell you clearly why it is called 'Maharashtra' ('the great land') 308. The Mahātmā Śrī Datta, at whose lotus feet all holy places reside, lives in the Sahyādris, and so it is called Maharashtra in the family of sages well-known from the Purāṇas. 309. There are twelve Jyotirliṅgas; six of them are in Maharashtra. Nine of the twelve

> Mahāliṅgas are there. 310. Phaḷasthaḷ [Phalṭaṇ] destroys the sin of killing a woman; Ātmatīrtha destroys the sin of killing a Brāhmaṇ; Sarvatīrtha provides liberation to one's ancestors; Vijñāneśvar gives the state of liberation. 311. And on both banks of the Gaṅgā [the Godāvarī] is a crowd of all holy places. This is why Maharashtra is at the crown of all lands."

The "crowd" of holy places in the last verse of this passage could be the numerous Mahānubhāv holy places along the Godāvarī. However, there are also many non-Mahānubhāv holy places there, and these may be included in the "crowd." Similarly, because Dattātreya is one of the Mahānubhāvs' divine incarnations, places touched by his "lotus feet" are holy for Mahānubhāvs; but such places are also holy for non-Mahānubhāvs, since Dattātreya is a god for mainstream Hindus as well. The places Kṛṣṇamuni names in verse 310 are Mahānubhāv holy places, but the reasons he gives for their importance—destruction of stereotypical sins, including Brāhmaṇ-murder; liberation for one's ancestors; even ultimate liberation for oneself—are drawn from (though not, strictly speaking, exclusive to) Brāhmaṇical orthodoxy. Most strikingly, in locating six of the 12 Jyotirliṅgas, as well as nine of an analogous set of places, the Mahāliṅgas ("great *liṅgas*"), in Maharashtra (verse 309), Kṛṣṇamuni is claiming that Maharashtrian places predominate in one of the most important sets of non-Mahānubhāv pilgrimage places of all of India.

Earlier in his work, Kṛṣṇamuni discusses the Jyotirliṅgas in more detail. First he gives his list of the 12 of them (verses 123–26): (1) Tryambak; (2) Ghusameśvar (Ghṛṣṇeśvar) in Yeḷaur (Ellora, Verūḷ); (3) Somnāth in Saurāṣṭra; (4) Vaidyanāth in Paraḷī; (5) Nāgnāth in Āṃvaḍhe or Amardaka;[73] (6) Bhīṣmeśvar (Bhīmaśaṅkar) in Ḍākinī; (7) Viśvanāth in Kāśī; (8) Kedār(nāth) near Badri(nāth); (9) Kāleśvar at Māthanī (Manthanī); (10) Mahākāḷ in Ujjain; (11) Rāmeśvar, "at Setubandhu in the south"; and (12) the Jyotirliṅga at Māndhātā (on the Narmadā). Of these, the six that verse 309 refers to as being in Maharashtra must be Tryambak, Ghusameśvar, Vaidyanāth, Nāgnāth, Bhīṣmeśvar, and Kāḷeśvar.[74]

Kṛṣṇamuni then lists the 12 Mahāliṅgas (verses 127–30):

> [1] Mallikārjun; [2] Mahābaḷeśvar; [3] Bhīmaśaṅkar;[75] [4] Gaṅgāsāgar; [5] Madhyameśvar on the bank of the Gaṅgā (Godāvarī) [in modern Nasik District]; [6] Ghaṭsiddhanāth [also on the Godāvarī, in modern Ahmadnagar District]; three famous *liṅgas* in Pratiṣṭhān (Paiṭhaṇ): [7] Ḍhoreśvar, [8] Pīmpaḷeśvarī, and [9] Siddhanāth; also [10] Vijñāneśvar, established by Śrī Datta [at Āpegāv, Ambaḍ Taluka, Aurangabad District, on the Godāvarī]; [11] Ambanāth in Aḷarkāvatī (Amrāvatī); and [12] Haṭakeśvar in Ṛddhipūr.

Ten of these, rather than the nine that verse 309 claims, would belong to Maharashtra by either of Kṛṣṇamuni's definitions of Maharashtra (note 18, earlier); Gaṅgāsāgar, in distant Bengal, and Mallikārjun, at Śrīśaila in less distant Andhra Pradesh, would not.

The set of Mahāliṅgas is by no means as famous, as a set, as the Jyotirliṅgas are. It appears to be a replica of the set of Jyotirliṅgas, a way of enabling 12 more *liṅga* temples to share in a religious importance analogous to that of the Jyotirliṅgas—another example of the strategies we examined at length in chapter 5. For Kṛṣṇamuni, the fact that Maharashtra contains almost all of these Mahāliṅgas, as well as half of the 12 Jyotirliṅgas, shows Maharashtra's importance to a major pilgrimage tradition of all of India.

With respect to another very important set of pilgrimage places located throughout India and visited by pilgrims from all over the country, Kṛṣṇamuni makes a claim that is similar, but clearer and bolder. The set is that of the Saptapurī, the seven cities that each provide liberation (see chapter 4 and map 4.1); Kṛṣṇamuni's claim is that a complete replica of this set is to be found in Maharashtra. After giving his list of the Seven Cities of all of India—Ayodhyā, Mathurā, Māyā (Gayā), Kāntī (Kāñcīpuram), Kāśī (Vārāṇasī, Banaras), Dvārkā or Dvārāvatī, and Avantī (Ujjain)[76]—Kṛṣṇamuni claims that the bases or abodes (*adhiṣṭhānem*) of these seven are found in Maharashtra (verse 139). He spells out the correspondences as follows: "140. Chinnapāp is called Ayodhyā; Aḷkāpur [Amrāvatī] is called Mathurā; Vāṅkī on the bank of the Sīnā [in modern Ahmadnagar District] is the *tīrtha* Māyā. 141. Phaḷasthaḷ [Phalṭaṇ] is called Kāntī; Prateṣṭān [Pratiṣṭhān, Paiṭhaṇ] is called Kāśī; Ṛddhipūr is Dvārāvatī; [and] Avantī is Yeḷaur [Ellora, Verūḷ]." Kṛṣṇamuni then supports these identifications by means of a series of analogies and mythological connections between each pair of places:

> 143. Because Rām made Daśarath's funeral offerings there, Chinnapāp's name is Ayodhyā [Rām's capital]. 144. Kṛṣṇanāth went to Aḷarkāvatī on his way to Rukmiṇī's engagement ceremony; he made an offering to Ambināth; therefore it's known to be Mathurā [Kṛṣṇa's town]. 145. Gayā is called Māyā because the demon Māyā was burned to ashes there. Since the demon Bhasma was burned to ashes (*bhasma*) at Vāṅkī, the *tīrtha* Vāṅkī is Māyā.[77] 146. Just as Rukmāṅgad was released through the Ekādaśī vow [at Kāntī?], Rām was released [at Phaḷasthaḷ?] from the sin of killing a woman.[78] Therefore Phaḷasthaḷ is called Kāntī. 147. The Bhogāvatī [river?][79] came from the underworld to meet the Gautamī (Godāvarī) at Pratiṣṭhān; therefore [Pratiṣṭhān] is said to be a mite better than Kāśī. 148. Just as the Jyotirliṅga Mahākāḷ resides in Ujjain, the Jyotirliṅga Ghusameśvar is in Yeḷaur. Therefore Yeḷaur's name is said to be Avantī. 149. Descending in the

Kali Age, the Lord showed Dvārkā to the Brāhmaṇ Lakṣmīdharbhaṭ [in Ṛddhipūr].[80] Therefore Ṛddhipūr is called Dvārāvatī.

All seven of the Maharashtrian places are pilgrimage places for Mahānubhāvs because of the places' connection with the lives of the Mahānubhāv incarnations. But for only one of the seven identifications Kṛṣṇamuni makes—that of Ṛddhipūr with Dvārkā—does the equivalence rest on an exclusively Mahānubhāv story. The story of Kṛṣṇa and Rukmiṇī, in connection with which Kṛṣṇamuni identifies Aḷarkāvatī with Mathurā, is told both by Mahānubhāvs and by non-Mahānubhāv Hindus. The other stories and analogies that Kṛṣṇamuni uses are not, as far as I know, otherwise at all prominent in the Mahānubhāv tradition. Thus, although the seven Maharashtrian places that Kṛṣṇamuni identifies with the Saptapurī are of sectarian importance to Mahānubhāvs, the reasons he gives for the identifications are overwhelmingly non-Mahānubhāv. The stories are found in Purāṇic Hindu traditions, though not necessarily in connection with the places where Kṛṣṇamuni locates them. More fundamentally, the seven liberating cities, and the 12 Jyotirliṅgas as well, are as irrelevant to Mahānubhāv theology as they are important to non-sectarian (and, in the case of the Jyotirliṅgas, Śaiva) Hindu pilgrimage traditions. According to Mahānubhāv theology, only the one, absolute God grants liberation; no place can grant it, nor can any merely relatively important deity like Śiva (Feldhaus 1980).

It is thus something of a mystery where Kṛṣṇamuni got the idea of making these identifications, and what audience he intended them for. Were they intended to convince non-Mahānubhāvs of the importance of the Mahānubhāv places? It would appear so. However, if, like other Mahānubhāv texts, Kṛṣṇamuni's *Ṛddhipūr Māhātmya* was copied and preserved in manuscripts written in secret codes, it would have been available only to Mahānubhāvs until the early twentieth century, for it was only then that the codes were revealed outside the sect. Was, then, Mahānubhāv exclusivism less strict in the early seventeenth century than it is in our own time or than it was at the beginnings of the sect? Was Kṛṣṇamuni simply an anomalous liberal? Or was he perhaps caught up in the ironies of using the rhetoric of praise in a *bhakti* context?

In any case, Kṛṣṇamuni's work has been preserved—and thereby implicitly accepted—by subsequent generations of Mahānubhāvs. And what Kṛṣṇamuni has done in these passages is to assert that Maharashtra replicates the religious geography of all of India. Using a quite typical Hindu rhetoric of glorification, Kṛṣṇamuni is able to identify the religious importance of Maharashtra as that of all of India, and thus to give the fullest possible rationale for the command to stay in Maharashtra. One should stay in

Maharashtra because every place worth going to is there. Maharashtra is a microcosm of India.

With the claims of Kṛṣṇamuni, then, the positive valuation of Maharashtra has gone far beyond the moral and physical benefits ascribed to it in some *Sūtrapāṭh* commentaries, beyond the reverence for it implicit in Mahānubhāv pilgrimage traditions, and into a completely different realm of values from that of Cakradhar's unexplained or negatively motivated command to stay in Maharashtra. From having been equivalent (or almost so) to the "end of the land," Maharashtra has here become the totality of the world—of all of the world that matters.

Despite its power as a religious, cosmological statement, Kṛṣṇamuni's positive valuation of Maharashtra has remained locked within the same sectarian confines as *Sūtrapāṭh* commentaries and Mahānubhāv pilgrimage traditions. None of these has had any noticeable effect on the outside world. The rest of Maharashtra has remained by-and-large oblivious to Mahānubhāv religious-geographical traditions, as the Mahānubhāvs have remained isolated from the rest of Maharashtra. In the twentieth century, the secret codes have been revealed outside the sect, the literary texts have been published in uncoded Marathi, and college and university students have begun to read small samples of Mahānubhāv literature in Marathi courses. But the rich religious-geographical traditions of the Mahānubhāvs have played little or no role in the formation of the state of Maharashtra or of any other political unit. In the conclusion I will suggest that the Vārkarī traditions, unlike those of the Mahānubhāvs, did have an influence on the mid-twentieth-century movement for a United Maharashtra.

Chapter 7

Conclusion

In their ground-breaking book *Mental Maps*, Peter Gould and Rodney White (1986:82–83) report a conversation overheard in London. A young woman was enthusiastically telling a friend about her recent vacation in Majorca. When the friend asked, "Where is Majorca?" the woman who had traveled there replied, "I don't know exactly. I flew."

The people in this book have a clearer idea than this woman did of where they go when they travel—and perhaps also of where they are the rest of the time. The book has examined these people's words and actions in order to understand their geographical experiences, images, and ideas. Because the people's words and actions give coherence and meaning to the areas they live in, travel through, and think about, I have called the areas "regions." Because these regions consist of places that people bring together—with their minds, with their imaginations, and most concretely with their bodies—I have named the book "Connected Places."

Regions are produced by human beings. It is people who create regions, in their experience and in their imaginations. People connect places by picturing them as different parts of a single body, by thinking of them as the homes of sisters married to different men, by counting them as members of specific, numbered sets. People bring regions into being by moving across the landscape, or by picturing themselves—or a palanquin, a pole, a bedstead, a *kāvaḍ*, or a river—moving across the landscape. They tell stories about the travels of the gods, then imitate those journeys in their own pilgrimages. They remember the biography of a divine incarnation, and they visit, physically or in acts of recollection, places where he sat, slept, spoke, ate, or even defecated. People differentiate one region from others to which it is opposed, but they also connect places in one region with those in another.

Much of the first four chapters of this book, as well as a good part of the sixth, has focused on the circulation of people, gods, rivers, and ritual objects throughout various small and large regions in the area covered by the modern state of Maharashtra. Chapter 1 began with a story about a river moving through an area, connecting places along the riverbank. The chapter ended with descriptions of people walking around rivers, of people carrying gods from various villages to a nearby river, and of yet other people carrying water from rivers to nearby or distant gods. Chapter 2 elaborated on one of the water-carrying rituals, pointing out the nested set of regions that the pilgrimage to Śiṅgṇāpūr enables its participants to experience and imagine.

Chapter 3 focused on stories about goddesses who move from one place to another in order to be closer to a faithful devotee, to kill a demon, or to get married. Chapter 3 also described pilgrimage festivals that replicate the journeys of two goddesses who came to their devotees' homes, as well as a pair of festivals that jointly replicate the demon-killer goddess's journey, bringing together seven different places where the goddess stopped. Chapter 3 also pointed out the journeys implied in saying that goddesses in several (often seven) different places are one another's sisters: to get to those places, the sisters must have once married and moved from their common home to their various in-laws' houses.

While most of chapter 3's sets of seven-sister-goddess places do not get connected by pilgrims who travel to all of them, most of the sets of places in chapter 4 are held together not only by the number that names each set but also by the circulation of pilgrims among the places that make up the set. The Mahānubhāv places discussed in chapter 6 are connected not only by the remembered peregrinations of the Mahānubhāvs' divine incarnations but also by the present-day pilgrimages of their followers. Even the introduction included an example of a region formed by someone moving around in it: the Deccan Plateau, and especially the Godāvarī valley, are identified as the Daṇḍakāraṇya, the forest through which Rām and his wife and brother wandered in exile. Many of the regions this book has examined have been formed, then, by people moving around within them, by people imagining an historical or mythological, human or divine person to have moved around within them in the past, or by people transporting water, gods, palanquins, poles, or even an empty bed through them.

People often highlight a region's identity by means of contrast and opposition. In this book, we have looked at oppositions expressed in stories, rituals, and verbal usages. The clearest examples are found in chapters 1, 2, 5, and 6, but there are also examples in chapter 4 and the introduction. The book begins with the opposition between Koṅkaṇ and Deś, the coastal plain and the Deccan Plateau, that I first experienced as I traveled up the mountains from Bombay. We saw mythological reflections on this contrast in the stories of Paraśurām in the introduction and Jogāī in chapter 3.

The stories of Agastya and Rām in the introduction highlight a contrast on an even larger scale: that between North and South India. This same contrast forms the underlying assumption of the many asserted connections between Maharashtrian places and North Indian ones cataloged in chapter 5 and echoed at the end of chapter 6. Other parts of chapter 6 present the contrast between Maharashtra and lands to its south in the views of Cakradhar, as well as the contrast between Varhāḍ and the upper Godāvarī valley in his early followers' experience.

We have also seen oppositions between regions on a smaller scale. Chapter 1 ends with some stories and a tug-of-war ritual pitting against each other places on opposite sides of a river. The rivalry between the two principal *kāvaḍ*s in the pilgrimage to Śiṅgṇāpūr in chapter 2 sets two parts of Purandar Taluka (Sāsvaḍ and the Pañcakrośī villages) against each other,[1] while the pilgrimage as a whole brings out the larger-scale contrast between two regions that are opposed as "Śakti's side" and "Śiva's side," the bride's and groom's sides in Śiva's wedding with the Bhātāṅgaḷī pole (alias Pārvatī).

In many of these cases, the opposition between two places or regions is expressed as an opposition between a woman's parental home (her *māher*) and her in-laws' house (her *sāsar*). This is true of Bhātāṅgaḷī and Śiṅgṇāpūr for the pole in chapter 2, of Varhāḍ and the Godāvarī valley for Cakradhar's followers in chapter 6, of the Koṅkaṇ and the Deś for Jogāī in chapter 3, and of Śendī and Pokhardī for women in the tug-of-rope ritual in chapter 1. In chapter 3, I have argued that the ties among widely separated places said to be the homes of seven sister goddesses are grounded in the implication that the sisters share a common *māher*. The contrast between *māher* and *sāsar* is an extremely common, and very poignant, way of expressing geographical contrasts.

The many regions identified in this book overlap, crisscross, and exclude one another, becoming salient in different religious contexts. Almost all of these regions are found within more or less the area of the modern state of Maharashtra. However, only a few of them get identified as "Maharashtra." Often the regions have names other than "Maharashtra," or they have no name at all.

What, then, is Maharashtra? In one sense, a reader of this book might conclude that Maharashtra is a network of overlapping regions that interweave to form a richly textured whole. And yet, I hesitate to affirm that the regions studied here form a "network" or are "interwoven" in the sense that any person or group makes significant connections among them. For the regions are, by-and-large, mutually oblivious. They coexist, next to one another or superimposed on one another, without any person or group of people necessarily connecting them in their minds. When different regions overlap in a single area, one region becomes important in one context, and another region in another context.

Take, as an example, Jejurī. A town that lies 50 kilometers southeast of Pune on the old highway and the railway lines that lead from Pune to Satara, Jejurī made its principal appearance in this book as the starting point and terminus of the pilgrimage in which the goddess Jāṇāī travels by palanquin to her temple at Navkhaṇ (chapter 3). Jejurī is more famous, however, as the site of an important temple of the god Khaṇḍobā, family god to people of many different groups in Maharashtra (Sontheimer 1989a, 1997). Jejurī lies on the bank of the Karhā river; it is one of the places along the upper reaches of the Karhā that not only the river connects, but also the story of the river's origin narrated at the beginning of chapter 1. And Jejurī is one of the early, important stops on the route of the large *kāvaḍs* that travel from Sāsvaḍ, the Pañcakrośī villages, and other places in Purandar Taluka (in which Jejurī itself also lies) to Śiṅgṇāpūr.

In addition, Jejurī is a major, overnight stop on the route of Jñāneśvar's palanquin, the most famous of those that travel to Paṇḍharpūr on the Vārkarī pilgrimage (Maharashtra's largest pilgrimage festival, discussed later in this conclusion). Situated close to Morgāv, the principal member of the Aṣṭavināyak set of Gaṇeś temples (chapter 4), Jejurī also falls within the triangle formed by Maharashtra's three-and-a-half principal goddess temples (also in chapter 4). But it lies outside the region formed by the Eleven Mārutis (chapter 4), outside the region formed by the story and pilgrimage festival of Maḷāī (chapter 3), and outside the region of the pilgrimage in which the bedstead and palanquin travel to Tuḷjāpūr (chapter 3). Moreover, it is completely irrelevant to Mahānubhāv pilgrimage traditions (chapter 6).

Thus, while Jejurī surfaces in various regions formed by different religious images and pilgrimages within the modern state of Maharashtra, there are many other religiously defined regions in Maharashtra to which Jejurī has no particular connection. In addition, the various regions in which Jejurī *does* participate are not necessarily connected to one another. The overnight stay of the Vārkarīs in Jejurī causes congestion that hardly anyone living there can fail to notice. Yet the passage of the Śiṅgṇāpūr *kāvaḍs* through town causes less of a stir. People can live in Jejurī without being aware of the Śiṅgṇāpūr festival, without knowing the story of the origin of the Karhā river, and even without taking cognizance of the pilgrimage festival of Jāṇāī. Most people in Jejurī are probably aware of Morgāv and the Aṣṭavināyak set of places, many know of the three-and-a-half principal goddesses of Maharashtra, but hardly anyone in Jejurī knows about the palanquin and bedstead that travel to Tuḷjāpūr (one of the three-and-a-half goddess places) in time for the Navarātra festival. Finally, many people in Jejurī know that goddesses come in sets of seven sisters located at different places (chapter 3), but almost every citizen of Jejurī, when asked, would come up with a different list of the seven sisters and their locations.

In other words, a number of different regions intersect in Jejurī, but they do not necessarily meet there. There is no one person or group that puts them together into a single imaginary unit. And this is the situation in many other places in what is now Maharashtra, as well as for Maharashtra as a whole. This book has shown a number of different ways in which religious imagery and pilgrimage traditions enable people in Maharashtra to experience and conceptualize regions. Each of the approaches has yielded a number of examples of regions, no two of them congruent with each other. Together the regions form a congeries, with the residents of each region normally aware of and acting in terms of their own region but not the others—even though these other regions are sometimes ones in which, by someone else's definition, they live. Rather than a network, then, Maharashtra as a whole is better represented as an overlapping, ragged, unfinished patchwork of regions.

The complexity of the picture, the vast number of religiously sanctioned but by-and-large mutually oblivious regions that fill up and spill out of the area now known as Maharashtra, would be enhanced even further were we to take into account Maharashtra's non-Hindu religious-geographical and pilgrimage traditions. The traditions that this book has discussed are almost exclusively Hindu. And yet, alongside its majority Hindu population, Maharashtra is also home to Jains, Sikhs, Christians, Jews, Buddhists, and especially Muslims. Situated between the great centers of Jain population and pilgrimage, Karnataka to the south and Gujarat and Rajasthan to the north, Maharashtra has not only a significant contemporary Jain population, but also—especially in southern Maharashtra—important archaeological remains of Jain images and buildings. Maharashtra hosts such important non-Hindu pilgrimage festivals as the Sikh one at Nāndeḍ in honor of Guru Govind Singh and the Christian one to Mary in the Mumbai suburb of Bandra. And Maharashtra is the site of numerous ancient Buddhist cave-temples and -monasteries, not only at the famous archaeological tourist sites of Ajanta and Ellora but also in various passes that lead through the Sahyādri Mountains (the Western Ghats). Modern Maharashtrian Buddhists, formerly-Untouchable Mahārs who have converted to Buddhism since Dr. B. R. Ambedkar's conversion in 1956, hold these caves in great reverence.

Most notably, Maharashtra is home to a very large number of Muslim shrines (*dargās*) and mosques. Many of the shrines attract Muslim and Hindu pilgrims from great distances and are the sites of important festivals not unlike many of those in this book. In addition to the individual importance of such shrines, those that mark the graves of people who are linked by the spiritual relationship of teacher and disciple presumably form networks like many of those examined here.[2] And, like the many Hindu replicas of North Indian places that are listed and classified in chapter 5, Maharashtra also has a replica of the Tāj Mahāl, the most famous Muslim building in India. This is the Bibīkā Makbarā in Auraṅgābād, the grave of Aurāṅgzeb's wife Rābiyā Durāṇī.

Besides regions formed by these non-Hindu religious-geographical and pilgrimage traditions, there are numerous other regions in Maharashtra that are important to people in contexts that have mostly not been covered in this book. These regions include tribal areas and former small kingdoms (see, e.g., Skaria 1999), earlier administrative divisions (Raychaudhuri 1960:44–53), and the districts and talukas of the modern state. All of these regions hold or have held meaning for people who have lived in them or within mental range of them. Besides these regions, many of which have very old names, there are other regions that people have experienced, imagined, and conceptualized, but to which no one has given a name. Thus, the many regions discussed in this book are only a few dozen of the hundreds of regions in what is now called Maharashtra.

The many regions that intersect in the area of modern Maharashtra State do not add up to the whole of Maharashtra, nor is any one of the regions studied in this book coextensive with the one that became the state of Maharashtra in 1960. There is one possible exception to this rule, one religiously defined region that closely approaches congruence with the modern Maharashtra State. This is the region defined by the Vārkarīs' pilgrimage to Paṇḍharpūr (map 7.1). In their most important annual pilgrimage, Vārkarīs accompany palanquins that travel from all corners of the plateau area (the Deś) of Maharashtra to Paṇḍharpūr, the site of the principal temple of the god Viṭhobā. Each of the palanquins contains silver representations of the footwear of a poet-saint devoted to Viṭhobā who lived or died (or went into a permanent trance, *samādhi*) at the place from which the palanquin sets out. As they walk, the pilgrims sing songs of devotion that the saints composed.

In the late 1940s, the sociologist Iravati Karve accompanied the most famous Vārkarī palanquin, that of the thirteenth-century saint Jñāneśvar, as it made its two-week journey from his *samādhi* temple at Āḷandī to Paṇḍharpūr. When Karve took part in the Vārkarīs' pilgrimage, the Saṃyukta Maharashtra movement, the political agitation to form a "United Maharashtra," was well under way. Karve's experience of the pilgrimage was colored by the politicized regionalism that people like her were very conscious of at the time, and that brought the movement for a United Maharashtra its ultimate success. In summing up her account of

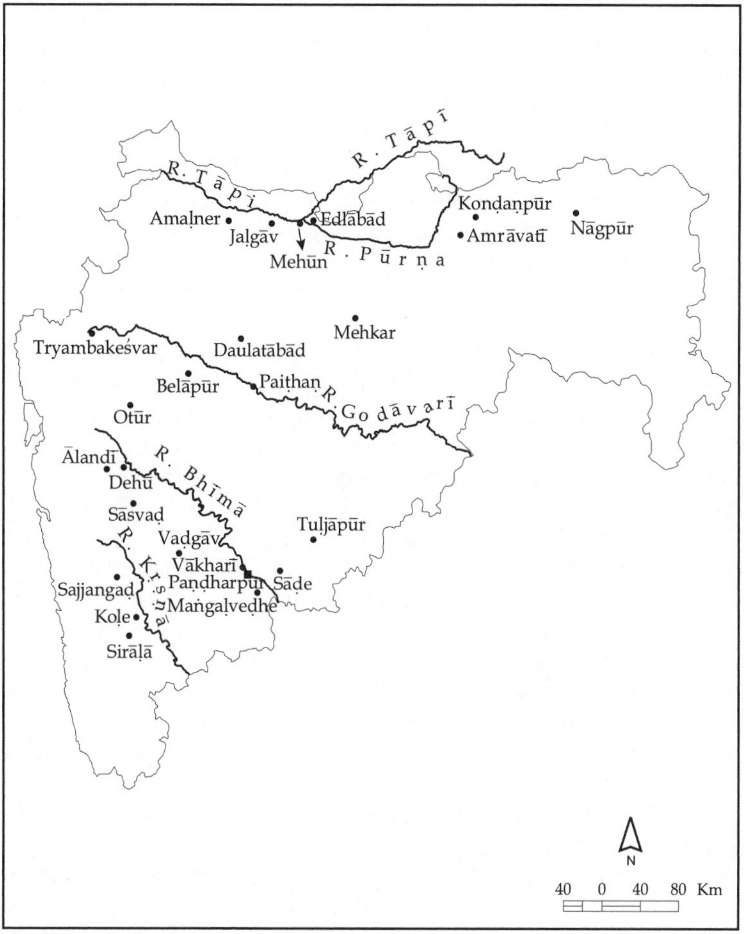

Map 7.1 The Vārkarī pilgrimage

the pilgrimage (Karve 1949, 1962:22), Karve stated:

> So, I was getting to know my Maharashtra anew every day. I found a new definition of Maharashtra: the land whose people go to Pandharpur for pilgrimage. When the palanquin started from Poona, there were people from Poona, Junnar, Moglai, Satara, etc. Every day people were joining the pilgrimage from Khandesh, Sholapur, Nasik, Berar. As we neared Pandharpur, the pilgrimage was becoming bigger and bigger. All were Marathi-speaking people—coming from different castes, but singing the same songs, the same verses of [the] Vārkari cult, speaking to each other, helping each other, singing songs to one another.

For Karve, the pilgrimage to Paṇḍharpūr was a way to experience Maharashtra, a way of "getting to know" it. The pilgrimage was a way to think about Maharashtra, to give it "a new definition." And it was a way to deepen her own identification with the region ("*my* Maharashtra"). Iravati Karve was a member of the Maharashtrian elite. She was a Brāhmaṇ, she was a highly educated woman, and she was a professor of Sociology. Her essays were widely read. Her experience of the Vārkarī pilgrimage must have captivated her readers' imaginations and strengthened the movement for a United Maharashtra. The pilgrimage became for others, too, a way of thinking about Maharashtra, and it helped them to articulate their demand for the founding of the state.

Sadāśiv Ātmārām Jogaḷekar's book *Sahyādri* provides further evidence of the importance of the Vārkarī tradition for Maharashtrian writers and intellectuals who dreamed of a United Maharashtra in the years before 1960. Jogaḷekar was a prolific popular and scholarly writer. His works range from a Marathi biography of Giuseppe Mazzini (1923) to a Marathi translation of and commentary on Hāla's Maharashtri Prakrit work *Gāthāsaptaśatī* (1956). Jogaḷekar's *Sahyādri*, which appeared in 1952, was named for the Sahyādri mountains, or Western Ghats. Identified on its title page as "Mahārāṣṭra Stotra," "A Paean to Maharashtra," *Sahyādri* is a geography of Maharashtra that aims to awaken and foster regional consciousness and pride on the part of its readers. For example, in one passage, given an unusually generous definition of the territorial extent of Maharashtra, and then stretching it a bit further, adding some unusual interpretations of place names and tossing in a bit of mathematical fudging, Jogaḷekar (1952:38–39) claims to find within Maharashtra eight of the 12 Jyotirliṅgas of all of India—an even greater number than the Mahānubhāv author Kṛṣṇamuni found.[3]

In another passage, a masterpiece of cosmological systematization, Jogaḷekar relates the valleys of the Godāvarī, Bhīmā, and Kṛṣṇā rivers to one another, to the mountain ranges that frame these valleys, to their biggest cities, to their most popular gods and goddesses, and to a variety of other philosophical and religious categories, including the river valleys' best-known saints (Jogaḷekar 1952:39):

> The valley between the Sātmāḷā and Bālāghāṭ ranges is that of the Godāvarī; Tryambakeśvar is the Lord of this valley. The valley between the Bālāghāṭ and Mahādev ranges is that of the Bhīmā; Bhīmaśaṅkar is the Lord of this valley. The valley to the south of the Mahādev hills is that of the Kṛṣṇā; Mahābaḷeśvar is the Lord of this valley. The Godāvarī's character (*vṛtti*) is *sāttvic*, and the Kṛṣṇā's character is *tāmasic*.[4] The Bhīmā harmonizes these characters. The *Bhīmaśaṅkar Māhātmya* calls the Bhīmā the boundary (*sīmā*) of liberation (*mokṣa*). The valley of the Godāvarī is Prabhu Rāmcandra's

> land;[5] the valley of the Bhīmā is that of the king of Paṇḍharī [Viṭhobā of Paṇḍharpūr]. The Godāvarī valley is the land of Mahiṣāsuramardinī of Saptaśṛṅgī; the Bhīmā valley, that of Bhavānī of Tuḷjāpūr; and the Kṛṣṇā valley, that of Ambābāī of Kolhāpūr.[6] Tukārām, in the Bhīmā valley, harmonized Nāmdev of the Kṛṣṇā valley and Jñāneśvar of the Gaṅgā valley. Nāsik, in the Godāvarī valley, is a religious center (*dharmakṣetra*); Sātārā, in the Kṛṣṇā valley, is a center for heroism (*vīrakṣetra*); and Pune, in the Bhīmā valley, is a center for work (*karmakṣetra*).[7] In this center for work, the religious center and the center for heroism get harmonized; and only when such a harmonization takes place is the culture of Maharashtra made manifest.

In this passage, Jogaḷekar classifies the valleys of the three central rivers of Maharashtra in terms of a variety of categories. Through the notion of harmonization (*samanvay*), he brings together the three valleys that he has distinguished in these different ways. And then he identifies the harmonized whole as Maharashtra.

The Vārkarī tradition is central to what Jogaḷekar is doing in this passage. This fact can be seen most clearly in the way he connects the three rivers with the three most popular Vārkarī poet-saints, Jñāneśvar, Tukārām, and Nāmdev. Jñāneśvar was born at Āpegāv, on the Godāvarī, and Tukārām lived in Dehū, on a tributary of the Bhīmā. Nāmdev, who is supposed to have lived and died in Paṇḍharpūr, on the Bhīmā, presumably gets assigned to the Kṛṣṇā because he is not quite as popular as Jñāneśvar or Tukārām, because the Kṛṣṇā is the river that is left over, and because his own river, the Bhīmā, eventually flows into the Kṛṣṇā.

It is also significant that the most popular of the Vārkarī saints, Tukārām, is the one who gets to keep the Bhīmā, and that it is this river that, in this and the other relevant categories in the passage, "harmonizes" the other two. The reason that the Bhīmā is held responsible for "harmonizing" the other two rivers could be that, in terms of physical geography, it lies between them. And yet something more is going on as well. In terms of "character" (*vṛtti*), where the Godāvarī is said to be *sāttvic* and the Kṛṣṇā *tāmasic*, one would expect the Bhīmā to be called *rājasic*, neatly matching the three rivers to the three *guṇa*s. But this is *not* what happens. Rather than taking this course, which would be easy, but which would rank the Bhīmā *lower* than the Godāvarī, Jogaḷekar instead states simply that the Bhīmā "harmonizes" the other two rivers' characters, without assigning it a character of its own. The very next sentence singles out the Bhīmā as the "boundary of liberation" without saying anything equivalent about the other two rivers.

Finally, the categorization of the Bhīmā valley as the "land" of the "King of Paṇḍharī"—that is, of the Vārkarīs' god Viṭhobā, whose main temple is at Paṇḍharpūr on the Bhīmā—indicates a more important reason than central location for the Bhīmā's prominence in this passage. Jogaḷekar makes the association between the Bhīmā and Viṭhobā even though he has an equivalent association only for the Godāvarī and none for the Kṛṣṇā. For all these reasons, it seems likely that the Bhīmā is the most prominent river in this passage, and the river that Jogaḷekar sees as the agent of the integration of Maharashtra, because this river is associated with Paṇḍharpūr and the Vārkarīs. The Vārkarī tradition and the Bhīmā river, then, are central to Jogaḷekar's view of Maharashtra as an integrated cosmos—a cosmos that, by implication, *deserved* the statehood it achieved a mere eight years after *Sahyādri* was published.

But to what extent can Karve's experience of the Vārkarī pilgrimage or Jogaḷekar's view of the centrality of the Vārkarī tradition to the religious geography of Maharashtra represent the experiences and views of people who are Vārkarīs by family tradition or personal piety rather than by virtue of intellectual gymnastics or cultural tourism? Even though the Vārkarī pilgrims eventually all converge on Vākharī, a place three kilometers outside Paṇḍharpūr where the palanquins meet and form a triumphant procession into the town, it is probably only very few of the hundreds of thousands of pilgrims who join this procession who experience it as the dramatization of the unity of Maharashtra that Karve saw in it. Most of them are intent on the goal of Paṇḍharpūr and joyful at having reached it. They are worried about where to spend the night, how to evade the pickpockets, and how long they will have to wait in line for the bus back home. The unity they experience is mostly that of the *immediate* group of pilgrims with whom they have been traveling for many days, rather than some imagined Maharashtrian whole.

Besides, *no* one who makes the Vārkarī pilgrimage travels throughout the *whole* region it covers. Each pilgrim accompanies only *one* of the palanquins that converge on Paṇḍharpūr. When Karve says, "I was getting to know my Maharashtra anew every day," even she is not thinking about the pilgrims who have travelled with the many palanquins that come from various points in Maharashtra to Paṇḍharpūr. She is referring, rather, to the pilgrims from *various* places who join *her* part of the pilgrimage, the largest and best-known group, the one that accompanies the palanquin of Jñāneśvar from Āḷandī to Paṇḍharpūr. In reflecting on the way the pilgrimage brings Maharashtra together, even Karve is referring not to the whole area that the pilgrimage covers, but only to one of its lines.

Still, the area that came into being as the State of Maharashtra in 1960 corresponds more closely to the region covered by the Vārkarī pilgrimage than it does to any of the other religious-geographical regions that have been highlighted in this book. Of the many regions that *could* have attained existence as a political unit, this is the one that has in fact done so. In the years leading up to 1960, the region covered by the Vārkarī pilgrimage had two great advantages over the other regions studied here: it corresponded closely to the Marathi linguistic region that formed the basic definition of the state, and it had well-known authors like Karve and Jogaḷekar to sing its praises.

Unlike the Vārkarīs' pilgrimage, the other pilgrimages and religious-geographical imagery in this book have not yet had elite interpreters like Karve and Jogaḷekar, nor have they contributed to the formation of modern political entities like Maharashtra State. In some cases, we have seen adumbrations of political movements and kingdoms past or present. The Aṣṭavināyak region (chapter 4), for instance, corresponds to the heartland of the Peśvās' kingdom, and Cakradhar's Godāvarī valley (chapter 6) corresponds to the kingdom of the much-earlier Yādavas, while at least one modern author with Hindu-nationalist leanings has pointed out the correspondence of the Akrā Mārutī region (chapter 4) to the core area of Śivājī's power. Nevertheless, for the most part the pilgrimages, concepts, and images the book has examined have not affected the political aspirations of the people who participate in the pilgrimages or hold the concepts and images in their minds. And yet these pilgrimages, concepts, and images have provided, and do provide, important means for people to experience, to think about, and to imagine a variety of regions—including some that get called "Maharashtra."

There are many religiously defined, meaningful regions that coexist within or overlap with the one that happened to become the state of Maharashtra. The fact that the region defined by the Vārkarī pilgrimage became a political unit is the exception that proves the rule. Through their large number, great variety, and lack of systematic order, the many religiously sanctioned regions of Maharashtra illustrate the vast array of possibilities from among which the political and administrative units of modern India have been chosen. But the many religiously meaningful regions of Maharashtra also inspire hope, both for the rest of India and for other fragile, fissiparous areas of the contemporary world. For these regions show that people can experience, imagine, conceptualize, and value a region in religious terms without feeling the need to make it into a politically separate entity.

In places around the world where regionalistic and nationalistic political movements have arisen—as ever-smaller units of Eastern Europe, Central Asia, Africa, and Indonesia aspire to nationhood, and as ever-smaller areas of northeastern India (Baruah 1999) aspire to become states within a federally organized modern nation—scholars can look back at imagery, concepts, and pilgrimages like those examined in this book and interpret them as expressions of "proto-nationalism" (Hobsbawm 1990).

But what of the cases where political movements do *not* arise? Although an understanding of the roots of potential regionalistic and nationalistic political movements is one of the contributions of a study such as the one undertaken here, another, more timely contribution is to point out the multiplicity of intersecting, overlapping, but often mutually ignorant regions that can coexist in one large place.

The fact that people attach religious meanings to regions makes those regions important, but it does not make them nations, nor does it mean that they *must* become political or administrative units. For religious meaning does not automatically bring with it political consequences, nor does the religious valuation of a region necessarily have a political teleology. When a part of the world to which people attach religious meanings does become a nation-state, the meanings can strengthen the bonds that hold the people together. When people attach *different* religious meanings to the *same* part of the world, the meanings can ignite the bombs that the people hurl at one another. But there is also still a chance, even now, that religious imagery can enrich the lives of individuals and small communities without engendering bloodshed and hatred. This book has sought to illustrate that possibility.

Notes

Introduction

Notes to Pages 1–5

1. Adele Fiske, a scholar of Greek and Latin Classics and a Professor of Religion at Manhattanville College, had done postdoctoral studies in Sanskrit and Buddhism at Columbia University. In the course of these studies, she had spent a year in India learning about modern forms of Buddhism there. In the summer of 1970, when she was returning to India to learn about popular Hinduism, she invited me to travel with her.
2. The train is probably more immediately named for Pune (Poona), which in British times was called the "Queen of the Deccan" (Frank Conlon, personal communication).
3. The southern border of Maharashtra corresponds roughly to a change from the heavy, black cotton soil called "Deccan trap" to the looser, reddish soil of the former Mysore State. See Chen 1996:122 and Spate and Learmonth 1967:98–99.
4. According to some, Khāndeś is named for Kṛṣṇa or Kānha, the god of the Ābhīras (R. C. Dhere, personal communication, 2001); according to others, it is named for the Yādava king Kānherdev (*BSK*, Volume 2, p. 635), or its name derives from Seuṇadeśa, a name of the Yādava kingdom (ibid.). Another etymology would derive its name from the Persian honorific title "Khān," reminiscent of the area's Muslim rulers.
5. According to *BSK*, Volume 8, p. 687–88, present-day usage restricts the term "Varhāḍ" to Akola, Amravati, Yavatmal, and Buldhana Districts, and applies the name "Vidarbha" to the area covered by these districts plus Vardha, Nagpur, Canda (Candrapur), and Bhandara Districts.
6. Aurangabad, Jalna, Parbhani, Nanded, Bid, Latur, and Usmanabad Districts.
7. For a fuller description of my fieldwork techniques, see Feldhaus 1995:9–15 and Feldhaus 2000:47–63.
8. Such a region is what Burton Stein (1977) called a "cognitive" or "formal" region, what Bernard Cohn (1967) called a "historical" region, and what others call a "naively given," "experienced," or "subjective" region (Lodrick 1994:3–4, quoting Schwartzberg 1967:89–90).
9. For an excellent survey of this literature, see Feld and Basso 1996b. Cultural geographers interested in place have had to extract themselves from a notion of

social science as exclusively concerned with scientific rationality. See, e.g., Entrikin 1989:40–41.

10. Casey 1996b:39, citing Bachelard and Heidegger; cf. Bourdieu 1971.
11. Entrikin 1989:30, e.g., uses "the terms 'place' and 'region' such that, except for the differences in geographical scale, their meanings are essentially equivalent." Agnew 1993:263, pointing out that "the sense of place need not be restricted to the scale of the locality," identifies "place" as "discrete if 'elastic' areas in which . . . social relations are located and with which people can identify." If place is "elastic," whole regions can be places.
12. They do, however, also know and speak of these directional terms (and have special terms not only for the cardinal directions, but for the intermediate ones, for which people in Kansas are left simply with the hybrids of the cardinal directions, "southwest," "northwest," and the others). People in Maharashtra use the cardinal and intermediate directions in architecture as well. For example, when possible, homes and temples are oriented to the east, and the Vāstu Puruṣa (see Kramrisch 1976) is installed in the (or a) southeast corner of many homes—even in flats in large apartment buildings. Although some people say that Muslims build mosques oriented to the west (the general direction of Mecca), mosques are in fact oriented to Mecca itself (an angle of 280 degrees from India. Catherine Asher, personal communication), rather than to the west. For the importance of the cardinal directions to the compilers of a medieval Marathi religious-geographical text, the *Sthānpothī*, see chapter 6.
13. Lee Schlesinger first made me aware of this linguistic phenomenon during the mid-1970s, when he was doing field work in a village in Satara District, Maharashtra.
14. Feldhaus 1995:24–25; cf. the section of chapter 5 titled "The Maharashtrian Gaṅgā."
15. See Berdoulay 1989:125 on the connotations of the term "*lieu*" in French geography.
16. See, e.g., Keith and Pile 1993.
17. I am grateful to Eleanor Zelliot for her help in formulating the information presented here. For modern definitions of Maharashtra before 1960, see Feldhaus 1986:536, n.8.
18. Quite apart from recent immigration to European countries, the situation is complicated by the fact that Belgium and Switzerland were founded as multilingual nation-states, as well as by the fact that several European languages are spoken in more than one nation-state: German, e.g., in Austria and Switzerland as well as in Germany. See Karna 2000:81.
19. See Karna 2000:84 for three "patterns of language diversity" in formerly colonized countries.
20. Kolte 1982a:92; *ASM* I.133–34. See chapter 6.
21. For further arguments in support of this statement, see the section "Maharashtra's Southern Identity" at the end of chapter 5.
22. Sontheimer 1991; Feldhaus 1995:98–101. There are also stories about the *Mahābhārata* heroes spending their period of exile in Maharashtra. See, e.g., the story of the origin of the Karhā river, at the beginning of chapter 1.

23. Paraśurāmbhakta n.d.:17; cf. Mate 1962:111.
24. For further explanations of the Citpāvans' connection with Āmbejogāī, see the section "The Goddess as Bride: Jogāī" in chapter 3.

1 Rivers and Regional Consciousness

1. Some of the villages along this river have names that connect them with this story. The place where the sage ran out of *bel* leaves for worshiping Śivaliṅgas is called Belsar ("*sar*" comes from the verb "*saraṇe*," "to give out," "to be expended"). The village just upstream from Pāṇḍeśvar is at the spot where Arjun and Nakul heard their eldest brother, Yudhiṣṭhir, calling out impatiently, "Arjun! Where are you?"—"I'm nearby (*javaḷ*)!" Arjun replied. And thus the place that Arjun had reached is now called Javaḷārjun.
2. Cf. Jackson 1994 on roads.
3. These texts are listed in the abbreviations at the end of the bibliography as *NM*, *TM*, *PM*, *GM*.Mar., *BM*, *KM*.Mar., *GM*.Skt., and *KM*.Skt., respectively. Full bibliographical information is given there.
4. *KM*.Mar. 60.21–22; *KM*.Skt. 60.23–25.
5. *durlabh*. *TM* 75.53. Cf. *TM* 78.51.
6. *KM*.Skt. 58.37–38; *KM*.Mar. 58.29.
7. *PM* 27.39–40 and *PM* 39.51 give the same list; *PM* 22.100–01, a partially different list.
8. Lele (1885:131) quotes a Sanskrit verse from "the Purāṇas" naming four places on the Bhīmā which are especially precious (*durlabh*); he also (1885:160) lists the five most important confluences (*saṅgams*) and the five most important holy places (*kṣetras*) along the Kṛṣṇā. For the Siṃhastha, see chapter 5 in this book.
9. See also Kāgalkar 1969:30–31.
10. T. Nīlakaṇṭh Kavīśvar Śāstrī gives a strikingly similar interpretation of an analogous image of the Kṛṣṇā. The image is found in a verse of a poem by Ṭembe Svāmī entitled "Kṛṣṇālaharī": "Your mouth is at the base of the Sahyādris; / You have Narahari's compassionate heart; / Your navel is in a town in Andhra; / Your two feet are in the east." Although the verse does not name specific *tīrtha*s or *kṣetras*, T. N. K. Śāstrī and other interpreters (Jośī 1950:13; oral information from a priest at Narsobācī Vāḍī) identify Wāī as the Kṛṣṇā's mouth or face (*mukha*), Narsobācī Vāḍī as its heart, and Kurugaḍḍī or Kuravapūr in Andhra Pradesh as its navel, with the feet being the two mouths by which the Kṛṣṇā reaches the ocean. Śāstrī explains that Wāī is called the mouth of the Kṛṣṇā because many Brāhmaṇs live in Wāī, and Brāhmaṇs are the mouth of Viṣṇu (whom Śāstrī identifies with the Vedic Puruṣa). Since "the scriptures" identify Viṣṇu with the Kṛṣṇā river (Śāstrī 1982:122), this river too is ultimately one with the Puruṣa of the Puruṣasūkta.
11. The mouth of the Sarasvatī river is understood to be at Prabhās, now called Somnāth, in Saurāṣṭra (Bhardwaj 1973:46–47).

12. In some accounts, the moon emerged from the ocean, which is thus its father. The story of the origin of the Pūrṇā or Payoṣṇī river (see later) shows it to be the daughter of the moon. This makes the river the granddaughter of the ocean.
13. See Feldhaus 1995 for more on gender imagery used in relation to rivers.
14. See Eck 1982:40–41, 320–21, 351–53.
15. For instance, Ujjain, Tryambakeśvar, Oṃkār Māndhātā (Kāgalkar 1969:9), Karāḍ (Gupte 1927:6), and Ṛddhipur (chapter 6 in this book).
16. *KM*.Mar. 54.11; 60.23; *KM*.Skt. 54.15; 60.26.
17. *PM* 1.49–6.90; cf. Feldhaus 1995:108–09.
18. I am not sure where either Belkuṇḍ or Vāramtīr is. It may be that Belkuṇḍ is the place that the Census of India 1991 *District Census Handbook for Amravati District* (1995) lists as Belkheda, near Vishroli. Vishroli lies on the east bank of the Pūrṇā river in Cāndūr Bājār Taluka.
19. More precisely, Brahmā accomplished the sacrifice despite the obstructions caused by his wives. See Feldhaus 1995:41–42, 78; cf. Malik 1993.
20. A Marathi-speaking pandit in Dharmapurī used a play on words to link Dharmapurī not only with Bāsar, but also with Kāleśvaram, another holy place on the Godāvarī in Andhra Pradesh: *Vā*sar (= Bāsar), he explained, is upstream (*va*r), and if one goes there one gets knowledge (*vi*dyā, the gift of Sarasvatī, who is the goddess of learning); *Kā*leśvaram is downstream (*khā*lī); if one goes there, one is spared an untimely death (a*kā*la mṛtyu); while in *Dharma*purī one gets *dharma*—religious, morally correct behavior.
21. In the *Godāvarī Māhātmya*, the demon's head is said to have fallen on Mt. Meru (*GM*.Skt. 36.39), or on the Sahyādri mountains (*GM*.Mar. 15.29).
22. The places the man named are Māhulī, Vāḍkheḍ, Limb, Marḍh, and Dhāvaḍśī. For more on Agastya (and Paraśurām), see the introduction to this book.
23. Some other texts do use marital imagery with respect to other rivers. See Feldhaus 1995:43.
24. Eck 1982:213, 1996:138. The Sanskrit *Godāvarī Māhātmya* names two sets of *six* rivers, one in North India and one in South India (*GM*.Skt. 1.23–24; cf. *GM*.Mar. 1.31–33).
25. In some versions of the story of the descent of the Gaṅgā (e.g., in NM. 40), when the water from Brahmā's waterpot flows down from Viṣṇu's toes, it goes first to the Pole Star and from there to the constellation of the Seven Sages, before falling to the peak of Mt. Meru. If we remember that the Godāvarī *is* the Gaṅgā (see chapter 5 in this book, and Feldhaus 1995:24–25), we can see the association of the Godāvarī delta with the Seven Sages as complementary to the river's passing through the *constellation* of the Seven Sages before coming to earth. The symmetry thus produced also suggests a cycle in which the river goes from sky to earth and back, as water does in the cycle of rain. The replication on earth of a constellation in the sky is, further, reminiscent of the very old notion of the Milky Way as a river in the sky. See Witzel 1984:213–79. In Marathi this river is called "Ākāśgaṅgā," "the Gaṅgā (or river) in the sky." However, the materials I have found about the Godāvarī delta express no direct connection to the Seven Sages constellation. Dāsagaṇu's Marathi *Godāvarī*

Māhātmya (*GM*.Mar. 29.34–39 etc.) makes use of an entirely different set of meanings of the Seven Sages: their identity as Brāhmaṇs living lives of piety, learning, and asceticism in the forest.

26. To perform a complete circumambulation of a holy place, pilgrims travel around the outer limits of its *pañcakrośī*.
27. Dāṇḍekar also wrote a nonfiction, albeit meditative and impressionistic, account of the Narmadā and of his own travels to and along it (Dāṇḍekar 1949). The influence of the Narmadā *parikrama* may perhaps also be seen in the *Narmadā Māhātmya*. This text, rather than following the source-to-mouth order of the other river Māhātmyas I have examined, treats first the places on the north bank of the Narmadā river, from source to mouth, and then the places on the south bank, from mouth to source. This order, however, is the opposite of the order one should follow in performing *pradakṣiṇā*: if one goes downstream on the north bank of the Narmadā and upstream on the south bank, the river stays on one's left instead of one's right.
28. Using this method, of course, means that one has the river on one's right only half the time.
29. I am not sure what this means for pilgrims who want to visit the island temple of Oṃkār Māndhātā in the course of their *parikrama* of the Narmadā.
30. So that all performing the *parikrama* will be equal, Kāgalkar explains.
31. Kāgalkar (1969:21–25) gives a vivid description of the difficulties of performing the *parikrama*.
32. This is especially the case for pilgrims who do the *parikrama* only a bit at a time, returning each time to take up the circumambulation at the place where they left off the last time. For instance, Śrīrāj Sant Mahārāj of Gujarat performed the *parikrama* in 108 days, living the whole time on nothing but jaggery water (Kāgalkar 1969:24)—but that included only the days on which he was actually walking and not the days of rest in between (Kāgalkar 1969:44).
33. SSG, Eknāth, no. 363.3.
34. Oral information, Rākṣasbhuvan; Kāgalkar (1969:17). *GM*.Mar. 31.81 recommends performing *pradakṣiṇā* of the Godāvarī during the Siṃhastha period. For more on the Siṃhastha and its significance for the Godāvarī, see chapter 5 in this book.
35. Kāgalkar 1969:17; oral information in Dhanorā, Rākṣasbhūvan, and Paiṭhaṇ.
36. Where the enormous Jāyakvāḍī dam provides a new barrier to further travel.
37. Oral information, Dharmapurī.
38. This is probably the one named Gautamī, the name otherwise given to the river as a whole.
39. Oral information, Paiṭhaṇ.
40. Oral information, Rākṣasbhuvan.
41. The "bright half" of a month is the fortnight during which the moon is waxing. The fortnight of the waning moon is called the "dark half."
42. See Deleury 1960, Karve 1962, and Mokashi 1987, as well as the conclusion of the present book.
43. Phiraṅgāī from Kurkumbh, Ambikāmātā from Khorvaḍī, and Śirsāī from Śirsuphaḷ.

44. Bhairavnāth or Navkhaṇḍīnāth from Jiregāv; Bhairavnāth from Maḷad, Pāṇḍharevāḍī, and Mirgaḷvāḍī; Birobā or Mhasnobā from Mhasnarvāḍī; Birobā from Yeḍevāḍī; Mhasobā from Māḷvāḍī; Mhaskobā from Gopāḷvāḍī; and Nāth from Girīm.
45. The group that had brought the palanquin of the god Bhairavnāth from Pāṇḍharevāḍī.
46. For more on *huīk* or *bhāganūk*, see Sontheimer 1989a:214n., 228.
47. Unless we asked them specifically about her connection with their god. Then they would say either that there is no connection, or that Kṛṣṇābāī is their god's "sister"—a categorical term that people often use in answering this sort of question.
48. I am grateful to Lee Schlesinger for attending the Saṅgam Māhulī festival and to Sudhir Waghmare for attending the Karāḍ festival in 1987, and to both of them for writing lengthy descriptions of what they saw.
49. I have described such rituals in Feldhaus 1995:29–36. There I presented a number of interpretations of the rituals, emphasizing the one most pertinent to the gender imagery on which that book focuses. Here I am interested in a different interpretation of the water-carrying rituals.
50. I owe this insight to Günther Sontheimer, for whom—from his shepherd-centered point of view—rivers' role as obstacles was primary.
51. One man in Wāī, on the Kṛṣṇā river, described the Godāvarī rather than the Narmadā as the dividing line between North and South India. This statement, although somewhat idiosyncratic, is nevertheless interesting in that it reveals the importance of the Godāvarī in the geographical thinking of people all over Maharashtra.
52. The Paingaṅgā, e.g., which was once a border between the Nizām's territory and that of the British in Vidarbha (Kandhārkar 1909:188), still separates the Vidarbha division of Maharashtra from Marāṭhvāḍā. The Vardhā river separates Vardha and Candrapur Districts, east of the river, from Amravati and Yavatmal Districts, to the west. The Godāvarī river separates Aurangabad, Jalna, and Parbhani Districts, to the north, from Ahmadnagar and Bid Districts, to the south, while the Nirā river separates Pune District from Satara District.
53. Young 1980; Eck 1982:34–35. The corresponding imagery is used quite widely in Marathi devotional (*bhakti*) literature. The seventeenth-century poet-saint Tukārām, for instance, rejoices, "The obstacle that the river of existence posed has disappeared. It has dried up; I can walk right through" (SSG, Tukārām 1833.1). More elaborately, Nāmdev, in the fourteenth century, makes Paṇḍharpūr a ferry boat and Viṭhobā the ferryman who gets people across (Nāmdev 1970, no. 400; cf. Nāmdev 440.1). See also Tukārām 1973, no. 1549, in which the name of God is the boat, and the poet is the porter who carries its treasures. I am grateful to Dr. S. G. Tulpule for finding these poems for me and reading them with me.
54. Sontheimer 1989a:37, 77–83; Sontheimer 1982:119.
55. Sontheimer 1989a:207–38 and passim. The version narrated here is summarized from an oral account given to me by a Gurav (non-Brāhmaṇ) priest at the temple in Vīr.

56. This is a common motif in the stories of the travels of gods and goddesses. See chapter 3, note 2, in this book.
57. There is also a Ghoḍe Udān near Kāmbaḷeśvar, where the goddess Bhivāī's brother Dhuḷobā jumped over a small river on his horse; another at Jejurī, where Khaṇḍobā jumped over the Karhā river on *his* horse; and yet others at places where other pastoral gods crossed rivers in this way—generally more successfully and gracefully than in the story from Vīr (cf. Sontheimer 1989a:76, 98, 197 on Ghoḍe Udān).
58. I am grateful to Thakur Raja Ram Singh, who not only accompanied me to this place and to several others along the Godāvarī in Andhra Pradesh but also conducted interviews for me, and who dictated to me his translation of this version of the story.
59. John Abbott (1932:161–62) reports a number of these, including a prohibition in the *Viṣṇusmṛti* (63.44) against crossing a river unnecessarily. The *GBP* 1883 (Nāsik):527 mentions that pilgrims to Nāsik used to avoid crossing the river there until they had completed their pilgrimage: "Before the opening of the railway . . . [pilgrims] always approached Nâsik from the east or from the west; and were careful to keep the rule against crossing the river until all pilgrim rites were over . . . ."
60. Some of these rules are listed in a Dhangar shepherds' epic (*ovī*) that Sontheimer has translated (Sontheimer 1989a:82): "Before you get into the boat / Take off your sandals / Make a salutation / Then step into the boat / Do not let a menstruating woman / Sit in the boat / Unless you are not told about it." My conversations with ferrymen in a number of different places in Maharashtra and Karnataka indicate that they still adhere more or less closely to rules like these.
61. 75,000, according to the 1961 census volume *Fairs and Festivals in Maharashtra* (1969: 379).
62. For a photograph of this procession, with the village headman who represents Khaṇḍobā crossing the river enveloped in a cloud of turmeric powder, seated on an elephant, and surrounded by parasols made of marigolds, see the jacket of Sontheimer 1997.
63. A footnote explains: "The local belief is that the non-observance of this fighting custom is followed by a failure of rain or if rain falls it produces a rat plague. A stone fight duly waged is followed by a plentiful rainfall." *GBP* 1884 (*Ahmadnagar)*:722–23. The *Gazetteer*'s source of this information is given as "Mr. Sinclair in Ind. Ant. V. 5."
64. Cāndekar 1984:6. Although the article was written by A. Mo. Cāndekar, the story was collected by Sureś Jośī, executive trustee of the historical museum of Ahmadnagar District, from one or several aged resident(s) of Śeṇḍī.
65. The third of the four world-ages (*yugas*), the one preceding the present age.
66. This ritual gesture, called *oṭī bharaṇeṃ*, is performed to married or marriageable women to express good wishes for their fertility and prosperity. In "filling the lap" of a woman, one puts a coconut, a piece of cloth for a sari blouse, some grain, red (*kuṅkuṃ*) powder, yellow (turmeric) powder, and perhaps a dried date or a knobbed turmeric root into the part of the woman's sari that covers her midriff.
67. Despite the statements of some pilgrims quoted toward the end of that chapter.

2 The Pilgrimage to Śiṅgṇāpūr

1. For a photograph of the mountain, see Feldhaus 1995, after page 64.
2. The temple also has a Sanskrit name, Amṛteśvar ("Lord of Nectar").
3. Ḍhere (1992a:13) gives a tantalizing series of quotations from poems of Vārkarī saints who refer to *kāvaḍs*, Śiṅgṇāpūr, and the worship of Śiva in various combinations. The collection of poems (*gāthā*) by Tukārām, the seventeenth-century poet who is the most popular of the Vārkarī saints, includes a series of five *abhaṅgas* about carrying a *kāvaḍ*. The eighteenth-century hagiographer Mahīpatī (1715–1790) builds these poems into a story about Tukārām going on pilgrimage to Śiṅgṇāpūr during the month of Caitra. The story, which appears in Mahīpatī's *Bhaktalīlāmṛt* (37.72–93), does not, however, explicitly state that Tukārām or any of his companions carried a *kāvaḍ* to Śiṅgṇāpūr.
4. "*Śaṅkarācī piṇḍ*" is the term I used, and the woman accepted its use.
5. Clearly there is a story here, one that seemed to involve some tension between the woman and her in-laws. But we did not pry too deeply into what seemed a private matter.
6. *Āratī* is a ritual in which one person waves a tray of lighted oil lamps or burning camphor in a circular motion in front of someone or something while others clap in rhythm to a song that the whole group sings. The ritual is performed in order to honor the person or thing to whom or which it is done, as well as to ward off evil.
7. The longer beams are called *āḍvat* or *dāṇḍī* and the crossbars *piḍī*.
8. On the significance and use of this "sail," see later. It may be because the cloth is seen as a sail that the pole it hangs from is called "*śīḍ*," a term that means "sail" in Marathi. For a photograph that gives a side view of one of the large *kāvaḍs* being carried to Śiṅgṇāpūr, see Feldhaus 1995, after page 64.
9. The principal *kāvaḍs* also have some distinctive, relatively permanent decorations. The front of the Pañcakrośī *kāvaḍ*, e.g., is covered with brass, with an image of Śiva and Pārvatī in relief on its right side and a relief of Bhutojī Telī on its left side. Bhutojī Telī is portrayed wearing three strands of *rudrākṣa* beads around his neck and holding a fourth strand in his left hand; his right hand is raised in a gesture of blessing. Beneath the image of Śiva and Pārvatī is an inscription that reads, "Oṃ Homage [to] Śiva [and] Pārvatī / Śikhar Śiṅgṇāpūr / Caitra Śu. 1 Śake 1912 / 27-3-1990," indicating the date (March 27, 1990) when this *kāvaḍ* was first put into use. Beneath the image of Bhutojī Telī is an inscription identifying him and naming and locating the five villages that cooperate in conveying this *kāvaḍ* to Śiṅgṇāpūr: "Sant Bhutojī Mahārāj (Telī) Pañcakrośī Kāvaḍ / Khaḷad, Ekhatpūr, Muñjavaḍī, Khānavaḍī, Kumbhār Vaḷaṇ, Purandhar Tālukā, Puṇe District." On the front crossbar of the *kāvaḍ* are some more images in brass: a double *piṇḍ* (Śivaliṅga), a Nandī, a tortoise, and a woman prostrating herself. On the back of the *kāvaḍ* are more, shallower brass reliefs with inscriptions identifying them as Śrī Sopāndev Mahārāj (a Vārkarī saint whose *samādhi* is in Sāsvaḍ) and the *advaita* philosopher and Śaiva *guru* Śrīmad Ādya Śaṅkarācārya.

The Sāsvaḍ *kāvaḍ*, which is older than the one from the Pañcakrośī villages, has inscriptions on both its water pots. Each of the pots bears the name of a king of Sātārā, Ābāsāheb Mahārāj (d. 1848?), who donated them; a number indicating the weight of the pot (in each case this is 66—standing for 66 seers, or approximately 66 kilograms); and another number (22-1/2 on one of the pots, 23-1/4 on the other) that no one was able to explain to me. The Sāsvaḍ *kāvaḍ* is decorated in silver, and in 1995 it had a new silver image of Nandī, Śiva's bull, that had been installed on its crossbar just in time for the pilgrimage.

10. The retinue of the Sāsvaḍ *kāvaḍ* includes horn players as well.
11. These two parts are sometimes distinguished as Malṭaṇ and Phalṭaṇ.
12. Although the Pañcakrośī *kāvaḍ* goes to the right, and the Sāsvaḍ *kāvaḍ* to the left, in relation to the movement of the procession, the people explaining the ritual to me as I watched it in Phalṭaṇ called the Pañcakrośī *kāvaḍ*'s position "left" (*ḍāvaṃ*) and the Sāsvaḍ *kāvaḍ*'s position "right" (*ujvaṃ*)—taking the point of view of someone (Mahādev, perhaps, at Śiṅgṇāpūr? Or themselves, as they stood with me on the far side of the river bed) watching the procession approach. The two principal *kāvaḍs* perform the *ujvī-ḍāvī* rite at least once more on the way to Śiṅgṇāpūr.
13. My companions and I have gathered different, conflicting views about the meaning and etymology of this name. One story we have heard recounts that this place, whose name means something like "Battle (*raṇ*) Cairn (*khiḷā*)," was the site of a battle between proponents of rival *kāvaḍs*. Another suggestion is that the name means "hard road" and refers to the difficulty of the unpaved, rocky cross-country road that cuts through from Baraḍ to Kothaḷe/Āndrūḍ via the *place* called Raṇkhiḷā.
14. According to its printed program, the Sāsvaḍ *kāvaḍ* "meets" three other *kāvaḍs*: that of Deśmāne Telī from Jintī Khānavaṭe, that of the Cāndguḍes from Mhasobācī Vāḍī, and finally that of Dhoṇḍībā Sāhebrāv Kavaḍe (who is also from Mhasobācī Vāḍī). According to the Pañcakrośī villages' printed program, their *kāvaḍ* "meets" others from "Śaṭphaḷ Gaḍeṃ," Śirsūphaḷ (Śirsuphaḷ), Saṇsar, Māḷegāv, "and so on." Such a meeting is called "*bheṭ*."
15. Men describing this to me before I had seen it called it too "Right-and-Left" (*ujvī-ḍāvī*): a "Right-and-Left Meeting." Some men also called it "Ramming" (*ṭakkar*). Later, when my companions and I were discussing the pilgrimage festival with members of the Āḍhāv families of Guṇavare, the "guides" of the two principal *kāvaḍs*, these men interpreted these meetings as simply "play" (*kheḷ*).
16. See the story about the epiphany at this place, under "Devotion to Śiva," later. For the *cambū*, see figure 2.2.
17. The men who described this method to me called it "*puḍhcī māḷ*," "the chain of the one in front."
18. According to some men I spoke with in the Grāmpañcāyat office at Śiṅgṇāpūr during the festival in 1994, 25% of the pilgrims at the festival come from "Marāṭhvāḍā and Vidarbha." According to another man, a former headman (Sarpañc) of Śiṅgṇāpūr, more than 80% of the festival pilgrims come from Marāṭhvāḍā. I have not yet figured out how to reconcile these vastly different estimates, nor do I have a firm basis for choosing between them.

19. The Marathi term "*dhaj*" may be derived from (Sanskrit and Marathi) *dhvaj*, flag. In 2002, the year I observed the *dhaj*-raising ceremony, the *dhaj* consisted of four strands of cloth that were wrapped around one another as the *dhaj* made its way from the top of the upper temple to the top of Baḷī's temple. The *dhaj* weaver explained that only one of the strands was the one he weaves; others had been offered by other people in fulfilment of *navas* vows.
20. The pole is called a *kāṭhī* (the more usual term for such a ritual object) or a *mānācā patāka*, an "honorary flag."
21. Usmanabad District is generally classified as belonging to the Marāṭhvāḍā division of Maharashtra rather than to Vidarbha. However, there is a tendency among people involved in the Śiṅgṇāpūr festival to identify the *dhaj*, and also the Bhātāṅgaḷī pole (which also comes from Usmanabad District), as coming from "Vidarbha."
22. The person making this statement used the term "*anna*." This word, which refers to most vegetables, lentils, rice, wheat bread, and millet bread, might best be translated "proper meals." During a fast, although one does not eat *anna*, one can still have many kinds of food, including certain root vegetables and fruits. Cf. note 52, later.
23. As a turban for the bridegroom Śiva, the *dhaj*-carrier explained when I talked with him in Caitra 2002. See later, under "Śiva's Wedding."
24. When my companions and I met and interviewed Kāḷ Gāvḍā in 1999, he told us that he now wears tennis shoes, although the previous practice was to wear leather footwear into the temple.
25. Men in Bhātāṅgaḷī explained that they count their pilgrimage by solar days, not lunar days (*tithī*s), starting with the first day of Caitra, Guḍhī Pāḍvā. They leave Śiṅgṇāpūr on the twelfth *day* after Guḍhī Pāḍvā, whether or not that day is Caitra Bāras.
26. In addition to the one from Bhātāṅgaḷī, my companions and I met or learned of *kāṭhī*s that come to Śiṅgṇāpūr from Ausā (Latur District), Ḍhavaḷī (Vāḷvā Taluka, Sangli District), Dhāyrī-Vaḍgāv (Havelī Taluka, Pune District), "Lātūr" (probably some particular place in Latur District), Phursuṅgī (Havelī Taluka, Pune District), Taḷegāv Ḍhamḍhere (Śirur Taluka, Pune District), Dhārkheḍ (Gaṅgākheḍ Taluka, Parbhani District), Sagaruḷī (Ausā Taluka, Latur District), and possibly also Yenegur (Umargā Taluka, Usmanabad District) and Porle (Panhāḷā Taluka, Kolhapur District), as well as places named Amboḷī, Jāgjī, Jīvaḷī, and Śivatī (taluka and district not identified). There are also probably several more. In the cases where my notes describe these *kāṭhī*s, each has a brass image affixed to it. Dhārkheḍ's has an image of Śaṅkar (Śiva) and his bull, Nandī, toward the bottom, while Dhāyrī-Vaḍgāv's has images of Śaṅkar and Nandī at its top. On top of the Phursuṅgī *kāṭhī* is what the people traveling with it called a "*vāgh*," a tiger. The group who carry this *kāṭhī* to Śiṅgṇāpūr are Buddhists, former Untouchables who have followed B. R. Ambedkar in converting to Buddhism; in 1995 they identified themselves as followers of Ambedkar by carrying bright blue flags in front of their *kāṭhī*. This particular blue is the color associated with the Ambedkar Buddhists and with the political party Ambedkar founded.

27. This is the interpretation of the men who carry the pole to Nātepute and Śiṅgṇāpūr. In the view of Brāhmaṇ priests (Baḍves) whom my companions and I spoke with in Nātepute, the pole is Śiva's sister (his *karavalī*), rather than his wife. The roles of bride and groom in the wedding that these priests perform at Nātepute are played by two men: the headmen (Pāṭīls) of Nātepute and the neighboring town of Māḷśiras, respectively. See note 37 in this chapter.
28. Compare the Navakalevara ceremony in the cult of Jagannāth (Tripathi 1978; Marglin 1985:263–64; cf. Eschmann 1978).
29. One man in Bhātāṅgaḷī estimated that the total weight of the silver ornaments on the *kāṭhī* is 15 kilograms; another suggested it could be four times as much. A priest in Śiṅgṇāpūr estimated the total weight of the pole, including its ornaments, at 50 kilograms. The men in Bhātāṅgaḷī told us that each of the silver bands affixed to the pole costs 100–150 rupees or more.
30. These *mānkarīs* include a torch-bearer (Maśāḷī), who is a Cāmbhār (Leatherworker) by caste, and three musicians: a Śiṅgyā, who plays a horn (*śiṅg*); a Halkyā, who plays a kind of tambourine (a *halkī* or *halgī*); and a Vājantrī, who plays an oboe-like wind instrument, the *śanāī*.
31. The bull is called a *kaṭālyā*, a *vaḷavūn*, or a Nandī bull.
32. One of these *kāvaḍs* belongs to Bhātāṅgaḷī's police Pāṭīl, another to the other (administrative) Pāṭīl, who is a Māḷī (Gardener) by caste, and the third to the "Pavārs." These last are, presumably, the Untouchables of the village. All three *kāvaḍs* travel all the way to Śiṅgṇāpūr, but the two Pāṭīls' *kāvaḍs* have their primary ritual function along the road: throughout the heat of the day, from about ten in the morning to four in the afternoon, men are supposed to pour water from them continually over the Nandī on the pole's crossbar.
33. "An especially important thing . . . is that the bamboo is 40 feet tall. It has to be carried upright, by one man. Carry it any distance, carry it one kilometer, carry it half a kilometer, it has to be carried upright."
34. Three of the stopping places on the pole's route are temples: that of the goddess Bhavānī in Tuḷjāpūr, that of Narasiṃha at Nīrā Narasiṅgpūr, and a temple in Dhāmangāv (or Dhāmaṇgāv). In each place, the men circumambulate the temple and cause the pole to "meet" it—this presumably means that they touch the pole to the top of the temple doorway, the way the men carrying a large *kāvaḍ* do with the *kāvaḍ*'s *śīḍ*-pole.
35. Again, by touching the top of its doorway.
36. Molesworth (1857:697) defines "*rukhvat*" as "The ceremony, in weddings, of the father and friends of the bride taking refreshments to the abode of the bridegroom, for him to make a repast previously to their conducting him to the house where the nuptials are to be celebrated," or "The articles of refreshment so taken: also the repast so made." Thus, in its normal usage this term refers to gifts made by the bride's party to the groom's party, ones that would thus be more appropriate for the men accompanying the bride from Bhātāṅgaḷī to her wedding to *give* than to *receive*. Priests in Nātepute see the *kāṭhī* not as the bride but rather as the groom's sister, his *karavalī*, and hence as a member of *his* wedding party (see note 27, earlier). On this interpretation, the use of the term "*rukhvat*" makes more sense.

37. In 1999, Sudhir and Pushpa Waghmare and Sakharam Lakade observed this wedding for me. I was able to see it for myself in 2002. In both years, the wedding was performed as stated in note 27, earlier. The headmen of Nātepute and Māḷśīras, who play the roles of Pārvatī and Śiva, respectively, wore wedding crowns, clean pants, and clean, white shirts. Two other men held up a marriage curtain (*āntarpāṭ*) between them and the crowd of onlookers periodically tossed grains of rice over the couple, while a priest recited the wedding verses (*maṅgaḷāṣṭaka*). In 2002, the pole from Bhātāṅgaḷī arrived late, but before this wedding ceremony took place. By the time the wedding was over, the men who had come with the pole were sound asleep. Despite the fact that I could meet and talk with these men again after they reached Śiṅgṇāpūr in 2002, and despite asking many other people in Nātepute and Śiṅgṇāpūr, I have not yet been able to determine if the Bhātāṅgaḷī *kāṭhī* is involved in a particular ritual that the men who accompany it see as its wedding.

In addition to the wedding (or weddings) at Nātepute, Śiva and Pārvatī's wedding is also performed on Caitra Aṣṭamī elsewhere in the vicinity, including inside the small, crowded sanctuary of the main temple at Śiṅgṇāpūr.

38. They lower the pole, they said, only to pass through the arched gateways along the steps and at the entrance to the temple courtyard.

39. Paṇḍharpūr is the center of the better-known of the two major medieval *bhakti* movements of Maharashtra, the Vārkarīs' cult of the god Viṭhobā. It is the goal of the Vārkarīs' pilgrimage in honor of Viṭhobā. For more on the Vārkarīs and their pilgrimage, see the conclusion of this book. Śiṅgṇāpūr lies less than 100 kilometers west-northwest of Paṇḍharpūr, and is visible for a long stretch of the route of the largest group of Vārkarī pilgrims, those who accompany the palanquin of the saint Jñāneśvar from his tomb (*samādhi*) in Āḷandī to Paṇḍharpūr. Many Vārkarīs visit Śiṅgṇāpūr on the twelfth day of the "bright" fortnight of Āṣāḍh (June–July), following the climax of the Paṇḍharpūr pilgrimage on the eleventh day (Ekādaśī) of that fortnight. The Brāhmaṇ priests of Śiṅgṇāpūr have the surname Baḍve, as do the most numerous and important group of Brāhmaṇs in Paṇḍharpūr. Mahādev Koḷīs are also quite prominent in both Śiṅgṇāpūr and Paṇḍharpūr. Finally, as Ḍhere (1992a:22) points out, just as the Vārkarī saints insist that their god, Viṭhobā (whom they also identify as 'Kānaḍā,' coming from Karnataka), is Kṛṣṇa, and thus came from Dvārkā, in Saurāṣṭra, so they repeatedly affirm that Mahādev of Śiṅgṇāpūr likewise came from Saurāṣṭra.

40. See Sontheimer 1989a:131–50 and Sontheimer 1975. One of the two principal Dhangar *vāḍā*s that Sontheimer describes lies within sight of Śiṅgṇāpūr, at a distance of 17 kilometers by road.

41. For the Mahānubhāvs and their literature, see chapter 6 in this book.

42. Although Cakradhar tells this story in connection with a "Vandev" temple in Hivaraḷī, Jalna District, Ḍhere argues (convincingly, I think) that this Vandev, as well as three others mentioned in the *Līḷācaritra*, are replicas (*upakṣetra*s) of Śiṅgṇāpūr. See Ḍhere 1992c:18–19.

43. Tulpule 1979:373. See also Ḍhere 1977:98–115.

44. For example, three temples in Rāśīn (Karjat Taluka, Ahmadnagar District) were built eight generations ago by a Liṅgāyat (Jaṅgam) named Akāppā

(or Akhobā) Śeṭe, whose family still has an important role in the goddess Yamāī's annual festival at Rāśīn.

45. The wood used in making the *kāvaḍs* is wood from the *umbar* or *audumbar*, a tree especially connected with the god Datta or Dattātreya, rather than Śiva. But, as a man who was telling us about the Beḷsar *kāvaḍ* explained when I asked him *why* it is so important that "no wood except that of the *umbar* tree gets used for a *kāvaḍ*": "They say it's a divine (*daivī*) tree . . . the *audumbar*, where Guru Datta's place (*ṭhikāṇ*) used to be, Datta's original (*mūḷ*) place. Datta's origin is Śiva. The original god in the tradition (*paramparā*) of Datta is Śiva. The Navnāth came from Śiva, Datta came from the Navnāth, and therefore this tree is important. And its root is Śiva."
46. The story as the present Kāḷ Gāvdā told it is an excellent example of the sort of story discussed at the beginning of chapter 3 in this book.
47. In fact, most *samādhis*—grave markers or memorial monuments—are quite naturally found in or near current or former cremation grounds.
48. Although this statement was true when I first wrote it, it is no longer so. When my companions and I visited Ekhatpūr in August 1999, the remains of the "Burning House" were being bulldozed to make way for a temple on the site. The oil mill was still standing, in the middle of the leveled plot of land.
49. That is, on the ninth lunar day of the month of Caitra. The two principal *kāvaḍs* each have a "setting-out" (*prasthān*) ceremony on the eighth day (the Aṣṭamī), but really leave home on the ninth.
50. Another man, citing the "ancestors" (*pūrvīcī lokaṃ*), told of a miraculous phenomenon that further confirms Bhutojī Buvā's "*tathya*"—and that also adds to the Śaiva imagery in the festival: the sand in Bhutojī's *kāvaḍ* turned into five *piṇḍs* (lumps, Śivaliṅgas) that can still be seen near Baḷī's temple.
51. There is also, generally, a "Buvā" who travels with the Śivarī *kāvaḍ*. This position, however, is not hereditary, but is given to a local person who is chosen for his devotion and his interest in serving. In August 1995, when we visited Śivarī and asked about the *kāvaḍ* from there, we were told that the last Buvā, Bājīrāv Kāmaṭhe, had died two years before and had not yet been replaced. He was a performer of *kīrtans* and had served as "Buvā" for 35 or 40 years.
52. As is generally the case with Hindu fasts, the Buvās' fast permits them to eat "snacks" (*pharāḷā*), including milk, fruits, nuts, potatoes, and some other root vegetables, but not wheat, rice, or most vegetables. See note 22, earlier.
53. Both the current Buvās are relatively new at their positions, having inherited them from their fathers in the early or mid-1990s. It is perhaps for this reason that they are not yet quite as tough as their founding ancestor is reputed to have been.
54. My companions and I have spent many hours trying to trace the water in the *kāvaḍs* and seeking to understand how much of it actually comes from rivers. In fact, very little of the water that gets poured in the temples at Śiṅgṇāpūr is river water; and, indeed, very little of it actually comes from pilgrims' home villages. The small *kāvaḍs* that people bring by bus must be stowed as luggage on the top of the bus. There the *kāvaḍs* lie on their sides, and so, because they have no lids (or because any lids they do have are not watertight), they cannot hold

water. The large *kāvaḍs* likewise generally arrive at Śiṅgṇāpūr empty. They are simply too heavy to carry full for great distances; moreover, at the last stage of the journey, as they go up the steepest part of Muṅgī Ghāṭ, it is impossible to keep them upright. The small *kāvaḍs* that people bring to Śiṅgṇāpūr on foot or by bicycle do, in many cases, have water in them; but the water often comes from a well or a faucet, rather than a river. The vast majority of *kāvaḍs*, it seems, get filled at Māḷojī's tank at Śiṅgṇāpūr. In 1995, when there was a drought, some people filled their *kāvaḍs*, as well as their own drinking-water containers, from tankers sent by the government.

There are, however, some important exceptions to all of this, cases in which the water that people bring to Śiṅgṇāpūr is in fact water from home, even water from a river at home. Men in Pisarve, the home village of the young man whose shrine is in Muṅgī Ghāṭ, insisted that they carry their rather large *kāvaḍ* full of water all the way from home, and that they then refill it once they have reached Śiṅgṇāpūr. Men from the Pañcakrośī villages told us that their *kāvaḍ* gets filled at the Karhā river on the Guḍhī Pāḍvā day, when they wash it before setting it up in the village. When they are about to leave for Śiṅgṇāpūr, before they go to circumambulate Bhutojī's *samādhi* temple, they pour out almost all of the water, allowing only a couple of inches of Karhā water to remain at the bottom of the *kāvaḍ*'s pots. In addition, the men who travel with the Sāsvaḍ, the Pañcakrośī, and some of the other large *kāvaḍs* bring along with them a small, closed container of water that they call a "*cambū*" or "*ghaḍavā*" (see figure 2.2). The men from Sāsvaḍ and the Pañcakrośī villages fill their *cambū*s with water from the Karhā river, then carry them with elaborate care and respect all the way to the temple at Śiṅgṇāpūr.

In any case, whether or not the *kāvaḍs* in fact arrive at Śiṅgṇāpūr filled with water brought from home, bringing water from home is clearly the *idea* behind the *kāvaḍ* festival. In discussing the fact that their *kāvaḍ* nowadays goes empty to Śiṅgṇāpūr, men in Śivarī explained that this was not the case in the past. In former times, these men told us, not only did the *kāvaḍ* go to Śiṅgṇāpūr full of water, people used to carry it the whole way themselves, on their heads, instead of putting it into a bullock cart for much of the journey, as they do now. People are not what they used to be, these men told us—a sentiment frequently implied or expressed in reminiscences about the festival's former glory. A former Sarpañc of Śiṅgṇāpūr, noticing my disappointment that most *kāvaḍs* arrive there empty these days, explained that, in the past, more people would come to the festival on foot, and that later they began to come in bullock carts and finally by State Transport bus. In the old days, the man implied, when people traveled on foot or by bullock cart, they could bring their *kāvaḍs* filled with water from home. Finally, even when it arrives empty and is filled at the tank at Śiṅgṇāpūr, a *kāvaḍ* is basically an implement for carrying water. Thus, the implication of bringing a water pot from home is that one is bringing water from home to pour on the god in the temple. A statement in the printed program of the Pañcakrośī *kāvaḍ* from 1995 makes this idea explicit: "*kāvaḍs* come to Śiṅgṇāpūr from all over Maharashtra, bringing the water of holy rivers to pour on the god."

55. According to the Hindu calendar, a lunar day (a *tithī*) starts at sunrise, and continues until sunrise the next day. Thus, midnight on the Aṣṭamī is midnight of the night following the Aṣṭamī day. The turmeric (*haḷdī*) ceremony preceding the wedding is performed on the Pañcamī (the fifth lunar day) of Caitra in the temple at Śiṅgṇāpūr. This is the day on which the *Bhāratiya Saṃskritikoś* says that Pārvatī and Śiva were reunited at Śiṅgṇāpūr.
56. See note 36, earlier.
57. But within its *kṣetra,* its holy area.
58. The flyer says "*dvaj*" ("flag"), not "*dhaj.*" For a fuller translation of the flyer's statement, see note 90, later.
59. The narrator could not at the moment remember the names of any more places. When he repeated this part of the story, later, he named Nātepute and referred to Umbareśvar.
60. There is also a tradition that there are eight holy places (*aṣṭatīrtha*) in and around Śiṅgṇāpūr. People naming the eight give differing lists of eight temples.
61. The hair atop the *kāvaḍ*'s pole, these men explained, comes from the tail of a *vangāy* (a wild cow), and is extremely expensive and hard to obtain. (It is sold by weight, using the same measures as for gold, and can be bought—or bought at a reasonable price—only in Bombay. The clump on the Śivarī *kāvaḍ* cost 3,000 rupees, the men said.) When I asked why no other kind of hair would do, the men said that it's silky, that "nothing [else] has hair like that." Ramdas Atkar clarified this, explaining that the hair is extremely soft. "Like a woman's," I suggested, and one of the men said, "The hair is even finer (*bhārī* or *bārik*) than a woman's."
62. "Tāī" means "Elder Sister." It is a polite yet affectionate term of address for a woman.
63. This is the road from Sāsvaḍ to Jejurī, the old Puṇe–Sātārā (Mumbai–Bangalore) road.
64. This is clearly a highly idealized statement. For example, it does not tell us if this obligation falls on *all* households of the village, even those of Dalits (Untouchables), nor does it indicate what sanctions are imposed (and by whom) on someone who does not pay.
65. Similarly, a man we talked to in Khāmasvāḍī about the weaver who makes the *dhaj* that comes to Śiṅgṇāpūr said that the man does so as a servant (*nokar*) of the village of Khāmasvāḍī, and that the village pays him for his work. Although the weaver is the one who gets to carry the *dhaj* to Śiṅgṇāpūr on his head, the honorary right of the *dhaj* belongs to "all the citizens of the village of Khāmasvāḍī." With only one exception that I am sure of, the offerings made to each of the large *kāvaḍs* and *kāṭhīs* become the property of the whole village from which it comes. The exception is the Sāsvaḍ *kāvaḍ,* which is the private property of its Buvā.
66. And was intended, I think, as a contribution to the festival as a whole, not just to the Pañcakrośī *kāvaḍ*'s pilgrimage.
67. I put the word "whole" in quotation marks because generally, in my conversations with these men, I accepted such statements at face value, without pressing the men to reveal whether or not their *kāvaḍ* or *kāṭhī* actually goes to the Dalit neighborhood (the former Mahārvāḍā) of the village, whether it travels

to outlying hamlets (this seems *not* to be the case), and so on. The point that is important here is that the men describing such a procession *thought* of it as going throughout what they *thought* of as their whole village. See Feldhaus 1995:156. The Buvā of the Sāsvaḍ *kāvaḍ* explained that it gets carried around three different parts of the town of Sāsvaḍ on three different days: the night of the "setting out" (*prasthān*) ceremony; the next day, as it actually leaves town; and the day of its return.

68. For *oṭī bharaṇ or oṭī bharaṇeṃ*, see chapter 1, note 66.
69. Although the man who told us about this did not say so, "everybody" quite likely means "everybody but Harijans" or "everybody but Harijans and Vāṇīs." For my suspicions about the inclusiveness of terms like "everybody" and "everywhere," see note 67.
70. I am not sure what the man was referring to. I doubt that he meant the (largely Brāhmaṇical) *sandhyā* rite, in which a man offers water to the sun while reciting the Gāyatrī *mantra*. Possibly he was using "*snān-sandhyā*," "bath and *sandhyā*," as a fancy term for "ritually important bath."
71. That is, they clap and sing in unison a rhythmic song of praise, while one person waves a tray of lighted oil lamps or camphor in a circular motion.
72. In the 1981 Census of India (1986), this village's population is given as 2,405, while none of the other villages has more than 1,000 people: Kumbhārvaḷaṇ, 961; Khānavaḍī, 732; Ekhatpūr, 609; and Muñjavaḍī, 295. According to the 1991 Census of India (1995), Khaḷad's population was 2,532, Kumbhārvaḷaṇ's 1,154, Khānavaḍī's 865, Ekhatpūr's 643, and Muñjavaḍī's 299.
73. On the 1981 census map, these two villages appear to have been formed by splitting what was once a single village. The 1991 census map places them (mistakenly, I believe) on opposite sides of the river.
74. These men also pointed out connections and parallels between Ekhatpūr and other famous places and historical figures. Ekhatpūr's name, the men said, derives from "Vikhatpūr" ("Purchase-ville"), and provides a rather unusual link to Kāśī (Banāras, Vārāṇasī; for other sorts of links, see chapter 5). At some time in the past, Ekhatpūr was a center for the slave trade, and so—according to these men—was Kāśī. Slaves that did not sell at Kāśī's twice-yearly bazaar would be sent to Ekhatpūr to be sold, and vice-versa. "They used to bring at least 400 or 500 people," one man said. And another added: "They'd bring the left-over children and sell them here." "Yes," said the first man, "children, women, men, whatever you need."
75. "Sopān Kākā" ("Uncle Sopān"), said the other man; both men were referring to the Vārkarī saint Sopān or Sopāndev, the brother of Jñāneśvar whose *samādhi* is at Sāsvaḍ. See note 9, earlier, for the inscription on the Ekhatpūr *kāvaḍ* that refers to Sopān.
76. A similar story, but with a happier ending, accounts for Beḷsar's having a *kāvaḍ* now. According to a man in Beḷsar, some Bhutojī Telī (whether in Sāsvaḍ or Ekhatpūr is not clear, nor is it clear when these events are supposed to have taken place) pawned his *kāvaḍ* to Beḷsar because he had financial difficulties. A decade or two later, he paid back the loan and redeemed the *kāvaḍ*. The people of Beḷsar had come to like having the *kāvaḍ*, so they started their own.

77. In essence, the argument was that if the man in Sāsvaḍ to whom the widow of Bhutyā Telī gave the *kāvaḍ* had been her husband's legitimate heir, there would have been no need for the people of the Pañcakrośī villages to adopt a Telī from Sātārā in recent times. See later.
78. I am not sure if he meant the notebook I was writing in, or the book I had said I was hoping to write.
79. See note 9.
80. I did not ask to see these inscriptions or documents, because the matter seemed to be such a contentious one, and besides nobody seemed to know exactly where they were. For my purposes, the fact that the men claim to have such evidence is what is important, not whether it really exists or what the inscriptions and documents actually say.
81. A Marathi inscription on the outer wall of the *samādhi* temple gives the details.
82. A man in Āndrūḍ gave a good illustration of the combination of devotion and personal friendship that can cause such a stop to be added:

> My father . . . used to be a very devoted (*gahire*) *bhakta* of Śambhū Mahādev. And by [Mahādev's] mercy, the worship of Śambhū Mahādev's *kāvaḍ* takes place here. And because my father was a *bhakta* . . . . Because the *kāvaḍ*'s Buvā and my father were friends, [the Buvā] began to bring the *kāvaḍ* here . . . to our . . . house in the village of Āndrūḍ. Previously the *kāvaḍ* did not come here, but from the time that our father and the Buvā became friends, it has come to our house.

83. Besides such coordination of various government officials and pilgrim leaders, which takes place on the local and taluka level, the state government also provides direct financial support for the festival arrangements. For example, I was told that, in 1994, the government of Maharashtra gave a grant of 300,000 rupees for the festival.
84. The man said "Nagar" here, but he clearly meant "Sāsvaḍ" and not "(Ahmad)nagar."
85. Another man who was present suggested that the reason has to do with crowd control and public health concerns: "An enormous crowd comes, and besides the fact that lots of people come, it's the hot season. And there's a disturbance in the water [supply]. Diseases increase. So when this group has left, that group comes."
86. Strictly speaking, Muṅgī Ghāṭ is on the northern face of the Śiṅgṇāpūr mountain. However, the prominent *kāvaḍ*s that climb this Ghāṭ come from the northwest.
87. And like the two opposed areas of Vidarbha and the Godāvarī valley in the Old Marathi period (chapter 6). For the story and ritual at Śeṇḍī and Pokharḍī, see the end of chapter 1.
88. The northernmost places from which my companions and I found *kāvaḍ*s to have come were in Śirūr Taluka of Pune District and Deglūr Taluka of Nanded District. We also found at least one *kāvaḍ* that had come from a village in Basav Kalyān Taluka, Bidar District, in Karnataka.
89. When I asked this man if he also meant to include the *kāvaḍ*s that come from the south and from Vidarbha and Marāṭhvāḍā, to the east and northeast, he said that he did: "All of them come into that village, through it, and then they

climb up. Because the stipulation (*saṅket*) is that *that* is the *ghāṭ* that one has to climb up by, through Kothaḷe."

90. The flyer's statement is as follows: "Śikhar Śiṅgṇāpūr in Maharashtra, the beginninglessly perfect and puranically famous, historical, living temple of Lord Śaṅkar, the family god of Maharashtra, the family god of Śrīmant Chatrapati Śivarāya, is known as the Kailās of southern India. The pilgrimage festival of this Śambhu Mahādev takes place every year, beginning on the first day of the bright half of Caitra. This pilgrimage festival celebrates the wedding of Śiva and Pārvatī. The turmeric ceremony is on the 5th, the flag-raising is on the 8th, and the wedding takes place that evening. Afterwards, on the bright 12th of Caitra, *kāvaḍs* come to Śiṅgṇāpūr from all over Maharashtra, bringing the water of holy rivers to pour on the god. Hundreds of thousands of devotees come to have a sight of the god." ("Śrī Kṣetra Śiṅgṇāpūr Yātrā," flyer distributed by the Pañcakrośī Ekhatpūr, Khaḷad, Khānavaḍī, Muñjavaḍī, Kumbhārvaḷaṇ pilgrimage festival committee, 1995.)
91. May 29, 1994, p. 6.
92. As far south as the Tuṅgabhadrā river and as far north as the Narmadā. See later.

3 Traveling Goddesses

1. Sometimes, but relatively infrequently, the devotee is a woman.
2. The goddess Sākaḷāī, whose complicated route is detailed in note 36, followed a devotee at least the last part of the way to the site of her present temple; when the devotee looked back, the goddess disappeared at the spot where her temple now stands. This "Orpheus" motif is quite common in these stories.
3. In this form, the "old *bhakta*" story is an intra-regional form of a kind of replication we will examine in chapter 5: "God G has followed devotee D from Y to X."
4. The *Gazetteer of the Bombay Presidency* (Khândesh 1880, 437n.) reports a story of this sort in which it is not a god but the Ganges river (Gaṅgā) that follows a faithful devotee to Maharashtra. For more examples of this kind of replication, see the section of chapter 5 entitled "Other Physical Connections Between Holy Places."
5. See note 2.
6. It would be interesting and informative to map the replicas of each of the three-and-a-half goddesses. However, such maps would not represent conceptual regions of the kind that this book is concerned with. Rather, the maps would show the spheres of influence of the four goddesses, the areas throughout which each goddess is the most important one, the one most worth replicating. Such areas would be regions in an "objective" sense, a matter of facts and statistics rather than of regional conceptions in any devotees' minds. For the devotees, the important connection in each case is the dyadic one between *their* goddess's local temple and her more distant, more famous one. The author of the *Maḷāī Māhātmya* (see the section of this chapter entitled "Maḷāī Kills the Demon"),

who has compiled a list of temples of Maḷāī that he views as replicas intentionally created by other devotees, is, as far as I can tell, quite exceptional.

For a study of six replicas of the goddess Vindhyavāsinī in Banaras, see Humes 1993. Humes reports a phenomenon that I have not found to be the case with the Maharashtrian goddesses: fear on the part of the goddess's priests that her powers in her principal temple may become weakened if she follows too many devotees to their various homes (Humes 1993:183).

7. See the introduction for a story that a schoolteacher in Jejurī told. This story shows Jāṇāī to be a form of Pārvatī. If she is Pārvatī, she cannot be a sister of Khaṇḍobā, who is widely (if not universally) understood to be an incarnation of Śiva, Pārvatī's husband.
8. People who have made the trip by road estimated the distance at "sixty or seventy" or "100 or 125" kilometers rather than the 20 that one can see on a map.
9. In addition, the goddess came from Saḷve to Navkhaṇ because she would be well guarded by the 12 Bhairīs (fierce forms of Śiva) in the village land surrounding her temple at Navkhaṇ.
10. I have combined parts of two different tellings of the story here.
11. The house is called "Meṇḍhke Vāḍā." The Meṇḍhke Vāḍā is named after its former residents, who were Dhangar shepherds. Probably Meṇḍhke was their surname, although it is also the honorific plural of "*meṇḍhkā*," "shepherd." The *vāḍā* (here a term for a large house with an inner courtyard) is now the residence of some of Jejurī's many priests.
12. For a description of *lejhīm*, see the discussion of the Dauṇḍ festival in chapter 1.
13. The first food offering is of vegetables and flat millet bread (*bhākrī*); the second is of sweet, stuffed, flat wheat bread (*poḷī* or *puraṇ-poḷī*); the mutton meal is the third and final offering.
14. Gondhaḷīs are small troupes of musicians, singers, and actors of a particular traditional type who perform in honor of goddesses. Their performance is called a Gondhaḷ. See Ḍhere 1988.
15. Also sometimes called *kāniyā*, this is a dish made by boiling whole grains.
16. See chapter 1, note 66.
17. In 1995, about 100 or 150 people were served.
18. At one point while Mrs. Jhagaḍe was possessed, an old woman with leucoderma asked about her son, who lived in Bombay; later this woman herself became possessed, and one of the drummers asked her about another woman, who had been missing for ten years. Later, a drummer asked yet another possessed woman—who happened to be his wife—about what he had done to offend the goddess; the conversation went on for a long time and brought in a number of other people, including another drummer and Mrs. Jhagaḍe.
19. As far as I could tell. I am not sure whether the "everyone" invited to the meal would have included Dalits and Muslims. It did not, of course, include Brāhmaṇs or other vegetarians. Cf. chapter 2, note 67.
20. This name, which means "Mother," is often used as a name of Śaiva goddesses.
21. The brief version of this story in the *Maḷāī Māhātmya* (7.64–66) suggests that the prospective bridegroom was a Muslim ruler, a "Bādśāh."

22. The monastery of Bhāratī Buvā in Tuḷjāpūr has a room where the goddess is still understood to come and play parcheesi with the head of the monastery every day (Jansen 1995:31–32).
23. When I interviewed high-ranking members of the Tīḷvan Telī Samāj in Ghoḍegāv in November 1995, the Sutār who had most recently been responsible for making the bedstead, Tātyā Kātārī, had just died. Already, when he had become old and weak, paternal relatives of his in Pune had made the pieces of the bedstead, and Tātyā Kātārī had assembled them in Ghoḍegāv.
24. The Telīs I talked with explained that the bedstead leaves on the day after Gaṇapati or Gaṇeś is installed for his ten-day festival in August–September, unless that next day falls on a Tuesday (a day of the week especially important for goddesses). In that case, the Telīs insist on keeping the bedstead in Ghoḍegāv until the following day, a Wednesday.
25. That is, Bhavānī of Tuḷjāpūr.
26. The (admittedly far-fetched) impression I received is that he makes himself look pregnant.
27. As *prasād*, food that has been offered to a god and is then consumed by the worshippers.
28. They are also invited to Tuḷjāpūr, where multiple prestations are made on the Dasarā day. The carpenter and the blacksmith used to attend the festival there, but they no longer do so, as the honorarium they would receive would no longer suffice to cover the cost of the trip.
29. The *story* that motivates the pilgrimage, however, connects only Tuḷjāpūr and Burhāṇnagar: the goddess of Tuḷjāpūr comes to Burhāṇnagar, and after she disappears Jānkojī travels from Burhāṇnagar to Tuḷjāpūr, where he finds her again.
30. In the mid-1990s, Bhagat was still living in Ciñcolī, one of the principal places of Maḷāī, where he granted me an extensive interview and sang a number of his own compositions.
31. *MM* 2.43. The same verse includes another explanation of the name as well: "There was *dhuḥdhuḥkār* (hissing) on all sides, so they called him Dhūmrākṣa." I do not find in the text any attempt to explain the rest of Dhūmrākṣa's name, but the word "*akṣa*" means "eye." Thus, the whole name means "Smoke Eyes."
32. Śiva came as an ascetic, carrying a begging bag, a conch shell, and a *ḍamarū* drum; he settled in the cremation ground. Brahmā came in the guise of an astrologer, a Brāhmaṇ. He wore a sacred thread and looked up people's fortunes in an almanac. Kubera, the god of wealth, became a poor potter (a Kumbhār); he took a mule through the streets and collected dung from the road. Agni became a washerman, and Indra became a barber.
33. The text specifies many of these places in an extraordinarily extensive list that takes in a large geographical swath and jumps around with no apparent order. The list includes numerous places in India, along with places in Pakistan, Bangla Desh, Nepal, Tibet, and Sri Lanka.
34. At this point, the narrative goes into a series of long excurses, telling of numerous goddesses in Maharashtra and beyond, giving etymologies of some goddess- and place-names, narrating stories about the goddesses, and including

such other materials as the author's comments on radio and television, all under the general rubric of the battle with the demons. Finally the narrative returns to the Dhūmrākṣa story.

35. The same place where the palanquin and bedstead meet on their way to Tuḷjāpūr. See earlier.
36. Maḷāī seems, in some respects, to be another example of the "seven sisters" to be discussed later in this chapter. A related set of goddesses, Sākaḷāī, sometimes numbers 14, or perhaps even 28. Sākaḷāī's devotees connect her to Maḷāī, although she does not seem to be included in Maḷāī's festival. Sākaḷāī's principal pilgrimage place is on a hilltop near Koregāv in Śrīgondā Taluka, Ahmadnagar District. Both a Gurav priest at the temple and a prominent priest-devotee (*bhakta*) of Sākaḷāī in Ahmadnagar said that there are 14 goddesses in all, each with a different name, who are collectively referred to as Sākaḷāī. According to the Gurav, "Sākaḷāī" is a "nickname" for all the goddesses together. One of the goddesses in the set that is Sākaḷāī is named Maḷāī, and all of them together came to Sākaḷāī's present location from other places prominent in Maḷāī's cult: Ciñcolī, Nighoj, and the Kuṇḍ.

    Sākaḷāī's *bhakta* in Ahmadnagar knows of a quite complex route by which the goddesses traveled: they started in Kāśī (Banaras), came from there to the Koṅkaṇ, and from the Koṅkaṇ onto the Deccan Plateau. On the Deccan, they went first to Ciñcoḷī, then to Nighoj, then to the Kuṇḍ in the Kukaḍī river, and from there to Sākaḷāī's hill, called Maiṇḍū Ḍoṅgar. There seven of them remained on the highest peak of the hill, where they are worshipped in the form of a set of stones out in the open, while the others came down to a slightly lower level, where they are worshipped in a temple. Thus, although more elaborate, Sākaḷāī's route follows the basic core of Maḷāī's: from Kāśī, to Ciñcolī, to Nighoj, to the Kuṇḍ.
37. These include Ahmadnagar, Bābhūḷvāḍī (Pārner Taluka), Bāmburī (Rāhurī Taluka), Belāpūr, Bhiṅgār, Ḍhoḷvaḍ, Khāmgāv, Khāndlī, Nevāse, Pārner, Pimpaḷvandī (Junnar Taluka), Pimparī, Śeṇḍī (Ahmadnagar District), Śrīgondā, Umbar (Rāhurī Taluka), and Umbraj. The *Maḷāī Māhātmya*'s list of places from where people came for the goddess's (apparently aborted) wedding on the seventh day of the dark half of Caitra may indicate places where poles (*kāṭhī*s) come from now (*MM* 8.69–71).
38. When my companions and I attended the festival at Ciñcolī in 1995, we did not see the palanquin from Nevāse, but at the festival in Nighoj in 1994, when we interviewed people who had come with the palanquin from Nevāse, they said that they had come to Nighoj via Ciñcolī. However, they had set out from Nevāse by truck ("tempo") on the eight day of the fortnight, thus reaching Ciñcolī *after* the festival (including the parade) on the seventh day of the fortnight there was over.
39. In a gentle version of *gāḍī-bagāḍ*, "hook-swinging." At Nighoj (and, as far as I know, everywhere else where the *bagāḍ* is still used), rope slings at the ends of a pivoting wooden beam substitute for the hooks from which devotees were hung in earlier times.
40. This last element of the festival, which has been the focus of a good deal of outside attention in recent years on the part of "uprooters of superstition" and

journalists, is not particularly important for my analysis. It seems to parallel the Māhātmya's account of the goddess emerging from the water with a pot of nectar in her hands. A step-well is a well with steps inside that can be used to walk down to the level of the water.

41. For *lejhīm*, see the description of the Dauṇḍ festival in chapter 1.
42. Or Neharābād-Araṇgāv.
43. One version of this story (Kāḷegāṃvkar 1987:30–33) connects it with the story of Pārvatī's testing of Rām in the Daṇḍakāraṇya (see the introduction), and makes both stories part of the ongoing, tense relationship between Śiva and his wife. This version explains Yogeśvarī's reluctance to marry Paraḷī Vaidyanāth on the grounds of the other episode, and at the same time provides an explanation for an old cave temple filled with monumental sculptures at Āmbejogāī.
44. There are other goddesses too who travel from the Koṅkaṇ to the Deś. Vajrāī (see Feldhaus 1995:59 and passim) came from the Koṅkaṇ to her place on the Nirā river near Aklūj. Sakaḷāī, whose complex wanderings are discussed in note 36, moved from the Koṅkaṇ to the Deś in the course of her travels. Finally, a Dhangar shepherd claimed that the goddess Bhivāī, whose principal pilgrimage place is on the Nirā river near Phalṭaṇ (Feldhaus 1995), originally came from a place at the eastern edge of the Koṅkaṇ, near the Ghāṭs; she traveled up, against the stream of waterfalls in the Ghāṭs, to the headwaters of the Nirā on the eastern side of the mountains.
45. Whitehead 1921:29, 32, 39; Elmore 1913:12. The seven sisters discussed by Whitehead and Elmore appear to be the kind that are found together (see later), whereas those Erndl discusses are geographically dispersed, like the sets on which the present discussion will concentrate.
46. Often with a male figure, who represents their "brother." See Feldhaus 1995:48, 55, and the illustrations after page 64.
47. The three-and-a-half Śakti Pīṭh goddesses of Maharashtra also include Ambābāī or Mahālakṣmī of Kolhāpūr. See chapter 4.
48. That is, Maharashtra's three-and-a-half Śakti Pīṭh goddesses. See chapter 4.
49. For another etymology, see the story about Rām in the introduction.
50. For *āratī*, see chapter 2, note 6.
51. It is possible that people would tell the story of various local goddesses' identity with Pārvatī (the story of Rām, Sītā, and Pārvatī narrated in the introduction) and at the same time assert that the goddesses are one another's sisters. However, I do not remember anyone doing this.
52. This is the case even when, as most often happens, the goddesses in the various locations are not married to any husbands in particular.
53. By "us," the woman could have meant humans or women; she addressed this remark to me, and used the inclusive form of the first-person-plural pronoun, the form that includes the person being spoken to in a group to which the speaker also belongs.
54. For a subtle analysis of women's uses of the imagery of the parental home and the in-laws' house, see Raheja and Gold 1996:73–148.
55. The kind of connection between places that the bonds of married sisterhood imply is different from the connection between "Śiva's side" and "Śakti's side"

in the wedding imagery at Śiṅgṇāpūr. Whereas Śiva and Śakti are complementary opposites that do get united, the longing of married sisters for one another is predicated on their very separation.

4 The Arithmetic of Place: Numbered Sets of Places

1. Or, in a variant list, Gayā.
2. Or, in another variant list, Prayāg (Allāhabād). According to Bharati (1970:97–98), "only the most learned" authorities, especially South Indian Brāhmaṇs, would name Kāñcīpuram (Kāñcī) rather than Prayāg among the seven holiest cities.
3. The exact list varies. A widely known Maharashtrian version includes Tryambakeśvar near Nāsik, Bhīmaśaṅkar at the source of the Bhīmā river, Ghṛṣṇeśvar at Ellora (Verūḷ), Vaidyanāth in Paraḷī, Nāgnāth in Auṇḍhe (all, according to this version, located in Maharashtra), Kedārnāth in the Himālayas, Somnāth in Saurāṣṭra, Mahākāl in Ujjain, Omkareśvar at Māndhātā on the Narmadā, Rāmeśvaram at the beginning of the string of islands leading to Sri Lanka, Mallikārjun at Śrīśailam, and Viśvanāth in Vārāṇasī. With the exception of Vaidyanāth, which is shown in its more generally recognized location at a Paralī in eastern India, these are the places shown on map 4.1.
4. The conjoined *liṅga* and *yoni* are at one and the same time male and female genitals and the stone shaft and pedestal of the normal, aniconic representation of Śiva in shrines and temples.
5. Why the number of the Jyotirliṅga places is 12 is not clear. The numbers more often associated with Śiva are five (e.g., his five forms or five faces) and 11 (the number of the Rudras, an old form of Śiva). Some scholars suggest that the Jyotirliṅgas stand for the 12 Ādityas (*BSK* 3:686), and others point to a list of 12 elements that the *Taittirīya Upaniṣad* identifies as Jyotirliṅgas (ibid.).
6. The Melā is held at Haridvār when the sun is in Aries and Jupiter is in Aquarius. It is held at Allāhabād (Prayāg) when the sun is in Capricorn and Jupiter is in Taurus, at Ujjain when both the sun and Jupiter are in Scorpio, and at Nāsik and Tryambakeśvar when both the sun and Jupiter are in Leo (Bhujaṅg n.d.:19–20).
7. The text has "Haridvār," the Vaiṣṇava version of the Śaiva name "Hardvār."
8. The *Matsya, Skanda, Padma,* and *Devībhāgavata Purāṇa*s place the number at 108, while other (mostly Tantric) sources, including the late-seventeenth- or early-eighteenth-century Bengali Sanskrit text that Sircar (1948, 1973) edits, give the number as 51. Sircar (1948:11–31) mentions traditions of 3, 4, 7, 8, 9, 10, 18, 42, and 50, as well as 51 and 108 Śakti Pīṭhs.
9. The three worlds are heaven, earth, and underworld, or earth, atmosphere, and sky.
10. Prabhudesāī 1967–1968:Volume 1, pp. 280–82; Sircar 1948, 1973. According to Prabhudesāī (1967–1968:Volume 1, p. 290), the places where parts of the

goddess's body above her heart fell are right-handed Tantric places, and those where parts of her body below her heart fell are left-handed Tantric places.

11. The majority of the places listed in the textual traditions are found far to the northeast of Maharashtra, in Bengal, Assam, and Orissa. Prabhudesāī 1967–1968:Volume 1, p. 290.
12. According to Govaṇḍe (1981:3), there are three principal Śaktī Pīṭhs. In addition to Kāmākhyā, these include Amarnāth in Kashmir, where the goddess's neck fell to earth, and Kāñcī in Tamil Nadu, where her bones fell.
13. A variant list of pilgrimage places names eight Dhāms. According to Bhaṇḍārī (1992:104), "These eight Dhāms are Trijugī Nārāyaṇ in the Himālayas, Muktināth in Nepal, Badrināth, Jagannāth-Purī, Raṅganāth, Gayā, Paṇḍharpūr, and Tirupatī."
14. These four are located at Jyotirmaṭh in the Himālayas (not far from Badrināth and Kedārnāth) and at Dvārkā, Purī, and Śṛṅgerī (*BSK*, Volume 9, p. 187). The only significant difference of this list from that of the four Dhāms, then, is in the south, where the Śaṅkarācārya Pīṭh is at Śṛṅgerī (in Karnataka) and the Dhām at Rāmeśvaram (in Tamil Nadu).
15. It is not clear whose "deliberate" intention Sopher thought it was that chose to consider places on the edges of India holy.
16. Maps in Bhardwaj (1976:62, 66) show all four of the places included among the *tīrtha*s listed in the *Garuḍa* and *Matsya Purāṇa*s, but only Dvārkā among those listed in the *tīrthayātrā* section of the *Mahābhārata* (1976:44). How old the four Dhāms are as a *set* I have not yet discovered.
17. McKean is quoting here from the English guidebook distributed at the temple: *Bharat Mata Mandir: A Candid Appraisal*, p. 13.
18. Setubandha is the chain of islands running from Rameśvaram to Sri Lanka.
19. In his *Hindutva*, e.g., Savarkar (cited in de Bary 1958:333) addresses Jains and Sikhs, among others, as Hindus, urging them to reinforce their organic unity with (other) Hindus.
20. See, e.g., Damrel (forthcoming) and Ernst 1995.
21. Earth at Kāñcī, wind at Kālahastī (in Andhra Pradesh), water at Tiruvanaikkaval. Ramesan does not name the locations of the *liṅgas* of fire and ether.
22. At Kolanupāka, in Andhra Pradesh, I was told a slightly different list of the Vīraśaiva places, one that included Kolanupāka and did not include Balehalli.
23. And referred to in Kulkarṇī 1971:52.
24. *jāśī Prayāgī prātaḥsnān / Pāñcāleśvarī karī anuṣṭhān / Karvīrpurīmājī karī bhīkṣāṭan mādhyānhīṃ / mādhyānh astamānāvarī Sahyādrī śikharī Mātāpurī / śayan karī Dattarāj māuḷī*. Cendavaṇkar (1964a:32) explains that almsgiving is especially important in Kolhāpūr because Datta comes here regularly to beg. For a partially different set of Datta places, see Pain (n.d.:8), citing the text *Datta Prabodh* 50.223–26.
25. Haṇamante (1964:54), Dāte and Karve (1942:Volume 1, p. 216), and Cendavaṇkar (1964a:9) list the three as Bhavānī of Tuljāpūr, Reṇukā of Mātāpūr/Māhūr, and Yogeśvarī of Āmbejogāī, while the half place, according

to them, is that of Lakṣmī of Kolhāpūr. Mate (1962:27) gives the standard list of four, but states that people disagree as to whether it is Saptaśṛṅga or Kolhāpūr that is to be considered the half place. For Āmbejogāī, see chapter 3.

26. Numerous physical evidences of the goddess's fight are to be seen at Saptaśṛṅga. The head of the Buffalo Demon appears at the foot of the 475 steps leading up to Saptaśṛṅgī's mountain-peak shrine. A hole in a mountain visible off to the north of Saptaśṛṅgī's mountain was cut out when a (different?) demon's body passed through it. The goddess killed the Buffalo Demon, according to local traditions here, at Caṇḍikāpūr, to the north of the mountain with the hole in it.
27. As Rāmvaradāyinī, the one who gave a boon to Rām.
28. See the section of the introduction entitled "Geographical Stories" for the story of Rām giving Pārvatī the name Tukāī (among others) when she appeared to him in the form of Sītā.
29. Govaṇḍe 1981:10–11; Kulkarṇī 1971:50–51.
30. According to Kulkarṇī (1971:51), pilgrims to Tirupatī understand their pilgrimage there to be complete only after they have also traveled to Kolhāpūr. In other contexts, Mahālakṣmī of Kolhāpūr is only rarely the wife of Viṣṇu. As Śakti, she is more likely to be implicitly Śiva's wife than Viṣṇu's, but in most contexts she appears as an independent goddess, also called Ambābāī, "Mother."
31. The word derives from Sanskrit *ardhacaturtha*, "half [less than]four," analogous to German *halbvier*. Dāte et al. 1932–1938:499.
32. *Muhūrta*s. Haṇamante 1964:54; Sontheimer 1989a:133, n.4.
33. Dāte and Karve (1942:Volume 1, p. 216) list two proverbs using the term "three-and-a-half *ghaṭakā*s" to indicate a brief period of time. A *ghaṭakā* (Sanskrit, *ghaṭikā*) is a period of 24 minutes. Dāte and Karve also quote a verse by the *bhakti* poet Tukārām to the effect that all one needs when one is dead is three-and-a-half arms' lengths of space, so it is pointless to exert oneself to get more: *auṭ hāt tujhā jāgā, yer siṇasī vāügā.*
34. But see note 25.
35. Tuḷjāpūr has a megalith that may indicate that the place was a prehistoric cult site (Jansen 1995:68–84), and thus perhaps older than Kolhāpūr. However, in the thirteenth century, Tuḷjāpūr was apparently not sufficiently prominent for Cakradhar to prohibit his followers from visiting it too, along with Māhūr and Kolhāpūr (see note 42). In terms of another kind of time-reckoning, of course, Tukāī/Bhavānī's connection with Rām and Sītā carries Tuḷjāpūr back to the Tretā Age.
36. Kolhāpūr is also the only one of the four to appear in a list of the 12 most important Śakti Pīṭhs in the *Tripurārahasya Māhātmyakhaṇḍ* 48:71–75 (quoted in Desāī 1969:2–3 and Govaṇḍe 1981:4). In addition, Kolhāpūr is the only one of the four places about which people make a clear and detailed claim that it is the "southern Kāśī" (Banaras). See chapter 5.
37. In such contexts, Kolhāpūr is most often called Karvīr.
38. Desāī (1975:111) repeats this scheme in all its details, but in the opposite order.
39. A reference to the goddess Tuḷjā in Nepal.

40. "The half Pīṭh, Saptaśṛṅga, is considered better than the three places [goddesses] Mahālakṣmī of Kolhāpūr, Mahāsarasvatī of Tuḷjāpūr, and Mahākālī of Māhūr. Here the seat of *dharma*, the feminine form of Brahman itself composed of the three *guṇa*s Mahākālī, Mahālakṣmī, and Mahāsarasvatī, is established in the form of the syllable *Om* . . . . The goddess Saptaśṛṅg[ī] is Mahālakṣmī, and she is also Mahākālī and Mahāsarasvatī" (Nerkar 1977:2). Nerkar ascribes his scheme of correspondences in part to the *Devībhāgavata Purāṇa*. Writing about Āmbejogāī, Kāḷegāvkar (1987:12) finds a way to show Āmbejogāī's superiority to all four of the three-and-a-half places: "Although in Maharashtra there are the principal *pīṭh*s of the goddess—Kolhāpūr, Tuḷjāpūr, Māhūr, and Saptaśṛṅgī—as well as many subsidiary *pīṭh*s, Āmbejogāī is the one and only Śakti Pīṭh in existence that is known by the name of the Mother (Ambā)."
41. See the introduction.
42. Although I have not heard or read any statements by contemporary Maharashtrians ascribing such a function to the goddesses of Kolhāpūr, Tuḷjāpūr, and Māhūr, the thirteenth-century Mahānubhāv text *Sūtrapāṭh* juxtaposes some of the commands of the Mahānubhāvs' founder, Cakradhar, in a way that I find suggestive. Just after the commands to avoid the "Kannada land" and the "Telugu land" and to "stay in Maharashtra" (see chapter 6), the text records another command of Cakradhar's: "Do not go to Mātāpūr [Māhūr] or to Kolhāpūr." The *sūtra* expressing this command does not, however, support the view that the places are declared off limits because they are somehow on the edge of the "Kannada land" or the "Telugu land." Moreover, although this *sūtra* links Māhūr and Kolhāpūr, it is important to note that neither the *sūtra* nor any of the commentaries I have examined indicates a view of these two places as belonging to a set of three-and-a-half goddess places.

    Mention in the *Gāthā* of Jñāneśvar (P. N. Jośī 1969, *abhaṅg* 488) of "*āūṭ pīṭhīṃcī duraguḷī*," "Durgā of the three-and-a-half *pīṭh*s," could be read as referring to the Śakti Pīṭhs of Maharashtra, even though this is not the way that Tulpule interprets "*āūṭpīṭh*" in this passage (Tulpule and Feldhaus 1999:s.v.). If the passage in the *Gāthā* does indeed date from the time of Jñāneśvar, and if it does refer to the Maharashtrian Śakti Pīṭhs, this would enable us to trace the recognition of a set of three-and-a-half goddesses to the Yādava period.
43. L. Preston 1980; 1989:16, 92–121; see also Courtright 1985:211–16.
44. Preston 1980:108, citing the *GBP*, Poona 1885:438.
45. For example, Ahilyābāī built the large temple sanctuary at Siddhaṭek (Govaṇḍe 1995:26).
46. Wolpert 1962:67–70; Barnouw 1954; Courtright 1985:226–47; 1988. Tilak's revival of this festival is a clear example of what would now be called an "invented tradition" (Hobsbawm and Ranger 1983).
47. L. Preston 1980:108, citing Ghurye 1962: 71, 91; *contra* Courtright 1985:4.
48. A *navas* is a promise made to a god in asking for a favor. When one has received what one asked for, one must fulfil the vow. Generally this involves making a particular offering or performing a particular ritual.
49. An exception to this is the Māgh Caturthī festival (Māgh Śuddha 4) at Mahaḍ, which was said in 1980 to attract 10,000 pilgrims each year (Govaṇḍe 1995:62).

People believe that receiving a coconut as *prasād* here on this day guarantees the birth of a son (ibid.: 63).

50. On the question of the order in which to visit the places, see later.
51. Ballāḷeśvar at Pālī, Varadavināyak at Mahaḍ, Girijātmaja at Leṇyādri, Vighneśvar at Ojhar, Mahāgaṇapatī at Rāñjaṇgāv, Cintāmaṇī at Theūr, Siddhivināyak at Siddhaṭek, and Moreśvar (or Mayūreśvar) at Morgāv.
52. Govaṇḍe 1995:3–5, 16–18, 24–26, 35–37, 42–44, 50, 57–60, 66–69.
53. One notable exception is a narrative connection between Leṇyādri and Morgāv: according to the story Govaṇḍe narrates about Leṇyādri, Pārvatī practiced asceticism there for 12 years in order to get Gaṇeś as her son. He was "born" to her at Leṇyādri, had his thread ceremony performed there, and lived the first 15 years of his life there. But people also say, according to Govaṇḍe, that "it was in this same area that Gaṇeś's descent to earth (*avatār*) as Mayūreśvar took place" (Govaṇḍe 1995:50). Mayūreśvar is the name under which Gaṇapati killed the demon Kamalāsur and the evil king Sindhū at Morgāv (Govaṇḍe 1995:3–5). In other words, the god spent his childhood at Leṇyādri first, and then moved on to Morgāv to kill the demon.
54. Guravs are a caste of non-Brāhmaṇ priests who generally serve in temples of Śiva or goddesses. See Bapat 2001.
55. Presumably they are related by various ties of marriage and consanguinity, like other temple priests of any one caste. In addition, as Irina Glushkova has pointed out to me (in June 2001), Morgāv serves as "a kind of headquarters" for the other seven places.
56. One of the temples (Leṇyādri, the former Buddhist cave) even faces toward the inauspicious south. However, the Gaṇeś image inside faces north into the moutainside, his back to his worshippers.
57. Or, more appropriately, guardians of Ciñcvaḍ, the home of Morobā Gosāvī and the Devs.
58. Gutschow (1977:310), discussing the eight goddesses who often serve as directional guardians of towns in Nepal, finds a similar tension between geometry and topography: "The ideal symmetrical pattern (which we find expressed in a *maṇḍala*) is in reality modified by the two factors of topography and of history: that [is,] by the structure of the terrain, and by a tendency to reuse the shrines of older gods and goddesses which have become reinterpreted and newly consecrated, to fit into the new system."
59. The exception is Theūr, which lies directly between Siddhaṭek and Pune.
60. Two major exceptions are the pairs of places near Junnar (Leṇyādri and Ojhar) and in the Koṅkaṇ (Mahaḍ and Pālī). Each of these places is more easily accessible from its close neighbor than from Pune or any of the other Aṣṭavināyak places. In addition, the route from Pune to Siddhaṭek passes close to Theūr.
61. The same seemed to be true of the Aṣṭavināyak Gaṇeś images that were painted inside the dome of the central hall of the temple at Ojhar when I visited there in 1997. The positions of the Gaṇeś images do not correspond to the geographical locations of the eight temples.

62. On the everyday character, and therefore importance, of Hanumān/Māruti, see the forthcoming Ph.D. dissertation by Jeffrey Brackett (University of Pittsburgh).
63. But see Sontheimer 1991 and Feldhaus 1995:98–101.
64. For an important exception—a village with*out* a Māruti—see Sontheimer 1991:122–27.
65. Another exception is Jarandeśvar, near Sātārā. See the forthcoming work by Brackett.
66. *rājkīya khalavata.* Harṣe 1983:47; cf. Gokhale 1973:141. According to Gordon (1993:81), citing Pawar 1971, "recent research has shown that Shivaji did not meet or know Ramdas until late in his life."
67. Harṣe 1983:44–45; cf. Merusvāmī, *Rāmsohaḷā* 1.8.36–58, pp. 40–41.
68. The temple was renovated in 1972.
69. On connections between political power and pilgrimage places in another region of India, Orissa, cf. Kulke 1978 and Kulke 1978–1979.
70. The Marathi here is strange: *ādilśāhīcyā dhoraṇāce vāremāp gheṇārī.*
71. *BSK,* Volume 10, p. 261. Māruti's name is a patronymic derived from the Maruts, another set of Vedic deities (wind gods), who generally number seven or 49, but not 11.
72. Harṣe 1983:34–36.
73. Describing the Māruti temple at Mājgāv, e.g., Harṣe (1983:44) writes:

> The temple has a tiled roof. The temple is made of mud and bricks. No flag flies over the temple. The floor is not paved. The temple does not have a proper door. It has not been painted, it is not clean. There is electricity, but sometimes the electricity has been cut off because the bill has not been paid. There is not even enough oil to keep a lamp burning before the god. There must not be enough red-lead (*śendūr*) either.

That is, the god's image is not sufficiently covered with red-lead, and so there must not have been enough red-lead to coat it properly.

5 The Algebra of Place: Replication of North Indian Religious Geography in Maharashtra

1. In discussing Nancy Munn's *The Fame of Gawa* (1986), e.g., Casey (1996b:42) writes: "An important aspect of being in a place or region is that one is not limited altogether by determinate borders (i.e., legal limits) or perimiters (i.e., those established by geography) . . . . Distinct and impenetrable borders may belong to sites as legally and geographically controlled entities, and hence ultimately to 'space,' but they need not (and often do not) play a significant role in the experience and knowledge of places and regions."
2. The context is a discussion of the purification requirements for someone who has a relative die in "a different country." The text is quoting an earlier legal authority, Bṛhaspati.

3. Because I gathered most of the examples in this chapter in the course of my study of religious meanings of the rivers of the Deccan, many of the examples refer to rivers or to holy places on the banks of rivers. As the major rivers that flow through Maharashtra also flow beyond its borders, a few of the examples are of places outside of Maharashtra.
4. In an article to be published separately, I will discuss the heightened paradoxes involved in the Vārkarī poet-saints' use of such forms of praise for their principal holy place, Paṇḍharpūr.
5. There are many other examples of the replication of the three-and-a-half major goddesses of Maharashtra, including the replica of Tuḷjāpūr at Burhāṇnagar discussed in chapter 3 and several replicas of Reṇukā of Māhūr discussed in Stark-Wild 1997.
6. This must be the same place as Bahe, or Bahe-Borgāv, the site of one of the Eleven Mārutis discussed in chapter 4. See that chapter for the story of Rām installing and worshipping a Śivaliṅga at Bahe-Borgāv, something he did at Rāmeśvaram as well.
7. *KM*.Skt. 18.4, 27; *KM*.Mar. 18.5. The Kali Yuga is the present, degenerate age of the world.
8. As I mentioned in the introduction, the name "Deccan" comes from "*dakṣiṇ*," "southern."
9. My sources for these examples are as follows: for Alampūr, oral information; for Dhom, oral information; for Karāḍ, Gupte 1927:1, 6; for Kolhāpūr, Lele 1885:157; for Nandikeśvar, *GBP*, Bijāpur, 1884:665; and for Nevāse, Paiṭhaṇ, and Wāī, oral information.
10. Oral information.
11. Phaḍke provides an elaborate explanation of this last identification:

> The confluence of the Bhogāvatī (Gaṅgā) and the Kāsārī (Yamunā) is about three miles west of Karvīr [Kolhāpūr]; the place is also called Prayāg. The Gaṅgā has the name Gaṅgā in heaven. In the world of mortals its name is Bhāgīrathī (because it was brought by Bhagīratha), and in the underworld it has the name Bhogāvatī. Because the holy area of Karvīr is in the south (in the underworld), the name that [the Gaṅgā here] has gotten is Bhogāvatī. The Kāsārī has gotten the name Kāsārī because it flows through very difficult terrain, and is as tough (*kaṭhīn*) as Yamunā, the sister of Yama [the god of death. A Kāsārī is a brass-maker woman or a woman who sells glass bangles; the implication is that such a woman is likely to be a shrew]. That is, just as in the north there is the Prayāg of the Gaṅgā and the Yamunā, so this is the Prayāg of the Gaṅgā and Yamunā of southern Kāśī.

Complex though this explanation is, it in fact finds North Indian equivalents for only two of the five (*pañca*) rivers (*gaṅgā*) that form the Pañcagaṅgā. The other three rivers are the Tuḷśī, the Kumbhī, and the Brāhmaṇī.

12. For example, at *KM*.Mar. 23.16; cf. *KM*.Skt. 23.23.
13. Kṛṣṇābāī is the Kṛṣṇā river, personified as "Lady Kṛṣṇā." See note 75.
14. In chapters 3, 47, and 72.
15. For Wāī and its Brāhmaṇs, see Feldhaus 1995:146–72.
16. For the versions of these places in (northern) Vārāṇasī, see Eck 1982.
17. See chapter 4, note 3.
18. *KM*.Skt. 53.66–68; cf. *KM*.Mar. 53.51–52.

19. Cf. Sontheimer 1989:225–30.
20. KM.Mar. 56.51; KM.Skt. 56.66.
21. Udās 1891:48, quoting the *Kṣetravarṇan*.
22. For instance, the *Payoṣṇī Māhātmya* claims that one gets liberation at Koṭi *tīrtha*, Rām *tīrtha*, Kṛtaśauca *tīrtha*, and Śukla *tīrtha* on the Pūrṇā river just as one does at Vārāṇasī (*PM* 22.102), and that Viśāla *tīrtha*, also on the Pūrṇā, gives the reward of "Karāḍ and Kolhāpūr" (*PM* 13.15).
23. This story is an interesting cross between two stories that are otherwise distinct: the story of Bhairav with the skull, and the story of Indra's brahminicide.
24. Such is the claim the *Tāpī Māhātmya* makes when it states that by just the *darśan* of Śivayoga at Gupteśvar *tīrtha* one gets the reward of ten pilgrimages to Kedār (*TM* 53.7). This is also the claim that the *Bhīmā Māhātmya* makes when it states that at Bhīmā *tīrtha* one gets a hundred times as much merit as one does at Setubandha (Rāmeśvaram) and a crore of times as much as one does at Vārāṇasī (*BM* 20.70).
25. For instance, after asserting that Gupteśvar *tīrtha* gives one the reward of ten pilgrimages to Kedār, the *Tāpī Māhātmya* claims, seven verses later, that just going to that same Gupteśvar *tīrtha* without performing almsgiving or practicing asceticism there gives one the benefit of having bathed in the Gaṅgā at Kedār—presumably only once (*TM* 53.14). Claims of the form "going to X = *n*(doing ritual R at Y)" must also certainly be made; however, I omit this possibility here, as I have not noted any examples of it.
26. The merit one gets at the Godāvarī during the Siṃhastha period, e.g., can be obtained at Prakāś *kṣetra* on the Tāpī at any time (*TM* 46.29). For a discussion of the astrological juncture called Siṃhastha and its significance in Maharashtrian religious geography, see later, under "Containing Other Places." At the confluence of the Payoṣṇī and the Tāpī, one gets a hundred times the benefits to be obtained at Kurukṣetra during an eclipse of the sun (*PM* 39.31).
27. Mahādevśāstrī Jośī (1950:10) cites a statement from the *Skandapurāṇa* that makes a claim of this sort with respect to the Godāvarī (or Godā) river: "One should practice asceticism on the bank of the Revā [Narmadā], one should lay down one's body [that is, die] on the bank of the Gaṅgā, and one should give alms at Kurukṣetra: such is the fame of these *kṣetras*. But by doing all of these things on the bank of just the Godā, one is rewarded with the same amount of merit."
28. Such is the assertion of the *Kṛṣṇā Māhātmya* when it states that baths in the Bhāgīrathī, the Gomatī, the Godāvarī, the Bhīmā (*KM*.Skt. 25.16–17), and the Narmadā (*KM*.Mar. 25.16) are limited in their rewards, while a bath at the confluence of the Pañcagaṅgā and the Kṛṣṇā is unlimited (in its rewards? Cf. Lele 1885:159).
29. Examples of the first of these two equations include the *Godāvarī Māhātmya*'s claim that one bath in the Godāvarī—and the *Kṛṣṇā Māhātmya*'s that one bath in the Kṛṣṇā during the Kanyāgat period—is equivalent to 60,000 years of bathing in the Bhāgīrathī (the Ganges river of North India. *GM*.Mar. 4.33; 30.60; cf. *GM*.Skt. 7.30;105.84; *KM*.Skt. 54.17; *KM*.Mar. 54.14.), and the *Tāpī Māhātmya*'s assertion that making *piṇḍa* offerings once at Dharmaśilā

tīrtha on the Tāpī is equivalent to making *piṇḍa* offerings at Gayā for 60,000 years. A relatively modest example of the second equation is the *Gurucaritra*'s claim that bathing at Cakratīrtha, one of the eight *tīrtha*s (Aṣṭatīrtha) of Gāṇgāpūr (a pilgrimage place of the god Dattātreya on the Bhīmā river), gives four times the merit of bathing at Dvārāvatī (Dvārkā; Pujārī 1935:11, citing *Gurucaritra* 49); a more pretentious example is the *Bhīmā Māhātmya*'s claim that by bathing at Dharmakṣetra on the Bhīmā one gets ten million times (one crore) the merit to be obtained by bathing at Kurukṣetra during an eclipse of the sun (*BM* 12.14).

30. See Kane 1973:604–09. In the south, Śrīśailam is known for this—as the *Tāpī Māhātmya* story of King Gajadhvaja (*TM* 53.54–61), cited earlier, illustrates.
31. Lele (1885:115, n.3) reports a tradition that the Godāvarī gets its name because a bath in this river gives the rewards of donating (*dā*) thousands of cows (*go*), properly adorned and accompanied by their calves, at Prayāg to worthy recipients during a solar or lunar eclipse.
32. Examples of both these formulas are found in the *Tāpī Māhātmya*. In one passage, Hanumān tells some pious Brāhmaṇs at the Gaṅgā that one gets eight times as much merit by *thinking* of the Tāpī as one gets by lifelong service of the Gaṅgā (*TM* 60.62). In another passage, the Māhātmya declares, in its own voice, that by listening to it one gets a crore of times the merit one gets by worshipping all the Jyotirliṅgas and bathing in all *tīrtha*s (*TM* 78.55; cf. *TM* 1.60).
33. For the four Dhams, see chapter 4. For this man, the four Dhāms also included the Seven Cities (Saptapurī) and the 12 Jyotirliṅgas, as well as a number of other places.
34. In this latter case, although the claim takes the form, "going to X completes a pilgrimage to Y," the reason given for saying that going to Gupteśvar completes a pilgrimage to Kedār is that [the god of] Kedār is himself at Gupteśvar. This reason, then, takes the form, "God G of place Y is at X"—a formula we will see in several of its variants in the next section of this chapter.
35. The Kṛṣṇā, in whose Māhātmya this passage is found, is the river about which people most often stress that it is a *mahānadī*, a river that reaches the ocean. See chapter 1.
36. Cf. Mani 1975. The *Kṛṣṇā Māhātmya* makes a similar claim, not particularly clear in either the Marathi or the Sanskrit version of the text (*KM*.Skt. 60.33–34; *KM*.Mar. 60.31–32), that whereas the Sarasvatī causes purification or sanctification in three days, the Yamunā in seven, the Bhāgīrathī immediately, and the Narmadā by the sight (*darśan*) of it, the Kṛṣṇā is even more powerful than these; this passage also mentions the Bhīmarathī (Bhīmā) and the Godāvarī, but it is hard to tell how they are supposed to fit into the table of equivalences.
37. It is not clear whether this means 100 *tīrtha*s *and liṅga*s or 100 *tīrtha*s that *are liṅga*s.
38. Oral information.
39. *GM*.Mar. 4.40; 31.15; *GM*.Skt. 7.34.
40. Oral information.
41. Oral information.

42. Mani 1975, citing *Padmapurāṇa* 13.
43. Oral information, in both cases.
44. Oral information; Kuḷkarṇī 1988:18–19.
45. Oral information.
46. *PM* 39.57–79. The exact arrangement of gods and *tīrtha*s at this place is hard to decipher, but it is clear that the intention is to assign them to the cardinal and intermediate directions.
47. See Gutschow 1977; Levy 1990:153–56, 228–31; Eck 1982:294–96; Feldhaus 1987; and chapter 6 of this book.
48. See Feldhaus 1995:23.
49. Eliade 1969:219–45; Varenne 1976:155–56; Kramrisch 1976:67–97; Beck 1976; White 1996:218–62; Bouillier and Tarabout 2002.
50. *PM* 13.16; cf. *PM* 22.99, *PM* 24.3, and *PM* 36.15.
51. *KM*.Skt. 58.39; *KM*.Mar. 58.31.
52. Oral information from a Paṇḍharpūr Koḷī. This man recited a Marathi verse that names the Gomatī, the Godāvarī, the Narmadā, the Sarasvatī, the Tuṅgabhadrā, and the Bhāgīrathī (= Gaṅgā), and states that they join the Candrabhāgā at noon (*madhyāhnakālīṃ*). See Nāmdev 399. The Koḷī interpreted the verse to mean that *all* rivers come to the Candrabhāgā, and that they do so at midnight rather than noon.
53. The author who quotes this verse takes it to mean that all *tīrtha*s and all deities live in the Godāvarī during the Siṃhastha period.
54. A specific form of the claim that a distant, famous river or place (Y) comes to, or comes to meet, a nearby river or place (X) is the claim that

    Y bathes at X.

    Such, e.g., is the claim that the Gaṅgā and all other rivers bathe in the Tāpī during the month of Āṣāḍh (*TM* 70.25), the claim that the Gaṅgā bathes in the Narmadā once a year (*Imperial Gazetteer* 1909:177), or the claim that Prayāg, Naimiṣa, Gayā, Vārāṇasī, Kurukṣetra, Prabhās, and Gokarṇa Mamaleśvar always bathe at Koṭitīrtha on the Payoṣṇī (*PM* 23.55, 57).
55. The numerous confluences where the Sarasvatī river reappears from underground could also be included here. I have already discussed them under the formula "X is the hidden Y."
56. See earlier, under "X has what Y has."
57. See Feldhaus 1995:41–42.
58. See chapter 1 and Feldhaus 1995:29–36.
59. Udās 1891:45–46; Phaḍke 1931:225. The astrological juncture at which this is said to happen is the Kapilā Ṣaṣṭhī Yog.
60. Ratnagiri District. Phaḍke 1931:120–24; Enthoven 1924:102; oral information.
61. Phaḍke 1931:120, based on information given by Rājvāḍe about the annual income of the place, estimates that "this Gaṅgā must have been known about for two or three hundred years."
62. For connections among rivers, women, cows, and milk, see Feldhaus 1995.
63. Yellow turmeric and red *kuṅkūṃ* are the two powders that are used on the forehead of an auspicious (married or marriageable, unwidowed) woman. For the femininity of rivers and their auspiciousness in Maharashtra, see Feldhaus 1995.

64. The man told me this story twice, once in 1985 and again in 1988. Here I give the 1988 version.
65. At Narsobācī Vāḍī, e.g., when the Kanyāgat period is about to start, men carry a festival image from the main temple to Śukla *tīrtha*, some distance upstream, and give it a bath. After this bath, the Gaṅgā is understood to have come into the Kṛṣṇā, to remain in it for a year.
66. For a description of this festival, see Feldhaus 1995:146–72.
67. Oral information.
68. Contrast the equality of the Kṛṣṇā and Koynā at their "love confluence" in Karāḍ (chapter 3).
69. And the underworld river Bhogāvatī (see Feldhaus 1991).
70. The *Tāpī Māhātmya* gives another example of this motif: to edify a doubting Brāhmaṇ, Śiva himself throws his own staff and water pot into the confluence of the Sarasvatī and the ocean at Prabhās; they come up at the confluence of the Tāpī and the ocean at Ulkeśvar (*TM* 67.88–101).
71. Usmanabad District. Sontheimer 1989a:210–14.
72. The pamphlets I have consulted (Burāṇḍe 1987, Jośī 1979, Ruīkar 1982, and Lāde 1983) tell of Jyotibā's coming to Ratnāgiri in order to kill a demon. He is born to the *ṛṣi* Paugaṇḍa and his wife, Vimalāmbujā, after they have prayed to Kedārnāth for a child. This does not, however, seem to be a version of the "old devotee" story discussed in chapter 3 (Ruīkar 1982:5).
73. Probably this is the Rāmtīrtha near Athni in Belgaum District (Karnatak), described in the *GBP*, Belgaum 1884:598–99.
74. I say "doing ritual R at Y" here rather than "doing ritual R′ at Y" because "giving *piṇḍas*" and "doing *śrāddha*" refer to the same ritual.
75. Kṛṣṇābāī, "Lady Kṛṣṇā," is a name used in some contexts to refer to the Kṛṣṇā river. It is also the name of the goddess who embodies the river, and whose festival is celebrated in late winter in Wāī and other towns along the river. See Feldhaus 1995:50–53, 146–72.
76. For a description and discussion of this temple, see Feldhaus 1995:21.
77. A more detailed version of the story can be found in Feldhaus 1995:24–25.
78. Jośī (1950:10) reports a popular tradition that the Godāvarī is linked with the Gaṅgā through an underground passage. This tradition, which differs from the Māhātmya's account (according to which the connection is more properly celestial than subterranean), follows the praise formula, "Y is connected with X by an underground passage," discussed earlier.
79. *GM*.Skt. 8.1–2; *GM*.Mar. 5.36; 31.119–21, 133. In addition, according to *GM*.Mar. 31.121, the Narmadā is the Gaṅgā of Vaiśyas, and the Kāverī is the Gaṅgā of Śūdras.
80. A man from another village who was listening to this corrected the speaker: the river is called "Godāvarī" at Nāsik too, at the river's source, this other man objected; but he did not challenge the statement that the Gaṅgā-Godāvarī is also the Candrabhāgā at Paṇḍharpūr.
81. Except, of course, in the *Narmadā Māhātmya*, where places on the Narmadā are the nearby, not the distant ones.
82. The information was obtained by making notecards with statements of this sort on them, then listing the places used as standards of comparison in the

statements, and counting the numbers of times each place occurs. The material so indexed is not complete, nor could it be, nor is it completely indexed, nor is it a "scientifically" valid sample, nor has it been checked for accuracy. Nonetheless, I think it does support the sort of rough conclusions I have drawn from it. In order to avoid a deceptive appearance of precision, I have intentionally refrained from mentioning any exact numbers. To indicate the general range of numbers involved: I have counted between 20 and 25 occurrences each of Kāśī, Kurukṣetra, and Prayāg as standards of comparison in the river Māhātmyas that I have used, and about four dozen occurrences of Kāśī in oral sources (including modern texts based primarily on oral sources).

83. For a major exception, see Cakradhar's command to his followers to stay out of the "Kannada and Telugu lands" (chapter 6). Cakradhar was a Gujarati, and hence a North Indian.
84. Rāmeśvaram and Śrīśailam are sometimes standards of comparison for Maharashtrian places.
85. I am grateful to Christian Novetzke for a lively discussion of the views I present here, and for reminding me of aspects of Maharashtrian culture that relate it more closely to the North than to the South of India. For instance, the script used for writing Marathi is the North Indian, *devanāgarī* script rather than any of the South Indian scripts; Marathi is classified as a North Indian, Indo-European, rather than a South Indian, Dravidian, language; and the kind of classical music that is prevalent in Maharashtra is North Indian, Hindustani music rather than South Indian, Carnatic music. On the other hand, Marathi vocabulary owes a great deal to its southern neighbor-language, Kannada (Lokāpur 1994), and many of the most prominent Hindustani musicians in Maharashtra have come from Karnataka. For additional evidence, see the section of the introduction entitled "Geographical Stories."
86. See the writings of Günther Sontheimer, including Sontheimer 1989b.

6 Pilgrimage and Remembrance: Biography and Geography in the Mahānubhāv Tradition

1. For the literature, see Raeside 1960. For the codes, see Raeside 1970.
2. The *Līḷācaritra* (Kolte 1982b).
3. *Ṛddhipurlīḷā* or *Ṛddhipurcaritra* (Kolte 1972), translated in Feldhaus, translator 1984.
4. In addition to Cakradhar and Guṇḍam Rāüḷ, these are Cāṅgdev Rāüḷ, Dattātreya, and Kṛṣṇa. See Feldhaus 1983b.
5. *Smṛtisthaḷ* (Deśpāṇḍe 1961), translated in Feldhaus and Tulpule, translators 1992.
6. For *bhakti* disdain for special places, see, e.g., Ramanujan 1973:26. For ascetic renunciation, see, e.g., Olivelle 1977 and 1995.
7. The numbering of *sūtras* follows that in Feldhaus 1983a. On the notion of attachment (*sambandh*), see Feldhaus 1994.

8. This last place is probably Purī, in Orissa. Māhūr and Kolhāpūr are two of Maharashtra's principal 3-1/2 goddess places, discussed in chapter 4.
9. Nipāṇīkar (1980) argues that the names "Kānaḍdeś" and "Telaṅgadeś" in this *sūtra* refer to particular villages with goddess temples rather than to regions. Tuḷpuḷe (1981) argues, convincingly, for the more traditional interpretation adopted here.
10. The young man had died and was being carried to the cremation ground just as a previous incarnation, Cāṅgdev Rāūḷ, left his body. Cāṅgdev Rāūḷ was an ascetic who was being harrassed by a lascivious woman (*LC*, "Pūrvārdha" 16–17).
11. *te marhāṭī tar anāvara bolati. LC*, "Uttarārdha"13.
12. The text does not use the names "Gujarat" and "Maharashtra" at this point.
13. Tulpule 1972, chapter 7: *to desu pārkā. tetha jāoṃ nai e.*
14. Kolte 1982b, "Pūrvārdha" 20. Cakradhar's father also objects on the grounds that his family are "*rāje*"—Kṣatriyas, perhaps—and hence should send a Brāhmaṇ on the pilgrimage in their stead. If, as S. G. Tulpule suggested to me in conversation, "*rāje*" refers to Brāhmaṇs engaged in royal service, then perhaps Cakradhar's father wants to send on the pilgrimage another *kind* of Brāhmaṇ, one engaged in religious rather than governmental work.
15. Perhaps the strong physical boundaries on Maharashtra's northern border—the Vindhya and Sātpuḍa mountains and the Narmadā and Tāpī rivers—make it unnecessary to articulate the sort of prohibition the *Sūtrapāṭh* expresses with respect to the south. See the introduction. See also the section of chapter 5 entitled "Maharashtra's Southern Identity."
16. Kolte 1982a:92; *Ācār Sthaḷ Mahābhāṣya* (Pañjābī n.d.b) Volume 1, 133–34.
17. VI.5.29, cited in Sircar 1971a:94.
18. Another Mahānubhāv text that explicitly defines Maharashtra is Kṛṣṇamuni Kavi Ḍimbh's *Ṛddhipur Māhātmya* (Kṛṣṇamuni 1967). This early-seventeenth-century (Raeside 1960:494) text gives two quite different definitions of Maharashtra. In one passage (verse 306), Kṛṣṇamuni identifies Maharashtra as the area "from Tryambak to Kāḷeśvar at Māthanī, and from the Kṛtamāḷā to the Tābraparṇī." The mention of Tryambak, at the source of the Godāvarī river, and of "Kāḷeśvar at Māthanī"—probably the Kāḷeśvar at the confluence of the Godāvarī and the Prāṇhitā, near modern Manthanī (Karimnagar District, Andhra Pradesh), at the farthest eastern border of modern Maharashtra with modern Andhra Pradesh—makes the upper Godāvarī valley the northern limit of Maharashtra. But the rest of the definition extends Maharashtra far to the south. The Kṛtamālā (now Vaigai) and Tābraparṇī (Tāmraparṇī) rivers both flow well to the south of the Kannada and Telugu lands that the *Sūtrapāṭh* explicitly distinguishes from Maharashtra.

    By Kṛṣṇamuni's other definition (verses 103–04), Maharashtra extends less far south, but farther north. By this definition, Maharashtra is the region south of the Vindhya mountains, north of the Kṛṣṇā river, and west of the "*jhāḍī maṇḍaḷ*" to the Koṅkaṇ. The "*jhāḍī maṇḍaḷ*" is, literally, the "treeful region," the forested region comprising the present-day districts of Canda (or Candrapur) and Bhandara (Dāte et al. 1932–1938, Volume 3:1353). By this definition, then, too, Maharashtra extends a good bit beyond the Godāvarī valley, though not into any territory that the *Sūtrapāṭh* explicitly excludes. Again, though, this definition does not give firm evidence about the *Sūtrapāṭh*'s use of the term "Maharashtra," since the *Sūtrapāṭh* was composed a full three centuries earlier than Kṛṣṇamuni's text.

19. M. S. Mate (1975:79) identifies these as the two "nuclear areas" of Marathi culture.
20. Mahānubhāv teachings hold that Cakradhar did not die but "left for the north" (*uttarāpanthe*).
21. Kolte 1972; Feldhaus, translator 1984 (slightly revised), chapter 88; cf. *LC*, "Pūrvārdha" 585. For Guṇḍam Rāüḷ as mad, see Feldhaus 1982 and Feldhaus, translator 1984.
22. That is, in the Godāvarī valley. For "Gaṅgā" as a name of the Godāvarī, see chapter 5.
23. Kolte 1972; Feldhaus, translator 1984, chapter 102.
24. This is equivalent to *sīvanadeś*, or Seunadeś, another name for the Yādava kingdom, the kingdom of King Seunacandra. Altekar 1960:516.
25. Kolte 1972; Feldhaus, translator 1984, chapter 235.
26. Deshpande 1961:203; Pañjābī 1968:184; *VMM* 206. *VMM* gives two other interpretations in addition to the one cited here. See also *LC*, "Ajñāt Līḷā" 148.
27. Deshpande 1960; Feldhaus and Tulpule, translators 1992, chapter 246.
28. Dr. S. G. Tulpule suggested (personal communication) that the reason for the Mahānubhāvs' pleasant associations with Vidarbha and their unpleasant associations with the Godāvarī valley is that Cakradhar met his guru, Guṇḍam Rāüḷ, in Vidarbha, and was killed in the Godāvarī valley. Cf. *MP*, verses 268–84.
29. These are Sanskrit pronouns.
30. Deshpande 1960; Feldhaus and Tulpule, translators 1992, chapter 66.
31. *yeṇeṃ mājhiyā mhāṃtārīyā nāgavatil.* Ibid., chapter 15.
32. Kolte 1982a:82–84; *ASM* I, 126–29. Other commentaries—*Niruktaśeṣ* (Deśpāṇḍe 1961:4), *Prakaraṇvaś* (Pañjābī 1968:17), and *Vicār Ācār Prakaraṇācā Vacan Sambandha Artha* (Pañjābī n.d.d:73)—do not explain the command.
33. The sub-commentary *ASM* gives Marwar as an example.
34. That is, they have large populations? Or does this mean that the people who live in these countries are tall? *ASM* gives as examples Gujarat and Panjab.
35. *Aiśvarya*. *ASM* gives "Arabasthān" (Arabia) as an example.
36. Here *ASM*'s example is the Koṅkaṇ.
37. *ASM* gives "Gauḍ Bengāl" as an example of a land great in witchcraft (*kauṭalya*), and the Kannada and Telugu countries as examples of lands great in lust.
38. The three *guṇas*—*rajas*, *tamas*, and *sattva*—are explained later.
39. *Sūtrapāṭh* XII.20, 57, 67; XIII.40, 41, 43, 81, 131, 132, 188, and 189.
40. Deshpande 1960; Feldhaus and Tulpule, translators 1992, chapter 115.
41. *Niruddeś*, *Sūtrapāṭh* XIII.40.
42. This section appears in the second edition (1976), but not the first (undated), of Kolte's edition of the work. Another undated edition, prepared by Mādhavrāj Pañjābī (n.d.c), includes a section entitled "Atha Ruddhipūr Sthāne."

43. Kolte 1982b. Kolte has included at various places in his edition passages from a number of texts that he believes to have originally belonged to the *Līḷācaritra*, even though the texts are generally not found in *Līḷācaritra* manuscripts. See note 46 and Kolte's introduction to his edition, p. 84 f.
44. In Kolte's edition, "Ekāṅka" does not form a separate section of the *Līḷācaritra*, but its chapters are included in "Pūrvārdha." For Kolte's reasons for considering "Ekāṅka" as part of "Pūrvārdha" rather than a separate section, see his introduction, 1982b:62–63.
45. This interpretation also makes sense of the fact that the section of the *Sthānpothī* entitled "Ṛddhipur Sthāneṃ" includes many places outside the village of Ṛddhipūr. Although these places are not found in Ṛddhipūr, they are, by and large, found in the *Ṛddhipurcaritra*.
46. The *Līḷācaritra*, in the course of narrating episodes of Cakradhar's life, several times makes statements like, "Then the Gosāvī [Cakradhar] taught '*x*,' " naming a section of the *Sūtrapāṭh*; or "Then the Gosāvī taught the '*y*' *dṛṣṭānta*," naming one of the parables in the *Dṛṣṭāntapāṭh*. In preparing his edition of the *Līḷācaritra*, Kolte has added the appropriate *sūtra*s and *dṛṣṭānta*s at these points, providing a crutch for those readers who do not share early Mahānubhāvs' ready knowledge of the *sūtra*s and *dṛṣṭānta*s. In the *Dṛṣṭāntapāṭh*, each of the parables is joined with a *Sūtrapāṭh sūtra* that it is supposed to illustrate, as well as with a moral (a *dārṣṭāntika*) that relates the *dṛṣṭānta* to the *sūtra*. The *Sūtrapāṭh* does not make explicit references to episodes of the *Līḷācaritra*, and yet it does state that its *sūtras* must be interpreted in terms of their context (*prakaraṇa*; see *Sūtrapāṭh* XII.148 and XI.135). By *prakaraṇa* is meant not primarily the *Sūtrapāṭh* context of a *sūtra*, its relationship to the *sūtra*s that precede and follow it, but its context in Cakradhar's life: to whom he spoke the *sūtra* and on what occasion or in answer to what question. This information can be found not only in the *Līḷācaritra*, but also in two distinctive *Sūtrapāṭh* commentaries: *Prakaraṇvaś* (Pañjābī 1968) and *Niruktaśeṣ* (Deśpāṇḍe 1961).
47. More precisely, "The Garland of Verses about Holy Places."
48. For a photograph of a Mahānubhāv *oṭā*, see Feldhaus 1988:273.
49. See Feldhaus, translator 1984.
50. Mahant Gopīrāj Mahānubhāv, Ṛddhipūr, July 1, 1983.
51. Personal communication, June 28–29, 1982. In Maharashtrian villages, Buddhist neighborhoods are the neighborhoods of formerly Untouchable Mahārs who have converted to Buddhism. In converting, they are following the lead of Dr. B. R. Ambedkar, who was formally initiated as a Buddhist shortly before his death in 1956.
52. People frequently use the term "*sāmārthya*" as a synonym for "*śakti*" in this sense.
53. One informant stated that *māyā śakti* has the more "pragmatic" effects and *kṛpā śakti* the more "transcendent" ones. For a thorough discussion of Mahānubhāv *śakti* theory, see Kolte 1975:71, 122–26 and Kolte 1973:312–17.
54. Mahant Pāc Rāūt Bābā Mahānubhāv, Ṛddhipūr, June 26, 1983.
55. Mādhavrāj Pañjābī, Amrāvatī, July 7, 1982.
56. The Collector is a high administrative official, the head of a district.

57. This title is borrowed from that of an article by James Foard (1995).
58. Like much of the rest of early Mahānubhāv literature, the text of the *Sthānpothī* includes within itself a number of variants. Some of these variants come from differing recollections of early Mahānubhāvs who had memorized an original version of the text. This version was lost (see the next note), and a number of these disciples together reconstructed the text from memory. (See Deśpāṇḍe 1932; Nene 1936, 1939; Feldhaus 1983a:10–11, 15; and Feldhaus, translator 1984:39–40.) Since the disciples' recollections did not always agree, the reconstructed text includes a number of different versions. A variant version is introduced by the name of the disciple from whom it comes—Hīrāïseṃ, Paraśarāmbās, and so on—or by the words "*śodh*" or "*tathā*," or both. Other variants introduced by the words "*śodh*" or "*tathā*" seem to indicate the work of a subsequent editor.
59. The claim that the writing of the *Sthānpothī* began with Bāïdevobās would mean that there was an early version of the text in existence before approximately 1309 C.E. Y. K. Deśpāṇḍe states that the *Sthānpothī* was written in Śaka 1275 (1353 C.E.) by Munivyās Koṭhī. This Munivyās is best known for having built the aniconic stone blocks or pedestals (*oṭās*) that mark the Mahānubhāv holy places. (See later.) Kolte finds no evidence to support the claim that Munivyās wrote the *Sthānpothī*; rather, Kolte suggests, in the course of building (or rebuilding) the *oṭās*, Munivyās may have revised a version of the *Sthānpothī* that was already in existence. Kolte identifies the "Ciḍale" whom he holds responsible for the authorship of *Sthānpothī* in its present form (the form of its present manuscript tradition) as a man belonging to the line of disciples of Dāyābās Ciraḍe.

    Kolte cites no evidence besides *Smṛtisthaḷ* 115 for the claim that Bāïdevobās made notes on the holy places visited in the course of the pilgrimage described in that chapter. Thus, the claim seems to rest on an interpretation of "*sthān-nirdeśeṃ*" as meaning that Nāgdev instructed Bāïdevobās to wander not "according to the *sthāns*" or "in the direction of the *sthāns*" but "writing down notes describing the *sthāns* as you go along." This interpretation does not seem warranted to me, as the text itself says only that Bāïdevobās went along "bowing" (*namaskarītaci*) to the *sthāns*, not writing anything down.

    One bit of evidence for the existence of an early, written version of the *Sthānpothī*, whether it was written by Bāïdevobās or by someone else, is the fact that a text called "Itihās," which gives an account of the loss of several Mahānubhāv texts at the time of a raid by the "sultan of Delhi" (probably the raid by Malik Kāpūr in 1308), lists "*sthānācī pothī*" among the texts that were lost. "Itihās," an Old Marathi text that was published in 1932 (Deśpāṇḍe 1932:45–57), is undated, however, and the other two extant Mahānubhāv accounts of the loss of the early texts—one in Kṛṣṇamuni's "Anvaymālikā" (Nene 1939) and the other in another "Anvaysthaḷ" (Nene 1936)—do not mention the *Sthānpothī* among the texts that were lost.

    The evidence that Munivyās Koṭhī wrote or edited a version of the *Sthānpothī* is almost as weak as the evidence that Bāïdevobās wrote one. And, finally, Kolte is unable to discover who precisely the fifteenth-century redactor named "Ciḍale" was.

60. Further evidence of this can be seen in the large number of major manuscript variants included in Kolte's edition (appendix 1). This suggests that the process of checking the book against the places and emending it accordingly was an ongoing one for some time, with different emendations being made by people who took special interest in different places.
61. Kolte 1976:4–7, 24–30; Paṭhāṇ 1973:47–57.
62. The texts are "Paiṭhaṇcā Vṛddhācār," published in Paṭhāṇ 1973:50–57; and "Caritra Abāb," quoted in Kolte 1976:6. These texts also say nothing about Munivyās's having written—or even revised—the *Sthānpothī*.
63. For example, Mahant Gopīrāj of Ṛddhipūr told me this in June 1983, and Mahant Yakṣadev of Ṛddhipūr said it to me in July 1982.
64. For instance, Mahant Pāc Rāüt Bābā of Ṛddhipūr told me this in July 1982, as well as in the statement quoted later, and Mahant Yakṣadev knew of one set of cases in which the *Sthānpothī* had been used in deciding where to place *oṭā*s.
65. The Narasiṃha temple that was Guṇḍam Rāüḷ's principal residence in Ṛddhipūr.
66. Something Guṇḍam Rāüḷ once did, according to *Ṛddhipurcaritra*, chapter 72 (Kolte 1972; Feldhaus, translator 1984).
67. On the other hand, some *Mahānubhāvs* have complained to me that the *Sthānpothī* is in fact difficult to use for finding new *sthān*s. Purushottam Nagpure, e.g., a prominent Mahānubhāv layman and author in Amravati District, told of making repeated efforts to determine the length of the "*pāṇḍā*" and other measures used in the text: measuring the distances between several different pairs of places given in the *Sthānpothī* failed to produce any uniform values for the *Sthānpothī*'s measures. Such a complaint highlights the belief that the *Sthānpothī ought* to be of help in locating *sthān*s.
68. See Feldhaus 1980.
69. For examples of this process in Ṛddhipūr, see Feldhaus 1987:77–80.
70. The *Sthānpothī* gives a survey of the deities who had temples in the Marāṭhvāḍā and Vidarbha areas of Maharashtra half a millennium or more ago. It tells us the directions in which the temples faced and sometimes on what side of a town or village they were found. Frequently it also names the deities whose temples were clustered together and describes the configurations of the clusters in terms of the directional relationships of the temples to one another.

    This is a rich store of information. So far only a few scholars have made use of it, but the kinds of use they have made of it indicate its potential value. Kolte (1976:21) points out that the *Sthānpothī* mentions no temples of Viṭṭhal/Pāṇḍuraṅg/Viṭhobā, the god of Paṇḍharpūr, who now has numerous temples all over Maharashtra; Kolte interprets this absence as evidence that the cult of Viṭhobā was not particularly widespread when the *Sthānpothī* was composed—or at the time when Cakradhar was wandering around visiting temples. This conclusion is probably correct. It is also possible, though, that Cakradhar's antipathy toward the cult of Viṭhobā—as recorded, e.g., in his derogatory explanation of the cult in *LC*, "Uttarārdha" 519—would have led him to avoid any Viṭhobā temples that he came upon in the course of his travels. Since places where Cakradhar did *not* go are generally *not* included in *Sthānpothī*, its failure to mention Viṭhobā temples does not constitute incontrovertible proof that there were no temples of this god in the villages and towns that Cakradhar visited. Kolte also notes the strong predominance of Śaiva deities among those in whose temples Cakradhar sat or stayed (Kolte 1976:20–21); this confirms the fundamentally Śaiva character of Maharashtrian Hinduism, prior to—and still today, in spite of—the Vaiṣṇava-Kṛṣṇaite overlay of the Vārkarī tradition.

The *Sthānpothī* can also facilitate more detailed kinds of historical research. The historian Setumādhavrāv Pagaḍī carried out such research in Paiṭhaṇ and Auraṅgābād Talukas of Aurangabad District in the early 1950s (Pagaḍī 1985). He visited a number of places described in the *Sthānpothī* and compared his observations with the *Sthānpothī*'s descriptions of the places. He found some very interesting changes. At one place (Pūrṇagāv) he found a Śiva temple on what the *Sthānpothī* describes as the site of a Nārāyaṇ (Viṣṇu) temple (Pagaḍī 1985:4). At three other places (Sāvkheḍā, Nāgamṭhāṇ, and Āvaḷ) he found Śiva temples on what the *Sthānpothī* describes as the site of Āditya temples (Pagaḍī 1985:5, 6, and 7). Although Pagaḍī himself takes the last three cases to mean that the sun god Āditya is now called Śiva, to me it seems more likely that the cult of Āditya, like that of Nārāyaṇ, has waned since the time of the *Sthānpothī*, while the cult of Śiva has continued to rise in popularity. And finally, in three further villages Pagaḍī found mosques—some of them dilapidated or in ruins—on sites that he is reasonably confident the *Sthānpothī* describes as those of Hindu temples: a Narasiṃha temple at Sarāḷmālā (Pagaḍī 1985:5–6), a Narasiṃha or Sarālādevī temple at Bādṭhāṇā (Pagaḍī 1985:2), and a cluster of three temples—to Mahālakṣmī, Śiva, and Gaṇapati—at Kaḍeṭhāg (Pagaḍī 1985:15–16). All three of the temples had been replaced by mosques at some point between the last editing of the *Sthānpothī* and 1952.

71. See, e.g., Beck 1976, Das 1982, Kramrisch 1976, and Levy 1990.
72. Some of the Mahānubhāv pilgrimage places are not purely sectarian in their importance. Besides places like Tryambakeśvar and Māhūr, which Mahānubhāvs share with non-Mahānubhāv Hindus, there are also Mahānubhāv pilgrimage places that are reputed, within the sect but even more so outside it, to have special power to cure ghost possession. See Stanley 1988:36–37.
73. I have taken "*āṃvaḍhe nāganātha amardaka tapovana*" in verse 124 to refer to a single place. Kolte identifies "Amardaka" as an older name of Auṇḍhe, a village in Parbhani District, Maharashtra (Kolte 1982b:807). The *Bhāratīya Saṃskṛtikoś* (Joshi 1962–1979, Volume 3:685) identifies Auṇḍhe as the location of the Dārukāvan in which the *Śivapurāṇa* places Nāgnāth. For the 12 Jyotirliṅgas, cf. map 4.1 and chapter 4, note 3.
74. According to one of Kṛṣṇamuni's definitions of Maharashtra (*Ṛddhipūr Māhātmya* 306; see note 18, earlier), Rāmeśvar would also be included in Maharashtra, for on that definition Maharashtra extends as far south as the Tāmraparṇī river, in far southern Tamil Nadu.
75. This is identical with "Bhīṣmeśvar in Ḍākinī" in the previous list.
76. This list agrees with the standard one given by Eck (1982:38) and Bharati (1970:97) and in chapter 4, except that Māyā is more usually identified as Hardvār than as Gayā. That Kṛṣṇamuni identifies it as Gayā can be seen from verse 145, cited later.

77. "The demon Māyā" may refer to Maya, Namuci's brother, one of the Dānavas. Anyone who put his hand on the head of the demon Bhasma was turned to ashes. Viṣṇu destroyed Bhasma by getting him to touch his hand to his own head (Citrāv 1932).
78. On Rukmāṅgad's devotion to the Ekādaśī vow, see the *Nāradapurāṇa* 2.36 (Veṅkaṭeśvara Press edition). By killing Rāvaṇa, Rām incurred *brahmahatyā*, the sin of killing a Brāhmaṇ, not *strīhatyā*, the sin of killing a woman. Perhaps the reference is to Rām's having Lakṣmaṇ cut off the nose and ears of Śūrpanakhā, Rāvaṇa's sister.
79. According to Goḍbole (1928:262), Bhogāvatī is a name of the Sarasvatī river. The *Gautamī Māhātmya* (*GM*.Skt. 41) tells of the marriage of a Princess Bhogavatī to a snake (a creature of the underworld) at Pratiṣṭhān. See Feldhaus 1991 for more on the serpents of Paiṭhaṇ.
80. This story is widely known in Ṛddhipūr today. See Feldhaus 1987:76. In literature, the story is found in Kṛṣṇamuni's *Ṛddhipur Māhātmya*, verses 639–94, and it forms the basic plot of Maheśvarpaṇḍit's *Ṛddhipur Māhātmya*. Both of these are elaborations of a story found in chapter 213 of the biography of Guṇḍam Rāūḷ (Kolte 1972; Feldhaus, translator 1984).

CONCLUSION

1. I have not seen similar regionalistic consequences of the rivalry between the bedstead- and palanquin-carriers on the pilgrimage to Tuḷjāpūr, although there is regionalistic potential in the fact that the two objects start out from different places: Rāhurī and Ghoḍegāv.
2. I have not been able to discover any studies of South Asian Muslim religious geography that examine networks of Muslim pilgrimage shrines from this perspective. Damrel (forthcoming) and Ernst 1995 make a good start at the study of the Muslim religious geography of India, but they do not reach the regional level.
3. I count seven rather than the eight Maharashtrian Jyotirliṅgas that Jogaḷekar claims his calculations add up to. But, in any case, even seven out of 12 would present a powerful religious-geographical argument for the superiority of Maharashtra to other parts of India. For Kṛṣṇamuni, see chapter 6. For the Jyotirliṅgas, see chapter 4.
4. *Sattva* ("purity"), *rajas* ("passion"), and *tamas* ("darkness") are the three *guṇa*s of Sāṅkhya-style Hindu philosophy, frequently used for classifying groups of three as, respectively, best, medium, and worst. The Godāvarī is the holiest river of Maharashtra in terms of the Brāhmaṇical-Sanskritic religious geography of India as a whole. See Feldhaus 1995:24–25 and chapter 5 of this book. I do not know why Jogaḷekar describes the Kṛṣṇā as *tāmasic*. I will discuss later why he refrains from describing the Bhīmā as *rājasic*.
5. As we have seen in the introduction, the valley of the Godāvarī river is identified as the Daṇḍakāraṇya, the forest in which Rām and his wife and brother spent most of their years of exile. See also Feldhaus 1995:98–99.

6. Saptaśṛṅgī, Tuljāpūr, and Kolhāpūr are three (or, rather, two-and-a-half) of the three-and-a-half Śakti Pīṭhas of Maharashtra, discussed in chapter 4.
7. Nāsik, identified here as a *dharmakṣetra,* is one of four sites of the 12-year cycle of the Kumbha Melā (see chapter 4) and a principal place in Maharashtra for performing *śrāddha* ceremonies. Sātārā, here called a *vīrakṣetra,* is still thought of as the center of the Marāṭhā military power. Pune, the *karmakṣetra,* was presumably already in Jogaḷekar's time beginning its rise as the industrial center it now is.

Selected Bibliography

[Anonymous.] N.d. *Sārtha Saptaśṛṅga Mahātmya*. Thane: Sādhanā Prakāśan.

[Anonymous.] N.d. *Śrī Catuḥśṛṅgī Devasthān*. Puṇe: Śrī Catuḥśṛṅgī Devasthān Trustees.

[Anonymous.] 1920. " 'Ālī Siṃhasthaparvaṇī, Nhāvyāṃ Bhatāṃ Jhālī Dhanī.'" *Mahārāṣṭra Sāhitya* 2.

[Anonymous.] 1967. "The Hindu Calendar and the Kumbh Mela." *The India Cultures Quarterly* 24:25–26.

Abbott, John. 1932. *The Keys of Power: A Study of Indian Ritual and Belief*. Reprint, Seacaucus: University Books, 1974.

Adams, Paul C., Steven Hoelscher, and Karen E. Till, editors. 2001. *Textures of Place: Exploring Humanist Geographies*. Minneapolis: University of Minnesota Press.

Agnew, John. 1993. "Representing Space: Space, Scale and Culture in Social Science." In Duncan and Ley, editors, 1993, pp. 251–71.

—— and James S. Duncan, editors. 1989. *The Power of Place: Bringing Together Geographical and Sociological Imaginations*. Boston: Unwin Hyman.

——, Doreen Massey, and Allan Cochrane, with Julie Charlesworth, Gill Court, Nick Henry, and Phil Sarre. 1998. *Rethinking the Region*. London: Routledge.

Altekar, A. S. 1960. "The Yādavas of Seuṇadeśa." In Yazdani, editor, 1960, pp. 513–74.

Anderson, Benedict. 1991. *Imagined Communities: Reflections on the Origin and Spread of Nationalism*. Revised edition, London: Verso.

Appadurai, Arjun. 1986. "Theory in Anthropology: Center and Periphery." *Comparative Studies in Society and History* 28:356–61.

——. 1990. "Topographies of the Self: Praise and Emotion in Hindu India." In Lutz and Abu-Lughod, editors, 1990, pp. 92–112.

——. 1991. "Global Ethnoscapes: Notes and Queries for a Transnational Anthropology." In *Recapturing Anthropology: Working in the Present*. Santa Fe: School of American Research Press, pp. 191–210. (Reprinted in Appadurai 1996a, pp. 48–65.)

——. 1996a. *Modernity at Large: Cultural Dimensions of Globalization*. Minneapolis: University of Minnesota Press.

——. 1996b. "The Production of Locality." In Appadurai 1996a:178–99.

(Auṇḍhekar), Bālkṛṣṇa Dhuṇḍirāj Ṛṣī. 1991. *Śrī Āmardaka Mahātmya Kathāsār arthāt Jyotirliṅg Auṇḍhā Nāgnāth*. Auṇḍhā (Nāgnāth): Śrī Nāgnāth Saṃsthān Viśvasta Maṇḍaḷ.

Babb, Lawrence A. 1970. "The Food of the Gods in Chhattisgarh: Some Structural Features of Hindu Ritual." *Southwestern Journal of Anthropology* 26:287–304.

Bachelard, Gaston. 1964. *The Poetics of Space*, translated by M. Jolas. New York: Orion Press.

Baker, Alan R. H. and Gideon Biger. 1992. *Ideology and Landscape in Historical Perspective: Essays on the Meanings of Some Places in the Past.* Cambridge: Cambridge University Press.

Balibar, Etienne and Immanuel Wallerstein. 1991. *Race, Nation, Class: Ambiguous Identities*, Balibar translated by Chris Turner. London: Verso.

Ballāḷ, Tryambak. 1913. *Payoṣṇī Māhātmya.* Bombay: Śaṅkar Printing Press.

Bapat, Jayant Bhalchandra. 1998. "A Jatipura (Clan-history Myth) of the Gurav Temple Priests of Maharashtra." *Asian Studies Review* 22 (1998):63–78.

——. 2001. *The Gurav Temple Priests of Maharashtra: A Problem of Hierarchy and Status.* Ph.D. thesis, La Trobe University, Melbourne, Australia.

Barnouw, Victor. 1954. "The Changing Character of a Hindu Festival." *American Anthropologist* 56:74–86.

Baruah, Sanjib. 1997. "Politics of Subnationalism: Society versus State in Assam." In *State and Politics in India*, edited by Partha Chatterjee. Delhi: Oxford University Press.

——. 1999. *India Against Itself: Assam and the Politics of Nationality.* Philadelphia: University of Pennsylvania Press.

Basso, Keith. 1984. " 'Stalking with Stories': Names, Places, and Moral Narratives among the Western Apache." In *Text, Play, and Story: The Construction and Reconstruction of Self and Society*, edited by Edward Bruner. Washington, D. C.: 1983 Proceedings of the American Ethnological Society, pp. 19–55.

——. 1988. " 'Speaking with Names': Language and Landscape among the Western Apache. *Cultural Anthropology* 3:99–130.

——. 1996. "Wisdom Sits in Places: Notes on a Western Apache Landscape." In Feld and Basso, editors, 1996a, pp. 53–90.

Bayly, C. A. 1998. *Origins of Nationality in South Asia: Patriotism and Ethical Government in the Making of Modern India.* Delhi: Oxford University Press.

Beck, Brenda E. F. 1976. "The Symbolic Merger of Body, Space and Cosmos in Hindu Tamil Nadu." *Contributions to Indian Sociology*, n.s. 10:213–43.

Berdoulay, Vincent. 1989. "Place, Meaning, and Discourse in French Language Geography." In Agnew and Duncan, editors, 1989, pp. 124–39.

Bhagat, Sakhārām Bāḷājī. N.d. *Śrī Maḷāīdevī Māhātmya.* Ciñcolī, Pārner Taluka, Ahmadnagar District: Sakhārām Bāḷājī Bhagat.

Bhaṇḍārī, Śāntīlāl. 1992. "Tīrtharāj 'Tirumal Tirupatī'cā Tīrthapatī." *Prasād* 46:57–62.

Bhandarkar, D. R. 1937. "Daṇḍakāraṇya." In *Jhā Commemoration Volume. Essays on Oriental Subjects*, edited by S. K. Belvalkar et al. Poona: Oriental Book Agency, pp. 47–57.

Bhandarkar, R. G. 1895. *Early History of the Dekkan down to the Mahomedan Conquest.* Reprint, New Delhi: Asian Educational Services, 1981.

Bharati, Agehananda. 1970. "Pilgrimage Sites and Indian Civilization." In *Chapters in Indian Civilization.* Revised edition, Volume I, edited by Joseph W. Elder. Dubuque: Kendall/Hunt Publishing Company, 85–126.

Bhardwaj, Surinder Mohan. 1973. *Hindu Places of Pilgrimage in India: A Study in Cultural Geography*. Berkeley: University of California Press.

Bhavāḷkar, Nīḷakaṇṭh Baḷavant and Harī Nārāyaṇ Nene, editors. 1937. *Śrī Sarvajña Cakradharnirūpit Dṛṣṭānta-Pāṭh*. Nāgpūr: Harī Nārāyaṇ Nene.

Bhiḍe, Ga. Raṃ. and Pu. La. Deśpāṇḍe, editors. 1971. *Kolhāpūr Darśan: Śrīmān Madanmohan Lohiyā Abhinandan Granth*. Puṇe: International Publishing Service.

Bhujaṅg, Sadāśiv Bhāskar. N.d. *Sacitra Tryambakeśvar Darśan*. Tryambakeśvar: Svadeśī Stores.

Blu, Karen I. 1996. " 'Where Do You Stay At?': Home Place and Community among the Lumbee." In Feld and Basso, editors, 1996a, pp. 197–227.

Bolle, Kees W. 1969. "Speaking of a Place." In *Myths and Symbols: Studies in Honor of Mircea Eliade*, edited by Joseph M. Kitagawa and Charles H. Long. Chicago: The University of Chicago Press, pp. 127–39.

Bouillier, Véronique and Gilles Tarabout, editors. 2002. *Images du corps dans le monde hindou*. Paris: CNRS Editions.

Bourdieu, Pierre. 1971. "The Berber House or the World Reversed." In *Rules and Meanings*, edited by Mary Douglas. Harmondsworth: Penguin, pp. 98–110.

Buḷe, Śakuntalābāī Nārāyaṇrāv. N.d. *Śrīnarmadāmāhātmya*. Dādar: Narendra Book Depot.

Burāṇḍe, Sa. Śa. 1987. *Dakkancā Rājā Śrī Jotibā*. Kirloskarvāḍī: Kīrti Prasād Burāṇḍe.

Buttimer, Anne. 1984. "Musing on Helicon: Root Metaphors and Geography." In Richardson, editor, 1984, pp. 55–62.

Cahill, James. 1992. "Huang Shan Paintings as Pilgrimage Pictures." In *Pilgrims and Sacred Sites in China*, edited by Susan Naquin and Chün-fang Yü. Berkeley: University of California Press.

Caitanya, Māyānand. 1919. *Parikramāsahit Narmadāpañcāṅg*. Poona: Indira Press.

Cāndekar, A. Mo. 1984. "Māherpaṇāsāṭhī Mahilāṃcī 'Laḍhāī.'" *Sakāḷ* (Pune), August 29, p. 6.

Casey, Edward S. 1993. *Getting Back into Place: Toward a Renewed Understanding of the Place-World*. Bloomington: Indiana University Press.

——. 1996. "How to Get from Space to Place in a Fairly Short Stretch of Time: Phenomenological Prolegomena." In Feld and Basso, editors, 1996a, pp. 3–52.

——. 1997. *The Fate of Place: A Philosophical History*. Berkeley: University of California Press.

——. 2001. "Body, Self, and Landscape: A Geophilosophical Inquiry into the Place-World." In Adams, Hoelscher, and Till, editors, 2001, pp. 403–25.

Cauhan, D. V. 1971. "Maharashtra Dharma—Its Origin." In *Maratha History Seminar (May 28–31, 1970) Papers*, convened by A. G. Pawar. Kolhapur: Shivaji University, pp. 7–14.

Cavhāṇ, Vijay Śaṅkarrāv. 1999. *Bhātāṅgaḷīcā Mahādev Kāṭhī*. Bārśī: Media Offset Printers.

Cendavaṇkar, Sadānand. 1964a. *Āmcyā Dahā Devatā*. Girgāṃv (Mumbaī): Sāhitya-Ras Mālā Prakāśan.

——. 1964b. *Aṣṭavināyak*. Girgāṃv (Mumbaī): Sāhitya-Ras Mālā Prakāśan.

——. 1965. *Mahārāṣṭrātīl Mahāgaṇapati*. Mumbaī: Nirṇaysāgar Press Prakāśan.

Census of India 1961. 1969. *Census of India 1961*. Volume X *Maharashtra*. Part VII-B *Fairs and Festivals in Maharashtra*. Bombay: Maharashtra Census Office.

Census of India 1981. 1986. *District Census Handbook: Pune*. Bombay: The Director, Government Printing, Stationery and Publications, Maharashtra State.

Census of India 1991. 1995. *District Census Handbook: Pune*. Mumbai: The Director, Government Printing and Stationery, Maharashtra State.

Chatterjee, Partha. 1999. "On Religious and Linguistic Nationalisms: The Second Partition of Bengal." In *Nation and Religion: Perspectives on Europe and Asia*, edited by Peter van der Veer and Hartmut Lehmann. Princeton: Princeton University Press, pp. 112–28.

Chen Han-Seng. 1996. "Twenty-one Regions of the South Asian Subcontinent." In *Ecological and Agrarian Regions of South Asia circa 1930*, edited by Daniel Thorner. Karachi: Oxford University Press, pp. 55–141.

Chitgopekar, Nilima. 1998. *Encountering Śivaism: The Deity, the Milieu, the Entourage*. New Delhi: Munshiram Manoharlal.

Ciñcolkar, Sunīl. 1983. "Akrā Mārutīñce Ajñāt Mahattva." In Harṣe 1983, pp. 6–8.

Citrāv, Siddheśvarśāstrī. 1932. *Bhāratvarṣīya Prācīn Caritrakoś*. Puṇe: Bhāratvarṣīya Caritrakoś Maṇḍaḷ.

Clothey, Fred W. 1972. "Pilgrimage Centers in the Tamil Cultus of Murukan." *Journal of the American Academy of Religion* 40:79–95.

——. 1978. *The Many Faces of Murukaṉ: The History and Meaning of a South Indian God*. The Hague: Mouton Publishers.

Cohn, Bernard S. 1967. "Regions Subjective and Objective: Their Relation to the Study of Modern Indian History and Society." In Crane, editor, 1967, pp. 5–37.

—— and McKim Marriott. 1958. "Networks and Centers in the Integration of Indian Civilization." *Journal of Social Research* 1:1–9.

Cosgrove, Denis and Stephen Daniels. 1987. *The Iconography of Landscape: Essays on Symbolic Representation, Design and Use of Past Environments*. Cambridge: Cambridge University Press.

—— and Mona Domosh. 1993. "Author and Authority: Writing the New Cultural Geography." In Duncan and Ley, editors, 1993, pp. 25–38.

Courtright, Paul. 1985. *Gaṇeśa: Lord of Obstacles, Lord of Beginnings*. New York: Oxford University Press.

——. 1988. "The Ganesh Festival in Maharashtra: Some Observations." In Zelliot and Berntsen, editors, 1988, pp. 76–94.

Crain, Mary M. 1997. "The Remaking of an Andalusian Pilgrimage Tradition: Debates Regarding Visual (Re)presentation and the Meanings of 'Locality' in a Global Era." In Gupta and Ferguson, editors, 1997a, pp. 291–311.

Crane, Robert I., editor. 1967. *Regions and Regionalism in South Asian Studies: An Exploratory Study*. Durham, NC: Duke University Program in Comparative Studies on Southern Asia.

Damrel, David. Forthcoming. "Muslim Spaces in South Asia." In *Sacred Space in Asia*, edited by Ron Lukens-Bull. Tempe: Program for Southeast Asian Studies, Arizona State University.

Dāṇḍekar, Gopāḷ Nīlkaṇṭh. 1949. *Narmadecyā Taṭākīṃ*. Puṇeṃ: Maṅgal Sāhitya Prakāśan.

———. 1957. *Kuṇā Ekācī Brahmaṇgāthā*. 4th printing, Mumbāī: Mauj Prakāśan, 1982.

Daniel, E. Valentine. 1984. *Fluid Signs: Being a Person the Tamil Way*. Berkeley: University of California Press.

Das, R. K. 1964. *Temples of Tamilnad*. Bombay: Bharatiya Vidya Bhavan.

Das, Veena. 1982. *Structure and Cognition: Aspects of Hindu Caste and Ritual*. 2nd edition, Delhi: Oxford University Press.

Dāsagaṇū. 1921 (Śake 1843). *Śrī Gautamī Māhātmya*. Nāndeḍ: Dāmodhar Vāman Aṭhavale.

———. 1952. *Śrī Śambhūmahādev athavā Śrī Māṅgeś Māhātmya Sārāmṛt*. Mumbaī: Mādhavrāv Gāṅgalā.

Dāte, Yaśvant Rāmkṛṣṇa and Cintāmaṇ Gaṇeś Karve, editors. 1942. *Mahārāṣṭra Vākasampradāy Koś*. 2 volumes. Puṇeṃ: Mahārāṣṭra Kośmaṇḍaḷ.

——— Cintāmaṇ Gaṇeś Karve, Ābā Cāndorkar, and Cintāmaṇ Śaṅkar Dātār, editors. 1932–1938. *Mahārāṣṭra Śabdakoś*. 7 volumes plus supplement (1950). Puṇe: Maharāṣṭra Kośmaṇḍaḷ.

Dattakiṅkar. 1886. *Śrī Bhīmā Māhātmya*. Bombay: Jagadīśvar Press.

de Bary, William Theodore, editor. 1958. *Sources of Indian Tradition*, Volume 2. New York: Columbia University Press.

Deegan, Chris. 1995. "The Narmada in Myth and History." In *Toward Sustainable Development: Struggling Over India's Narmada River*, edited by William F. Fisher. Armonk, NY: M. E. Sharpe, pp. 47–68.

Deleury, G. A. 1960. *The Cult of Viṭhobā*. Poona: Deccan College Postgraduate and Research Institute.

Desāī, Pa. Sa. 1969. *Sacitra Karvīrnivāsinī Śrīmahālakṣmī (Paurāṇik va Aitihāsik Māhitīsaha, Nityanaimittik Upāsanā)*. 3rd (revised) printing, Kolhāpūr: Vasantrāv Śaṅkarrāv Mevekarī (originally 1963).

Desāī, Sītārām Gaṇeś. 1975. *Devī-Darśan: Goṣṭīrūp Saptaśatī va Pāṭvidhi*. 2nd printing, Puṇe: Jośī Brothers Booksellers and Publishers.

Deshpande, Madhav M. 1983. "Nation and Region: A Socio-Linguistic Perspective on Maharashtra." In *National Unity: The South Asian Experience*, edited by Milton Israel. New Delhi: Promilla, pp. 111–34.

Deśpāṇḍe, Yaśvant Khuśāl. 1929. "Mahānubhāvīya Vāṅmayānt Ālele Yādavkālīn Aitihāsik Ullekh." *Bhārat Itihās Saṃśodhak Maṇḍaḷ Quarterly* 10:78–87.

———. 1932. "Mahānubhāvāṃce Caritra-Granth." *Bhārat Itihās Saṃśodhak Maṇḍaḷ Quarterly* 13:45–57.

———, editor. 1929. *Śrī Ṛddhipūrvarṇan: Paṇḍit Nārāyaṇvyās Bahīḷiye Kṛt*. Yavatmāḷ: Śāradāśram.

———. 1960. *Smṛtisthaḷ*. Puṇe: Venus Prakāśan, 2nd edition (originally 1939).

———. 1961. *Paṃ. Bhīṣmācārya Saṅkalit Niruktaśeṣ*. Nāgpūr: Vidarbha Saṃśodhan Maṇḍaḷ.

Dev, Vighnahari Bhālcandra. 1995. *Sadguru Śrīmorayā Gosāvī*. Puṇe: Anamol Prakāsan.

Dharmādhikārī, Vā. Rā. 1986. *Śrī Karvīr Nivāsinī Mahālakṣmī, Kolhāpūr*. Kolhāpūr: Vasantrāv Śaṅkarrāv Mevekarī, 9th printing. (Mostly a word-for-word copy of Desāī 1969.)

Dhavalikar, M. K. 1960. "The Origin of the Saptamātṛkās." *Bulletin of the Deccan College Research Institute* 21:19–26.

Ḍhere, Rāmcandra Cintāmaṇ. 1977. *Cakrapāṇī [Ādya Marāṭhī Sāṃskṛtik Pārśvabhūmī]*. Puṇe: Viśvakarmā Sāhityālay.

——. 1984. *Śrīviṭṭhal: Ek Mahāsamanvay*. Puṇe: Śrīvidyā Prakāśan.

——. 1988. "The Gondhali: Singers for the Devi," translated by Anne Feldhaus. In Zelliot and Berntsen, editors, 1988 pp. 174–89.

——. 1992a. "Yā re vanduṃ Śikharācaḷ! Santsāhityātīl ullekhāṃtūn ghaḍavilelī Śikharśiṅgṇāpūrcyā Śambhumahādevācī akṣaryātrā." *Santkṛpā* 17:1 (March 1992):11–22.

——. 1992b. "Baḷī bhāvārthī ananya." *Santkṛpā* 17:2 (April 1992):10–21.

——. 1992c. "Mahānubhāvīya vāṅmayātīl Baḷīpa-kathā." *Santkṛpā* 17:3 (May 1992):12–23.

——. 1992d. "Kṛṣṇadās Dāmā yācī samṛddha Baḷīpa-kathā." *Santkṛpā* 17:4 (June 1992):14–23.

——. 1992e. "Śahājīrājāñcyā mūḷ puruṣācī kathā." *Santkṛpā* 17:5 (July 1992):14–27.

——. 1992f. "Baḷīpa: Bhosale kuḷācā mūḷ puruṣ." *Santkṛpā* 17:6 (August 1992):17–27.

——. 1993. "Śikhar Śiṅgṇāpūr: pāc ṭipaṇe." *Santkṛpā* 17:10 (January 1993):17–21.

——. 2001. *Śikhar Śiṅgṇāpūrcā Śrīśaṃbhumahādev: Śivachatrapatīñcā kuḷasvāmī Śrīśaṃbhumahādev āṇi Śikharkṣetrāt tyācī pratiṣṭhāpanā karṇāre Bhosle gharāṇe yāñcyā dakṣiṇ-saṃbandhācī śodhkathā*. Puṇe: Śrīvidyā Prakāśan.

Diddee, Jayamala, S. R. Jog, and V. S. Datye. 1985. "Pilgrimage Circulation at Bhimashankar on Mahashivratri Day." *Geographical Review of India* 47, 3:30–33.

Dowson, John. 1957. *A Classical Dictionary of Hindu Mythology and Religion, Geography, History, and Literature*. 9th edition, London: Routledge & Kegan Paul Ltd.

Duara, Prasenjit. 1995. *Rescuing History from the Nation: Questioning Narratives of Modern China*. Chicago: University of Chicago Press.

Dumont, Louis. 1957. *Une Sous-Caste de l'Inde du Sud*. Paris: Mouton and Company.

Duncan, James and David Ley, editors. 1993. *Place/Culture/Representation*. London: Routledge.

Durkheim, Emil and M. Mauss. 1963. *Primitive Classification*. Chicago: University of Chicago Press.

Eade, John, and Michael J. Sallnow, editors. 1991. *Contesting the Sacred: The Anthropology of Christian Pilgrimage*. London: Routledge.

Eck, Diana L. 1982. *Banaras: City of Light*. New York: Alfred A. Knopf.

——. 1996. "Gaṅgā: The Goddess Ganges in Hindu Sacred Geography." In *Devī: Goddesses of India*, edited by John S. Hawley and Donna M. Wulff. Berkeley: University of California Press.

—— and Françoise Mallison, editors. 1991. *Devotion Divine: Bhakti Traditions from the Regions of India*. Groningen: Egbert Forsten/Paris: École Française d'Extrême-Orient.

Edney, Matthew H. 1997. *Mapping an Empire: The Geographical Construction of British India, 1765–1843*. Chicago: The University of Chicago Press.

Eliade, Mircea. 1969. *Yoga: Immortality and Freedom*. 2nd edition, Princeton: Princeton University Press (originally 1958).

Elmore, W. T. 1913. *Dravidian Gods in Modern Hinduism*. Reprint, New Delhi: Asian Educational Services, 1984.

Embree, Ainslie T. 1977. "Frontiers into Boundaries: From the Traditional to the Modern State." In Fox, editor, 1977, pp. 255–79.

Ensink, J. 1979. "Hindu Pilgrimage and Vedic Sacrifice." In *Ludwik Sternbach Felicitation Volume, Part One*. Lucknow: Akhila Bharatiya Sanskrit Parishad, pp. 105–17.

Enthoven, R. E. 1924. *The Folklore of Bombay*. Oxford: Clarendon Press.

Entrikin, J. Nicholas. 1981. "Royce's 'Provincialism': A Metaphysician's Social Geography." In *Geography, Ideology and Social Concern*, edited by D. R. Stoddart. Totowa, NJ: Barnes and Noble Books.

——. 1989. "Place, Region, and Modernity." In Agnew and Duncan, editors, 1989, pp. 30–43.

——. 1991. *The Betweenness of Place: Towards a Geography of Modernity*. Baltimore: The Johns Hopkins University Press.

Erndl, Kathleen. 1993. *Victory to the Mother*. New York: Oxford University Press.

Ernst, Carl. 1995. "India as a Sacred Islamic Land." In *Religions of India in Practice*, edited by Donald S. Lopez, Jr. Princeton: Princeton University Press, pp. 556–63.

Eschmann, Anncharlott. 1978. "Prototypes of the Navakalevara Ritual and Their Relation to the Jagannātha Cult." In Eschmann, Kulke, and Tripathi, editors, 1978, pp. 265–83.

——, Herman Kulke, and Gaya Charan Tripathi, editors. 1978. *The Cult of Jagannath and the Regional Tradition of Orissa*. New Delhi: Manohar.

Feld, Steven and Keith H. Basso, editors. 1996a. *Senses of Place*. Santa Fe: School of American Research Press.

——. 1996b. "Introduction." In Feld and Basso, editors, 1996a, pp. 3–11.

Feldhaus, Anne. 1980. "The *devatācakra* of the Mahānubhāvas." *Bulletin of the School of Oriental and African Studies, University of London* 43:101–9.

——. 1982. "God and Madman: Guṇḍam Rāüḷ." *Bulletin of the School of Oriental and African Studies, University of London* 45:74–83.

——. 1983a. *The Religious System of the Mahānubhāva Sect: The Mahānubhāva Sūtrapāṭha*. New Delhi: Manohar.

——. 1983b. "Kṛṣṇa and the Kṛṣṇas: Kṛṣṇa in the Mahānubhāva Pantheon." In *Bhakti in Current Research, 1979–1982*, edited by Monika Thiel-Horstmann. Collectanea Instituti Anthropos, Volume 30. Berlin: Dietrich Reimer Verlag, pp. 133–42.

——. 1986. "Maharashtra as a Holy Land: A Sectarian Tradition." *Bulletin of the School of Oriental and African Studies, University of London* 49:532–48.

——. 1987. "The Religious Significance of Ṛddhipur." In Israel and Wagle, editors, 1987, pp. 68–91.

Feldhaus, Anne. 1988. "The Orthodoxy of the Mahanubhavs." In Zelliot and Berntsen, editors, 1988, pp. 264–79.

——. 1991. "Paiṭhaṇ and the Nāgas." In Eck and Mallison, editors, 1991, pp. 91–111.

——. 1994. "Separation, Connection and Obedience among the Early Mahānubhāvs." In *Studies in South Asian Devotional Literature*, edited by Alan W. Entwistle and Françoise Mallison. New Delhi: Manohar/Paris: École Française d'Extrême-Orient, pp. 154–68.

——. 1995. *Water and Womanhood: Religious Meanings of Rivers in Maharashtra.* New York: Oxford University Press.

——. 1998. "Goddesses and the Domestic Realm in Maharashtra." In *House and Home in Maharashtra*, edited by I. Glushkova and A. Feldhaus. Delhi: Oxford University Press, pp. 73–81.

——. 2000. "On My Way of Living in India." In *Ethnography and Personhood: Notes from the Field*, edited by Michael W. Meister. Jaipur: Rawat Publications, 2000, pp. 47–63.

——. Forthcoming. "*Sthānapothī*: The Mahānubhāva 'Book of Places.'" In the Proceedings of the Third International Conference on Devotional Literature in New Indo-Aryan Languages (Leiden, December 1985), edited by G. Schokker.

——, translator. 1984. *The Deeds of God in Ṛddhipur.* New York: Oxford University Press.

—— and S. G. Tulpule, translators. 1992. *In the Absence of God: The Mahānubhāvs' Early Years.* Honolulu: University of Hawaii Press.

Flueckiger, Joyce Burkhalter. 1996. *Gender and Genre in the Folklore of Middle India.* Ithaca: Cornell University Press.

Foard, James H. 1995. "Text, Place, and Memory in Hiroshima." *Senri Ethnological Studies* 38:65–76.

Foucault, Michel. 1984. "Space, Knowledge, and Power." In *The Foucault Reader*, edited by Paul Rabinow. New York: Pantheon (interview originally 1982), pp. 239–56.

Fox, Richard G., editor. 1977. *Realm and Region in Traditional India.* Durham, NC: Duke University Program in Comparative Studies on Southern Asia.

Freed, Ruth S. and Stanley A. Freed. 1964. "Calendars, Ceremonies and Festivals in a North Indian Village: Necessary Calendric Information for Fieldwork." *Southwestern Journal of Anthropology* 20:67–90.

Freeman, Edward A. 1879. "Race and Language." In *Historical Essays*, 3rd series. London: Macmillan and Company.

Fuller, Jonathan. 1992. *The Camphor Flame: Popular Hinduism and Society in India.* Princeton: Princeton University Press.

Gāḍgīḷ, Amarendra. 1968. *Śrīgaṇeśkoś.* Mumbaī: Vorā and Company Publishers.

Gaige, Frederick H. 1975. *Regionalism and National Unity in Nepal.* Berkeley: University of California Press.

Gāṅgaḷ, Manohar. 2000. *Samarthāṃcī Smṛtisthāne.* Śrīvardhan (Raygad District): Manohar Gāṅgaḷ.

Gautamī Māhātmya. 1906. Printed separately at the end of *Śrī Brahmapurāṇa.* Bombay: Veṅkaṭeśvara Press; reprint, Delhi: Nag Publishers, 1985.

Gazetteer of the Bombay Presidency. Bombay: Government Central Press.
1880. Vol. XII. *Khândesh*.
1883. Vol. XVI. *Nāsik*.
1884. Vol. XVII. *Ahmadnagar*.
1884. Vol. XXI. *Belgaum*.
1884. Vol. XXIII. *Bijāpur*.
1885. Vol. XVIII, Part III. *Poona*.
1885. Volume XIX. *Sātāra*.

Geertz, Clifford. 1973. "The Integrative Revolution: Primordial Sentiments and Civil Politics in the New States." In *The Interpretation of Cultures*. New York: Basic Books, pp. 255–310.

——. 1983. "Centers, Kings, and Charisma: Reflections on the Symbolics of Power." In *Local Knowledge: Further Essays in Interpretive Anthropology*. New York: Basic Books, pp. 121–46.

Gellner, Ernest. 1983. *Nations and Nationalism*. Ithaca: Cornell University Press.

——. 1994. *Encounters with Nationalism*. Oxford: Blackwell.

——. 1997. *Nationalism*. London: Weidenfeld & Nicolson.

Ghāṇekar, Pra. Ke. 1993. "Cār Dhām Yātretīl Badrī va Kedār." *Prasād* 47:33–45.

Ghoḍke, Nivṛttināth Eknāth. 1989. *Śrī Saptaśṛṅg Devīce Avatār Māhātmya*. 4th printing, Kāregāv (Nevāse Taluka, Ahmadnagar District): Kailāsnāth Nivṛttināth Ghoḍke.

Ghurye, G. S. 1962. *Gods and Men*. Bombay: Popular Book Depot.

Goḍbole, Raghunāth Bhāskar. 1928. *Bhārat Varṣīya Prācīn Aitihāsik Koś*. Puṇe: Citraśāḷā Press.

Gokhale, Puruṣottam Pāṇḍuraṅg. 1973. *Śrīrām-Samartha*. Cāphaḷ: Śrīrām Devasthān Trust.

Gokhale-Turner, Jayashree. 1980. "Region and Regionalism in the Study of Indian Politics: The Case of Maharashtra." In *Images of Maharashtra: A Regional Profile of India*, edited by N. K. Wagle. London: Curzon Press.

Gold, Ann Grodzins. *Fruitful Journeys: The Ways of Rajasthani Pilgrims*. Berkeley: University of California Press, 1988.

Gole, Susan. 1989. *Indian Maps and Plans from Earliest Times to the Advent of European Surveys*. New Delhi: Manohar.

Gordon, Stewart. 1993. *The Marathas 1600–1818*. The New Cambridge History of India, II.4. Cambridge: Cambridge University Press/New Delhi: Foundation Books.

Gould, J. and R. White. 1986. *Mental Maps*. 2nd edition, Harmondsworth: Penguin (originally 1974); reprint London: Routledge, 1992.

Govaṇḍe, Śrīkānt. 1981. *Karvīr-Nivāsinī Śrīmahālakṣmī Ambābāī (Kṣetra Māhitī va Upāsanā)*. Pune: Anamol Prakāśan.

——. 1995. *Śrī Aṣṭavināyak Darśan Yātrā*. Puṇe: Anamol Prakāśan (originally 1980).

Guha, Sumit. 1999. *Environment and Ethnicity in India 1200–1991*. Cambridge: Cambridge University Press.

Gupta, Akhil and James Ferguson, editors. 1997a. *Culture, Power, Place: Explorations in Critical Anthropology*. Durham: Duke University Press.

Gupta, Akhil and James Ferguson, editors. 1997b. "Culture, Power, Place: Ethnography at the End of an Era." In Gupta and Ferguson, editors, 1997a, pp. 1–29.

Gupta, S.L. 1967a. "The Kumbh Mela, an Interpretation." *The India Cultures Quarterly* 24:44–49.

——. 1967b. "The Number Twelve and the Four Kumbh Mela Sites." *The India Cultures Quarterly* 24:50–57.

Gupte, Yaśvant Rājārām, editor. 1927. *Karhāḍ*. Revised edition, Puṇe: Bhārat Itihās Saṃśodhak Maṇḍal, 1929.

Gutschow, Niels. 1977. "Ritual as Mediator of Space: Kāṭmāṇḍu." *Ekistiks* 265 (December):309–12.

Haberman, David. 1994. *Journey through the Twelve Forests: An Encounter with Krishna*. New York: Oxford University Press.

Haṇamante, Śrī. Śā. 1964. *Saṅket-Koś*. Solāpūr: Kamalābāī Bendre.

Harley, J. B. 1987. "Maps, Knowledge, and Power." In Cosgrove and Daniels, editors, 1987, pp. 277–312.

—— and David Woodward, editors. 1992. *Cartography in the Traditional Islamic and South Asian Societies* (The History of Cartography, Volume 2, Book 1). Chicago: The University of Chicago Press.

Harrison, Selig S. 1960. *India: The Most Dangerous Decades*. Princeton: Princeton University Press.

Harṣe, Pu. Vi. 1983. *Samartha Sthāpit Akrā Mārutī*. Reprint, Mumbaī: Jyotī Dhanañjay Ḍhavaḷe and Keśav Bhikājī Ḍhavaḷe, 1995.

Haynes, Douglas. 1999. "Market Formation in Khandesh, c 1820–1930." *Indian Economic and Social History Review* 36:275–302.

Heaney, Seamus. 1980. "The Sense of Place." In *Preoccupations: Selected Prose, 1968–1978*. New York: Farrar Strauss Giroux, pp. 131–49.

Hirsch, Eric and Michael O'Hanlon, editors. 1995. *The Anthropology of Landscape: Perspectives on Place and Space*. Oxford: Clarendon Press.

Hobsbawm, E. J. 1990. *Nations and Nationalism Since 1780: Programme, Myth, Reality*. 2nd edition, Cambridge: Cambridge University Press.

—— and Terence Ranger, editors. 1983. *The Invention of Tradition*. Cambridge: Cambridge University Press.

Humes, Cynthia Ann. 1993. "The Goddess of the Vindhyas in Banaras." In *Living Banaras: Hindu Religion in Cultural Context*, edited by Bradley R. Hertel and Cynthia Ann Humes. Albany: State University of New York Press, pp. 181–204.

Imperial Gazetteer of India. 1909. *Provincial Series. Bombay Presidency*. Calcutta: Superintendent of Government Printing.

Irschick, Eugene F. 1994. *Dialogue and History: Constructing South India, 1795–1895*. Berkeley: University of California Press.

Israel, Milton and N. K. Wagle, editors. 1987. *Religion and Society in Maharashtra*. Toronto: University of Toronto Centre for South Asian Studies.

Jackson, John Brinckerhoff. 1994. *A Sense of Place, a Sense of Time*. New Haven: Yale University Press.

Jackson, Peter. 1989. *Maps of Meaning: An Introduction to Cultural Geography*. London: Unwin Hyman.

Jahāgirdār. N.d. *Māhūrgaḍ Darśan: Śrīkṣetra Māhūrgaḍācī Māhitī*. Māhūr: Govindrāv Arādhye.

Jansen, Roland. 1995. *Die Bhavani von Tuljapur: religionsgeschichtliche Studie des Kultes einer Göttin der indischen Volksreligion*. Stuttgart: Franz Steiner Verlag.

Jogaḷekar, Dā. Vi. 1990. *Narmadā Parikammā (Pradakṣiṇā)*. Mumbāī: Dhananjay Bāḷkṛṣṇa Ḍhavaḷe and Keśav Bhikājī Ḍhavaḷe.

Jogaḷekar, Sadāśiv Ātmārām. 1952. *(Mahārāṣṭra-Stotra) Sahyādri*. Puṇeṃ: Prasād Prakāśan.

Jośī, Arvind Sadāśivrāv. 1994. *Trailokya Sāmrājya Cakravartī Śrī Jñāneśvar Mahārājāṃcā Pālkhī Sohaḷā*. Puṇe: Indrāyaṇī Sāhitya Prakāsan.

Jośī, Kāśināth Anant, editor. 1979. *Śrī Kedār Vijay: Sacitra-Kathāsār*. Karāḍ: Prabhākar Granth Bhāṇḍār.

Jośī, Mahādevśāstrī. 1950. "Kṛṣṇātīrīṃ Narahari." *Prasād* 3, 1 (June).

——. 1951. *Tīrtharūp Mahārāṣṭra*. 2 volumes. Puṇe: Jñānrāj Prakāśan.

——, editor. 1962–1979. *Bhāratīya Saṃskṛtikoś*. 10 volumes. Puṇe: Bhāratīya Saṃskṛtikoś Maṇḍaḷ.

Jośī, Pralhād Narhar. 1978. *Māhurgaḍvāsinī Śrīreṇukā*. Pune: Continental Prakāśan.

——, editor. 1969. *Sārtha Śrījñāndev Abhaṅga-Gāthā*. Puṇe: Suvicār Prakāśan Maṇḍaḷ.

Jośī, Raṃ. Ma. (Nirmaḷgurujī). 1985. *Bhagavān Śaṅkarācī Bārā Jyotirliṅg*. Puṇe: Ādarś Vidyārthī Prakāśan.

Juergensmeyer, Mark. 1994. *Religious Nationalism Confronts the Secular State*. Delhi: Oxford University Press.

Kāgalkar, Mu. Nā. 1969. *Śrī Narmadā Māhātmya (Dhārmik va Bhaugolik)*. Nānded.

Kakati, Bani Kanta. 1948. *The Mother Goddess Kāmākhyā: Or Studies in the Fusion of Aryan and Primitive Beliefs of Assam*. Gauhati: Lawyer's Book Stall.

Kāḷe, Kalyāṇ. 1983. "Gaṅgaṃkaḍaṃ an Rākisākaḍaṃ." *Bhāṣā āṇi Jīvan* 1, 1:11.

Kāḷegāṃvkar, Lakṣmaṇrāv Śā. 1963. *Manohar Ambānagarī*. Ambājogāī: La. Śā. Kāḷegāṃvkar.

——. 1987. *Śrī Yogeśvarī Mahātmya Darśan*. Ambājogāī: Ratnākar Prakāśan.

Kālgāvkar, Āṇṇābuvā. 1973. *Akrā Mārutī*. Cāphaḷ: Śrīrām Devasthān Trust.

Kandhārkar, Dattātreya Anant. 1909. "Śrīkṣetra Māhūr," *Lokmitra* 18:188–94.

Kane, Pandurang Vaman. 1973. *History of Dharmaśāstra (Ancient and Mediaeval Religious and Civil Law)*, Volume 4. 2nd edition, Poona: Bhandarkar Oriental Research Institute.

Kāṇṇav, Ravindrakumār Rāmbhāū. 1987 (Śake 1909). *Māhūrgaḍ: Śrīkṣetra Māhūrcī Māhitī*. Māhūr: author.

Kapadia, B. H. 1962. "The Four-fold Division of the Heavenly River in the Purāṇas." *Purāṇa* 4:146–53.

Kapferer, Bruce. 1988. *Legends of People, Myths of State: Violence, Intolerance, and Political Culture in Sri Lanka and Australia*. Washington: Smithsonian Institution Press.

Karambelkar, V. W. 1955. "Matsyendranātha and his Yoginī Cult." *Indian Historical Quarterly* 31:362–74.

Karmarkar, A. P. 1938. "Boundaries of Ancient Mahārāṣṭra and Karṇāṭaka." *Indian Historical Quarterly* 14:779–86.

Karna, M. N. 2000. "Language, Region and National Identity." In *Nation and National Identity in South Asia*, edited by S. L. Sharma and T. K. Oommen. New Delhi: Orient Longman, pp. 75–96.

Karve, Irāvatī. 1949. "Vāṭcāl." In *Paripūrti*. 2nd edition, revised and expanded, Puṇe: Deśmukh āṇi Company, pp. 120–43.

——. 1962. "On the Road: A Maharashtrian Pilgrimage." *Journal of Asian Studies* 22:13–29 (translation of Karve 1949).

——. 1968. *Maharashtra—Land and Its People*. Maharashtra State Gazetteer, General Series. Bombay: Directorate of Government Printing, Stationery and Publications, Maharashtra State.

Kavaḍī, Nareś. 1960. *Bharlī Candrabhāgā: Solāpūr Jilhyāṃtīl Loksāhitya*. Solāpūr: Mahārāṣṭra Sāhitya Pariṣad, Śākhā Solāpūr.

Kaviraj, Sudipta. 1992a. "The Imaginary Institution of India." In *Subaltern Studies VII. Writings on South Asian History and Society*, edited by Partha Chatterjee and Gyanendra Pandey. Delhi: Oxford University Press, pp. 1–39.

——. 1992b. "Writing, Speaking, Being: Language and the Historical Formation of Identities in India." In *Nationalstaat und Sprachkonflikte in Süd- und Südostasien*, edited by Dagmar Hellmann-Rajanayagam and Dietmar Rothermund. Stuttgart: Franz Steiner Verlag, pp. 25–65.

Keith, Michael and Steven Pile, editors. 1993. *Place and the Politics of Identity*. London: Routledge.

Khare, Ga. Ha. 1966. "Śikhar-Śiṅgṇāpūr va Śivachatrapatīñce Pūrvaj." *Bhārat Itihās Saṃśodhak Maṇḍaḷ Traimāsik* 44:85–88.

Kidd, Colin. 1999. *British Identities Before Nationalism: Ethnicity and Nationhood in the Atlantic World, 1600–1800*. Cambridge: Cambridge University Press.

Kiernan, Victor. 1991. "Languages and Conquerors." In *Language, Self, and Society: A Social History of Language*, edited by Peter Burke and Roy Porter. Cambridge: Polity Press, pp. 191–210.

Kodumaguḷḷa, Parāṅkuśācārya. 1979. *Śrī Vāsar Jñān Sarasvatī Māhātmya*, translated by Gauripeddidurgā Malleśvar Śarmā. Second printing, Vāsar (Ādilābād, Āndhra Prades): Devāday Dharmādāyśākhā, Vāsar Kṣetra, 1983.

Kolte, Vi. Bhi. 1962. *Mahānubhāv Saṃśodhan: 1*. Malkāpūr: Aruṇ Prakāśan.

——. 1973. *Mahānubhāvāñcā Ācārdharma*. Reprint, Malkāpūr: Aruṇ Prakāśan (originally 1948).

——. 1975. *Mahānubhāv Tattvajñān*. 4th edition, Malkāpūr: Aruṇ Prakāśan (originally 1945).

——, editor. 1972. *Mhāiṃbhaṭ-Saṅkalit Śrī Govindprabhu Caritra*. Malkāpūr: Aruṇ Prakāśan.

——, editor. 1976. *Sthān Pothī*. 2nd edition, Malkāpūr: Aruṇ Prakāśan (originally undated).

——, editor. 1982a. *Ācārband*. Malkāpūr: Aruṇ Prakāśan.

——, editor. 1982b. *Mhāīmbhaṭ Saṅkalit Śrīcakradhar Līḷā Caritra*. 2nd edition, Mumbaī: Mahārāṣṭra Rājya Sāhitya-Saṃskṛti Maṇḍaḷ (originally 1978).

Kosambi, Damodar Dharmanand. 1962. *Myth and Reality*. Bombay: Popular Prakashan.
Kosambi, Meera. 1988. "Indigenous and Colonial Urban Development in Western Maharashtra." In *City, Countryside and Society in Maharashtra*, edited by D. W. Attwood, M. Israel and N. K. Wagle. Toronto: University of Toronto Centre for South Asian Studies, pp. 1–34.
Kramrisch, Stella. 1976. *The Hindu Temple*. Reprint, Delhi: Motilal Banarsidass (originally 1946).
Kṛṣṇā Māhātmya. 1885 (Śake 1807). Edited by V. S. S. Gaṅgādharaśāstrī Abhyaṅkara. Wāī: Virāja Vaibhava Press.
Kṛṣṇamuni Kavi Ḍimbh. 1967. *Ṛddhipur Māhātmya*, edited by Yu. Ma. Paṭhāṇ. Solāpūr: Prācīn Sāhitya Prakāśan.
Kulkarni, A. R. 1996. *The Marathas (1600–1848)*. New Delhi: Books and Books.
Kulkarṇī, Cidambar Śrīpādrāv. 1988. *Śrī Kṣetra Gāṇagāpūr Mahātmya*. 21st edition, Beḷgāṃv: Sarasvatī Pustak Bhāṇḍār.
Kulkarṇī, Dattātray Mādhavrāv. 1920. *Mahārāṣṭrācī Kulsvāminī Śrītuljābhavānī*. Reprint, Bārśī (Solapur District): Acal Niśikānt Govardhan and Bakuḷ Keśav Jośī, 1990.
Kulkarṇī, Sītārām. 1971. *Āmcī Tīrthakṣetre, Āmcī Daivate*. Puṇe: Jagannāthrāv Nīlkaṇṭhrāv Kulkarṇī.
——. 1972. *Bhāratātīl Ekvīs Tīrthakṣetre*. Puṇe: Avināś Prakāśan.
Kulke, Hermann. 1978. "Royal Temple Policy and the Structure of Medieval Hindu Kingdoms." In Eschmann, Kulke, and Tripathi, editors, 1978, pp. 126–37.
——. 1978–1979. "Jagannatha—The State Deity of Orissa." In *Reflections of Indian Art and Culture*. Department of Museums, Gujarat State, *Museum Bulletin* 28:69–89.
Lāde, Rāmdās Dagaḍū. 1983. *Śrī Kṣetra Jotībā*. Kolhāpūr: Rāmdās Dagaḍū Lāde.
Laine, James W. 2003. *Shivaji: Hindu King in Islamic India*. New York: Oxford University Press.
Lele, Gaṇeś Sadāśivśāstrī. 1885. *Tīrthayātrā Prabandh*. Reprint/2nd edition, Puṇe: Deśmukh āṇi Company, 1964.
Lele, Jayant. 1982. "Chavan and the Political Integration of Maharashtra." In *Contemporary India: Socio-Economic and Political Processes* (Professor V. M. Sirsikar Felicitation Volume), edited by N. R. Inamdar et al. Poona: Continental Prakashan, pp. 29–54.
Leonard, Karen. 1997. "Finding One's Own Place: Asian Landscapes Re-visioned in Rural California." In Gupta and Ferguson, editors, 1997a, pp. 118–36.
Levy, Robert I. with Kedar Rāj Rājopādhyāya. 1990. *Mesocosm: Hinduism and the Organization of a Traditional Newar City in Nepal*. Berkeley: University of California Press.
Lewis, Martin W. and Kären E. Wigen. 1997. *The Myth of Continents: A Critique of Metageography*. Berkeley: University of California Press.
Lodrick, Deryck O. 1994. "Rajasthan as a Region: Myth or Reality?" In Schomer, Erdman, Lodrick, and Rudolph, editors, 1994, Volume I, pp. 1–44.
Lokāpur, Raṅganāth Śāmācārya. 1994. *Jñāneśvarkālīn Marāṭhī Bhāṣevar Kannaḍcā Prabhāv*. Beḷgāṃv: Niśānt Prakāśan.

Lutz, Catherine A. and Lila Abu-Lughod, editors. 1990. *Language and the Politics of Emotion*. Cambridge: Cambridge University Press.

Madan, P. L. 1997. *Indian Cartography: A Historical Perspective*. New Delhi: Manohar.

Mahābaḷeśvarkar, V. S. N.d. *Śrī Saptaśṛṅgī Darśan*, 5th edition, Thane: Sadhana D. Joshi.

Mahājan, Śāntārām Gajānan. 1994. *Himālayātīl Cārī Dhām Yātrā*. Puṇe: Utkarṣa Prakāśan.

Maheśvarpaṇḍit. N.d. *Ṛddhipur Māhātmya*. Photographed copy of an unpublished ms. in the Marathi Department Library, Dr. Babasaheb Ambedkar Marathwada University, Aurangabad.

Mahīpatī. 1935. *Kavi-Mahīpatīkṛt Bhaktalīlāmṛt (Ovībaddha Prākṛt Granth)*. Mumbaī: Dāmodar Sāṃvaḷārām āṇi Maṇḍaḷī.

Malik, Aditya. 1993. *Das Puṣkara-Māhatmya: Ein religionswissenschaftlicher Beitrag zum Wallfahrtsbegriff in Indien*. Stuttgart: Franz Steiner Verlag.

Mandelbaum, David. 1970. *Society in India*. Volume 2. *Change and Continuity*. Berkeley: University of California Press.

Mandlik, Rāo Sāheb Vishvanāth Nārāyan. 1870. "The Shrine of the River Krishṇā at the Village of Mahābaleśvara." *Journal of the Bombay Branch of the Royal Asiatic Society* 9:250–61.

Mani, Vettam. 1975. *Purāṇic Encyclopedia*. Delhi: Motilal Banarsidass.

Marāṭhe, Nandkumār. 1998. *Kolhāpūr Darśan*. Sāṅglī: Gokhale Granth Prakāśan.

Marglin, Frédérique Apffel. 1985. *Wives of the God-King: The Rituals of the Devadasis of Puri*. Delhi: Oxford University Press.

Markovits, Claude, Jacques Pouchepadass, and Sanjay Subrahmanyam, editors. 2003. *Society and Circulation: Mobile People and Itinerant Cultures in South Asia 1750–1950*. Delhi: Permanent Black.

Massey, Doreen. 1992. "A Place Called Home?" *New Formations* 17:3–15; reprinted in Massey 1994:157–73.

——. 1993a. "Politics and Space/Time." In Keith and Pile, editors, 1993, pp. 141–61.

——. 1993b. "Questions of Locality." *Geography: Journal of the Geographical Association* 78:142–49.

——. 1994. *Space, Place, and Gender*. Cambridge: Polity Press.

——. 1999. "Spaces of Politics." In Massey, Allen, and Sarre, editors, 1999, pp. 279–94.

Massey, Doreen, John Allen, and Philip Sarre, editors. 1999. *Human Geography Today*. Cambridge: Polity Press.

Mate, M. S. 1962. *Temples and Legends of Maharashtra*. Bombay: Bharatiya Vidya Bhavan.

——. 1975. "Marāṭhī Rājā Koṇās Mhaṇāveṃ?" *Bhārat Itihās Saṃśodhak Maṇḍaḷ Quarterly* 54:79–84.

McDonald, Ellen E. 1968. "The Growth of Regional Consciousness in Maharashtra." *Indian Economic and Social History Review* 5:223–43.

McKean, Lise. 1996. *Divine Enterprise: Gurus and the Hindu Nationalist Movement*. Chicago: University of Chicago.

Merusvāmī. 1920 (Śake 1842). *Rāmsohalā*, edited by S. S. Dev. Dhule.

Metcalf, Barbara D. 1990. "The Pilgrimage Remembered: South Asian Accounts of the *Hajj*." In *Muslim Travellers: Pilgrimage, Migration, and the Religious Imagination*, edited by Dale F. Eickelman and James Piscatori. Berkeley: University of California Press, pp. 85–107.

Misra, O. P. 1989. *Iconography of the Saptamātrikās*. Delhi: Agam Kala Prakashan.

Mitchiner, John E. 1982. *Traditions of the Seven Ṛṣis*. Delhi: Motilal Banarsidass.

Mohapatra, Bishnu N. 1996. "Ways of 'Belonging': The *Kanchi Kaveri* Legend and the Construction of Oriya Identity." *Studies in History* (n.s.) 12:203–21.

Moin, M. 1951. "The Number 'Seven' and Nizâmī's Haft Paykar (The Seven Images)." In *Professor Poure Davoud Memorial Volume*, No. II. Bombay: The Iran League.

Mokashi, D. B. 1987. *Palkhi: An Indian Pilgrimage*, translated by Philip C. Engblom. Albany: State University of New York Press.

Molesworth, James Thomas. 1857. *Molesworth's Marathi–English Dictionary*. Corrected reprint, Poona: Shubhada-Saraswat, 1975.

Morinis, E. Alan. 1984. *Pilgrimage in the Hindu Tradition: A Case Study of West Bengal*. Delhi: Oxford University Press.

Morley, David and Kevin Robins. 1995. *Spaces of Identity: Global Media, Electronic Landscapes and Cultural Boundaries*. London: Routledge.

Morphy, Howard. 1991. *Ancestral Connections: Art and an Aboriginal System of Knowledge*. Chicago: The University of Chicago Press.

——. 1995. "Landscape and the Reproduction of the Ancestral Past." In Hirsch and O'Hanlon, editors, 1995, pp. 184–209.

Morris, Henry. 1878. *A Descriptive and Historical Account of the Godavery District in the Presidency of Madras*. London: Trübner & Co.

Morwanchikar, R. S. 1985. *The City of the Saints: Paithan through the Ages*. Delhi: Ajanta Publications.

Mulay, Sumati. 1972. *Studies in the Historical and Cultural Geography and Ethnography of the Deccan*. Poona: Deccan College Post-graduate and Research Institute.

Munn, Nancy. 1986. *The Fame of Gawa: A Symbolic Study of Value Transformation in a Massim (Papue New Guinea) Society*. Cambridge: Cambridge University Press.

——. 1990. "Constructing Regional Worlds in Experience." *Man* 25:1–17.

Nāmdev. 1970. *Śrī Nāmdev Gāthā*. Mumbaī: Śāsakīya Madhyavartī Mudraṇālay.

Nene, Harī Nārāyaṇ. 1936. "Anvaysthaḷ." *Bhārat Itihās Saṃśodhak Maṇḍaḷ Quarterly* 17:55–59

——. 1939. "Kṛṣṇamunīceṃ Anvaysthaḷ." *Bhārat Itihās Saṃśodhak Maṇḍaḷ Quarterly* 20:57–71.

——, editor. 1937. *Sūtra-Lāpikā-Ācār-Prakaraṇvaś-Vacansambandh-Sahit Ācārsthaḷ Tyāgprakaraṇ Sūtreṃ 1 te 26*. Singapore: Kumar Rājkumārī Bābū Govind Sahāy.

Nerkar, Arvind. 1977. *Saptaśṛṅga Darśan* (4th printing, 1989). Nasik: Śraddhā Prakāśan.

Neūrgāṃvkar, Sadaśiv Keśav. 1972. *Palkhī Sohaḷā*. 3rd edition, Āḷandī: Śrī Jñāneśvar Mahārāj Saṃsthān, 1994.

Nipāṇīkar, Rā. Pāṃ. 1980. " 'Asatī Parī' Madhīl Kānaḍ Deś va Telaṅga Deś." *Pratiṣṭhān* 28, 2:5–8.

Niphāḍkar, Yādav Vyaṅkaṭeś. 1915. "Bārā Jyotirliṅgeṃ." *Uṣā* 25:19–21.

Nitz, Hans-Jürgen. 1992. "Planned Temple Towns and Brahmin Villages as Spatial Expressions of the Ritual Politics of Medieval Kingdoms in South India." In Baker and Biger, editors, 1992, pp. 107–24.

Novetzke, Christian. 2003. *The Tongue Makes a Good Book: History, Religion, and Performance in the Namdev Tradition of Maharashtra*. Ph.D. thesis, Columbia University.

O'Brien, Michael. 1979. *The Idea of the American South*. Baltimore: The Johns Hopkins University Press.

O'Flaherty, Wendy Doniger, translator. 1975. *Hindu Myths: A Sourcebook Translated from the Sanskrit*. Harmondsworth: Penguin Books.

——. 1981. *The Rig Veda: An Anthology*. Harmondsworth: Penguin Books.

Olivelle, Patrick, editor and translator. 1977. *Vāsudevāśrama Yatidharmaprakāśa: A Treatise on World Renunciation*. Vienna: Publications of the De Nobili Research Library.

——. 1995. *Rules and Regulations of Brahmanical Asceticism: Yatidharmasamuccaya of Yādava Prakāśa*. Albany: State University of New York Press.

Padoux, André. 1987. "Vīraśaivas." In *The Encyclopedia of Religion*, edited by Mircea Eliade. New York: Macmillan Publishing Company, Volume 13, pp. 12–13.

Pagaḍī, Setu Mādhavrāv. 1985. "Mahāṇubhāv Sāhityātīl Bhūgol āṇi tyācā Itihās." *Pañcadhārā* (Quarterly of the Marāṭhī Sāhitya Pariṣad of Andhra Pradesh) 27/28:1–22.

Pain, Charles. N.d. "Gangapur: The Center of the Dattatreya Cult." Unpublished manuscript.

Pañjābī, Mādhavrāj, editor. 1968. *Prakarṇavas*. Amrāvatī: Mādhavrāj Pañjābī.

——. N.d.a. *Ācār Māḷikā Mahābhāṣya*. Amrāvatī: Bābūrāj Relkar.

——. N.d.b. *Ācār Sthaḷ Mahābhāṣya*. 2 volumes. Amrāvatī: Kiśor Prakāśan.

——. N.d.c. *Sthān-Pothī*. Amrāvatī: Mahānubhāv Viśvabhāratī.

——. N.d.d. *Vicār Ācār Prakarṇācā Vacan Sambandha Artha*. Ridhorā, Taluka Kāṭol: Mādhavrāj Pañjābī.

——. N.d.e. *Vicār Māḷikā Mahābhāṣya*. Amrāvatī: Bābūrāj Relkar.

Parāñjpe, Moreśvar Viṭṭhal. 1946. *Śrīkṣetra Harihareśvar Saṃkṣipta Varṇan*. Puṇeṃ: Bhārat Itihās Saṃśodhak Maṇḍaḷ.

Paranjpye, Vijay. 1990. *High Dams on the Narmada: A Holistic Analysis of the River Valley Projects*. Delhi: Indian National Trust for Art and Cultural Heritage.

Paraśurāmbhakta. N.d. *Bhagavān Śrī Paraśurām va Śri Kṣetna Paraśurām*. Paraśurām: Chairman, Paraśurām Devasthān Committee.

Parry, Jonathan P. 1994. *Death in Banaras*. Cambridge: Cambridge University Press.

Paryaṭan Sañcālanālay Mahārāṣṭra Śāsan. N.d. *Aṣṭa Vināyak*. Mumbaī: Paryaṭan Sañcālanālay Mahārāṣṭra Śāsan.

Pāṭaṇkar, Tryambakśāstrī Nathūśāstrī. 1984. *Ādya Jyotirliṅg Tryambakeśvar (Bārā Jyotirliṅgāñcyā Māhitīsaha)*. Tryambakeśvar: Candraśekhar Tryambakśāstrī Pāṭaṇkar.

Paṭhāṇ, Yu. Ma. 1973. *Mahānubhāv Sāhitya Saṃśodhan*, Volume 1. Auraṅgābād: Marāṭhvāḍā Vidyāpīṭh.
Patkī, Gopāl Dattātreya. 1917. *Śrīkarvīr-Māhātmya va Yātrā-Prakāś*. Reprint, Kolhāpūr: Paśyantī Prakāśan, 1988.
Pavār, Nārāyaṇrāv Dhoṇḍīrām. 1977. *Agastī Mahātma Granth*. Mhāsurṇe (Khaṭāv Taluka, Satara District): Haṇmantrāv Rāmcandra Māne.
Pawar, A. G. 1971. "Shivaji and Ramdas." In *Maratha History Seminar*, convened by A. G. Pawar. Kolhapur, pp. 51–79/80.
Pearson, Michael N. 1996. *Pilgrimage to Mecca: The Indian Experience, 1500–1800*. Princeton: Markus Wiener Publishers.
Peterson, Indira. 1982. "Singing of a Place: Pilgrimage as Metaphor and Motif in the *Tēvāram* Hymns of the Tamil Śaivite Saints." *Journal of the American Oriental Society* 102:69–90.
——. 1983. "Lives of the Wandering Singers: Pilgrimage and Poetry in Tamil Śaivite Hagiography." *History of Religions* 22:338–60.
Phaḍke, Govind Harī. 1931. *Mājhī Tīrthayātrā*, Part 4. *Mahārāṣṭra Pravās va Samudra Paryaṭaṇ*. Neraḷ: Govind Harī Phaḍke.
Phadke, Y. D. 1979. *Politics and Language*. Bombay: Himalaya Publishing House.
Pītdār, Śaṅkarrāv. 1983. "Āndhrapradeśāmadhīl Śrī Nṛsiṃhācī Devasthāne." *Prasād* 37:106–8.
Pollock, Sheldon. 1993. "Rāmāyaṇa and Political Imagination in India." *The Journal of Asian Studies* 52:261–97.
Prabhudesāī, Pralhād Kṛṣṇa. 1967–1968. *Ādiśaktīce Viśvasvarūp arthāt Devīkoś*, Volumes 1–2. Puṇe: Ṭiḷak Mahārāṣṭra Vidyāpīṭh.
Prasad, B. R. 1967. *The Chalukyan Architecture of Mahabubnagar District*. Ph.D. thesis, University of Poona (Deccan College).
Prasad, Leela. 1998. *Scripture and Strategy: Narrative and the Poetics of Appropriate Conduct in Sringeri, South India*. Ph.D. Dissertation, University of Pennsylvania.
Pravāsī, Ek ("A Traveller"). 1925. "Oṃkāreśvar Māndhātā." *Manorañjan* 30:238–43.
Presler, H. H. 1967. "The Kumbh Mela at Ujjain, M.P., India, April 13–May 12, 1968." *The India Cultures Quarterly* 24:27–43.
Preston, James J. 1980. "Sacred Centers and Symbolic Networks in South Asia." *The Mankind Quarterly* 20:259–93.
——. 1983. "Goddess Temples in Orissa: An Anthropological Survey." In *Religion in Modern India*, edited by Giri Raj Gupta. New Delhi: Vikas, pp. 229–47.
Preston, Laurence W. 1980. "Subregional Religious Centres in the History of Maharashtra: The Sites Sacred to Ganesh." In *Images of Maharashtra: A Regional Profile of India*, edited by N. K. Wagle. London: Curzon Press, pp. 102–28.
——. 1989. *The Devs of Cincvad: A Lineage and the State in Maharashtra*. Cambridge: Cambridge University Press.
Pujārī, Kṛṣṇambhaṭ Naraharbhaṭ. 1935. *Śrīkṣetra Gāṇgāpūr Varṇan*, edited by Gurubhaṭ Rāmbhaṭ Pujārī. Gāṇgāpūr.
Raeside, I. M. P. 1960. "A Bibliographical Index of Mahānubhāva Works in Marathi." *Bulletin of the School of Oriental and African Studies, University of London* 23:464–507.

Raeside, I. M. P. 1965. "The Pāṇḍuraṅga-Māhātmya of Śrīdhar." *Bulletin of the School of Oriental and African Studies, University of London* 28:81–100.

——. 1970. "The Mahānubhāva *sakaḷa lipī*." *Bulletin of the School of Oriental and African Studies, University of London* 33:328–34.

——. 1978. "A Note on the 'Twelve Mavals' of Poona District." *Modern Asian Studies* 12:399–417.

Raghavan, V. 1966. *The Great Integrators: The Saint Singers of India*. Delhi: Publications Division, Government of India.

Raheja, Gloria Goodwin and Ann Grodzins Gold. 1996. *Listen to the Heron's Words: Reimagining Gender and Kinship in North India*. Delhi: Oxford University Press (originally Berkeley: University of California Press, 1994).

Ramanujan, A. K. 1973. *Speaking of Śiva*. Harmondsworth: Penguin Books.

Ramaswamy, Sumathi. 1993. "En/gendering Language: The Poetics of Tamil Identity." *Comparative Studies in Society and History* 35:683–725.

——. 1994. "The Nation, the Region, and the Adventures of a Tamil 'Hero.'" *Contributions to Indian Sociology*, n.s., 28:295–322.

——. 1997. *Passions of the Tongue: Language Devotion in Tamil India, 1891–1970*. Berkeley: University of California Press.

——. 1998. "Language of the People in the World of Gods: Ideologies of Tamil before the Nation." *Journal of Asian Studies* 57:66–92.

Ramesan, N. 1969. *Temples and Legends of Andhra Pradesh*. Bombay: Bharatiya Vidya Bhavan.

Rānaḍe, Bhā. La. 1997. *Goṣṭīrūp Karvīr Māhātmya*. Sāṅglī: Gokhale Granth Prakāśan.

Ranade, M. G. 1900. *Rise of the Maratha Power*. Bombay; reprint, New Delhi: Publications Division, Ministry of Information and Broadcasting, 1961.

Raychaudhuri, Hemchandra. 1960. "Geography of the Deccan." In Yazdani, editor, 1960:1–63.

Relph, Edward. 1976. *Place and Placelessness*. London: Pion Limited.

——. 1981. *Rational Landscapes and Humanistic Geography*. Totowa, New Jersey: Barnes and Noble Books.

Richardson, Miles, editor. 1984. *Place: Experience and Symbol* (Geoscience & Man, Volume 24). Baton Rouge: Department of Geography and Anthropology, Louisiana State University.

Ruīkar, Prabhākar, editor. 1982. *Śrī Jyotibā: Sacitra Māhitī, Āratyā, Pade, Stotre, Bhūpāḷī, Ovī, Kavaca, Aṣṭaka Vagaire*. 2nd edition, Karāḍ: Prabhākar Granth Bhāṇḍār.

Ryden, Kent C. 1993. *Mapping the Invisible Landscape: Folklore, Writing, and the Sense of Place*. Iowa City: University of Iowa Press.

Ryerson, Charles A. 1988. *Regionalism and Religion: The Tamil Renaissance and Popular Hinduism*. Madras: Christian Literature Society.

Sack, Robert David. 1980. *Conceptions of Space in Social Thought: A Geographic Perspective*. Minneapolis: University of Minnesota Press.

Salomon, Richard. 1985. *The Bridge to the Three Holy Cities: The Sāmānya-praghaṭṭaka of Nārāyaṇa Bhaṭṭa's Tristhalīsetu*. Delhi: Motilal Banarsidass.

Śāstrī, Tryambak Nīlakaṇṭh Kavīśvar. 1982. "Śrīkṣetra Kuruvapur va Kṛṣṇece Vaiśiṣṭhya." *Śrīkṛṣṇāmāīce Nābhisthān Śrī Kṣetra Kuruvapūr*. Haiderābād: Hindu Vijay Prakāśan.

Satya, Laxman. 1997. *Cotton and Famine in Berar 1850–1900*. New Delhi: Manohar.

Sax, William S. 1991. *Mountain Goddess: Gender and Politics in a Himalayan Pilgrimage*. New York: Oxford University Press.

Schama, Simon. 1995. *Landscape and Memory*. New York: Alfred A. Knopf.

Schomer, Karine, Joan L. Erdman, Deryck O. Lodrick, and Lloyd I. Rudolph, editors. 1994. *Rajasthan: Explorations in Regional Identity*. Volume I *Constructions*. New Delhi: Manohar/American Institute of Indian Studies.

Schwartzberg, Joseph E. 1967. "Prolegomena to the Study of South Asian Regions and Regionalism." In Crane, editor, 1967, pp. 89–111.

——. 1992a. "Cosmographical Mapping." In Harley and Woodward, editors, 1992, pp. 332–87.

——. 1992b. "Geographical Mapping." In Harley and Woodward, editors, 1992, pp. 388–493.

——. 1992c. "Introduction to South Asian Cartography." In Harley and Woodward, editors, 1992, pp. 295–331.

——, editor. 1978. *A Historical Atlas of South Asia*. Chicago: University of Chicago Press. Second impression, with additional material, New York: Oxford University Press, 1992.

Seamon, David. 1984. "Heidegger's Notion of Dwelling and One Concrete Interpretation as Indicated by Hassan Fathy's *Architecture for the Poor*." In Richardson, editor, 1984, pp. 43–53.

Śendurṇīkar, Mādhav Rājārām. 1969. "Śrīkṛṣṇā-Samārādhan." In *Aitihāsik Lekh, Carcā* (Rājvāḍe Saṃśodhan Maṇḍaḷ-Granthamālā, No. 8). Dhuḷe: Rājvāḍe Saṃśodhan Maṇḍaḷ, pp.16–40.

Śevalīkar, Bhāskardādā, editor. 1981. *Tīrthamālikā*. Phalṭaṇ: Śrī Mahānubhāv Bhakta Saṅghaṭanā.

Śevalīkar, Dattarāj. 1970. *Sthān-Mārga-Darśak*. Ghogargāv, Taluka Śrīgondā.

Sharma, B. R. 1957. "On Saptá—in the Ṛgveda." *Bulletin of the Deccan College Research Institute* 18 (*Taraporewala Memorial Volume*):294–308.

Shields, Rob. 1991. *Places on the Margin: Alternative Geographies of Modernity*. London: Routledge.

Shulman, David Dean. 1980. *Tamil Temple Myths: Sacrifice and Divine Marriage in the South Indian Śaiva Tradition*. Princeton: Princeton University Press.

Siṃhasthasambandhī Māhitī. Lithograph in the library of the Bhandarkar Oriental Research Institute, Pune, 29606 (no publication information).

Sircar, D. C. 1948. "The Śākta Pīṭhas." *Journal of the Royal Asiatic Society of Bengal. Letters* 14:1–107.

——. 1971a. *Studies in the Geography of Ancient and Medieval India*. 2nd edition, Delhi: Motilal Banarsidass (originally 1960).

——. 1971b. *Studies in the Religious Life of Ancient and Medieval India*. Delhi: Motilal Banarsidass.

Sircar, D. C. 1973. *The Śākta Pīṭhas*. 2nd revised edition, Delhi: Motilal Banarsidass.

Skaria, Ajay. 1999. *Hybrid Histories: Forests, Frontiers and Wildness in Western India*. Delhi: Oxford University Press.

Soja, Edward W. 1989. *Postmodern Geographies: The Reassertion of Space in Critical Social Theory*. London: Verso.

Solaṅkī, Lukanāth. 1905 (Śake 1827). *Śrī Tāpī Māhātmya*. Puṇe: Āryavijay Press.

Sontheimer, Günther D. 1975. "The Dhangars: A Nomadic Pastoral Community in a Developing Agricultural Environment." In *Pastoralists and Nomads in South Asia*, edited by Lawrence Saadia Leshnik and Günther-Dietz Sontheimer. Wiesbaden, pp. 139–70.

——. 1982. "King Vikram and Kamaḷū Śinde, the Shepherd: *Bhakti* Episodes from an Oral Epic of the Dhangars of Maharashtra." *South Asian Digest of Regional Writing* 11:97–128.

——. 1985. "Folk Deities in the Vijayanagara Empire: Narasiṃha and Mallaṇṇa/Mailār." In *Vijayanagara—City and Empire: New Currents of Research*, edited by Anna Libera Dallapiccola in collaboration with S. Zingel-Avé Lallemant. Wiesbaden: Franz Steiner Verlag, pp. 144–58.

——. 1989a. *Pastoral Deities in Western India*, translated by Anne Feldhaus. New York: Oxford University Press.

——. 1989b. "Between Ghost and God: A Folk Deity of the Deccan." In *Criminal Gods and Demon Devotees: Essays on the Guardians of Popular Hinduism*, edited by Alf Hiltebeitel. Albany: State University of New York Press, pp. 299–337.

——. 1991. "The Rāmāyaṇa in Contemporary Folk Traditions of Maharashtra." In *Rāmāyaṇa and Rāmāyaṇas*, edited by M. Thiel-Horstmann. Wiesbaden: Otto Harrassowitz, pp. 115–37.

——. 1993. "King Khaṇḍobā's Hunt and His Encounter with Bāṇāī, the Shepherdess." In *Flags of Fame: Studies in South Asian Folk Culture*, edited by Heidrun Brückner, Lothar Lutze, and Aditya Malik. New Delhi: Manohar, pp. 19–80.

——. 1997. *Essays on Khaṇḍobā*, edited by Anne Feldhaus, Aditya Malik, and Heidrun Brückner. New Delhi: Indira Gandhi National Centre for the Arts/Manohar.

Sopher, David. 1968. "Pilgrimage Circulation in Gujarat." *Geographical Review* 58:392–425.

——. 1980a. "The Geographical Patterning of Culture in India." In *An Exploration of India: Geographical Perspectives on Society and Culture*. Ithaca: Cornell University Press, pp. 289–326.

——. 1980b. "The Message of Place: Addendum to a Geography of Indian Pilgrimage." Typescript of a paper presented at Columbia University, New York, April 1980.

Spate, O. H. K. and A. T. A. Learmonth. 1967. *India and Pakistan: A General and Regional Geography*. 3rd edition, Methuen & Co Ltd (originally 1954).

Spencer, George W. 1970. "The Sacred Geography of the Tamil Shaivite Hymns." *Numen* 17:232–44.

Śrīkhaṇḍe, Anil. 1988. "Ratnāgirīcī Devī Bhagavatī." *Sakāḷ*, October 20, p. 6.

Stanley, John M. 1977. "Special Time, Special Power: The Fluidity of Power in a Popular Hindu Festival." *Journal of Asian Studies* 37:27–43.

——. 1988. "Gods, Ghosts, and Possession." In Zelliot and Berntsen, editors, 1988, pp. 26–59.

Stark-Wild, Sonja. 1997. *Die Göttin Renuka in Mythos und Kultus: eine Analyse ihrer sakralen Präsenz unter besonderer Berüksichtigung ihrer Verbreitung in Maharashtra.* Ph.D. dissertation, University of Heidelberg.

Stein, Burton. 1967. "Comments on Bernard S. Cohn, 'Regions Subjective and Objective: Their Relation to the Study of Modern Indian History and Society.'" In Crane, editor, 1967, pp. 41–47.

——. 1969. "Integration of the Agrarian System of South India." In *Land Control and Social Structure in Indian History*, edited by Robert Eric Frykenberg. Madison: The University of Wisconsin Press, pp. 175–216.

——. 1974. "Dēvī Shrines and Folk Hinduism in Medieval Tamilnad." In *Studies in the Language and Culture of South Asia*, edited by Edwin Gerow and Margery D. Lang. Seattle: University of Washington Press.

——. 1977. "Circulation and the Historical Geography of Tamil Country." *Journal of Asian Studies* 37:7–26.

——. 1980. *Peasant State and Society in Medieval South India.* Delhi: Oxford University Press.

Stewart, Kathleen C. 1996. "An Occupied Place." In Feld and Basso, editors, 1996a, pp. 137–65.

Stoddard, Robert H. and Alan Morinis, editors. 1997. *Sacred Places, Sacred Spaces: The Geography of Pilgrimages.* (*Geoscience and Man*), Volume 34. Baton Rouge: Geoscience Publications, Department of Geography and Anthropology, Louisiana State University.

Stokes, Martin, editor. 1994. *Ethnicity, Identity and Music: The Musical Construction of Place.* Oxford: Berg.

Sunthankar, B. R. 1988. *Nineteenth Century History of Maharashtra.* Pune: Shubhada-Saraswat.

Tagare, Ganesh Vasudev, editor. 1980. *Śrī Karavīra Māhātmya.* Kolhapur: Shivaji University.

Talbot, Cynthia. 2002. *Precolonial India in Practice: Society, Region, and Identity in Medieval Andhra.* New York: Oxford University Press.

Thakur, Vasudha. 1991. *Paṇḍharpūrcī Vārī: Ek Samājśāstrīya Abhyās.* Ph.D. thesis, S. N. D. T. Women's University.

Thurston, Edgar. 1914. "The Number Seven in Southern India." In *Essays and Studies Presented to William Ridgeway on His Sixtieth Birthday*, edited by E. C. Quiggin. Cambridge: at the University Press, pp. 353–64.

Tripathi, G. C. 1978. "Navakalevara: The Unique Ceremony of the 'Birth' and the Death of the 'Lord of the World.'" In Eschmann, Kulke, and Tripathi, editors, 1978, pp. 223–64.

Tuan, Yi-fu. 1984. "In Place, Out of Place." In Richardson, editor, 1984, pp. 3–10.

——. 1997. "Sense of Place: What Does It Mean to Be Human?" *American Journal of Theology and Philosophy* 18:47–58.

Tukārām. 1973. *Śrī Tukārāmbāvāṃcyā Abhaṅgāṃcī Gāthā*. Mumbaī: Śāsakīya Madhyavartī Mudraṇālay.

Tuḷpuḷe, Śaṅ. Go. 1972. *Līḷācaritra Ekāṅk*. Nāgpūr/Puṇe: Suvicār Prakāśan Maṇḍaḷ.

——. 1979. *Classical Marāṭhī Literature from the Beginning to A.D. 1818*. Wiesbaden: Otto Harrassowitz.

——. 1981. "Līḷācaritrātīl Kannaḍ Deś va Telaṅg Deś." *Pratiṣṭhān* 28, 5:16–17.

—— and Anne Feldhaus. 1999. *A Dictionary of Old Marathi*. Mumbai: Popular Prakashan; New York: Oxford University Press, 2000.

Turner, Victor. 1973. "The Center Out There: Pilgrim's Goal." *History of Religions* 12:191–230.

Udās, Yaśvantrāv Ānandrāv. 1891. *Dhaummahābaḷeśvarvarṇan*. Mumbaī.

Underhill, M. M. 1921. *The Hindu Religious Year*. Calcutta: Association Press.

Vaidya, Gaṇeś Rāmkṛṣṇa. 1897 (Śake 1819). *Śrī Kṛṣṇā Māhātmya*. Bombay: Nirṇaysāgar Press; reprint, Wāī, 1983.

Valentine, Gill. 1999. "Imagined Geographies: Geographical Knowledges of Self and Other in Everyday Life." In Massey, Allen, and Sarre, editors, 1999, pp. 47–61.

Varenne, Jean. 1976. *Yoga and the Hindu Tradition*, translated by Derek Coltman. Chicago: The University of Chicago Press.

Vaudeville, Charlotte. 1987. "The Shaivaite Background of Santism in Maharashtra." In Israel and Wagle, editors, 1987, pp. 32–50.

——. 1993. *A Weaver Named Kabir: Selected Verses, with a Detailed Biographical and Historical Introduction*. Delhi: Oxford University Press.

Vora, Rajendra. 1999. "Maharashtra Dharma and the Nationalist Movement in Maharashtra." In *Writers, Editors and Reformers: Social and Political Transformations of Maharashtra, 1830–1930*, edited by N. K. Wagle. New Delhi: Manohar, pp. 23–30.

Wagle, Narendra K. 1989. "HindūMuslim Interactions in Medieval Maharashtra." In *Hinduism Reconsidered*, edited by Günther D. Sontheimer and Hermann Kulke. New Delhi: Manohar, reprinted 1991, pp. 51–66.

Wallace, Paul, editor. 1985. *Region and Nation in India*. New Delhi: American Institute of Indian Studies.

Walter, Eugene Victor. 1988. *Placeways: A Theory of the Human Environment*. Chapel Hill: The University of North Carolina Press.

Washbrook, David. 1991. " 'To Each a Language of His Own': Language, Culture, and Society in Colonial India." In *Language, History and Class*, edited by Penelope J. Corfield. Oxford: Basil Blackwell, pp. 179–203.

Weiner, James F. 1991. *The Empty Place: Poetry, Space, and Being among the Foi of Papua New Guinea*. Bloomington: Indiana University Press.

Wheatley, Paul. 1968. *City as Symbol*. London: H. K. Lewis and Co. Ltd.

White, David Gordon. 1996. *The Alchemical Body: Siddha Traditions in Medieval India*. Chicago: The University of Chicago Press.

Whitehead, Henry. 1921. *The Village Gods of South India*. Reprint, Delhi: Sumit Publications, 1976.

Winslow, Deborah. 1984. "A Political Geography of Deities: Space and the Pantheon in Sinhalese Buddhism." *Journal of Asian Studies* 43:273–91.

Witzel, Michael. 1984. "Sur le chemin du ciel." *Bulletin d'Études Indiennes* 2:213–79.

Wolpert, Stanley A. 1962. *Tilak and Gokhale: Revolution and Reform in the Making of Modern India*. Berkeley: University of California Press.

Yang, Anand A. 1998. *Bazaar India: Markets, Society, and the Colonial State in Bihar*. Berkeley: University of California Press.

Yazdani, G., editor. 1960. *The Early History of the Deccan*, 2 volumes. Reprint, New Delhi: Oriental Books Reprint Corporation, 1982.

Young, Katherine. 1980. "Tīrtha and the Metaphor of Crossing Over." *Studies in Religion* 9:61–68.

Yule, Henry and A. C. Burnell. 1903. *Hobson–Jobson*. Reprint, New Delhi: Munshiram Manoharlal, 1979.

Zelliot, Eleanor. N.d. "Ramdas and the Akara Maruti." Unpublished notes on a 1996 field trip.

—— and Maxine Berntsen, editors. 1988. *The Experience of Hinduism*. Albany: State University of New York Press.

Zimmermann, Francis. 1982. *La Jungle et le fumet des viandes: Un thème écologique dans la médecine hindoue*. Paris: Gallimard.

Abbreviations

AMM	*Ācār Māḷikā Mahābhāṣya*, edited by M. Pañjābī. N.d. Amrāvatī: Bābūrāj Relkar.
ASM	*Ācār Sthaḷ Mahābhāṣya*, edited by M. Pañjābī. N.d. Amrāvatī: Kiśor Prakāśan.
BM	Dattakiṅkar. 1886. *Śrī Bhīmā Māhātmya*. Bombay: Jagadīśvar Press.
BSK	*Bhāratīya Saṃskṛtikoś*, edited by Mahādevśāstrī Jośī. 1962–1979. 10 volumes. Puṇe: Bhāratīya Saṃskṛtikoś Maṇḍaḷ.
GBP	*Gazetteer of the Bombay Presidency*.
GM.Mar.	Dāsagaṇū. 1921 (Śake 1843). *Śrī Gautamī Māhātmya*. Nānded: Dāmodhar Vāman Aṭhavale.
GM.Skt.	*Gautamī Māhātmya*. 1906. Printed separately at the end of *Śrī Brahmapurāṇa*. Bombay: Veṅkaṭeśvara Press; reprint, Delhi: Nag Publishers, 1985.
KM	*Kṛṣṇā Māhātmya* (Sanskrit and/or Marathi).
KM.Mar.	Vaidya, Gaṇeś Rāmkṛṣṇa. 1897 (Śake 1819). *Śrī Kṛṣṇā Māhātmya*. Bombay: Nirṇaysāgar Press; reprint, Wāī, 1983.
KM.Skt.	*Kṛṣṇā Māhātmya*. 1885 (Śake 1807). Edited by V. S. S. Gaṅgādharaśāstrī Abhyaṅkara. Wāī: Virāja Vaibhava Press.
LC	*Mhāīmbhaṭ Saṅkalit Śrīcakradhar Līḷā Caritra*, edited by V. B. Kolte. 1982. 2nd edition, Mumbaī: Mahārāṣṭra Rājya Sāhitya-Saṃskṛti Maṇḍaḷ.
MM	Bhagat, Sakhārām Bāḷājī. N.d. *Śrī Maḷāīdevī Māhātmya*. Ciñcolī, Pārner Taluka, Ahmadnagar District: Sakhārām Bāḷājī Bhagat.
MP	*Muni Keśirāj Viracit Mūrtiprakāś*, edited by V. B. Kolte. 1962. Nāgpūr: Vidarbha Saṃśodhan Maṇḍaḷ.
NM	Buḷe, Śakuntalābāī Nārāyaṇrāv. N.d. *Śrīnarmadāmāhātmya*. Dādar: Narendra Book Depot.
PM	Ballāḷ, Tryambak. 1913. *Payoṣṇī Māhātmya*. Bombay: Śaṅkar Printing Press.

SSG	*Gāthāpañcaka arthāt Sakala-Santa-Gāthā*, edited by Tryambak Hari Āvaṭe. Puṇeṃ: Indira Chāpkhānā, 1924–1927.
TM	Solaṅkī, Lukanāth. 1905 (Śake 1827). *Śrī Tāpī Māhātmya*. Puṇe: Āryavijay Press.
VMM	*Vicār Māḷikā Mahābhāṣya*, edited by Mādhavrāj Pañjābī. N.d. Amrāvatī: Bābūrāj Relkar.

Index